ATLA BIBLIOGRAPHY SERIES
edited by Dr. Kenneth E. Rowe

1. *A Guide to the Study of the Holiness Movement,* by Charles Edwin Jones. 1974.
2. *Thomas Merton: A Bibliography,* by Marquita E. Breit. 1974.
3. *The Sermon on the Mount: A History of Interpretation and Bibliography,* by Warren S. Kissinger. 1975.
4. *The Parables of Jesus: A History of Interpretation and Bibliography,* by Warren S. Kissinger. 1979.
5. *Homosexuality and the Judeo-Christian Tradition: An Annotated Bibliography,* by Thom Horner. 1981.
6. *A Guide to the Study of the Pentecostal Movement,* by Charles Edwin Jones. 1983.
7. *The Genesis of Modern Process Thought: A Historical Outline with Bibliography,* by George R. Lucas, Jr. 1983.
8. *A Presbyterian Bibliography,* by Harold B. Prince. 1983.
9. *Paul Tillich: A Comprehensive Bibliography . . .,* by Richard C. Crossman. 1983.
10. *A Bibliography of the Samaritans,* by Alan David Crown. 1984.
11. *An Annotated and Classified Bibliography of English Literature Pertaining to the Ethiopian Orthodox Church,* by Jon Bonk. 1984.
12. *International Meditation Bibliography, 1950 to 1982,* by Howard R. Jarrell. 1984.
13. *Rabindranath Tagore: A Bibliography,* by Katherine Henn. 1985.
14. *Research in Ritual Studies: A Programmatic Essay and Bibliography,* by Ronald L. Grimes, 1985.
15. *Protestant Theological Education in America,* by Heather F. Day. 1985.
16. *Unconscious: A Guide to Sources,* by Natalino Caputi. 1985.
17. *The New Testament Apocrypha and Pseudepigrapha,* by James H. Charlesworth. 1987.
18. *Black Holiness,* by Charles Edwin Jones. 1987.
19. *A Bibliography on Ancient Ephesus,* by Richard Oster. 1987.
20. *Jerusalem, the Holy City: A Bibliography,* by James D. Purvis. 1987.
21. *An Index to English Periodical Literature on the Old Testament and Ancient Near Eastern Studies,* Volume I, by William G. Hupper. 1987.
22. *John and Charles Wesley: A Bibliography,* by Betty M. Jarboe. 1987.

John and Charles WESLEY:

A Bibliography

by

BETTY M. JARBOE

ATLA Bibliography Series, No. 22

The American Theological
Library Association
and
The Scarecrow Press, Inc.
Metuchen, N.J., & London
1987

Library of Congress Cataloging-in-Publication Data

Jarboe, Betty.

    John and Charles Wesley.

    (ATLA bibliography series ; no. 22)
    Bibliography: p.
    Includes index.
    1. Wesley, John, 1703-1791--Bibliography.
2. Wesley, Charles, 1707-1788--Bibliography.
I. Title. II. Series.
Z8967.J37 1987 [BX8495.W5] 016.287'092'2 87-13005
ISBN 0-8108-2039-0

CONTENTS

EDITOR'S FOREWORD

The American Theological Library Association Bibliography Series is designed to stimulate and encourage the preparation of reliable bibliographies and guides to the literature of religious studies in all its scope and variety. Compilers are free to define their field, make their own selections, and work out internal organization as the unique demands of the subject require. The Publication Committee of ATLA is pleased to publish Betty M. Jarboe's John and Charles Wesley: A Bibliography as number 22 in its series.

Betty M. Jarboe took her undergraduate and graduate training at Indiana University. Following public library posts in Montgomery County, Maryland, and Hobart, Indiana, Mrs. Jarboe joined the staff of the Indiana University Library where she currently holds the post of Assistant Head, Reference Department. Her previous publications include Studies on Indiana: A Bibliography of Theses and Dissertations, 1902-1977 (Indiana Historical Bureau, 1980) and Obituaries: A Guide to Sources (G. K. Hall, 1982).

Kenneth E. Rowe
Series Editor

Drew University Library
Madison, NJ 07940

v

INTRODUCTION

In preparation for a trip to England in 1983 to visit places of importance in the life of John Wesley, the absence of a recent, comprehensive bibliography of secondary Wesley writings became evident. After some reassurance from several contemporary Wesley scholars that such a bibliography was needed, the compiler enthusiastically began the task of searching, verifying, and preparing the bibliography.

John Wesley is recognized as a leading figure of the eighteenth century, with influences that reached into many aspects of English life--religious, social, medical, educational, and political. It was this diversity of activities that made him an attractive subject to the compiler, a general reference librarian. Initially it was felt that the skills of a librarian were sufficient to produce a useful bibliography. As time passed, it became evident that a lack of theological training and familiarity with the events and conditions of the time in which Wesley lived was a significant handicap; however, attempts were made to remedy this lack of expertise. One thing is certain--the endeavor has been exciting and there have been many personal rewards.

Scope

The bibliography covers writings about the Wesleys from 1791, the date of John Wesley's death, with a few exceptions. It was decided a bibliography on John Wesley alone would be almost impossible since one cannot study him without including his brother Charles and their parents, Susanna and Samuel. Thus the bibliography focuses on these four.

It is difficult to separate Wesley and Methodism, but an attempt was made to do so. Many books on Methodism were examined, but only those that had a section devoted to the Wesleys were included.

Methodology

A list of subject headings was established for searching library catalogs in the United States. This list included subjects closely associated with Wesley, such as conversion, class meetings, perfection, sanctification, along with the more general subjects of Methodism, the Church of England, hymns, and preaching. If a book was listed in a library's catalog with John, Charles, Susanna, or Samuel as a subject heading, the book was not examined. It was verified in the National Union Catalog, OCLC, the General Catalogue of Printed Books of the British Library, or the Methodist Union Catalog, and added to the bibliography. If it could not be verified, it was included in the bibliography and the library owning it would be indicated in the citation. All books without the Wesleys as subject headings were examined to ascertain the extent of Wesley material they contained. A location symbol is given for books that could not be verified in the standard verification tools.

The following indexes and abstracting services were searched manually:

Abstracts of English Studies. Boulder, Colo.: National Council of Teachers of English, 1958- . v. 1- .

Annual Bibliography of English Language and Literature. Cambridge: University Press, 1921- . v. 1- .

Bibliographic Index. New York: Wilson, 1938- .

Bibliographie der deutschen Zeitschriftenliteratur...., 1896-1964. Leipzig, 1897-1964.

Biography Index; a Cumulative Index to Biographical Material in Books and Magazines. New York: Wilson, 1947- . v. 1- .

British Humanities Index. London: Library Association, 1963- . v. 1- .

Catholic Periodical Index; a Cumulative Author and Subject Index to a Selected List of Catholic Periodicals, 1930-66. New York: Catholic Library Association, 1936-66. Continued by Catholic Periodical and Literature Index. Haverford, Pa.: Catholic Library Association, 1968- . v. 14- .

Christian Periodical Index. Buffalo, N.Y.: Christian Librarians' Fellowship, 1958- . v. 1- .

Cumulated Magazine Subject Index, 1907-1949. Boston: G. K. Hall, 1964. 2 vols.

Essay and General Literature Index, 1900-1933. New York: Wilson, 1934. Supplements, 1934- .

Humanities Index. New York: Wilson, 1974- . v. 1- .
Continues in part the Social Sciences and Humanities Index.

Index to Theses Accepted for Higher Degrees in the Univer-
    sities of Great Britain and Ireland. London: Aslib, 1953- .
    v. 1- .

Index-Catalogue of the Library of the Surgeon General's Of-
    fice, United States Army, Authors and Subjects. Ser. 1-5.
    Washington: Government Printing Office, 1880-1961. 61
    vols.

Internationale Bibliographie der Zeitschriftenliteratur aus allen
    Gebieten des Wissens. Osnabruck: Felix Dietrich, 1965- .
    v. 1- .

International Bibliography of Historical Sciences. Oxford:
    University Press; New York: Wilson, 1930- . v. 1- .

International Bibliography of Sociology. London: Tavistock;
    Chicago: Aldine, 1952- . v. 1- .

Library of Congress Catalog, Books: Subjects, 1950-1982.
    Ann Arbor: Edwards, 1955-1982.

A London Bibliography of the Social Sciences. London: London
    School of Economics, 1931-32. 4 vols. Supplements.

Methodist Periodical Index. Nashville: Methodist Publishing
    House, 1961-68. v. 1-8. Became United Methodist Period-
    ical Index. v. 9-20, 1968-80.

Music Index. Detroit, Mich.: Information Service, 1950- .
    1949- .

Nineteenth Century Readers' Guide to Periodical Literature,
    1890-1899. New York: Wilson, 1944. 2 vols.

Play Index, 1949-1952, 1953-1960, 1961-1967, 1968-1972, 1973-
    1977, 1978-1982. New York: Wilson, 1953-1983. 6 vols.

Poole's Index to Periodical Literature 1802-1909. Boston:
    Houghton, 1802-1907.

Readers' Guide to Periodical Literature, 1900- . New York:
    Wilson, 1905- . v. 1- .

Religious and Theological Abstracts. Youngstown, Ohio: Theo-
    logical Publications, 1958- . v. 1- .

Social Sciences and Humanities Index. Formerly International
    Index, 1907/15-1974. New York: Wilson, 1916-1974. v.
    1-61. Superseded by the Humanities Index and the Social
    Sciences Index.

Social Sciences Index. New York: Wilson, 1974- . v. 1,
   no. 1- . Continues in part the Social Sciences and Humanities Index.

Subject Index to Periodicals, 1915-1961. London: Library
   Association, 1919-1962.

Writings on American History, 1902- . Publisher varies,
   1904- .

Writings on British History, 1901-1933. London: Jonathan
   Cape, 1968-70. 5 vols. 1934- . v. 1- .

The following databases were searched by computer:

America: History and Life. 1964- .

Dissertation Abstracts Online. 1861- .

Historical Abstracts. 1973- .

MLA Bibliography. 1968- .

Religion Index. 1949- .

RILM Abstracts. 1971-1979.

RLIN.

    All articles retrieved were examined for accuracy of citations
with the exception of a few from non-English periodicals, which are
marked with an asterisk. All periodicals have been verified in the
Union List of Serials, New Serial Titles, OCLC, or British Union
Catalogue of Periodicals.

    In addition to runs of indexes, many subject bibliographies
were searched, as well as important bibliographies in such works as
Piette's John Wesley in the Evolution of Protestantism (no. 1301) and
Semmel's The Methodist Revolution (no. 1476). All bibliographies of
secondary material listed in the bibliography section were, of course,
searched. Judson's bibliography (no. 17) was very useful, particularly for its indexing of Wesley material in the Methodist Recorder.

    No attempt has been made to include book reviews. Those
found were included, but no searching was done. Nor did time per-
mit the listing of all editions of each work cited. No claim for complete coverage is made.

Arrangement

    The bibliography is classified by format:

Bibliographies
Books
Articles
Dissertations and theses
Poetry
Drama
Fiction
Juvenile works
Miscellanea

The bibliography concludes with a section of non-English publications.

Indexing

Authorities for index terms were the Library of Congress Sub-
ject Headings, indexing done by John A. Vickers in The Bicentennial
Edition of the Works of John Wesley, and the Encyclopedia of World
Methodism. On a few occasions, keyword indexing was used.

Every item in the bibliography deals with the Wesleys. However, some items are listed in the index under John Wesley and
Charles Wesley directly. In some cases, a subject will be listed
under John Wesley and also under the subject. An example of this
is "Ordination." Under John Wesley, it refers to his ordination. Under the word as a subject, it refers to Wesley's ordination of others.
"Conversion" and "Aldersgate," however, have been listed only under
the words, not under John Wesley, as it was often not easily determined when they applied to Wesley's own personal experiences or
when they had a broader meaning. The index is admittedly not as
precise as hoped for, and many entries could not be assigned a precise heading.

Resource Libraries

The following libraries were visited:

United States

Archives and History Center of the United Methodist Church, Madison,
    N.J.
Asbury Theological Seminary Library, Wilmore, Ky.
Christian Theological Seminary Library, Indianapolis, Ind.
Drew University Library, Madison, N.J.
Duke University Library, Durham, N.C.
Garrett-Evangelical Theological Seminary Library, Evanston, Ill.
Library of Congress, Washington, D.C.
Southern Methodist University, Perkins School of Theology Library,
    Dallas, Tex.
Vanderbilt University Library, Nashville, Tenn.

Great Britain

British Library, London
Cambridge University Library, Cambridge
Central Library, Lincoln
Dr. William's Library, London
Methodist Archives and Research Centre, John Rylands University
    Library of Manchester
Moravian Church House Library, London
National Library of Scotland, Edinburgh
National Library of Wales, Aberystwyth
Oxford University Library, Oxford
University of London Library, London
Wesley College Library, Bristol
Wesley Historical Society Library, Southlands College, London

Acknowledgments

    I wish to express my appreciation to the librarians who assisted
me and granted me access to their collections. It made my task much
easier. I also wish to thank Indiana University for the sabbatical
leave which allowed me to complete the bibliography within a reasonable
time, and I especially want to thank my husband for his encourage-
ment and assistance throughout the project. I would never have
managed the many trips without him.

ABBREVIATIONS

United States

DLC   Library of Congress
     Washington, D.C. 20540

GEU-T   Candler School of Theology Library
     Emory University
     101 Theology Bldg.
     Atlanta, Ga. 30322

IEG   Garrett-Evangelical Theological Seminary Library
     2121 Sheridan Rd.
     Evanston, Ill. 60201

InU-Lilly Lilly Library
     Indiana University
     Bloomington, Ind. 47405

KyWAT   B. L. Fisher Library
     Asbury Theological Seminary
     N. Lexington Avenue
     Wilmore, Ky. 40390

MBU-T   Boston University School of Theology Library
     745 Commonwealth Avenue
     Boston, Mass. 02215

NN   New York Public Library
     5th Avenue and 42nd Street
     New York, N.Y. 10018

NcD   William R. Perkins Library
     Duke University
     Durham, N.C. 27706

NcLjUM See NjMUM

NjMD   See next entry

NjMUM The Library
     United Methodist Archives

                P.O. Box 127
                Madison, N.J. 09740
                (Joint collections of Drew University Library and the
                   General Commission on Archives and History, United
                   Methodist Church)

RPB   John D. Rockefeller, Jr. Library
                Brown University
                Prospect Street
                Providence, R.I. 02912

TNMPH   Methodist Publishing House
                201 Eighth Avenue, South
                Nashville, Tenn. 37203

TxDaM-P   Bridwell Library
                Perkins School of Theology
                Southern Methodist University
                Dallas, Tex. 75275

Australia

AusVmQ   Queens College Library
                Parkville
                Melbourne, Victoria 3052

England

GtBBrP   Bristol Public Library
                Central Library
                College Green
                Bristol 1

GtBLDW   Dr. William's Library
                14 Gordon Square
                London, W.C. 1

GtBLM   See GtBMM

GtBLMor   Moravian Church House
                42 Onslow Gardens
                Muswell Hill
                London, N. 10

GtBLU   Library
                University of London
                Malet Street
                London WC1E 7Hp

GtBLW   Wesley Historical Society Library
               Southlands College
               Wimbledon, Parkside
               London SW19 SNN

GtBMM   Methodist Archives and Research Centre
               The John Rylands University Library
               University of Manchester
               Manchester M13 9PP

Germany

GDZS   Gesamtverzeichnis Deutschsprachiger Zeitschriften und
               Serien (Union List of German Language Serials)

Italy

IT   Biblioteca Nazionale Centrale
               Piazza Cavalleggeri 1B
               50122 Florence

Scotland

ScoE   National Library of Scotland
               George IV Bridge
               Edinburgh, EH1 1EW

Wales

AbN   National Library of Wales
               Aberystwyth, Dyfed

PART I:

ENGLISH-LANGUAGE PUBLICATIONS

BIBLIOGRAPHIES

1. Ayres, Samuel Gardiner. Supplement to 'Outlines of Wesleyan Bibliography,' by G. Osborn; Contained in the Library of Drew Theological Seminary and the Library of Garrett Biblical Institute. N.p. 1915. 389p. Typed manuscript. See no. 25. IEG

2. Baker, Frank. "More Additional Notes to Wesley Bibliography." Proceedings of the Wesley Historical Society 21 (1938): 132-33, 155-58.

3. _____. "Unfolding John Wesley: A Survey of Twenty Years' Study in Wesley's Thought." Quarterly Review (Nashville) 1, no. 1 (1980): 44-58. A bibliographical essay covering the Wesley scholarship for the years 1960-80.

4. _____. A Union Catalogue of the Publications of John and Charles Wesley. Durham, N.C.: Divinity School, Duke University, 1966. 230p.

5. Bassett, Paul Merritt. "Finding the Real John Wesley." Christianity Today 28, no. 16 (1984): 86-88. A bibliographical essay.

6. "Bibliography." In vol. 2 of The Encyclopedia of World Methodism, 2721-2814. Sponsored by the World Methodist Council and the Commission on Archives and History of the United Methodist Church, Nolan B. Harmon, General Editor; Albea Godbold, Louise L. Queen, Assistants to the Editor. 2 vols. Nashville: United Methodist Publishing House, 1974.

7. Bibliotheca Methodistica. Katalog. Zurich: Christliche Vereinsbuchhandlung/Methodist Publishing House, 1967. 228p.

8. Blanshard, Thomas. Catalogue of Books, Published by J. Wesley and the Preachers in Connexion with Him; Together with a Selection of Some of the Most Excellent and Useful Books Now Extant. London: T. Cordeux, Printer, 1816. 16p.

9. Bowmer, John C. "Twenty-five Years (1943-68): Methodist Studies." Proceedings of the Wesley Historical Society 37 (1969): 61-66.

10. A Catalogue of Books for the Year 1805, Published by the Late
     Rev. Mr. Wesley, and Others Sold at the New-Chapel, City Road,
     London, and at the Methodist Preaching-Houses in Town and
     Country. London: Printed at the Conference Office by George
     Story, Agent, 1805. 8p. NjMUM

11. Cavender, Curtis H. Catalogue of Works in Refutation of Method-
     ism, from Its Origin in 1729, to the Present Time. 2d ed. New
     York, 1868. 55p.

12. Fortney, Edward L. "The Literature of the History of Method-
     ism." Religion in Life 24 (1955): 443-51.

13. Green, Richard. Anti-Methodist Publications Issued During the
     Eighteenth Century.... 1902. Reprint. New York: Burt
     Franklin, 1973. 175p.

14. _____. "A List (Chiefly) of Published Biographies and Bio-
     graphical Notices of John Wesley." Proceedings of the Wesley
     Historical Society 3 (1902): 217-36.

15. _____. The Works of John and Charles Wesley: A Bibliog-
     raphy.... 2d ed. New York: AMS Press, 1976. 291p.

16. Jones, Arthur E. A Union Checklist of Editions of the Publi-
     cations of John and Charles Wesley; Based upon the 'Works of
     John and Charles Wesley; a Bibliography' by Richard Green....
     Madison, N.J.: Drew University, 1960. 74p. See no. 15.

17. Judson, Sandra. Biographical and Descriptive Works on the
     Rev. John Wesley. Thesis, University of London, 1963. 259p.

18. Lenhart, Thomas E. A Checklist of Wesleyan and Methodist
     Studies, 1970-1975. Evanston, Ill.: Institute for Methodist
     Studies and Related Movements, Garrett-Evangelical Theological
     Seminary, 1976. 19p.

19. McIntosh, Lawrence D. "The Place of John Wesley in the Chris-
     tian Tradition--a Selected Bibliography." In The Place of Wes-
     ley in the Christian Tradition, 134-59. See no. 88.

20. Melbourne University. Queen's College. Catalogue of Wesleyana
     in the Library of Queen's College, University of Melbourne.
     Melbourne, 1927. 15p.

21. Melton, J. Gordon. "An Annotated Bibliography of Publications
     about the Life and Work of John Wesley." Methodist History 7,
     no. 4 (1969): 29-46.

22. Newton, John Anthony. "Susanna Wesley (1669-1742): A Bib-
     liographical Survey." Proceedings of the Wesley Historical So-
     ciety 37 (1969): 37-40.

23. Norwood, Frederick A. "Methodist Historical Studies, 1930-59."
     Church History 28 (1959): 391-417; 29 (1960): 74-88.

24. _____. "Wesleyan and Methodist Historical Studies, 1960-70:
     A Bibliographical Article." Church History 40 (1971): 182-99.

25. Osborn, George. Outlines of Wesleyan Bibliography; or, A
     Record of Methodist Literature from the Beginning.. In Two
     Parts: The First Containing the Publications of John and Charles
     Wesley ... the Second, Those of Methodist Preachers. London:
     Wesleyan Conference Office, 1869. 220p.

26. Reed, Alfred Hamish. Notes on Autograph Letters of John and
     Charles Wesley in the Alfred and Isabel Reed Collection at the
     Dunedin Public Library. Dunedin, New Zealand, 1972? 8p.
     NjMUM

27. Rogal, Samuel J. "The Wesleys: A Checklist of Critical Com-
     mentary." Bulletin of Bibliography 28 (1971): 22-35.

28. Sharp, J. Alfred. A Catalogue of Manuscripts and Relics, En-
     gravings and Photographs, Medals, Books and Pamphlets, Pot-
     tery, Medallions, etc., Belonging to the Wesleyan Methodist
     Conference.... Together with Some of the Principal Books,
     MSS., etc.... London: Methodist Publishing House, 1921.
     217p.

29. Stampe, George. "List of Local Histories of Methodism." Pro-
     ceedings of the Wesley Historical Society 1 (1898): 3-14; 6
     (1907): 70-74.

30. Swift, Wesley F. "The Works of John Wesley." Proceedings of
     the Wesley Historical Society 31 (1958): 173-77. Brief biblio-
     graphical article listing the known editions.

31. United Methodist Studies: Basic Bibliographies, compiled by
     the Advisory Committee on United Methodist Studies, Board of
     Higher Education and Ministry, Division of Ordained Ministry; Ken-
     neth E. Rowe, editor. Nashville: Abingdon Press, 1982. 40p.

32. Wesleyana 1973. N.p.: Methodist Museum of South Georgia,
     1973. 12p.

33. Wesleyana: Selected Items from the Clark Collection of Wesleyana
     and Methodistica in the Library of the World Methodist Council
     and the Methodist Historical Society at Lake Junaluska, North
     Carolina, U.S.A. Lake Junaluska, N.C., 1962. 31p.

34. World Methodist Building. Methodistica; Selected Items from the
     Clark Collection of Wesleyana and Methodistica in the World Meth-
     odist Building at Lake Junaluska, North Carolina, U.S.A. Lake
     Junaluska, 1952. 42p.

BOOKS

35. Abbey, Charles John. "The English Church, 1714-60."
    Chap. 3 in vol. 1 of The English Church and Its Bishops
    1700-1800, 183-366. 2 vols. London: Longmans, Green and
    Co., 1887. Both volumes contain numerous references to the
    Wesleys.

36. Abbey, Charles John and J. H. Overton. "The Evangelical
    Revival: The Methodist Movement." Chap. 2 in vol. 2 of
    The English Church in the Eighteenth Century, 57-144. 2
    vols. London: Longmans, Green and Co., 1878.

37. The Abingdon War-Food Book. New York: Abingdon Press,
    1918. 58p. Contains a reprint of Wesley's pamphlet "Thoughts
    on the Present Scarcity of Provisions," with comments by
    Herbert Hoover and Vernon Kellogg.

38. Adams, Charles. The Poet Preacher: A Brief Memorial of
    Charles Wesley, the Eminent Preacher and Poet. New York:
    Carlton and Porter, 1859. 234p.

39. Adams, Samuel B. "John Wesley, the Founder of Methodism."
    In The Wesley Bi-Centenary Celebration in Savannah, Ga.
    Wesley's Only American Home. June 25-29, 1903, 17-32.
    Savannah, Ga.: Savannah Morning News Print, 1903. 163p.

40. Addison, William. "Apostolic Ministry." Chap. 13 in English
    Country Parson, 104-11. London: J. M. Dent, 1947. 246p.

41. Alcock, Joan Pilsbury. "John Wesley and the Beginnings of
    Methodism in the District." Chap. 1 in Methodism in Congle-
    ton..., 1-17. Congleton, Cheshire: Dean Crest Publicity,
    1968. 66p.

42. Alexander, Gross. "The Significance for Methodism of Mr.
    Wesley's Residence in Savannah." In The Beginnings of
    Methodism in the South, 3-8. Nashville: Publishing House of
    the Methodist Episcopal Church, South, 1897. 20p.

43. Allchin, Arthur M. "Our Life in Christ: John Wesley and the
    Eastern Fathers." In We Belong to One Another: Methodist,

Anglican and Orthodox Essays, edited by A. M. Allchin, 62-78. London: Epworth Press, 1965.

44. Allen, Cecil John. "John and Charles Wesley." Chap. 6 in Hymns and the Christian Faith, 55-66. London: Pickering and Inglis, 1966. 199p.

45. Allen, Richard. History of Methodism in Preston and Its Vicinity; With Notices of Its Introduction into East Lancashire and the Fylde. Preston: Toulmin, Printer, Guardian Office, 1866. 66p.

46. Allen, Ronald Wilberforce. Methodism and Modern World Problems.... London: Methuen and Co., 1926. 234p. Contains numerous references to John Wesley and his attitudes toward specific social problems.

47. Allen, W. H. Tiviot Dale Wesleyan Chapel Centenary, 1826-1926. Stockport: Edgeley Press, 1926. 119p.

48. Allendale Methodist Circuit, 1747-1947: Bi-Centenary Memorial. Allendale, n.d. 36p. GtBLW

49. Alley, James M. "The Influence of Wesley upon Ireland." In Wesley As a World Force, edited by John Telford, 31-43. London: Epworth Press, 1929. 144p.

50. Anderson, Arthur E. The Life of John Wesley. [Moline, Ill.: Strombeck Press, 1951]. 32p.

51. Anderson, Joan M. Early Methodism in Bedford: Published in Connection with the Bi-centenary of John Wesley's First Visit to Bedford, 1753. Bedford: Rush and Warwick, 1953. 31p.

52. Andrews, Edward Gayer. "The Decisive Year 1725." In Wesley Bicentennial, Wesleyan University, 180-87. Middletown, Conn.: Wesleyan University, 1904. 239p. Concerns Wesley's response to reading Thomas à Kempis's The Imitation of Christ.

53. Andrews, Stuart. "The Birth of Methodism," and "Methodism under Wesley." Chaps. 3 and 4 in Methodism and Society, 21-36, 37-55. Seminar Studies in History. Harlow: Longman, 1970. 140p.

54. Andrus, Paul C. Wesley's World Parish. Salem, Ohio: Schmul, 1980. 112p.

55. Annan, William. The Difficulties of Arminian Methodism; Embracing Strictures on the Writings of Wesley, Drs. Clarke, Fisk, Bangs and Others, in a Series of Letters.... 3d ed. Pittsburgh, Pa.: Luke Loomis, 1838. 342p.

56. Anstadt, Peter. Luther, Zinzendorf, Wesley: An Account of John Wesley's Conversion through Hearing Luther's "Preface to the Epistle to the Romans," Read in a Moravian Prayer Meeting in London, England. York, Pa.: P. Anstadt, 1902. 112p.

57. Ariarajah, S. Wesley. "Evangelism and Wesley's Catholicity of Grace." Chap. 5 in The Future of the Methodist Theological Traditions. Papers from the Seventh Oxford Institute of Methodist Theological Studies held July 26–August 5, 1982, 138–48. Nashville: Abingdon Press, 1985. 224p.

58. Armstrong, Anthony. The Church of England, the Methodists and Society, 1700–1850. London: University of London Press, 1973. 224p.

59. Armstrong, Richard A. Wesley and Wesleyanism: A Sermon Delivered at High Pavement Chapel, Nottingham. Nottingham: J. Derry, 1876. 14p. GtBLW

60. Armstrong, Thomas. "The Wesleys--Evangelists and Musicians." In Organ and Choral Aspects and Prospects, edited by Max Hinrichsen, 95–106. New York and London: Hinrichsen, 1958. 181p.

61. Arnett, William M. "The Wesleyan/Arminian Teaching on Sin." In Insights into Holiness: Discussions of Holiness by Fifteen Leading Scholars of the Wesleyan Persuasion, compiled by Kenneth Geiger, 55–72. Kansas City, Mo.: Beacon Hill Press, 1962. 294p.

62. _____. "What Happened at Aldersgate?" and "How Aldersgate Affected Wesley." Chaps. 1 and 2 in Methodism's Aldersgate Heritage, by Four Wesleyan Scholars, 11–22. Nashville: Methodist Evangelistic Materials, 1964. 62p.

63. Artingstall, George. A Man of One Book, an Introduction to John Wesley's Teaching on the Bible, Assurance, and Sanctification. London: Epworth Press, 1953. 23p. NjMUM

64. _____. Silver Threads amongst the Gold, 1873-1933-1958: The Methodist Central Hall, City Road, Chester. Chester: Courant Press, 1958. 72p. GtBLW

65. Arvine, Kazlitt. Cyclopedia of Moral and Religious Anecdotes.... New York: George A. Leavitt, 1852. 891p. Contains sixteen anecdotes about John Wesley.

66. Ashley, William. "Wesley's Influence on Christian Thought." In Wesley As a World Force..., 19-22. See no. 49.

67. Atkinson, John. "Mr. Wesley's Relation to the New Church."

Chap. 3 in Centennial History of American Methodism..., 51-
84. New York: Hunt and Eaton, 1884. 559p.

68. Atmore, Charles. "John Wesley" and "Charles Wesley." In
The Methodist Memorial: Being an Impartial Sketch of the
Lives and Characters, of the Preachers, Who Have Departed
This Life..., 453-86. Bristol: R. Edwards, 1801. 582p.

69. Atwood, Anthony. Methodism Defended and Prelatical Succession Refuted, Being a Reply to "Tracts for the People, no. 4."
Harrisburg, Pa.: Isaac G. M'Kinley, 1843. 30p. "Tracts for
the People, no. 4" claimed that Wesley never intended to form
a church in America.

70. Ayling, Stanley Edward. John Wesley. London: Collins,
1979. 350p.

71. Bagslate Wesleyan Chapel, 1810-1910. Methodism in Bagslate,
Being the Centenary Souvenir, compiled by S. L. Coupe, James
Howarth, and Hugh Taylor. Rochdale: Edwards and Bryning,
1910. 78p.

72. Bailey, Albert Edward. "The Age of the Wesleys." Chap. 5
in The Gospel in Hymns; Backgrounds and Interpretations, 73-
102. New York: Charles Scribner's Sons, 1950. 600p.

73. Baillie-Saunders, Margaret Elsie Crowther. "Charles Wesley in
Marylebone." In The Great Folk of Old Marylebone, 62-73.
London: H. J. Glaisher, 1904. 79p.

74. Baines-Griffiths, David. Wesley the Anglican. London: Macmillan, 1919. 140p.

75. Baker, Donald. Introduction to The American War under the
Conduct of Sir William Howe..., by Charles Wesley, 7-11. London: Keepsake Press, 1975. 37p.

76. Baker, Eric W. A Herald of the Evangelical Revival: A Critical
Inquiry into the Relation of William Law to John Wesley, and the
Beginnings of Methodism. London: Epworth Press, 1948.
203p. Dissertation with similar title, Edinburgh University,
1941.

77. Baker, Frank. Charles Wesley, As Revealed by His Letters.
Wesley Historical Society Lectures, no. 14. London: Epworth
Press, 1948. 152p.

78. _____. Charles Wesley's Verse, an Introduction. London:
Epworth Press, 1964. 110p.

79. _____. From Wesley to Asbury: Studies in Early American

Methodism. Durham, N.C.: Duke University Press, 1976.
223p.

80. _____. Introduction to Letters I 1721-1739, 1-140. Vol. 25
of The Oxford Edition of the Works of John Wesley, Frank
Baker, Editor-in-Chief. Oxford: Clarendon Press, 1980.
763p.

81. _____. Introduction to Representative Verse of Charles
Wesley, edited by Frank Baker, ix-lxi. London: Epworth
Press, 1962. 413p.

82. _____. "John Wesley and the Birth of the Methodist Episcopal Church." In Reflections upon Methodism during the American Bicentennial, Papers Presented at the 1984 Regional Conference of the World Methodist Historical Society Held at Asbury Theological Seminary, Wilmore, Kentucky, 1-11. Dallas:
Bridwell Library Center for Methodist Studies, 1985. 274p.

83. _____. John Wesley and the Church of England. Nashville:
Abingdon Press, 1970. 422p.

84. _____. "John Wesley, Postal Pastor." In Dig or Die: Pa-
pers given at the World Methodist Historical Society Wesley
Heritage Conference at Wesley College within the University of
Sydney, 10-15 August 1980, 37-45. Sydney: World Methodist
Historical Society, Australasian Section, 1981. 335p.

85. _____. Methodism and the Love-Feast. London: Epworth
Press, [1957]. 83p. Wesley's discovery of the love-feast
through the Moravians and its use in Methodism are described.

86. _____. The Methodist Pilgrim in England. Rutland, Vt.:
Academy Books, 1976. 110p. Five key areas which are unique-
ly significant in Wesley's life have been described: Epworth,
Oxford, London, Bristol, and Birmingham.

87. _____. "Origin: How Methodism Began." Part 1 of A
Charge to Keep; an Introduction to the People Called Methodists, 1-29. London: Epworth Press, 1947. 232p.

88. _____. "The Oxford Edition of Wesley's Works and Its
Text." Chap. 5 in The Place of Wesley in the Christian Tra-
dition, edited by Kenneth E. Rowe, 117-33. Metuchen, N.J.:
Scarecrow Press, 1976. 165p.

89. _____. "The People Called Methodists. Pt. 3. Polity."
Chap. 7 in vol. 1 of A History of the Methodist Church in
Great Britain, 213-55. London: Epworth Press, 1965.

90. _____. The Story of Cleethorpes and the Contribution of

Books   11

Methodism through Two Hundred Years. Cleethorpes: Trinity
Methodist Church, 1953. 182p.

91. _____. The Story of Methodism in Newland. Kingston-upon-
Hull: Newland Methodist Church, 1958. 67p.

92. _____. "Susanna Wesley: Puritan, Parent, Pastor, Pro-
tagonist, Pattern." In vol. 2 of Women in New Worlds: Historical Perspectives on the Wesleyan Tradition, edited by Rose-
mary Skinner Keller, 112-31. Nashville: Abingdon Press,
1982. Also contained in Dig or Die..., 77-88. See no. 84.

93. _____. A United Methodist Heritage Tour of England.
N.p., n.d. 32p.

94. _____. "Wesleyana and British Methodism." In Gnomon:
Essays for the Dedication of the William R. Perkins Library,
April 16, 1970, edited by John L. Sharpe, III, and Esther
Evans, 52-62. Durham, N.C.: Duke University Library,
1970. 95p.

95. Baker, H. W. The Story of Methodism in Caton. Lancaster:
Guardian Printing Works, 1936. 119p.

96. Baker, J. A. Asquith. A Short History of Methodism in Colchester, Essex. Colchester: Essex Telegraph Ltd., 1935.
23p. Issued in 1935 in connection with the centenary of
Oliver Street Church on January 14, 1936. First published
in serial form in the Essex County Telegraph in June 1935.

97. Baldwin, Stanley. "John Wesley." In This Torch of Freedom:
Speeches and Addresses, 94-99. London: Hodder and
Stoughton, 1935. 339p. A speech delivered at the 150th
anniversary meeting of Wesley's Chapel, London, November 1,
1928.

98. Ball, Raymond Oliver. There is Holy Ground: A History of
Methodism in Middleton, 1760-1950. N.p. 1950. GtBLW

99. Balleine, George Reginald. A History of the Evangelical Party
in the Church of England. London: Longmans, Green, 1908.
338p. Chaps. 1-4 are concerned with the Wesleys.

100. _____. Sing with the Understanding; Some Hymn Problems
Unravelled. London: Independence Press, 1954. 224p.
"Oh for a Thousand Tongues to Sing," "Love Divine, All Love
Excelling," and "Jesu, Lover of My Soul" are discussed on
pp. 94-111.

101. Banfield, Frank. John Wesley. London: K. Paul, 1900.
128p.

102.   Bangs, Carl O.   "Biblical Faith: The Wesleys," and "Faith-
       ful Theology: The Wesleys."   In Our Roots of Belief: Bib-
       lical Faith and Faithful Theology, 39-66.   Kansas City, Mo.:
       Beacon Hill Press, 1981.   79p.

103.   Bangs, Nathan.   A History of the Methodist Episcopal Church.
       ...   3d ed.   4 vols.   New York: Lane and Tippett, 1845.
       Vol. 1 covers the years 1766 to 1792.

104.   _____.   An Original Church of Christ: or, A Scriptural
       Vindication of the Orders and Powers of the Ministry of the
       Methodist Episcopal Church.   2d ed.   New York: T. Mason
       and G. Lane, 1837.   388p.

105.   _____.   Vindication of Methodist Episcopacy.   New York:
       Bangs and Mason, 1820.   193p.

106.   Banks, John.   "How Methodism Began."   Chap. 9 in A People
       Prepared.   The Methodist Way in Faith, History and Practice,
       44-47.   London: Epworth Press, 1961.   96p.

107.   _____.   Nancy Nancy: The Life Story of Ann Bolton Who
       Was the Friend, and Confidante, of John Wesley....   Wilmslow,
       Cheshire: Penwork, 1984.   151p.

108.   Barbeau, Alfred.   "Society in Bath: The Methodists."   Chap.
       6 in Life and Letters at Bath in the Eighteenth Century, 153-
       67.   London: Heinemann; New York: Dodd, Mead and Co.,
       1904.   328p.

109.   Barber, Frank L.   The Philosophy of John Wesley.   Toronto:
       Ryerson Press, 1923.   19p.

110.   Barber, William T. A.   "The Rise and Progress of Methodism."
       Chap. 1 in Methodism in the Modern World, edited by John
       Scott Lidgett and Bryan H. Reed, 11-34.   London: Epworth
       Press, 1929.   286p.   Contains very brief mention of the Wes-
       leys.

111.   Barclay, Wade Crawford.   "The Wesleyan Heritage."   In vol.
       1 of Early American Methodism, 1769-1844, xv-xli.   2 vols.
       History of Methodist Missions, Part 1.   New York: Board of
       Missions, The Methodist Church, 1949-50.   There are addi-
       tional references to John Wesley in other chapters of both
       volumes of this work.

112.   Baring-Gould, Sabine.   The Evangelical Revival.   London:
       Methuen, 1920.   360p.   Pp. 19-122 deal with Wesley and
       Methodism: Wesley's doctrines, methods, personality, and the
       results of his ministry.   The author questions Wesley's use of
       conversion, states Wesley's gospel was imperfect, claims that

Wesley and Whitefield "harped on two themes, the utter corruption of man's nature and justification by faith."

113. Barker, Esther T. Lady Huntingdon, Whitefield, and the
      Wesleys. Maryville, Tenn.: E. T. Barker, 1984. 144p.

114. Barker, Joseph. A Review of Wesley's Notions Respecting the
      Primeval State of Man and the Universe. N.p. 1848. Dis-
      cusses and criticizes Wesley's view of the universe before
      original sin. 22p. GtBLDW

115. Barnes, Annie Maria. Scenes in Pioneer Methodism. Nash-
      ville: Methodist Episcopal Church, South, 1889. 397p.
      Describes the beginnings of Methodism in England, Wales,
      and Ireland.

116. Barnes, Charles Wesley. "The Social Message of John Wesley.
      In Social Messages, the New Sanctification, 24-37. New York:
      Methodist Book Concern, 1915. 100p.

117. Barns, William. O'Connell Refuted; Wesley, Methodism, and
      the Protestant Bible Vindicated, and Popery Exposed. Harris
      burg, Pa.: Barrett and Parke, 1840. 40p.

118. Barr, Josiah Henry. Early Methodists under Persecution.
      1916. Reprint. Salem, Ohio: Schmul Publishers, 1978.
      256p.

119. Barratt, Thomas H. "The Lord's Supper in Early Methodism.
      In Methodism: Its Present Responsibilities: The Proceedings
      of the Methodist Church Congress Held in The Central Hall,
      Bristol, October 7-10, 1929, 71-81. London: Epworth Press
      1929. 319p.

120. Bartlett, Mabel, and Sophia Baker. "Susanna Wesley." In
      Mothers, Makers of Men; Biographical Sketches of Mothers of
      Famous Men, 65-69. 2d rev. ed. New York: Exposition
      Press, 1952. 100p.

121. Bashford, James Whitford. Commemorative Addresses. John
      Wesley As Related to the Eighteenth Century. John Wesley
      Related to Subsequent Times. Denver, Colo.: Shattuck Pr
      ing Co., 1891. 44p. The second address is by H. W. Warr

122. _____. Wesley and Goethe.... Cincinnati: Jennings an
      Pye; New York: Eaton and Mains, 1903. 97p.

123. Bassett, Ancel Henry. A Concise History of the Methodist
      Protestant Church from Its Origin: with Biographical Sketc
      of Several Leading Ministers of the Denomination. 2d ed.

Pittsburgh: James Robison, 1882. 504p. Only pp. 19-26
are devoted to the Wesleys.

124. Bate, A. G. Gleanings from the History of Priory Place
Wesleyan Methodist Church. Doncaster: Chronicle Co.,
1932. 32p. GtBLW

125. Baxter, Daniel Minort. "Origin of the Methodist Church."
Chap. 2 in Back to Methodism, 25-37. Philadelphia: A.M.E.
Book Concern, 1926. 205p.

126. Baxter, Matthew. "Rise of Methodism and Its Influence on the
Moral Condition of England." Chap. 2 in Methodism: Memorials of the United Methodist Free Churches, with Recollections
of the Rev. Robert Eckett and Some of His Contemporaries.
London: W. Reed, 1865. 514p. Includes Voltaire in the discussion.

127. Beach, Waldo and Helmut R. Niebuhr. "John Wesley." Chap.
12 in Christian Ethics; Sources of the Living Tradition, 353-
79. New York: Ronald Press, 1955. 550p.

128. Beal, William. Biographical Notices of the Rev. Bartholomew
Westley, Rector of Charmouth and Catherston, Dorset, 1645-
1662, and of the Rev. John Westley, M.A., His Son, Vicar of
Winterbourne Whitchurch, in the Same County, 1658-1662:
The Former, the Greatgrandfather, the Latter, the Grand-
father of the Late Rev. John and Charles Wesley. London:
John Mason, 1839. 32p.

129. _____. The Fathers of the Wesley Family and References
to Their Times. London: J. Mason, 1833. 122p.

130. Beard, John Relly. The Rise, Progress, and Present Influence
of Wesleyan Methodism. London: British and Foreign Unita-
rian Association, 1831. 60p. Published anonymously. Also
attributed to Robert Brook Aspland. This is an attack on
Wesley and Methodism, focusing on Wesley on pp. 10-25.

131. Beardsley, Frank Grenville. "John Wesley, the Founder of
Methodism." Chap. 3 in Heralds of Salvation; Biographical
Sketches of Outstanding Soul Winners, 38-51. New York:
American Tract Society, 1939. 218p.

132. Bebb, Evelyn Douglas. "John Wesley." In Nonconformity and
Social and Economic Life 1660-1800; Some Problems of the
Present as They Appeared in the Past, 115-19. London: Ep-
worth Press, 1935. 198p. Contains an analysis of Wesley's
sermon on "The Use of Money." There are many references to
John Wesley throughout the book.

133. _____. Wesley, a Man with a Concern. London: Epworth Press, 1950. 143p.

134. Beck, Brian E. "A Retrospect." Chap. 7 in The Future of the Methodist Theological Tradition..., 209-21. See no. 57.

135. Beckerlegge, John J. Two Hundred Years of Methodism in Mousehole, Penzance, St. Clements Methodist Church. N.p. 1954. 38p.

136. Beckerlegge, Oliver A. Free Methodism in Cornwall. Occasional Publications, no. 2. Truro: Cornish Methodist Historical Association, 1961. 26p.

137. _____. Introduction to A Roman Catechism with a Reply Thereto. London: Protestant Truth Society, 1968. 88p.

138. Beckett, W. James. Brunswick Wesleyan Methodist Church, Birkenhead, Centenary Souvenir, 1830-1930. Birkenhead: John Woolman, 1930. 104p. GtBMM

139. Beebe, George. The Optical Lantern Life of Wesley.... A Lecture to Accompany a Series of Sixty Photographic Transparencies. Bradford: Riley Brothers, 1891. 40p. "Many of this new and original set of slides are copied from the unique collection of pictures in the possession of Robert Teare, Esq., of King's Lynn, kindly lent for the purpose"--title page.

140. Beecham, John. "The Constitution of Methodism Previous to 1795 and 1797." In An Essay on the Constitution of Wesleyan Methodism: In Which Various Misrepresentations of Some of Its Leading Principles..., 1-30. 2d ed. London: J. Mason, 1850. 134p. The author describes the early organization of Methodism--"the highest department in the executive was filled by Mr. Wesley, who exercised a general superintendence over the whole connexion."

141. _____. "The Life of the Rev. John Wesley, A.M." In vol. 1 of Sermons on Several Occasions, by John Wesley, i-xlix. 3 vols. London: Wesleyan Conference Office, 1876.

142. Beetham, Thomas A. The Methodist Way: Notes on John Wesley's Rules. London: Atlantis Press, 1960. 40p.

143. Begbie, Harold. "The Age of Wesley." Chap. 7 in Seven Ages: A Brief and Simple Narrative of the Pilgrimage of the Human Mind As It Has Affected the English-Speaking World, 177-208. New York and London: G. P. Putnam's Sons, 1923. 218p.

144. Belshaw, Robert Redman. John Lee and Charles Wesley's

Hymns: An Appreciation. Dublin: Ponsonby and Gibbs, 1902. 19p.

145. Beltz, Roy Allen. John Wesley, a Great Leader. Hall-of-Fame Series. Des Moines: Boone Publishing Co., 1944. 48p.

146. Benedict, Samuel. Notes to The Duty of Constant Communion: A Sermon, by John Wesley, 19-24. Philadelphia: Lippincott Press, 1877. 24p.

147. Benjamin, Frederick Albert. A Facet of Life in Keswick 1757-1975: Methodism. Keswick: Keswick Southey Street Methodist Church Council, 1975. 33p.

148. Bennett, Herbert E. A History of Teddington Methodist Church. Dudley: W. H. Hill, 1939. 15p. GtBMM

149. Bennetts, George Armstrong. John Wesley versus Modernism. Gloucester: F. J. Brooke; London: Morgan and Scott, 1913. 20p.

150. Benson, Arthur Christopher, and H. F. W. Tatham. "John Wesley." In Men of Might: Studies of Great Characters, 144-63. London: E. Arnold, 1892. 295p.

151. Benson, Clarence Irving. John Wesley and the Beginning of Methodism. 2d ed. Melbourne: Methodist Publishing House, n.d. 20p. NcD

152. Benson, Joseph. An Apology for the People Called Methodists; Containing a Concise Account of Their Origin and Progress, Doctrine, Discipline and Designs: Humbly Submitted to the Consideration of the Friends of True Christianity. London: G. Story, 1801. 405p.

153. _____. The Beauties of the Rev. J. Wesley, Containing the Most Interesting Passages, Selected from His Whole Works. To Which is Prefixed, Memoirs of His Life, the Particulars of His Will, and an Account of His Last Illness and Death, by One of His Preachers. Nottingham: C. Sutton, 1802. 262p.

154. _____. "Particulars of the Death of Mr. Wesley." In vol. 6 of The Works of John Wesley..., 249-58. 2d ed. 17 vols. London: Conference Office, 1810. 416p.

155. _____. A Sermon Preached on the Sunday Evening Preceding the Opening of the Conference of the Preachers Lately, in Connexion with the Rev. John Wesley at Manchester, July 26, 1791. Birmingham: J. Thompson, 1791. 32p.

156. Benson, Louis F. "The Hymnody of the Methodist Revival."

Chap. 5 in The English Hymn: Its Development and Use in
Worship, 219-61. 1915. Reprint. Richmond, Va.: John
Knox Press, 1962. 624p.

157. _____. "Jesus, Lover of My Soul." Chap. 4 in Studies of
Familiar Hymns, 33-44. 2d series. Philadelphia: Westminster
Press, 1923. 314p.

158. _____. "The Wesleyan Hymns as Poetry." In The Hymnody
of the Christian Church, 115-22. 1927. Reprint. Richmond,
Va.: John Knox Press, 1956. 310p.

159. Beresford, John. "John Wesley." In From Anne to Victoria;
Essays by Various Hands, edited by Bonamy Dobrée, 204-16.
London: Cassell, 1927. 630p.

160. Berg, Johannes van den. "Methodism, Great Awakening and
Missions." Chap. 3 in Constrained by Jesus' Love: An In-
quiry into the Motives of the Missionary Awakening in Great
Britain in the Period between 1698 and 1815, 66-105. Kampen:
J. H. Kok, 1956. 238p.

161. Best, Ernest E. Religion and Society in Transition: The
Church and Social Change in England, 1560-1850. Texts and
Studies in Religion, vol. 15. New York: Edwin Mellen Press,
1982. 336p. Numerous discussions of John Wesley throughout
the book, especially in Chap. 6, "Faith, Thought and Life:
the Vital Issues at Stake," pp. 164-91.

162. Bett, Henry. The Hymns of Methodism in Their Literary Relations. Manuals for Christian Thinkers. London: C. H. Kelly,
1913. 131p.

163. _____. The Spirit of Methodism. London: Epworth Press,
1937. 254p.

164. _____. "Wesley's Journal." Chap. 6 in Studies in Literature, 103-20. London: Epworth Press, 1929. 193p. Chap.
1, "Evangelical Religion and Literature" has some mention of
the Wesleys.

165. Bevan, Frances A. John Wesley. True Stories of God's Ser-
vants. London: Alfred Holness, [187-?] 348p.

166. Bewes, Richard, ed. John Wesley's England: A Nineteenth
Century Pictorial History Based on an Eighteenth Century
Journal. London: Hodder and Stoughton, 1981. 110p. Ex-
cerpts from Wesley's journal with commentary by Bewes.

167. Bibbins, Ruthella Mary. How Methodism Came: The Beginnings of Methodism in England and America. Biographical

introduction by Laura Dempster Gronemeyer. Edited by
Richard Larkin Shipley and Gordon Pratt Baker. Baltimore:
American Methodist Historical Society, 1945. 190p.

168. Billington, Raymond John. "The Implications for Methodism:
The Methodist Heritage." Chap. 3 in The Liturgical Movement and Methodism, 109-41. London: Epworth Press, 1969.
217p.

169. Birks, William. Centenary of Wesley's Death, 1891: Rev. J.
Wesley and Methodism. Newark: J. Stennett, 1891. 14p.
A sermon.

170. Birrell, Augustine. John Wesley: Some Aspects of the Eighteenth Century in England. London: Epworth Press, 1938.
31p. This essay is contained in various collections of Birrell's
essays and in Scribner's Magazine 26 (1899):753-61. It is par-
tially reprinted in Letters of John Wesley (1914) and The Heart
of John Wesley's Journal (1903).

171. Birtwhistle, Allen. Seek Ye First: A Series of Six Meditations Based on Charles Wesley's Hymn, "Come O Thou Traveller Unknown." London: Epworth Press, 1949. 84p.

172. Bishop, John. Derby King Street Methodist Church: Centenary Souvenir Handbook, 1841-1941. Derby: Marper and
Sons, 1941. 39p. GtBLW

173. _____. "The History of Methodism in Perth." In Perth
Wesleyan Methodist Church: Diamond Jubilee Souvenir Handbook, 1880-1940, 5-11. Perth: R. K. Smith and Son, 1940.
32p. GtBLW

174. _____. "The Methodist Church--A Detailed Study of Its
Worship." Part 2 in Methodist Worship, in Relation to Free
Church Worship. London: Epworth Press, 1950. 164p.
Describes the origin and development of Methodist services--
baptism, communion, hymns. A revision of the author's M.A.
thesis, Bristol University, England, published under the title:
The Forms and Psychology of Worship in the Free Church with
Special Reference to Methodism.

175. Black, J. C. C. "Wesley Outside of Methodism." In The
Wesley Bi-Centenary Celebration in Savannah, Ga., 117-25.
See no. 39.

176. Blair, Ralph. Wesleyan Praxis and Homosexual Practice. New
York: HCCC, Inc., 1983. 30p. Based on an address given
at the Michigan Area United Methodist Pastor's School, August
22, 1983, on the campus of Ferris State College, Big Rapids,
Michigan.

177. Blanshard, Thomas W. Sketch of the History of Methodism in
     the Shotley Bridge Circuit. Consett: Robert Jackson,
     1872. 57p. GtBMM

178. Bloxam, M. "Evangelical Revivals." Chapter 43 in A New
     Guide to Knowledge of Church History, 255-61. London and
     Edinburgh: Marshall Bros., [1920]. 264p.

179. Bloye, G. Herbert. John Wesley, the Evangelist of England.
     The Lecture Library, no. 1. London: Francis Griffiths,
     1912. 64p. GtBLW

180. Body, Alfred Harris. John Wesley and Education. London:
     Epworth Press, 1936. 168p. His M.Ed. thesis, Manchester
     University, 1935.

181. Bogue, David, and James Bennett. The History of Dissenters
     from the Revolution in 1688 to the Year 1808. 4 vols. London,
     1808-12. Vol. 3, pp. 1-74 deal with Wesley and Methodism.

182. Boisen, Anton Theophilus. "From Sect to Church: A Case
     Study." Chap. 8 in Religion in Crisis and Custom: A So-
     ciological and Psychological Study. New York: Harper and
     Bros. 1945. 271p.

183. Bolitho, Herbert. Truly Rural: Lights and Shadows on the
     History of the North Hill Circuit (Cornwall) of the Methodist
     Church, 1743-1946. [Launceston, Eng., 1947]. 102p. IEG, NcD

184. Bolitho, Paul. Methodism in the Liskeard Circuit, 1751-1967.
     Liskeard: P. Bolitho, 1967. 74p.

185. Bolles, James A. "The Claims of Methodist Episcopacy."
     In The Episcopal Church Defended; with an Examination into
     the Claims of Methodist Episcopacy in a Series of Letters Ad-
     dressed to the Rev. Allen Steele, with His Replies, 75-166.
     Batavia, N.Y.: Frederick Follett, 1843. 198p.

186. Bolton, Sarah K. "Susanna Wesley." In Famous Types of
     Womanhood, 105-49. New York: T. Y. Crowell and Co.,
     1892. 350p.

187. Bonar, Andrew R. "John Wesley." In The Last Days of
     Eminent Christians, 241-47. Edinburgh: T. Nelson, 1841.
     320p.

188. Bond, Beverly Waugh. Life of John Wesley. Nashville:
     Southern Methodist Publishing House, 1885. 216p.

189. Bond, John. Golden Candlesticks: or, Sketches of the Rise
     of Some Early Methodist Churches. London: Elliot Stock,
     1873. 134p.

190. Bone, Florence. "John Wesley in the North Riding." In
Wesley Studies, 220-26. London: C. H. Kelly, 1903. 237p.

191. Bonino, José Miguez. "Wesley's Doctrine of Sanctification
from a Liberationist Perspective." In Sanctification and Liberation: Liberal Theologies in the Light of the Wesleyan Tradition, edited by Theodore Runyon, 49-63. Nashville: Abingdon Press, 1981. 255p. Paper presented at the Oxford Institute on Methodist Theological Studies, 6th, 1977 held under
the auspices of the World Methodist Council.

192. Boreham, Frank William. "John Wesley's Text." Chap. 19
in A Bunch of Everlastings or Texts That Made History; a
Volume of Sermons, 198-209. New York and Cincinnati:
Abingdon Press, 1920. 255p.

193. Borgen, Ole Edvard. Introduction to John Wesley; an Autobiographical Sketch of the Man and His Thought, Chiefly from
His Letters, by John Wesley, ix-xvi. Leiden: E. J. Brill,
1966. 116p.

194. _____. John Wesley on the Sacraments: A Theological
Study. Nashville: Abingdon Press, 1972. 307p. His dissertation, Drew University, 1968.

195. Boswell, John Wesley. A Short History of Methodism. Nashville: Publishing House, Methodist Episcopal Church, South,
1903. 188p.

196. Bourne, George. The Life of the Rev. John Wesley, A.M.,
with Memoirs of the Wesley Family. To Which Are Subjoined,
Dr. Whitehead's Funeral Sermon; and a Comprehensive History
of American Methodism. Baltimore: Printed by George Dobbin
and Murphy, for themselves, John Hagerty and Abner Neal,
1807. 351p.

197. Bouyer, Louis. The Spirit and Forms of Protestantism.
Translated by A. V. Littledale. Fontana Library of Theology
and Philosophy. London: Collins, 1963. 284p. Includes discussion of John and Charles Wesley, their hymns, and their
work in the revival, pp. 46-49, 219-25.

198. Bowden, Haygood Samuel. History of Savannah Methodism,
from John Wesley to Silas Johnson. Macon, Ga.: J. W. Burke
Co., 1929. 321p.

199. Bowen, Marjorie [pseud.]. Wrestling Jacob: A Study of the
Life of John Wesley and Some Members of His Family. London:
W. Heinemann, 1937. 395p.

200. Bowie, Walter Russell. "John Wesley." Chap. 17 in Men of

Fire; Torchbearers of the Gospel, 185-97. New York: Harper, 1961. 244p.

201. _____. "Susanna Wesley." Chap. 4 in Women of Light, 42-53. New York: Harper and Row, 1963. 205p.

202. Bowmer, John C. Pastor and People: A Study of Church and Ministry in Wesleyan Methodism from the Death of John Wesley (1791) to the Death of Jabez Bunting (1858). Fernley-Hartley Lecture, 1975. London: Epworth Press, 1975. 272p.

203. _____. The Sacrament of the Lord's Supper in Early Methodism. London: Dacre Press, 1951. 244p.

204. Boyd, Myron F. Flame of a Century, What Made It Burn? Radio Messages on John Wesley and Early Methodism. Winona Lake, Ind.: World Wide Gospel Broadcast, 1958. 64p.

205. Boyd, Wesley. John Wesley's Journal, a Spiritual Tonic. s.l.: Methodist Aldersgate Bi-centenary Commission, 1938. 19p.

206. Boyling, Percy L. John Wesley's Chapel. Rev. ed. London: Friends of Wesley's Chapel, 1949. 51p.

207. Brabrook, Edward W. Methodism in Lewisham. London: Wesleyan Conference Office, 1881. 32p. GtBMM

208. Bradburn, Samuel. Further Account of the Rev. John Wesley. Manchester: F. Radford, 1791? 27p.

209. _____. The Question, Are the Methodists Dissenters...? N.p. 1792.

210. _____. "A Sketch of Mr. Wesley's Character." In Select Letters, Chiefly on Personal Religion, by the Rev. John Wesley, 7-23. New York: T. Mason and G. Lane, 1838. 240p.

211. Bradshaw, David B. Methodist Centenary Church, St. Stephen's Green, Dublin: A Commemorative Record. Dublin: Robert T. White, 1943. 181p.

212. Brailsford, Mabel Richmond. Susanna Wesley, the Mother of Methodism. London: Epworth Press, 1938. 144p.

213. _____. A Tale of Two Brothers, John and Charles Wesley. London: Hart-Davis, 1954. 301p.

214. Braithwaite, Matthew. History of Methodism in the Bishop Auckland Circuit. Bishop Auckland: Matthew Braithwaite, 1885. 235p.

215. Brantley, Richard E. Locke, Wesley, and the Method of
English Romanticism. Gainesville: University of Florida
Press, 1984. 300p. (Rev. in no. 3888.)

216. _____. Wordsworth's "Natural Methodism." New Haven:
Yale University Press, 1975. 205p. In developing his thesis
that Wordsworth had a strong Methodist orientation, the author
has many references to Wesley throughout the book.

217. Brash, W. Bardsley. Methodism: The Faiths, Varieties of
Christian Expression, edited by L. P. Jacks. London:
Methuen and Co., 1928. 207p. The author tells how
Methodism arose--the story of the Wesleys and their helpers.

218. _____. "Wesley." In vol. 12 of Encyclopaedia of Religion
and Ethics, edited by James Hastings, 724-27. 13 vols. New
York: Charles Scribner's Sons, 1961.

219. Brawley, Benjamin Griffith. "Charles Wesley and His Age."
Chap. 5 in History of the English Hymn, 89-119. New York:
Abingdon Press, 1932. 256p.

220. Bready, John Wesley. England: Before and After Wesley;
the Evangelical Revival and Social Reform. New York: Russell and Russell, 1971. 463p.

221. _____. Faith and Freedom: The Roots of Democracy.
New York: American Tract Society, 1946. 149p. Based on
radio lectures delivered on the Canadian Broadcasting Corporation.

222. _____. Wesley and Democracy. Toronto: Ryerson Press,
1939. 65p. A series of talks given over a national network
by the Canadian Broadcasting Corporation. This book is a
digest of his England: Before and After Wesley, no. 220.

223. Bretherton, Francis Fletcher. Early Methodism in and around
Chester, 1749-1812. Chester: Phillipson and Golder, 1903.
296p. Based on material collected by Benjamin Smith.

224. _____. The Origin and Progress of Methodism in Margate:
Forming a Souvenir of Centenary Celebrations Held in 1908 to
Celebrate the Formation of the Margate Circuit in 1808. Mar-
gate: Bobby, 1908. 47p.

225. _____. Sans Street Methodist Mission, Sunderland: Historical Souvenir. Sunderland, 1937. 16p. GtBLW

226. Brett, Sidney Reed. John Wesley. London: Adam and
Charles Black, 1958. 96p.

227. Bridgman, Thomas. Remarks on a Review of Two Sermons by
Messrs. Bridgman and Beckwith Published in the Christian Instructor for February; with an Account of the Character and
Death of the Rev. J. Wesley. Perth, Eng.: R. Morison,
1819. 24p. NjMUM

228. A Brief Account of Peter Böhler, the Spiritual Father of John
and Charles Wesley. London: Printed for the Promoters of
the Böhler Memorial Chapel, 1877. 23p. NjMUM

229. Bridgden, Thomas E. "John Wesley." Chap. 3 in vol. 1 of
A New History of Methodism, edited by W. J. Townsend, H.
B. Workman, and George Eayrs, 159-234. 2 vols. London:
Hodder and Stoughton, 1909.

230. _____. John Wesley the Methodist: A Plain Account of
His Life and Work. New York: Eaton and Mains, 1903.
319p.

231. _____. "The Reading of Wesley's Preachers." In Wesley
Studies, 142-50. See no. 190.

232. _____. "The Teaching of Wesley's Mother." In Wesley
Studies, 135-41. See no. 190.

233. Brightwell, Cecilia Lucy. "Mrs. Susannah Wesley." Chap. 9
in Above Rubies; or, Memorials of Christian Gentlewomen,
219-43. London: T. Nelson and Sons, 1865. 304p.

234. Brindley, John. John Wesley: "A Burning and a Shining
Light." A Lecture, Delivered in the Music Hall, Birmingham,
on the Evening of Thursday, November 17, 1859. Birmingham,
Eng.: F. A. Harwood, [1859]. 16p. GEU-T

235. Bristol, John Wesley's Chapel. A Short Guide to John Wesley's
Chapel, Bristol; the New Room. Bristol: Rankin Bros., n.d.
12p. AbN

236. Broadley, William S. History of the United Methodist Free
Church, Meeting in Bethesda Chapel, Newchurch-in-Rossen-
dale, Lancashire from the year 1822 to 1907. Edinburgh:
Lorimer and Chalmers, 1908. 96p.

237. Brockett, Allan. "Whitefield and Wesley." Chap. 8 in Nonconformity in Exeter 1650-1875, 118-30. Manchester: Manchester University Press, 1962. 252p.

238. Bronson, Asahel. A Plain Exhibition of Methodist Episcopacy,
in Fourteen Numbers. Burlington, Vt.: Chauncy Goodrich,
1844. 259p. This author claims that Wesley was a "hearty
despiser of democracy in every form, and more especially of
democracy in things ecclesiastical."

239. Brook, David. "The Oxford Methodists." Chap. 2 in vol. 1
     of A New History of Methodism, 135-58. See no. 229.

240. Brook, H. M. The Methodist Church, Cleadon: Jubilee
     Celebrations, 1899-1949. [Cleadon, Eng.], 1949. NcD

241. Brown, Earl Kent. Women of Mr. Wesley's Methodism.
     Studies in Women and Religion, vol. 11. New York: Edwin
     Mellen Press, 1983. 261p.

242. _____. "Women of the World: Selected Leadership Roles
     of Women in Mr. Wesley's Methodism." In Women in New
     Worlds: Historical Perspectives on the Wesleyan Tradition,
     edited by Hilah F. Thomas and Rosemary Skinner Keller, 69-
     87. Nashville: Abingdon Press, 1981. 445p.

243. Brown, J. W. Wesleyan Methodist Church, Leith; Jubilee,
     1868-1918; Brief History of Methodism in Leith. Leith: Wil-
     liam R. Duff and Co., 1918. 8p. GtBMM

244. Brown, Robert. John Wesley; or, The Theology of Conscience.
     2d ed. London: Elliott Stock, 1868. 96p. NjMD, KyWAT

245. _____. John Wesley's Theology: The Principle of Its Vi-
     tality and Its Progressive Stages of Development. London:
     Jackson, Walford and Hodder, 1865. 52p.

246. Brown, William J. Wesley's Chapel, City Road, London; Its
     History and Associations. London: Hayman, Christy and
     Lilly, 1896. 45p.

247. Brownlie, John. "Charles Wesley." In Hymns and Hymn
     Writers of the Church Hymnary, 131-37. London and New
     York: H. Frowde, 1899. 364p.

248. Brownlow, William Gannaway. The Great Iron Wheel Examined;
     or, Its False Spokes Extracted, and an Exhibition of Elder
     Graves, Its Builder. Nashville, Tenn., 1856. 331p. A rebut-
     tal to J. R. Graves' The Great Iron Wheel..., with several
     chapters devoted to the story of the Wesleys. See nos. 692,
     840.

249. Bruce, William. Wesley and Swedenborg, a Review of the Rev.
     John Wesley's "Thoughts on the Writings of Baron Swedenborg."
     London: James Speirs, F. Pitman, 1877. 80p.

250. Bryan, John L. John Wesley, the First Methodist, 1703-1791;
     a Little Biographical Essay Designed to Introduce Modern Col-
     lege Students to the Most Distinguished Wesleyan. Greensboro,
     N.C., 1957. 16p.

251. Buck, Richard Hugh Keats. How Wesley's Society Lapsed
     into Schism: A Brief Sketch. London: Houlston and Sons,
     1874. 31p.

252. Buckley, Harry. Woodhouse Methodist Church, 1756-1940.
     N.p. 1940. 12p. GtBMM

253. Buckley, J. M. A History of Methodists in the United States.
     vol. 5 of American Church History Series. 2d ed. New
     York: Charles Scribner's Sons, 1899. Pp. 27-280 discuss
     Wesley's life, the religious movement he founded, and its in-
     troduction to America.

254. Budd, Leonard H. Days Multiplied: The Wesley Legacy.
     Lima, Ohio: C.S.S. Publishing Co., 1984. 37p. Book of
     devotional essays based on seven days in John Wesley's jour-
     nal.

255. Bullock, Frederick William Bagshawe. Evangelical Conversion
     in Great Britain, 1696-1845. St. Leonards-on-Sea: Budd and
     Gillatt, 1959. 287p. Discussion of John and Charles Wesley,
     pp. 44-54.

256. _____. "Religious Societies in Great Britain." In Volun-
     tary Religious Societies, 1520-1799, 173-256. St. Leonards-on-
     Sea: Budd and Gillatt, 1963. 264p.

257. Bullock, Thomas Austin. "Wesley's Influence on the Intellec-
     tual, Social, and Religious Life of the English Masses." In
     The Wesley Memorial Volume; or, Wesley, and the Methodist
     Movement, Judged by Nearly One Hundred and Fifty Writers,
     Living or Dead, edited by J. O. A. Clark, 98-127. New York:
     Phillips and Hunt; Cincinnati: Walden and Stowe, 1881. 743p.

258. Buoy, Charles Wesley. "Susannah, Mother of the Wesleys."
     In Representative Women of Methodism, 1-87. New York: Hunt
     and Eaton; Cincinnati: Cranston and Curts, 1893. 476p.

259. Burbridge, Alfred. Wesleyanism, a Sympathetic Study of the
     History of an Institution Which Was Founded Only for the Better
     Service of God in the Name of Christ. Rev. ed. Catholic
     Truth Society Historical Pamphlets, no. 29. London: Catho-
     lic Truth Society, 1932. 36p.

260. Burbridge, Charles. The Mecca of Methodism: A Collection
     of Permanent Photographs [of Wesley's House and Chapel] with
     Descriptive Sketch. London: C. H. Kelly, 1906. 18p.

261. Burgess, John. John Wesley and Cumbria. s.l.: Wesley His-
     torical Society, Cumbria Branch, 1979. 21p.

262. Burgess, William Penington. Wesleyan Hymnology; or, A

Companion to the Wesleyan Hymn Book. London: T. Riley,
1845. 282p.

263. Burns, James. "Wesley and the Evangelical Revival." Chap.
7 in Revivals, Their Laws and Leaders, 263-312. London:
Hodder and Stoughton, 1909. 312p.

264. Burroughs, R. A Centenary History of Old King Street
Wesleyan Chapel, Bristol. Bristol: W. Hemmons, 1895. 95p.

265. Burrow, Osbert Mordaunt. Epworth: The Home of the Wesleys. Epworth: Barnes and Breeze, 1936. 32p.

266. _____. A Sermon Preached in the Wesley Memorial Church,
Epworth, on Thursday, April 25, 1935, on the Occasion of the
Bi-centenary of the Death of Rev. Samuel Wesley, M.A., Rector of Epworth, 1697-1735. Epworth: Barnes and Breeze,
1935. 8p.

267. Burton, Jack Robert. The Richest Legacy: The Eucharistic
Hymns of John and Charles Wesley. Norwich, Eng.: F.
Crowe and Sons, 1981. 112p. (Rev. in no. 3960.)

268. Burton, John. "Wesley's Missionary Call: Advice concerning
Georgia." In Wesley Studies, 71-80. See no. 190.

269. Burwash, N. Introduction to Wesley's Doctrinal Standards,
v-xviii. 1881. Reprint. Salem, Ohio: H. E. Schmul, 1967.
A collection of Wesley's sermons with analysis and notes for each.

270. Butler, Dugald. John Wesley and George Whitefield in Scotland; or, The Influence of the Oxford Methodists on Scottish
Religion. Edinburgh: W. Blackwood, 1898. 318p.

271. Butler, Henry Montagu. Ten Great and Good Men; Lectures.
London: Edward Arnold, 1909. Includes an account of Wesley's life based on the works of Southey, Tyerman, and Wesley's journal.

272. Butterworth, Richard. "Wesley's Interviews with Famous
People." In Wesley Studies, 182-90. See no. 190.

273. Byrt, W. H., and Arthur E. Shooter. The Chapel by the
Toll Gate, Wesley Chapel, Baptist Mills, Bristol, 1837-1937.
Bristol: J. Cook and Co., 1936. 20p. GtBBrP

274. Cadman, S. Parkes. "The Influence of Wesley in America."
In Wesley As a World Force..., 53-70. See no. 49.

275. _____. The Three Religious Leaders of Oxford and Their
Movements, John Wycliffe, John Wesley, John Henry Newman.
New York: Macmillan, 1916. 596p.

276. Caine, Caesar. A Brief Chronicle of Wesleyan Methodism in
      Leyton, Essex, 1750-1895. Leyton: T. Hubbard, 1896. 96p.

277. Cairns, Earle Edwin. "The Sources of Evangelical Reform."
      Chap. 2 in Saints and Society: The Social Impact of Eight-
      eenth Century English Revivals and Its Contemporary Rele-
      vance, 29-43. Chicago: Moody Press, 1960. 192p.

278. Caldwell, Merritt. "The Wesleyan Theory." Chap. 7 in The
      Philosophy of Christian Perfection, 76-109. Philadelphia:
      Sorin and Ball, 1848. 159p.

279. Caldwell, Wayne E. "The View of John Wesley [on angels]."
      In A Contemporary Wesleyan Theology: Biblical, Systematic,
      and Practical, edited by Charles W. Carter, 1059-61. 2 vols.
      Grand Rapids, Mich.: Francis Asbury Press, 1983.

280. Cameron, Richard M. "John Wesley, the Molder of Methodism."
      In Methodism and Society in Historical Perspective, 31-72.
      Methodism and Society, vol. 1. Nashville: Abingdon Press,
      1961. 349p.

281. _____. The Rise of Methodism: A Source Book. New York:
      Philosophical Library, 1954. 397p. The purpose of this book
      is "to render accessible in convenient form the more crucial
      portions of the sources for the beginnings of the Methodist
      Revival." The extracts are mostly from the letters and jour-
      nals of Wesley and Whitefield, with introductory essays to each
      section.

282. Cameron, W. Comments on John Wesley's Plain Account of
      Christian Perfection. Liverpool: Edward Howell, 1883.
      35p. NjMUM

283. Camidge, William. York Wesleyan Methodist Juvenile Missionary
      Society: History, Birth and Growth. York: Yorkshire Ga-
      zette Office, 1898. 214p. GtBMM

284. Candler, Warren Akin. "The Man Wesley." In The Wesley
      Bi-Centenary Celebration in Savannah, Ga., 129-40. See
      no. 39.

285. _____. Wesley and His Work; or, Methodism and Missions;
      a Volume of Addresses. Nashville: Publishing House of the
      Methodist Episcopal Church, South, 1912. 223p.

286. Cannon, Thomas. An Appendix to the Sermon Preached at
      the City Chapel on the Death of Mr. John Wesley.... Lon-
      don, 1791. 2p. GtBMM

287. Cannon, William R. "Accomplishments to Wesley's Death." In

Methodism, edited by William Ketcham Anderson, 28-37. Cincinnati: Methodist Publishing House, 1947. 317p.

288. _____. The Theology of John Wesley, with Special Reference to the Doctrine of Justification. New York and Nashville: Abingdon-Cokesbury Press, 1946. 284p. Describes the historical background to Wesley's theology and expounds justification as Wesley's central doctrine. The author then deals with the concepts that arise out of the doctrine of justification.

289- Cannon, William Walters. Methodism and the Church of Eng-
290. land: A Comparison, by a Layman. London: Griffith Farran Okeden and Welsh, 1891. 184p. The author of this book had been a Methodist and rejoined the Church of England. He describes briefly the rise of Methodism with numerous references to Wesley and his doctrines, and compares them to the Church of England doctrines.

291. Carpenter, Eugene E. "Some Wesleyan Observations on Cosmology." In A Contemporary Wesleyan Theology: Biblical, Systematic, and Practical, 176-78. See no. 279.

292. Carpenter, Spencer Cecil. "John Wesley and the Beginnings of Methodism." Chap. 11 in Eighteenth Century Church and People, 194-216. London: John Murray, 1959. 290p.

293. Carpenter, William Boyd. "The Religious Revival A.D. 1703-1754." Chap. 31 in A Popular History of the Church of England, from the Earliest Times to the Present Day. New York: E. P. Dutton and Co., 1909. 517p. Pp. 365-76 deal with Wesley.

294. Carter, Charles Sydney. "John Wesley and the Growth of Methodism." Chap. 7 in The English Church in the Eighteenth Century, 55-66. London: Longmans, Green and Co., 1910. 128p.

295. Carter, Charles W. "The Ethics of John Wesley," and "Wesley's View on Moral Conditions in Eighteenth-Century Great Britain." In A Contemporary Wesleyan Theology: Biblical, Systematic, and Practical, 992-97. See no. 279.

296. _____. "John Wesley's Evaluation of Humanity." In A Contemporary Wesleyan Theology: Biblical, Systematic, and Practical, 220-28. See no. 279.

297. _____. "John Wesley's Understanding of Sin." In A Contemporary Wesleyan Theology: Biblical, Systematic, and Practical, 265-72. See no. 279.

298. _____. The Person and Ministry of the Holy Spirit: A
Wesleyan Perspective. Rev. ed. Grand Rapids, Mich.: Baker
Book House, 1974. 355p.

299. Carter, Charles W., and Everett N. Hunt, Jr. "Significant
Influences on Wesley's Preparation for Mission," and "Wesley's
Sense of Mission." In A Contemporary Wesleyan Theology:
Biblical, Systematic, and Practical, 665-72. See no. 279.

300. Carter, Henry. The Methodist; a Study in Discipleship. The
Fellowship Library, vol. 1. London: C. H. Kelly, 1914.
181p.

301. _____. The Methodist Heritage. London: Epworth Press,
1951. 246p. The author's aim is to reply to the question:
"What is there in Methodist history and experience which
bears directly on the new endeavour of Christ's Church on
earth to recover her unity, to bring together her scattered
spiritual wealth, to proclaim her Head as Lord, Redeemer,
and Renewer of mankind." He examines the heritage of the
Wesleys, and the heritage bequeathed by the Wesleys.

302. Carter, Kathy. London and the Famous: An Historical Guide
to Fifty Famous People and Their London Homes. London:
Frederick Muller, 1982. 157p. John Wesley, pp. 142-44.

303. Carter, Thomas. John Wesley As a Philanthropist and the Social Mission of Methodism. Nashville: Missionary Training
School, 1905. 40p.

304. Cary, Clement. "Did Mr. Wesley Change His View on Sanctification?" In Entire Sanctification, edited by S. L. C.
Coward, 73-80. Louisville: Pentecostal Herald Press, 1900.
371p.

305. Castleman, T. T. An Inquiry into the Origin of American
Methodism, with Selections from the Writings of the Rev. John
Wesley. Petersburg, Va., 1843. 43p. NjMUM

306. Cate, Margaret Davis. The Wesleys on Saint Simons Island.
St. Simons Island, Ga.: The Commission on Archives and
History, South Georgia Conference, United Methodist Church,
1971. 18p. NjMUM

307. Cell, George Croft. John Wesley's New Testament Compared
with the Authorized Version. Philadelphia and Chicago:
John C. Winston Co., 1938. 391p.

308. _____. The Rediscovery of John Wesley. New York: Henry
Holt and Co., 1935. 420p. (Rev. in no. 2549.)

309.   The Centenary of Methodism; Being a Condensed and Classi-
       fied History of the Rise, Extension and Continuance of That
       System Which Was Founded by Rev. John Wesley, A.M., in
       the Year 1739. Dublin: Primitive Wesleyanism Methodist Book
       Room, 1839. 366p.

310.   Chambers, Peggy. Six Great Christians: Edmund Campion,
       Vincent de Paul, George Fox, John Wesley, Mary Slessor,
       Gladys Aylward. London: Hamilton, 1958. 175p.

311.   Champness, Mary. "Charles Wesley and His Hymns." and
       "John Wesley's Hymns and Translations." Chaps. 1 and 2 in
       Half-hours with "The Methodist Hymnbook," 1-95. London:
       Robert Culley, 1904. 288p.

312.   Champness, Thomas. John of Epworth. London: "Joyful
       News" Book Depot, n.d. 16p. GEU-T

313.   Chancellor, Frank Beresford, and Henry S. Eeles. Celebrated
       Carthusians. London: P. Allan, 1936. 326p. Tells the story
       of Charterhouse School and some of its famous students, in-
       cluding John Wesley.

314.   Chandler, Douglas R. "John Wesley and the Uses of the Past."
       In Foundations of Theological Education; the 1972 Willson Lec-
       tures, 27-37. Washington, D.C.: Wesley Theological Seminary,
       1972. 46p.

315.   Chapman, E. V. John Wesley and Company (Halifax). Hali-
       fax: Halifax Printing Co., 1952. 80p.

316.   Chapman, John Arundel. John Wesley's Quest. Fellowship of
       the Kingdom Pamphlets, no. 7. London: Epworth Press,
       1921. 16p.

317.   Chappell, Edwin Barfield. Studies in the Life of John Wesley.
       Dallas: Publishing House, M. E. Church, South, Smith and
       Lamar, Agents, 1911. 239p.

318.   A Character of the Celebrated John Wesley, M.A., Late Fellow
       of Lincoln College, Oxford, Who Died March 2, 1791, aged 88
       years. 1 p. NjMD

319.   "Charles Wesley's Children." In The Homes, Haunts and
       Friends of John Wesley, 15-24. Rev. ed. London: C. H.
       Kelly, 1891. 154p.

320.   Chase, Gilbert. "Singing Dissenters." Chap. 3 in America's
       Music; from the Pilgrims to the Present, 41-64. N.Y.:
       McGraw-Hill Book Co., 1955. 733p.

321. Cheetham, S. A History of the Christian Church Since the
     Reformation. London: Macmillan, 1907. 474p. Contains a
     brief account of Wesley and Methodism.

322. Chicago Methodist Social Union.... John Wesley. Born 1703--
     Died 1791. Centennial Commemoration of Mr. Wesley's Death
     March 19th, '91. Chicago: W. J. Jefferson, 1891. 8p.

323. Chick, Elijah. A History of Methodism in Exeter and the
     Neighbourhood, from the Year 1739 until 1907. Exeter: S.
     Drayton, 1907. 180p.

324. Chiles, Robert Eugene. "Methodism's Theological Heritage."
     Chap. 1 in Theological Transition in American Methodism,
     1790-1935, 21-36. New York: Abingdon Press, 1965. 238p.

325. _____. Scriptural Christianity: A Call to John Wesley's
     Disciples. Grand Rapids, Mich.: Zondervan, 1984. 143p.

325a. Cho, John C. "John Wesley's View of Fallen Man." Chap. 5
     in A Spectrum of Thought: Essays in Honor of Dennis F.
     Kinlaw, edited by Michael L. Peterson, 67-77. Wilmore,
     Ky.: Francis Asbury Publishing Co., 1982. 188p.

326. Chowm, S. D. "Wesley's Influence in Canada." In Wesley
     As a World Force..., 71-79. See no. 49.

327. Christian Biography; Containing the Lives of Rev. George
     Whitefield, Rev. John Wesley, Rev. Augustus Hermann
     Francke, Rev. Jonathan Edwards. London: Religious Tract
     Society, 1835?

328. Christie, Thomas William. Methodism, a Part of the Great
     Christian Apostacy. A Review of the Life and Doctrines of
     John Wesley. London: Simpkin, 1881. 316p.

329. Christophers, Samuel Woolcock. Hymn Writers and Their
     Hymns. London: S. W. Partridge, 1866. 490p. References
     to the Wesleys throughout the book.

330. _____. The Poets of Methodism. London: Haughton, 1875.
     520p. American edition published under the title The Epworth
     Singers and Other Poets of Methodism.

331. Church, Leslie Frederic. The Early Methodist People. New
     York: Philosophical Library; London: Epworth Press, 1949.
     286p. Although this book is primarily about the ordinary
     people of Methodism who have been overshadowed by the Wes-
     leys in the histories of Methodism, there is considerable mate-
     rial dealing with the Wesleys.

332.   _____. Knight of the Burning Heart; the Story of John
Wesley. New York: Abingdon-Cokesbury Press, 1938. 185p.

333.   _____. More about the Early Methodist People. London:
Epworth Press, 1949. 324p. Sequel to The Early Methodist
People, no. 331. Although there is no one distinct section on
him, each of the six chapters in this book brings Wesley into
the discussion. The topics of the chapters are the social
relationships, occupations, and literacy of the early Methodist
people, their persecution, first local preachers, women
preachers, ventures in social service, and worship, public
and private.

334.   _____. "Religion in Georgia." Chap. 13 in Oglethorpe:
A Study of Philanthropy in England and Georgia. London:
Epworth Press, 1932. 335p. His dissertation, University of
London. The first part of this chapter describes Wesley's
experience in Georgia.

335. Clark, Davis. "John Wesley." In Death-bed Scenes; or,
Dying with and without Religion, 157-66. New York: Carlton
and Porter, 1851. 569p.

336. Clark, Elmer Talmage. An Album of Methodist History. New
York: Abingdon-Cokesbury Press, 1952. 336p.

337.   _____. Charles Wesley. Lake Junaluska, N.C.: World
Methodist Council; Association of Methodist Historical Society,
[1964?]. 20p.

338.   _____. Charles Wesley: The Singer of the Evangelical
Revival. Nashville: The Upper Room, 1957. 32p.

339.   _____. "Methodism." In The American Church of the
Protestant Heritage, edited by Vergilius Ferm, 313-30. New
York: Philosophical Library, 1953. 481p.

340.   _____. The Warm Heart of John Wesley. New York:
Association of Methodist Historical Societies, 1950. 78p.

341.   _____. The Wesley Family. Lake Junaluska, N.C.: World
Methodist Council; Association of Methodist Historical Societies,
[1964?]. 18p.

342.   _____. "What Happened at Aldersgate." Chap. 1 in What
Happened at Aldersgate: Addresses in Commemoration of the
Bicentennial of the Spiritual Awakening of John Wesley in Al-
dersgate Street, London, May 24, 1738, edited by Elmer T.
Clark, 11-42. Nashville: Methodist Publishing House, 1938.
239p.

343. Clark, Henry William. History of English Nonconformity from Wiclif to the Close of the Nineteenth Century. 2 vols. London: Chapman and Hall, 1911-13. Vol. 2, pp. 205-44, are concerned primarily with the Wesleys, Methodism, and the revival of religion.

344. Clark, James Osgood Andrew. "Wesley and Methodism." In The Wesley Memorial Volume, 51-75. See no. 257.

345. _____. "Wesley and the Evidence Writers, Essayists and Others." In The Wesley Memorial Volume, 404-17. See no. 257.

346. _____. "Wesley and the Methodist Movement Judged by Nearly One Hundred Writers, Living or Dead." In The Wesley Memorial Volume, 649-99. See no. 257.

347. _____. "Wesley in Savannah and the Wesley Monumental Church." In The Wesley Memorial Volume, 606-48. See no. 257.

348. Clark, Willie Thorburn. "Hark! the Herald Angels Sing." Chap. 12 in Stories of Fadeless Hymns, 68-73. Nashville: Broadman Press, 1949. 184p.

349. _____. "Jesus, Lover of My Soul." Chap. 18 in Hymns That Endure, 146-53. Nashville: Broadman Press, 1942. 168p.

350. Clarke, Adam. Memoirs of the Wesley Family; Collected Principally from Original Documents. London: J. and T. Clarke, 1823. 543p.

351. Clarke, Charles Philip Stewart. Short History of the Christian Church from the Earliest Times to the Present Day. London: Longmans, Green and Co., 1929. 531p. pp. 401-6 are concerned with Wesley.

352. Clarke, Eliza. Susanna Wesley. Boston: Roberts Bros. 1886. 301p. (rev. in nos. 3322, 3797.)

353. Clarke, James Freeman. "John Wesley and His Times." Chap. 12 in Events and Epochs in Religious History: Being the Substance of A Course of Twelve Lectures Delivered in the Lowell Institute, Boston, in 1880, 351-86. Boston: James R. Good and Co., 1881. 402p.

354. Clarke, Joseph M. Was John Wesley a Methodist? [Syracuse, N.Y., 189-?]. 36p. NjMUM

355. Claxton, Marshall. Prospectus of an Engraving of the Death

of John Wesley, Painted by Claxton, To Be Engraved by
W. O. Gellar. Philadelphia, 1849. 8p.

356.   Cleland, James T. "John Wesley on the Holy Communion."
       In Wherefore Art Thou Come? Meditations on the Lord's Sup-
       per, 51-56. New York and Nashville: Abingdon, 1961. 143p.

357.   Clifford, John. "The Prophet of the Eighteenth Century."
       In Wesley, the Man, His Teaching and His Work: Being Ser-
       mons and Addressed Delivered in City Road Chapel at the
       Centenary Commemoration of John Wesley's Death, 108-25.
       London: C. H. Kelly, 1891. 431p.

358.   _____. "Wesley's Influence on Theology and Life." In
       Wesley's House: Sermons and Addresses, 63-72. London:
       C. H. Kelly, 1898. 214p.

359.   [Coates, Edward]. A New Portrait of Methodism, Being a
       Circumstantial Account of the Dispute between the Rev. John
       Wesley and the Trustees of Millbourn Place Chapel at North
       Shields.... Leeds, Eng.: J. Heaton, 1815. 64p. NjMUM

360.   Cocking, Thomas. The History of Wesleyan Methodism in
       Grantham and Its Vicinity: With Preliminary Observations
       of the Rise, Progress and Utility, the Discipline and Doc-
       trines of the Connexion; the Life of Its Founder.... London:
       Simpkin, Marshall and Co., 1836. 418p.

361.   Coke, Thomas. The Life of the Rev. John Wesley, A.M.,
       Including an Account of the Great Revival of Religion, in
       Europe and America, of Which He Was the First and Chief
       Instrument. Harriesfield: Edward Bayley, 1792. 481p.

362.   _____. Preface to Samuel Wesley's The Life of Christ, a
       Poem, iii-xxii. 2 vols. London: A Paris, 1809.

363.   _____. The Substance of a Sermon Preached in Baltimore
       and Philadelphia on the First and Eighth of May, 1791, on the
       Death of the Rev. John Wesley. London: G. Paramore, 1791.
       20p. Also appeared in Methodist Recorder, 26 February 1891,
       167-68, as "Elijah and John Wesley, a Parallel."

364.   Cole, Richard Lee. A History of Methodism in Dublin. Dublin:
       R. T. White, 1932. 145p.

365.   _____. John Wesley's "Journal;" an Appreciation. Wesley
       Historical Society Lectures, no. 4. London: Epworth Press,
       1938. 47p.

366.   _____. Love-Feasts; a History of the Christian Agape.
       London: C. H. Kelly, 1916. 292p. Pp. 276-80 discuss
       Wesley's and Methodism's use of the Love-feast.

367. _____. The Wesleys Come to Dublin. Commemorating the Bicentenary of the Landing of John Wesley in Dublin, 9th August 1747. London: Epworth Press, 1947. 32p.

368. _____. The Wesleys in Cork. Cork: Guy, 1917. 11p.

369. Coles, Francis H. Louth Circuit Missionary Exhibition, April 1st-5th, 1946: Souvenir Handbook and Programme, 1946. N.p.: T. E. Wiggen and Son, 1946. 26p. GtBLW

370. Coles, George. "Mrs. Susannah Wesley." In Heroines of Methodism; or, Pen and Ink Sketches of the Mothers and Daughters of the Church, 25-36. New York: Carlton and Porter, 1857. 336p.

371. Colet, John Annesley. An Impartial Review of the Life and Writings, Public and Private Character of the Late Rev. Mr. John Wesley. Interspersed with a Variety of Curious, Entertaining, and Authentic Anecdotes.... London, 1791. 37p.

372. _____. A Letter to the Rev. Thomas Coke LLD. and Mr. Henry Moore Occasioned by Their Proposals for Publishing the Life of the Rev. John Wesley, A.M., in Opposition to That Advertised (under Sanction of the Executors) to Be Written by John Whitehead. Also, a Letter from the Rev. Dr. Coke to the Author on the Same Subject, Together with the Whole Correspondence and the Circular Letters Written on the Occasion, and a True and Impartial Statement of Facts Hitherto Suppressed.... London: J. Luffman, 1792. 56p. NjMUM

373. Colhouer, Thomas Henry. Non-Episcopal Methodism Contrasted with Episcopal Methodism; and the Polity of the Methodist Church; Illustrated and Defended. Pittsburgh, Pa.: Methodist Book Concern, 1869. 364p.

374. Collier, Frank Wilbur. Back to Wesley. New York and Cincinnati: Methodist Book Concern, 1924. 52p.

375. _____. John Wesley among the Scientists. New York and Cincinnati: Abingdon Press, 1928. 351p.

376. Colquhoun, Frank. Charles Wesley, 1707-88: The Poet of the Evangelical Revival. Great Churchmen Series, 8. London: Church Book Room Press, [1948?]. 35p.

377. _____. Hymns That Live: Their Meaning and Message. London: Hodder and Stoughton, 1980. 320p. Several of Charles Wesley's hymns are discussed.

378. Cook, Alice Isabel. "Susanna Wesley." In Women of the Warm Heart, 7-10. London: Epworth Press, 1952. 40p.

379. Cook, Isaac P. "Wesley and Lay Preaching." In Wesley Memorial Volume, 532-47. See no. 257.

380. Cooke, Corbett. The Opinions of the Rev. John Wesley, in Reference to the Relation Which Methodism Sustains to the Established Church, Fully and Fairly Stated and Its Present Ecclesiastical Position Vindicated.... Exeter: W. Balle, 1844. 51p.

381. Cooke, Joseph. "Containing a Statement of the Primitive and Final Sentiments of Mr. Wesley, on the Doctrine of Justification by Faith, and the Witness of the Spirit." Part 2 in Methodism Condemned by Methodist Preachers; or, a Vindication of the Doctrines Contained in Two Sermons, on Justification by Faith, and the Witness of the Spirit..., 43-108. Rochdale, Eng.: T. Wood, 1807. 280p.

382. Cooke, Richard Joseph. "Ordination of Wesley by a Greek Bishop," and "The Authority of Wesley." Chaps. 8 and 10 in The Historic Episcopate, a Study of Anglican Claims and Methodist Orders, 139-55, 181-202. New York: Eaton and Mains; Cincinnati: Curts and Jennings, 1896. 224p.

383. Cooke, William. "Wesley's Influence on the Religion of the World." In Wesley Memorial Volume, 213-44. See no. 257.

384. Coomer, Duncan. English Dissent under the Early Hanoverians. London: Epworth Press, 1946. 136p. Contains a brief discussion of the animosity of the Wesleys to Dissent, as well as the animosity of the Dissenters to Methodism.

385. Coope, William John. Wesley a Catholic! "Wesleys Sons," Invited. Falmouth Tracts, no. 4. Falmouth: M. Dunstone, 1868. 28p.

386. Cooper, Joseph. The Love Stories of John Wesley and Other Essays. Boston: R. G. Badger, 1931. 107p.

387. Copestake, Reginald Henry. Learning about John Wesley. Mowbray's Enquirer's Library. London: Mowbray, 1983. 32p.

387a. Coppedge, Allan. "John Wesley and the Issue of Authority in Theological Pluralism.: Chap. 6 in A Spectrum of the Thought: Essays in Honor of Dennis F. Kinlaw, 78-94. See no. 325a.

388. Corson, Fred Pierce. "The One Book of Wesley." In John Wesley's New Testament Compared with the Authorized Version, ix-xiv. Philadelphia: Winston, 1953. 391p.

389. _____. Preface and Introduction to John Wesley's New

Testament, Compared with the Authorized Version, vii-xiv.
Philadelphia: J. C. Winston Co., 1953. 391p.

390. Cosslett, Edith. Father of Methodism: A Sketch of the Life
and Labours of the Rev. John Wesley, M.A. London: Wesleyan Conference Office, 1879. 147p.

391. Courthope, William John. "Religious Lyrical Poetry in the
Eighteenth Century: Influence of the Methodist Movement."
In vol. 5 of A History of English Poetry, 337-45. 6 vols.
New York: Russell and Russell, 1962.

392. Coward, S. L. C. "Sketch of John Wesley." In Entire Sanctification, 1-24. See no. 304.

393. Cox, Harvey W. "Aldersgate and Christian Stewardship."
Chap. 13 in What Happened at Aldersgate, 175-82. See no.
342.

394. Cox, Leo George. John Wesley's Concept of Perfection. Kansas City, Mo.: Beacon Hill Press, 1964. 227p. His dissertation, University of Iowa, 1959.

395. Coxon, W. Vere. Wesleyan Methodist Church, Shepherds Bush
Road Souvenir Programme with a Short History of the Church.
Jubilee Celebrations, 1925. London: Belsham and Sons, 1925.
16p. GtBMM

396 Cozens, Samuel. John Wesley, the Papa of British Rome....
Willenhall, Eng.: W. H. Hughes, 1852. 36p.

397. Cragg, Gerald R. Introduction to The Appeals to Men of
Reason and Religion and Certain Related Open Letters, 1-36.
Vol. 11 of The Oxford Edition of the Works of John Wesley,
Frank Baker, Editor-in-Chief. Oxford: Clarendon Press,
1975. 593p. There are additional introductions to the letters
on pp. 37-42, 95-101, 327-31, 353-58, 437-40, 459-63.

398. _____. "Methodism and the Evangelical Revival." Chap. 10
in The Church and the Age of Reason, 1648-1789, 141-56.
Harmondsworth, Middlesex: Penguin Books, 1960. 299p.

399. Cragg, Gerald R., R. E. Morton, and J. D. Browning. "Wesley and the Renewal of English Religion." In Religion in the
Eighteenth Century, edited by R. E. Morton and J. D. Browning, 77-84. New York: Garland, 1979. 135p.

400. Crake, John W. The Person, Life, and Work of the Rev. John
Wesley, A.M., the Founder of Methodism, Illustrated by Engravings, Drawings, Photographs, etc., Together with Portraits, Views, etc. of Persons and Places Connected with the

History of Methodism. From the Collection of Rev. John W.
Crake. Huddersfield: Preston Bros., 1886. 12p.

401. Crane, Frank. "Sketch of Samuel Wesley [1666-1735]." In
The Life of Christ; a Poem, by Samuel Wesley, 505-16. Chicago: Union Book Co., 1900. 516p.

402. Crane, Jonathan Townley. Methodism and Its Methods. New
York: Nelson and Phillips, 1876. 395p.

403. Craps, John. A Caveat against the Puseyism of Mr. Wesley's
Treatise on Baptism. London: Houlston and Stoneman, 1844.
12p.

404. Crawford, Benjamin Franklin. Changing Conceptions of Religion, As Revealed in One Hundred Years of Methodist Hymnology 1836-1935. Carnegie, Pa.: Carnegie Church Press,
1939. 245p. Despite its title, chaps. 1 and 2 are concerned
with the Wesleys.

405. _____. "The First Official Hymn Book." In Religious
Trends in a Century of Hymns, 27-35. Carnegie, Pa.: Carnegie Church Press, 1938. 204p.

406. Creamer, David. Methodist Hymnology; Comprehending Notices of the Poetical Works of John and Charles Wesley ... and
Some Account of the Authors; with Critical and Historical Observations. New York, 1948. 470p.

407. Croft, George. Thoughts Concerning the Methodists and the
Established Church. London: F. and C. Rivington, 1795.
52p.

408. Crook, William. The Ancestry of the Wesleys; with Special
References to Their Connexion with Ireland. London: Epworth
Press, 1938. 84p.

409. _____. "Origin and Progress of Methodism amongst the
Palatines." Chap. 2 in Ireland and the Centenary of American
Methodism, 35-70. London: Hamilton Adams and Co.; Dublin:
Richard Yoakley, 1866. 263p.

410. Crooks, H. T. The Story of Biggleswade Methodism, 1934,
Trinity Methodist Church, 1834-1934. N.p. n.d. 27p.
GtBLW

411. Crookshank, Charles H. A Methodist Pioneer: The Life and
Labours of John Smith, Including Brief Notices of the Origin
and Early History of Methodism in Different Parts of the North
of Ireland. London: Wesleyan Conference Office, 1881.
136p.

412. _____. "Wesley and His Times." In vol. 1 of History of
      Methodism in Ireland. 4 vols. Belfast: R. S. Allen, 1885-
      88. 480p.

413. _____. "Wesley's Work in Ireland." In Wesley Studies,
      213-19. See no. 190.

414. Crothers, Samuel McChord. "The Leisurable Hours of John
      Wesley." In The Cheerful Giver: Essays, 22-40. Boston
      and New York: Houghton Mifflin Co., 1923. 242p. Discusses
      some of the books Wesley read during his travels, "when he
      rode with a slack rein."

415. Crowther, Jonathan. The Methodist Manual; or, A Short His-
      tory of the Wesleyan Methodists, Including Their Rise, Pro-
      gress, and Present State.... Halifax: J. Walker, 1813.
      216p.

416. _____. A Portraiture of Methodism; or, The History of the
      Wesleyan Methodists.... London: Edwards, 1815. 512p.

417. Culbreth, James Marvin. "Preparing a Man for the Task."
      Chap. 1 in Studies in Methodist History..., 7-18. Cokesbury
      Training Course. Nashville: Cokesbury Press, 1926. 141p.

418. Cumbers, Frank Henry. "Wesley and Literature." Chap. 1
      in The Book Room: The Story of the Methodist Publishing
      House and Epworth Press, 1-10. Wesley Historical Society
      Lectures, no. 22. London: Epworth Press, 1956. 153p.

419. Cumming, James Elder. "John Wesley." Chap. 11 in Holy
      Men of God, Dating Back to St. Augustine, 157-72. Chicago:
      Moody Press, 1961. 254p.

420. Cummings, Anson Watson. "Kingswood School, Bristol, Eng-
      land." Pt. 1, Chap. 1 in The Early Schools of Methodism,
      9-19. New York: Phillips and Hunt; Cincinnati: Cranston
      and Stowe, 1886. 432p.

421. Cummings, Arthur Dagg. A Portrait in Pottery. Wesley His-
      torical Society Lectures, no. 28. London: Epworth Press,
      1962. 48p.

422. Cunninggim, Jesse L. "John Wesley: Evangelical Arminianism."
      In The Theologians of Methodism, 38-47. Nashville: Publish-
      ing House of the Methodist Episcopal Church, South, 1895.
      138p. This book is a collection of theses by members of the
      senior class in the Biblical Department of Vanderbilt University.

423. Cunningham, George Godfrey. "John Wesley." In vol. 6 of
      A History of England in the Lives of Englishmen, 37-48. 8
      vols. Edinburgh: A Fullarton, 1855.

424. Curnock, George C. "The Wesleys and Westminster." In
     Wesley Studies, 56-61. See no. 190.

425. Curnock, Nehemiah. "Birth and Early Training." In Wesley
     Studies, 18-29. See no. 190.

426. _____. "The Group Round Wesley's Death-Bed." In The
     Homes, Haunts and Friends of John Wesley, 24-26. See no.
     319.

427. _____. Hinde Street Chapel, 1810-1910. London: Culley,
     1910. 126p.

428. _____. Introduction in vol. 1 of The Journal of the Rev.
     John Wesley..., vol. 1, 3-77. 8 vols. New York: Eaton and
     Graham, 1909-16. This introduction has discussions on John
     Wesley's unpublished diaries, the first Oxford diary, and Wes-
     ley's cipher.

429. _____. "John Wesley in Bristol." In The Homes, Haunts
     and Friends of John Wesley, 95-109. See no. 319.

430. _____. "New Light on Old Facts: Photographed Manu-
     scripts." In Wesley Studies, 41-55. See no. 190.

431. _____. "Our Venerable Father in the Gospel." In The
     Homes, Haunts and Friends of John Wesley, 1-4. See no. 319.

432. _____. "Wesley's House." In Wesley's House: Sermons
     and Addresses, 89-99. See no. 358.

433. Currie, Robert. "Ethic and Authority from Wesley to Bunting."
     Chap. 1 in Methodism Divided: A Study in the Sociology of
     Ecumenicalism, 17-43. Society Today and Tomorrow. London:
     Faber, 1968. 348p.

434. Curteis, George H. "The Wesleyans." Lecture 7 in Dissent
     in Its Relation to the Church of England, 339-394. Bampton
     Lectures, 1871. London and New York: Macmillan, 1872.
     448p.

435. Curtiss, George L. "Arminianism in Its Wesleyan Growth."
     Chap. 8 in Arminianism in History; or, The Revolt from Pre-
     destinationism, 156-237. New York: Hunt and Eaton, 1894.
     237p.

436. Curwen, John Spencer. "Methodist Psalmody." In Studies in
     Worship-Music, Chiefly As Regards Congregational Singing,
     24-40. London: J. Curwen and Sons, 1880. 225p.

437. Cushman, Ralph S. "The Meaning of Aldersgate." Chap. 6 in
     What Happened at Aldersgate, 91-102. See no. 342.

438. Cushman, Robert E. "Salvation for All." In Methodism, 103-
15. See no. 287. Also in Faith Seeking Understanding; Essays Theological and Critical, 63-74. Durham, N.C.: Duke
University Press, 1981. 373p.

439. _____. "Theological Landmarks of the Wesleyan Revival."
In his Faith Seeking Understanding; Essays Theological and
Critical, 51-62. See previous entry.

440. _____. "Wesley on Baptism." In The Doctrine of the
Church, edited by Dow Kirkpatrick, 82-88. Oxford Institute
on Methodist Theological Studies, 2d, 1962. New York:
Abingdon Press, 1964. 215p.

441. Cutts, Edward Lewes. Turning Points of English Church
History, 323-31. London: Society for the Promotion of
Christian Knowledge, 1924. 334p.

442. The Daily Telegraph. Christianity in Great Britain: An Outline of Its Rise, Progress, and Present Condition. London:
Hodder and Stoughton, 1874. 162p. GtBMM. This is a series
of articles contributed to The Daily Telegraph. The story of
Methodism told on pp. 53-81.

443. Daintree, Joseph. Methodism in Witton: Station Road Wesleyan Church Jubilee, October 31st, 1928. [Witton, Eng.,
1928.] 29p. GtBMM

444. Dale, Alan T., and John Lawson. Study Notes on Christian
Doctrine. London: Epworth Press, 1952. 88p. This book
is designed to assist students in studying Christian doctrine,
utilizing H. Maldwyn Hughes' Christian Foundations and Wesley's Forty-four Sermons.

445. Dale, R. W. The Evangelical Revival and Other Sermons....
London: Hodder and Stoughton, 1880. 286p. These are
sermons by a Congregationalist minister. The first in the collection, "The Evangelical Revival," does make mention of
Wesley.

446. _____. "The Theology of John Wesley." Chap. 9 in Fellowship with Christ; and Other Discourses Delivered on
Special Occasions, 216-46. New York: A. C. Armstrong,
1892. 368p. Also published in Wesley, the Man, His Teaching and His work, 69-90. See no. 357.

447. Dale, T. Cyril. "Durham Associations of John Wesley." In
Memorials of Old Durham, edited by Henry R. Leighton, 229-
38. London: Allen and Sons, 1910. 264p.

448. Dale, Thomas Pelham. "Life of John Wesley, the Methodist."

In A Life's Motto: Illustrated by Biographical Example, 107-
60. New York: Virtue and Yorston, [1868]. 345p.

449. Daniels, William Haven. The Illustrated History of Methodism
in Great Britain and America from the Days of the Wesleys to
the Present Time. New York: Methodist Book Concern,
Phillips and Hunt, 1880. 784p.

450. Darlington, U. V. W. "Our Personal Approach to Aldersgate."
Chap. 18 in What Happened at Aldersgate, 222-25. See no.
342.

451. Davenport, Frederick Morgan. "John Wesley and English So-
cial Evolution in the Eighteenth Century." Chap. 9 in
Primitive Traits in Religious Revivals; a Study in Mental and
Social Evolution, 133-79. New York: Macmillan, 1905. 323p.

452. Davey, Cyril. John Wesley and the Methodists. Basingstoke:
Marshall Pickering, 1985. 48p.

453. Davey, Cyril J. John Wesley. Foundery Pamphlets, no. 1.
London: Epworth Press, 1955. 19p.

454. _____. The Methodist Story. London: Epworth Press,
1955. 190p.

455. Davidson, Henry Martin Perkins. "John Wesley." In Good
Christian Men, 199-212. New York: Charles Scribner's Sons,
1940. 260p.

456. Davie, Donald. "The Classicism of Charles Wesley." Chap. 5
in Purity of Diction in English Verse, 70-81. London: Chatto
and Windus, 1952. 211p.

457. _____. "Dissent and the Wesleyans, 1740-1800." In A
Gathered Church: The Literature of the English Dissenting
Interest, 37-54. London and Henley: Routledge, 1978. 152p.
First appeared in The Journal of the United Reformed Church
History Society 1 (1977): 272-85.

458. Davies, Daisy. "Aldersgate and Enduement for Service."
Chap. 15 in What Happened at Aldersgate, 190-98. See no.
342.

459. Davies, Edward. The Life of John Wesley, A.M. Written from
a Spiritual Standpoint. Reading, Mass.: Holiness Book Concern, 1887. 261p.

460. Davies, G. C. B. The Early Cornish Evangelicals, 1735-60;
a Study of Walker of Truro and Others. London: Society for
the Promotion of Christian Knowledge, 1951. 229p. Pp. 88-
129 are concerned with Walker and the Wesleys.

461. Davies, Horton. "The Age of Toleration." Chap. 6 in The
English Free Churches, 119-42. 2d ed. London: Oxford
University Press, 1963. 208p. Much of this chapter is de-
voted to the Wesleys and Methodism.

462. _____. From Watts and Wesley to Maurice, 1690-1850.
Vol. 3 of Worship and Theology in England. London: Oxford University Press, 1961. 355p.

463. Davies, Rupert E. "The Church Revived." Chap. 5 in The
Church in Bristol; a Short History. Bristol: J. Wright, 1960.
105p. Pp. 61-72 of this chapter deal with John Wesley and
his activities in Bristol.

464. _____. "How Did Methodism Become Separate." Chap. 1
in Methodists and Unity, 1-12. London: A. R. Mowbray;
New York: Morehouse-Barlow, 1962. 100p.

465. _____. "John and Charles Wesley," "The Revival," and
"The Theology and the Hymns of the Revival." Chaps. 3-5
in Methodism, 38-104. London: Epworth Press, 1963. 184p.

466. _____. John Wesley in Modern Scholarship: A Lecture
Delivered to the Bristol Branch of the Wesley Historical Society, 5 November, 1977. N.p. 1977. 5p.

467. _____. "Justification, Sanctification, and the Liberation of
the Person." In Sanctification and Liberation, 64-82. See no.
191.

468. _____. "The People Called Methodists. Pt. 1. Our Doctrines." Chap. 5 in vol. 1 of A History of the Methodist
Church in Great Britain, 147-79. See no. 89.

469. _____. "Why Methodism?" Chap. 6 in What Methodists Be-
lieve, 89-102. London: Mowbrays, 1976. 128p. Tells briefly
the story of John Wesley and Methodism.

470. Davies, William. Early Methodism at Gornal Wood. London:
Epworth Press, 1939. 36p.

471. Davis, Angela Kirkham. Wesley and Early Methodism: An
Historical Text-Book for Church Lyceums and General Students.
New York: Phillips and Hunt, 1884. 142p.

472. Davis, Arman Leslie. History of the Christian Church and the
Origin of Methodism.... 2d ed. Germantown, Pa.: A. L.
Davis, 1934. 36p.

473. Davis, Valentine David. Twelve Hymns and Their Writers:
Biographical Sketches and Lesson Notes. London: Sunday

44   John and Charles Wesley

School Association, 1901. 128p. Includes Charles Wesley,
pp. 44-53.

474. Davison, Leslie. "Holiness in the Teaching of the Wesleys."
      In Pathway to Power; the Charismatic Movement in Historical
      Perspective, 51-75. London: Fountain Trust, 1971. 93p.
      A lecture given at the International Conference at the Uni-
      versity of Surrey, July 1971, sponsored by the Fountain
      Trust.

475. Davison, William Hope. Centenary Memorials of Duke's-Alley
      Chapel, Bolton-Le-Moors, Lancashire; Being Sketches of Its
      Pastors and Its Progress. Bolton: John Tillotson, 1854.
      158p. GtBLW

476. Daw, Leslie T. John Wesley. Makers of History Series,
      no. 10. Exeter: A. Wheaton, 1938. 59p.

477. Dawson, Arthur A. Wesley Not a Wesleyan; an Address.
      Swaffham: Brown and Gardner, 1880. 18p. GtBMM

478. Dawson, George. "John Wesley." In Biographical Lectures,
      edited by George St. Clair, 487-504. London: Kegan Paul,
      Trench and Co., 1887. 553p.

479. Dawson, Joseph, ed. Introduction to John Wesley on Preach-
      ing. London: C. H. Kelly, 1903. 214p.

480. Dawson, William James. Wesley and His Work: A Sermon
      Preached on the Centenary of the Death of John Wesley, in
      St. Giles' Cathedral, Edinburgh.... Glasgow and Edinburgh:
      John Menzies, 1891. 29p.

481. Dayton, Wilber T. "Aldersgate Is from God," and "Alders-
      gate Must Be Desired by Man." Chaps. 6 and 7 in Methodism's
      Aldersgate Heritage, 43-54. See no. 62.

482. _____. "Entire Sanctification: The Divine Purification and
      Perfection of Man." Chap. 13 in A Contemporary Wesleyan
      Theology: Biblical, Systematic, and Practical, 517-69. See
      no. 279.

483. _____. "Infallibility, Wesley, and British Wesleyanism."
      In Inerrancy and the Church, edited by John D. Hannah,
      223-54. Chicago: Moody Press, 1984. 422p. This book is
      part of a series of scholarly works sponsored by the Inter-
      national Council on Biblical Inerrancy.

484. _____. "A Wesleyan Note on Election." In Perspectives on
      Evangelical Theology: Papers from the Thirtieth Annual Meet-
      ing of the Evangelical Society, edited by Kenneth S. Kantzer

and Stanley N. Gundry, 95-103.   Grand Rapids, Mich.:
Baker Book House, 1979.   289p.

485.   Dearing, Trevor.   Wesleyan and Tractarian Worship: An Ecumenical Study.   London: Epworth Press, 1966.   166p.

486.   Dearmer, Percy.   Songs of Praise Discussed; a Handbook to the
Best-Known Hymns and to Others Recently Introduced.   Lon-
don: Oxford University Press, 1933.   559p.   Twenty-one of
Charles's hymns and 4 of John's are discussed.

487.   Deen, Edith Alderman.   "Susanna Wesley--Mother of John and
Charles Wesley."   In Great Women of the Christian Faith, 141-
49.   New York: Harper and Row, 1976.   410p.

488.   A Defence of the Rev. John Wesley.   Baltimore: Joseph
Robinson, 1860.   18p.   NcD

489.   Demaray, Donald Eugene.   "Homiletics: Incarnational Preaching
of God's Word."   Chap. 18 in A Contemporary Wesleyan Theology: Biblical, Systematic, and Practical, 779-828.   See no.
279.

490.   _____.   "John Wesley, Persistent Preacher."   In Pulpit
Giants; What Made Them Great, 155-60.   Chicago: Moody
Press, 1973.   174p.

491.   Dennis, John.   "John Wesley under Two Aspects."   In Studies
in English Literature, 226-49.   London: Edward Stanford,
1876.   444p.   Discusses Wesley's intellectual interests and activities.

492.   Deschner, John.   Wesley's Christology, an Interpretation.
Dallas: Southern Methodist University Press, 1960.   220p.

493.   Dewart, Edward Hartley.   "The Relationship of Wesley and of
Methodism to the Church of England."   Chap. 2 in High Church
Pretensions Disproved; or, Methodism and the Church of England, 9-32.   2d ed.   Toronto: Methodist Book Room, 1877.
59p.   NjMD

494.   Dickinson, Edward William.   John Wesley's Visit to York: With
Contemporaneous Facts.   York: Rusholmes, 192-?   57p.

495.   _____.   John Wesley's Visits to Whitby and Robin Hood's
Bay with Contemporaneous Facts.   3d ed.   Whitby, Eng.:
Horne, 1925.   71p.

496.   Dickons, James Norton.   Kirkgate Chapel, Bradford, and Its
Associations with Methodism.   Bradford, 1903.   134p.

497. Dimond, Sydney George. "The Human Wesley." In The
      Psychology of Methodism, 27-36. London: Epworth Press,
      1932. 154p.

498. _____. "The Mind of John Wesley," and "Wesley's Religious
      Sentiment." Chaps. 3 and 4 in The Psychology of the Metho-
      dist Revival; an Empirical and Descriptive Study, 42-103. New
      York: Oxford University Press, 1926. 296p.

499. Dingley, Edward Alfred. Footsteps of John Wesley in Wednes-
      bury. London: Epworth Press, 1938. 32p.

500. Dixon, James. "Wesley and Whitefield." In Lectures on Prot-
      estant Nonconformists, 345-419. London: Robert Theobald,
      1853. GtBLDW

501. Dobbin, Orlando T. "Ideas Wesley Developed in Organizing
      His Societies." In Wesley Memorial Volume, 191-212. See no.
      257.

502. _____. "John Wesley." In Sketches of Eminent Methodist
      Ministers, with Portraits and Other Illustrations, 9-67. New
      York: Carlton and Phillips, 1854. 370p.

503. Dobbs, A. E. Education and Social Movements, 1700-1850.
      London and New York: Longmans, Green and Co., 1919.
      257p. There are references throughout the book to John Wes-
      ley, Methodism, and religious revival, and their impact on
      education.

504. Doble, Gilbert Hunter. John Wesley and His Work in Cornwall.
      Liskeard, Eng.: Philp and Sons, 1935. 56p. Reprinted from
      The Cornish Times, 1935.

505. Dobrée, Bonamy. John Wesley. London: Duckworth; New
      York: Macmillan, 1933. 138p.

506. _____. Three Eighteenth Century Figures: Sarah Chur-
      chill, John Wesley, and Giacomo Casanova. London and New
      York: Oxford University Press, 1962. 248p.

507. Dodd, Thomas J. John Wesley: A Study for the Time. Cin-
      cinnati: Cranston and Stowe; New York: Hunt and Eaton,
      1891. 152p.

508. Doherty, Robert Remington. "John Wesley, and the Modern
      Evangelical Church." In Torchbearers of Christendom: The
      Light They Shed and the Shadows They Cast, 243-88. Cin-
      cinnati: Curts and Jennings; New York: Eaton and Mains,
      1896. 288p.

509. Doidge, Reginald J. John Wesley's Christian Library. Little
      Books of the Kindly Light, No. 45. London: Epworth Press,
      1938. 15p.

510. _____. Wesley and the Industrial Era. Little Books of the
      Kindly Light, No. 46. London: Epworth Press, 1938. 15p.

511. Dolbey, George W. The Architectural Expression of Methodism:
      The First Hundred Years. London: Epworth Press, 1964.
      195p. Part of a larger thesis submitted to Manchester Univer-
      sity in 1962.

512. Done, Agnes E. A Short Account of Our Great Church Mu-
      sicians (1540-1876) Specially Written for Choristers. London
      and New York: Frowde, 1903. 68p.

513. Doraisamy, Theodore R. What Hath God Wrought: Motives of
      Mission in Methodism from Wesley to Thoburn. Singapore:
      Methodist Book Room, 1983. His dissertation, Serampore Col-
      lege.

514. Dorchester, Daniel. The Why of Methodism. New York:
      Phillips and Hunt, 1887. 182p.

515. Doughty, William Lamplough. John Wesley, His Conferences
      and His Preachers. Wesley Historical Society Lectures, no. 10.
      London: Epworth Press, 1944. 79p.

516. _____. John Wesley in Lincolnshire. Wesley Bi-centenary
      Manuals, no. 9. London: Epworth Press, 1938. 55p.

517. _____. John Wesley, Preacher. London: Epworth Press,
      1955. 213p.

518. Douglas, Charles Winfred. "The Contribution of the Evangeli-
      cal Revival." In Church Music in History and Practice, 189-
      98. Rev. ed. New York: Charles Scribner's Sons, 1962.
      263p.

519. Douglass, George. "Wesley As a Revivalist." In Wesley
      Memorial Volume, 149-63. See no. 257.

520. Douglass, Paul Franklin. Wesley at Oxford; the Religion of
      University Men. Bryn Mawr, Pa.: Bryn Mawr Press, 1953.
      107p.

521. Douthwaite, Henry. "Wesley's Chapel at City Road, and Its
      Environments." In Wesley Centenary Handbook..., 41-72.
      London: C. H. Kelly, 1891. 72p.

522. Dove, John. A Biographical History of the Wesley Family,

More Particularly Its Earlier Branches. London: Hamilton,
Adams, and Co.; Leeds: H. W. Walker, 1840. 300p.

523. Downey, James. The Eighteenth Century Pulpit: A Study of
the Sermons of Butler, Berkeley, Secker, Sterne, Whitefield
and Wesley. Oxford: Clarendon Press, 1969. 254p.

524. Drakeford, John W. "The Man and His Work." Chap. 1 in
John Wesley, edited by John W. Drakeford, 13-36. Nashville:
Broadman Press, 1979. 414p. The remainder of the book is
a selection of Wesley's writings.

525. Drew, Samuel. "Memoirs of the Late Rev. John Wesley, the
Venerable Founder of Methodism." In Sermons on Several Occasions. 10th ed. 2 vols. London: J. F. Dove, 1828.

526. Drinkhouse, Edward Jacob. History of Methodist Reform,
Synoptical of General Methodism, 1703-1898, with Special and
Comprehensive Reference to Its Most Salient Exhibition in the
History of the Methodist Protestant Church. 2 vols. Balti-
more: Board of Publication of Methodist Protestant Church,
1899. vol. 1, 1703-1820.

527. Duffield, Samuel Willoughby. English Hymns: Their Authors
and History. New York and London: Funk and Wagnalls,
1886. 675p. References to both John and Charles Wesley
throughout the book.

528. Dugard, Donald. A Brief History of the Methodist Church
in Bromley from the Time When John Wesley First Came up to
the Year 1958. [Bromley, Eng., 1958.] GtBMM

529. Duncan, Ivar L. "John Wesley Edits Paradise Lost." In
Essays in Memory of Christine Burleson in Language and Lit-
erature, edited by Thomas G. Burton, 73-85. Johnson City,
Tenn.: East Tennessee State University, 1969. 163p.

530. Duncan, Joseph. "Rev. Charles Wesley's Hymn: Jesu, Lover
of My Soul.'" Chap. 5 in Popular Hymns: Their Authors and
Teaching, 38-46. London: Skeffington and Son, [1910?]
329p.

531. Duncan, Peter. A Letter of Exposure and Remonstrance Re-
spectfully Addressed to Isaac Taylor, Esq., in Which His Al-
legations against the Integrity and Ecclesiastical Order of
Wesleyan Methodism are Examined and Refuted. Bath, Eng.:
Wood Bros., 1852. 55p.

532. Duncan, Watson Boone. Studies in Methodist Literature.
Nashville: Publishing House of the Methodist Episcopal Church,
South, 1914. 173p. Two chapters are devoted to discussions

of Wesley's writings, which the author divides into four
classes: personal, polemical, educational, and miscellaneous.

533. Dunn, Samuel. Memoirs of Mr. Thomas Tatham, and of Wesleyan Methodism in Nottingham. London: Tegg, Snow,
Aylott, and Jones, 1847. 280p.

534. Durnbaugh, Donald F. "The People Called Methodists." In
The Believers' Church: The History and Character of Radical Protestantism, 130-45. New York: Macmillan Co., 1968.
315p.

535. Dutton, W. E., ed. Introduction to The Eucharistic Manuals
of John and Charles Wesley, 7-25. 2d ed. Charing Cross:
John Hodges, 1880. 174p.

536. Duvall, Sylvanus Milne. "The English Background and the
Educational Heritage of American Methodism." Chap. 1 in
The Methodist Episcopal Church and Education up to 1869,
1-12. Contributions to Education, no. 284. New York:
Teachers College, Columbia University, 1928. 127p. Issued
also as dissertation, Columbia University.

537. Dyer, Alfred Saunders. "The Wesleyan Methodists." In
Sketches of English Nonconformity, 65-75. London: William
Poole, 1881. 105p. Describes the history and organization
of Methodism, along with the similarities between its theological
doctrines and those of the Church of England, ending with the
hope that Methodism might return to the Church of England.

538. Dyson, John B. A Brief History of the Rise and Progress of
Wesleyan Methodism, in the Leek Circuit; with Biographical
Sketches of Several Eminent Characters. Leek: Edward
Hallowes, 1853. 92p.

539. _____. The History of Wesleyan Methodism in the Congleton
Circuit; Including Sketches of Character, Original Letters, etc.
London: John Mason, 1856. 186p.

540. _____. Methodism in the Isle of Wight: Its Origin and
Progress Down to Present Times. Ventnor: George M. Burt,
1865. 344p.

541. The Early Days of Methodism ... by a Wesleyan Local Preacher.
Manchester: John Heywood, 1880. 112p. GEU-T

542. "The Early Life and Christian Experience of the Rev. John
Wesley...." In The Journals of the Rev. John Wesley ... to
Which Is Prefixed an Account of His Early Life, iii-xi. Lon-
don: John Bennett, 1837. 902p.

543. Eayrs, George. British Methodism As It Is, As It Was, As It
      Will Be. A Handbook and Short History To Help the Union of
      Wesleyan, Primitive, United and Other Methodists. London:
      Hooks, 1920. 120p.

544. _____. "Developments, Institutions, Helpers, Opposition."
      Chap. 6 in vol. 1 of A New History of Methodism, 277-331.
      See no. 229.

545. _____. John Wesley, Christian Philosopher and Church
      Founder. London: Epworth Press, 1926. 288p.

546. _____. "Links between the Ejected Clergy of 1662, the
      Wesleys, and Methodism." In The Ejectment of 1662 and the
      Free Churches, by Alexander Maclaren, 97-119. London:
      National Council of Evangelical Free Churches, 1912. 143p.

547. _____. Our Founders and Their Story: A Short History
      of Three Churches and Their Union As the United Methodist
      Church. London: A. Crombie, 1907. 62p.

548. _____. "Wesley." Chap. 10 in Alfred to Victoria: Hands
      across a Thousand Years; Connected Historical Sketches of
      Great Lives (900 A.D. to 1900 A.D.), 161-77. London: S.
      Sonnenschein, 1902. 250p.

549. _____. Wesley and Kingswood, and Its Free Churches ...
      with an Account of the Wesley Memorial Church, Bryant's
      Hill, Bristol. Bristol: J. W. Arrowsmith, 1911. 326p.

550. Eddy, George Sherwood. "Discovery of God During the
      Protestant Reformation ... John Wesley...." Chap. 7 in Man
      Discovers God, 141-50. New York: Harper and Bros., 1942.
      170p.

551. Eddy, George Sherwood, and Kirby Page. "John Wesley--
      Freedom from Moral and Spiritual Insensibility." In Makers of
      Freedom; Biographical Sketches in Social Progress, 123-52.
      New York: George H. Doran Co., 1926. 311p.

552. Edmondson, George W. From Epworth to London with John
      Wesley, Being Fifty Photo-Engravings of the Sacred Places of
      Methodism.... Cincinnati: Cranston and Stowe, 1890.

553. Edwards, Eric. "John Wesley in Holyhead." In English
      Methodist Church, Holyhead: Jubilee Year, 1910-1960.
      Llangefni: W. O. Jones, 1960. 16p. GtBLW

554. Edwards, Maldwyn L. After Wesley; a Study of the Social and
      Political Influence of Methodism in the Middle Period (1791-1849).
      London: Epworth Press, 1935. 190p. Expansion of his dis-
      sertation, University of London.

555. _____. The Astonishing Youth; a Study of John Wesley As Men Saw Him. London: Epworth Press, 1959. 128p.

556. _____. Family Circle; a Study of the Epworth Household in Relation to John and Charles Wesley. London: Epworth Press, 1949. 192p.

557. _____. "John Wesley." Chap. 2 in vol. 1 of A History of the Methodist Church in Great Britain, 35-79. See no. 89.

558. _____. John Wesley. Lake Junaluska, N.C.: World Methodist Council; Association of Methodist Historical Societies, 1964. 20p.

559. _____. John Wesley and the Eighteenth Century; a Study of His Social and Political Influence. London: Allen and Unwin; New York: Abingdon Press, 1933. 220p.

560. _____. "John Wesley and War." Chap. 4 in This Methodism: Eight Studies, 67-91. London: Epworth Press, 1939. 152p.

561. _____. John Wesley, Including the Story of Wesley's Chapel City Road. People and Places in Early Methodism, Book 4. Manchester, Eng.: Penwork (Leeds) 1972. 14p.

562. _____. Methodism and England; a Study of Methodism in Its Social and Political Aspects During the Period 1850-1932. London: Epworth Press, 1943. 252p. Although the focus of the book is on a time period after Wesley, there are many references to him throughout it.

563. _____. My Dear Sister: The Story of John Wesley and the Women in His Life. Manchester, Eng.: Penwork (Leeds), 1980. 124p.

564. _____. Sons to Samuel. London: Epworth Press, 1961. 134p.

565. _____. The Wesley Family and Their Epworth Home. People and Places in Early Methodism, Book 2. Manchester, Eng.: Penwork (Leeds), 1972. 12p.

566-
567. _____. The Wesleys in Bristol. Manchester, Eng.: Penwork (Leeds), 1974. 20p.

568. Egermeier, Elsie Emilie. John Wesley, the Christian Hero. Anderson, Ind.: Gospel Trumpet Company, 1923. 131p.

569. Elliott-Binns, Leonard Elliott. "The Beginnings of the Move-
      ment." Chap. 1 in The Evangelical Movement in the English
      Church, 1-12. Garden City, N.Y.: Doubleday, Doran, 1928.
      171p. This author emphasizes Wesley's loyalty to the Church
      of England.

570. _____. The Early Evangelicals: A Religious and Social
      Study. Lutterworth Library, vol. 41. London: Lutterworth
      Press, 1953. 464p. (Rev. in no. 2486.)

571. Ellis, James Joseph. John Wesley. New York: Fleming H.
      Revell, 1891. 228p.

572. _____. John Wesley: The Man Who Revolutionised Britain
      in the Seventeenth [sic] Century. London and Glasgow:
      Pickering and Inglis, 1928. 64p.

573. Ellis, Sarah S. "The Mother of John Wesley." In The Mothers
      of Great Men, 309-47. London: Chatto and Windus, 1859.
      414p.

574. Eltzholtz, Carl Frederick. John Wesley's Conversion and
      Sanctification. Cincinnati: Jennings and Graham; New York:
      Eaton and Mains, 1908. 41p.

575. Emory, John. Defence of "Our Fathers," and of the Original
      Organization of the Methodist Episcopal Church, against the
      Rev. Alexander M'Caine, and Others; with Historical and
      Critical Notices of Early American Methodism. New York: N.
      Bangs and J. Emory, 1827. 92p. The classic work which
      opposes M'Caine's contention that the Methodist Episcopal or-
      ganization never had the sanction of John Wesley, and that
      episcopacy had been forced upon the Methodist societies.

576. _____. Preface in vol. 1 of The Works of the Rev. John
      Wesley, A.M...., iii-vii. 7 vols. New York: J. Emory and
      B. Waugh for the Methodist Episcopal Church, 1831.

577. England, Martha Winburn, and John Sparrow. Hymns Unbid-
      den: Donne, Herbert, Blake, Emily Dickinson and the Hymnog-
      raphers. New York: New York Public Library, 1966. 153p.

578. English, James Seymour. Methodism in Gainsborough. Gains-
      borough: Whiteswood Methodist Church, 1967. 16p.

579. English, John C. The Heart Renewed: John Wesley's Doctrine
      of Christian Initiation. Wesleyan Studies, no. 4. Macon, Ga.:
      Wesleyan College, 1967. 82p.

580. Ensley, Francis Gerald. John Wesley, Evangelist. Nashville:
      Tidings, 1955. 64p.

581. _____. Our United Methodist Heritage. Nashville: Discipleship Resources, 1979. 43p. Tells the story of John
Wesley at Bristol, Oxford, Epworth, and London.

582. Epworth and Its Surroundings. The Home of the Wesleys.
Epworth: Barnes and Breeze, [1898]. MBU-T

583. [Epworth League]. The Third Epworth Pilgrimage, 1897: A
Visit to the Home of Wesley, Organized by the Rev. James T.
Docking.... New York: T. Cook, 1897. 31p.

584. Epworth Press. Catalogue of an Exhibition of Wesleyana; Arranged by the Epworth Press and Methodist Publishing House
at Epworth House from July 5 to July 16, 1954. London: Epworth House, 1954. 9p.

585. Erdman, Walter Collins. "John Wesley." In Sources of Power
in Famous Lives, 147-52. Nashville: Cokesbury Press, 1936.
160p.

586. Essex, Walter. Faces in the Firelight. London: Epworth
Press, 1934. 26p. Brief story about Henry Perlee Parker,
the painter of the Epworth parsonage fire, 1709, and the
Wesley family.

587. Ethridge, Willie Snow. Strange Fires: The True Story of
John Wesley's Love Affair in Georgia. New York: Vanguard
Press, 1971. 254p.

588. Evans, Frederick, and Tom M. Dumwell. Eastbrook Chapel,
1825: Centenary Souvenir. Bradford: Harry Brearley,
1925. 176p. GtBLW

589. Evans, Seth. Methodism in Bradwell; Work and Worthies of
160 Years, Chapel Centenary Souvenir. New Mills, Eng.:
G. H. Bailey, 1907. 108p.

590. Everett, James. H. P. Parker's Historical Wesleyan Centenary
Picture, Representing the Rescue of the Founder of Methodism,
from the Fire of the Parsonage House at Epworth, Including
the Family Group in the Foreground.... Newcastle-upon-Tyne:
John Hernaman, 1839. 16p.

591. _____. Historical Sketches of Wesleyan Methodism, in Sheffield and Its Vicinity. Sheffield: Montgomery, 1823. 268p.

592. _____. Wesleyan Methodism in Manchester and Its Vicinity.
Manchester, Eng.: 1827. 191p. A detailed account of Methodism
in Manchester and vicinity, beginning with John Clayton and ending with the year 1749. Wesley's numerous visits to the area
are recounted.

54   John and Charles Wesley

593. Everson, F. Howell. "How It All Began." Chap. 16 in This
     Is Methodism, 96-102. London: Epworth Press, 1957. 108p.

594.   _____. The Manchester Round. Manchester, Eng.: Man-
     chester Districts of the Methodist Church, 1947. 39p. GtBLW

595. Ewing, Curtis Clair. Hosea and the Wesleyan Revival.
     Pasadena, Calif.: Church of the Covenants, [196-?] 4p.

596. Ewing, Walter Lee. "The Road to Aldersgate," and "The
     Expanding Church." Chaps. 4 and 5 in The Church That
     Was and Is to Be..., 41-63. New York and Cincinnati:
     Methodist Book Concern, 1936. 74p.

597. Failing, George E. "Developments in Holiness Theology After
     Wesley." In Insights into Holiness..., 11-31. See no. 61.

598. Fairchild, Hoxie Neale. "Evangelical Movements," and "The
     Saints and Their Foes." Chaps. 3 and 4 in vol. 2 of Re-
     ligious Trends in English Poetry, 78-130. 6 vols. New York:
     Columbia University Press, 1942.

599. Fallaw, H. F. and W. C. G. Low Fell Wesley Memorial Metho-
     dist Church: Jubilee Souvenir, 1882-1933. N.p. 1933. 16p.
     GtBLW

600. Faris, John Thomson. "Called to Save Souls; the Strenuous
     Life of John Wesley." Chap. 9 in Reapers of His Harvest,
     79-86. Philadelphia: Westminster Press, 1915. 160p.

601. Farrar, F. W. "John Wesley." In Prophets of the Christian
     Faith, 125-47. London: J. Clarke, 1897. 252p.

602. Faulkner, John Alfred. The Methodists. New York: Baker
     and Taylor, 1903. 264p.

603.   _____. "The Socialism of John Wesley." In Social Ideals:
     Papers on Social Subjects..., 103-24. London: Robert Culley,
     1909. 124p. Describes Wesley's thoughts on various social,
     political, and economic issues of his day--scarcity of food, war,
     luxury, slavery, concluding that Wesley was not a true social
     reformer, but rather a man intensely interested in his fellow
     man and what was required to improve his lot.

604.   _____. Wesley As Sociologists, Theologian and Churchman.
     New York: Methodist Book Concern, 1918. 173p.

605. Feather, James. The Life and Work of Wesley: A Lecture for
     the Optical Lantern. Leeds: Crowther and Hunt, 1891. 24p.

606. Feiling, Keith Graham. In Christ Church Hall. London: Mac-
     millan, 1960. 208p. Sketch of Charles Wesley, pp. 53-62.

607. Fendrich, Joseph Lowrey, Jr. "John Wesley--Reformer."
     Chap. 5 in Five Men Named John, 93-115. Philadelphia, Pa.:
     Moyer and Lotter, 1924. 115p. Fendrich, a Presbyterian
     minister, preached this sermon December 14, 1924, at the
     First Presbyterian Church of Chestnut Hill, Philadelphia.

608. Ferm, Robert O. The Psychology of Christian Conversion.
     Westwood, N.J.: Fleming H. Revell Co., 1959. 255p. The
     author discusses the "evangelical crises" in the lives of
     Jonathan Edwards, John Wesley, John Bunyan, and others.

609. Few, William Preston. "Aldersgate and Christian Education."
     Chap. 5 in What Happened at Aldersgate, 84-90. See no.
     342.

610. Findlater, John. Perfect Love; a Study of Wesley's View of
     the Ideal Christian Life. Leith: Leith Printing Co., 1914.
     182p.

611. Findlay, George G. "Methodism." In vol. 8 of Encyclopaedia
     of Religion and Ethics, 603-12. See no. 218.

612. Findlay, George G., and Mary Grace Findlay. Wesley's World
     Parish: A Sketch of the Hundred Years' Work of the Wesleyan
     Methodist Missionary Society. London: Hodder and Stoughton,
     1913. 224p. The last chapter was written by William Hare
     Findlay.

613. Findlay, George H. Christ Standard Bearer; a Study of the
     Hymns of Charles Wesley as They Are Contained in the Last
     Edition (1876) of "A Collection of Hymns for the Use of the
     People Called Methodists," by the Rev. John Wesley, A.M.
     London: Epworth Press, 1956. 74p.

614. Fish, Henry. Introductory essay in The Wesleyan Psalter: A
     Poetical Version of Nearly the Whole Book of Psalms, by the
     Rev. Charles Wesley, ix-xxiv. Nashville: E. Stevenson and
     F. A. Owens, 1855. 330p.

615. Fisher, Samuel Ware. John Calvin and John Wesley: An Ad-
     dress Delivered August 7, 1856, on the Nineteenth Anniversary
     of the Mt. Holyoke Female Seminary, South Hadley, Massa-
     chusetts. Cincinnati: Moore, Wilstach, Keys and Co., 1856.
     54p.

616. Fisher, Welthy Honsinger. "Aldersgate the Power Uplifting
     Womanhood." Chap. 14 in What Happened at Aldersgate, 183-
     89. See no. 342.

617. Fitchett, William Henry. Wesley and His Century: A Study in
     Spiritual Forces. London: Smith, Elder and Co., 1906. 537p.

618.   Fitzgerald, Oscar Penn. The Class-Meeting: In Twenty Short
        Chapters. Nashville: Southern Methodist Publishing House,
        1888. 104p.

619.   _____. "The Epworth Springs." Part 1 in The Epworth
        Book..., 9-40. Nashville: Southwestern Publishing House,
        1893. 318p. A retelling of the Wesley story.

620.   _____. "Susanna Wesley." In Eminent Methodists, 199-
        241. Nashville: Publishing House, M. E. Church, South,
        1897. 375p.

621.   Fitzgerald, William Blackburn. The Roots of Methodism.
        London: C. H. Kelly, 1903. 217p.

622.   Fletcher, G. Arthur. Records of Wesleyan Methodism in the
        Belper Circuit, 1760-1903. Belper, Eng.: Tom Brown,
        Printer, 1903. 68p.

623.   Flew, Robert Newton. The Hymns of Charles Wesley: A Study
        of Their Structure. Wesley Historical Society Lectures, 1953.
        London: Epworth Press, 1953. 79p.

624.   _____. "Methodism." Chap. 19 in The Idea of Perfection
        in Christian Theology, 313-41. London: Oxford University
        Press, 1934. 422p.

625.   Flint, Charles Wesley. Charles Wesley and His Colleagues.
        Washington: Public Affairs Press, 1957. 221p.

626.   Foakes-Jackson, F. J. "Life in the Eighteenth Century Il-
        lustrated by the Career of John Wesley." In Social Life in
        England, 1750-1850, 1-41. New York: Macmillan, 1916.
        338p.

627.   Foot, Isaac, and T. S. Gregory. The City of the Living God,
        Studies in Wesley's Catholicity. London: Epworth Press,
        1932. 31p.

628.   Ford, Jack. "A Comparison of Their Exposition of Holiness
        and Wesley's." In In the Steps of John Wesley: The Church
        of the Nazarene in Britain, 226-35. Kansas City: Nazarene
        Publishing House, 1968. 300p. Also his thesis, University of
        London.

629.   Fosdick, Harry Emerson. "On John Wesley." In Great Voices
        of the Reformation; an Anthology, 491-98. New York: Random
        House, 1952. 546p. This essay on John Wesley is followed by
        excerpts from his writings.

630.   Foss, Cyrus D. "Wesley and Personal Religious Experience."
        In Wesley Memorial Volume, 128-48. See no. 257.

631. Foster, Henry J. "The Society Room in Aldersgate." In
     Wesley Studies, 81-87. See no. 190.

632. Foster, William Horton. "Susannah Wesley." Chap. 2 in
     Heroines of Modern Religion, edited by Warren Dunham Foster,
     23-56. New York: Sturgis and Walton, 1913. 275p.

633. Fowler, James W. "John Wesley's Development in Faith."
     Chap. 6 in The Future of the Methodist Theological Traditions,
     172-92. See no. 57.

634. Frazer, George Stanley. Methodism, Its History, Teaching,
     and Government. 2d ed. Nashville: Publishing House of the
     M. E. Church, South, 1922. 57p. Written for the layman.

635. Freeman, James Midwinter. The Birthplace of Methodism.
     Oxford League Series, no. 3. New York: Phillips and Hunt,
     189-? 16p.

636. Freeman, John. Bilston Wesleyan Methodism: Notes on Its
     Origin and Progress.... Bilston: Freeman, 1923. 170p.

637. French, W. Maynard. The John Wesley Prayer Book. Nash-
     ville: Parthenon Press, [1956]. 133p.

638. Frere, W. H. "The Contributions of Congregationalism and
     Methodism." In Hymns Ancient and Modern; for Use in the
     Services of the Church..., lxxxii-lxxxix. London: Clowes,
     1909. 911p.

639. Friend of Sabbath Schools. The Life of the Rev. John Wesley,
     A.M.: Abridged from Authentic Sources. New York: Pub-
     lished by J. Emory and B. Waugh for the Methodist Episcopal
     Church, 1830. 104p.

640. Fries, Adelaide L. "Wesley, Ingham and Töltschig." In The
     Moravians in Georgia, 190-201. Winston-Salem, N.C.:
     Edwards and Broughton, 1905. 252p.

641. Frost, Brian. "The Idea of Fullness in the Hymns of Charles
     Wesley." In We Belong to One Another: Methodist, Anglican
     and Orthodox Essays, 48-61. See no. 43.

642. Frost, S. E. "John Wesley." In Great Religious Stories,
     268-72. Garden City, N.Y.: Garden City Publishing Co.,
     1945. 277p.

643. Fukamachi, Masanobu. "The Love-Feast." In Japanese Con-
     tributions to the Study of John Wesley, 69-78. Macon, Ga.:
     Wesleyan College, 1967. 98p.

644. Fuller, Margaret. "Methodism at the Fountain." In Art,
      Literature and the Drama, edited by Arthur B. Fuller, 342-
      51. Boston: Roberts Bros., 1875. 449p. An essay on John
      and Charles Wesley.

645. Funston, John Wesley. The Wesleys in Picture and Story:
      An Illustrated History of the Life and Times of John and
      Charles Wesley. Mount Morris, Ill.: Kable Bros., 1939.
      137p.

646. Fussell, James. A Refutation of Several Charges Alleged
      against the Late Rev. J. Wesley by the Rev. W. Ward, in His
      Work Entitled "The Fulfilment of Revelation." Diss, Eng.:
      E. E. Abbott, 1820. 56p. IEG

647. Galloway, Charles B. "Charles Wesley, the Hymnist of the
      Ages." In The Wesley Bi-Centenary Celebration in Savannah,
      Ga., 55-74. See no. 39.

648. _____. "Mrs. Susanna Wesley, 1670-1742." In Eminent
      Methodists, 199-241. Nashville: Barbee and Smith, 1896.
      375p.

649. Gamble, Thomas. The Love Stories of John and Charles
      Wesley. [Savannah: Review Publishing and Printing, 1927.]
      68p.

650. Garber, Paul Neff. That Fighting Spirit of Methodism.
      Greensboro, N.C.: Piedmont Press, 1928. 199p.

651. Garrett, Margueritte Bixler and William Beery. History and
      Message of Hymns. Elgin, Ill.: Elgin Press, 1924. 240p.
      Includes discussions on numerous hymns by Charles Wesley.

652. Gaskell, John. Wesley Methodist Church, Lamberhead Green:
      Brief History of the Last 170 Years, 1776-1946. Wigan: J.
      Starr, 1946. 27p. GtBLW

653. Gaskin, Robert Tate. The Rise of Methodism, Briefly Sketched.
      London: Whittaker and Co., 1863. 99p.

654. Gee, Charles H. Methodism in Heptonstall. London: Epworth
      Press, 1939. 24p.

655. Gee, Herbert Leslie. Easter at Epworth: Story of a Pil-
      grimage. London: Epworth Press, 1944. 69p.

656. Geissinger, James Allen. "The Appeal to Methodist History."
      Chap. 4 in The Democracy of Methodism, 31-50. New York
      and Cincinnati: Methodist Book Concern, 1920. 83p.

657. George, A. Raymond. "The Lord's Supper." Chap. 8 in
     The Doctrine of the Church, 140-60. See no. 440.

658. _____. "The People Called Methodists. Pt. 4. The Means
     of Grace." Chap. 8 in vol. 1 of A History of the Methodist
     Church in Great Britain, 259-73. See no. 89.

659. Gibbins, Henry de Beltgens. "Wesley and Wilberforce."
     Chap. 3 in English Social Reformers, 65-108. London:
     Methuen and Co., 1902. 229p. This author states that the
     noblest result of Wesley's work was "the stimulus he gave to
     all the noble and humane impulses of his time to work together
     patiently and hopefully for the relief of human misery and de-
     gradation in all its forms." He lists among Wesley's many
     contributions (Methodism being one of the least important) the
     growth of philanthropy, as seen in penal code reform, anti-
     slavery sentiment, and the growth of national consciousness.

660. Gifford, William Alva. John Wesley: Patriot and Statesman.
     Toronto: Ryerson Press, 1922. 29p.

661. Gilbert, Alan D. Religion and Society in Industrial England:
     Church, Chapel, and Social Change, 1740-1914. London and
     New York: Longman, 1976. 251p. There are references to
     Wesley throughout the book.

662. [Gilbert, Nathaniel]. An Answer to Mr. John Slack's Re-
     marks: By the Author of the Answer to J. Wesley's Mis-
     representations of the Catholic Doctrines. Manchester:
     Thomas Haydock, 1812. 274p.

663. Gilder, Richard Watson. John Wesley. N.p. 1903. 6p.
     Written for the celebration of the two hundredth anniversary
     of the birth of John Wesley, at Wesleyan University, Middle-
     ton, Connecticut, June, 1903.

664. Gilfillan, George. Modern Christian Heroes: A Gallery of
     Protesting and Reforming Men, Including Cromwell, Milton,
     The Puritans, Covenanters, First Seceders, Methodists, etc.
     London: Eliot Stock, 1869. 312p. John Wesley, pp. 264-78.

665. Gill, Frederick C. Charles Wesley, the First Methodist. Lon-
     don: Lutterworth Press, 1964. 238p.

666. _____. Glorious Company: Lives of Great Christians for
     Daily Devotion. London: Epworth Press, 1958.

667. _____. In the Steps of John Wesley. London: Lutter-
     worth Press, 1962. 239p.

668. _____. Introduction to John Wesley's Prayers, 9-17. Lon-
     don: Epworth Press, 1951. 102p.

669.   _____. Introduction to Selected Letters, by John Wesley.
        London: Epworth Press, 1956. 244p.

670.   _____. "The Wesleys." Chap. 2 in The Romantic Move-
        ment and Methodism: A Study of English Romanticism and
        the Evangelical Revival, 39-71. London: Epworth Press,
        1937. 189p.

671.   Gill, Josiah. The History of Wesleyan Methodism in Melton
        Mobray and the Vicinity, 1769-1909. Melton Mobray: Warner,
        1909. 268p.

672.   Gillman, F. J. "The Wesleys." Chap. 12 in The Evolution of
        of the English Hymn: An Historical Survey of the Origins and
        Development of the Hymns of the Christian Church, 214-31.
        London: George Allen and Unwin, 1927. 312p.

673.   Godley, Alfred Denis. Oxford in the Eighteenth Century.
        New York: G. P. Putnam's Sons; London: Methuen and Co.,
        1908. 291p. Pp. 265-80 describe the hostility at Oxford
        towards Methodism and the Wesleys.

674.   Godwin, George Stanley. "Wesley and the Methodist Revival."
        Chap. 8 in The Great Revivalists, 129-49. Boston: Beacon
        Press, 1950. 220p.

675.   Golding, Claud. "John Wesley's Virago-Wife." In Great Names
        in History, 356 B.C.-A.D. 1910, 185-90. Philadelphia: J. B.
        Lippincott and Co., 1936. 300p.

676.   Goldsack, R. S. Paul and John Wesley Compared with
        Swedenborg: Three Lectures. London: James Speirs, n.d.
        37p.

677.   González, Justo L. "Wesley and Methodism." In From the
        Protestant Reformation to the Twentieth Century, 279-87.
        Vol. 3 of A History of Christian Thought. Nashville: Abing-
        don Press, 1975. 407p.

678.   Goodloe, Robert Wesley. "Wesley's Conception of the Church
        and Ministry." Chap. 5 in The Principles and Development of
        Church Government, with Particular Application to Methodism,
        92-113. Nashville: Cokesbury, 1932. 271p.

679.   Goodsell, Buel. Animadversions on a Pamphlet, Entitled "A
        Series of Letters, on This Question: Whether True Saints Are
        Liable Finally to Fall from an Estate of Grace" ... and a Vindi-
        cation of the Sentiment and Arguments Contained in a Tract,
        Written by the Late Rev. John Wesley.... Plattsburgh, N.Y.:
        Frederick P. Allen, 1822. 77p.

680. Gordon, Alexander. "Charles Wesley." In vol. 20 of Dictionary of National Biography, 1213-14.

681. _____. "John Wesley." In vol. 20 of Dictionary of National Biography, 1214-25.

682. _____. "Samuel Wesley." In vol. 20 of Dictionary of National Biography, 1225-29.

683. Gordon, Fred G. Methodism in Enniskillen: Issued in Connection with the Jubilee of Darling Street Church, 1917. Enniskillan: William Trimble, 1917. 46p. GtBLW

684. Gorrie, Peter Douglass. "From the Birth of John Wesley, to the Introduction of Methodism into America." Chap. 1 in Episcopal Methodism, As It Was and Is..., 1-36. Auburn, N.Y.: Derby and Miller, 1852. 354p.

685. _____. "John Wesley." Chap. 1 in Lives of Eminent Methodist Ministers, 9-28. New York: Saxton, Barber, 1859. 408p.

686. Goucher, John F. "The Providential Preparation of Wesley." In The Wesley Bi-Centenary Celebration in Savannah, Ga., 101-14. See no. 39.

687. Gould, George C. Lest We Forget: The Record of Fifty Years Work in the Clacton-on-Sea Circuit of the Wesleyan Methodist Church, 1875-1925. London: Published by Authority of the Circuit Quarterly Meeting, 1925. 75p.

688. Gould, Joseph Glenn. Healing the Hurt of Man: A Study of John Wesley's "Cure of Souls." Kansas City, Mo.: Beacon Hill Press, 1971. 70p. Discusses "John Wesley's doctrine and methodology in dealing with the spiritual needs of men."

689. Grace Hill Methodist Church, Folkestone: Year Book 1955-56: The Story of the People Called Methodists. Ramsgate: Graham Cumming, 1956. 18p. GtBLW

690. Graham, William Creighton. John Wesley As a Letter Writer. Ryerson Essays, no. 24. Toronto: Methodist Book and Publishing House, 1923. 35p.

691. Grant, Johnson. "The Methodists." In vol. 3 of A Summary of the History of the English Church, and of the Sects Which Have Departed from Its Communion..., 205-83. 4 vols. London: J. Hatchard and Son, 1820.

692. Graves, James Robinson. The Great Iron Wheel.... Nashville: Graves, Marks and Rutland; New York: Sheldon,

Blakeman and Co., 1856. 570p. An attack on Wesley and
Methodism. See nos. 248, 840.

693. Gray, Andrew. Methodist Orders Examined: or, Modern
      Methodism Compared with the Writings of John Wesley. 2d ed.
      New York: James Pott and Co., 1894. 24p. NJmUM

694. Gray, Joseph Cross. The Father and Founder of Methodism.
      Holyoke, Mass., 1923. 30p.

695. Great Tributes to John Wesley and His Chapel, with forewords
      by Bishops F. W. McDowell and J. W. Hamilton. Washington:
      J. D. Milans and Sons, 1929. 24p. NjMUM

696. Greathouse, William M. "The Wesleyan Doctrine of Perfection."
      Chap. 10 in From the Apostles to Wesley: Christian Perfec-
      tion in Historical Perspective, 106-20. Kansas City, Mo.:
      Beacon Hill Press, 1979. 124p.

697. Greaves, J. George. Wesleyan Methodism in the City of the
      Proto-Martyr and the St. Albans Circuit; with Reminiscences
      of Folk-Lore. St. Albans: Gibbs and Bamforth, 1907. 152p.

698. Green, John Brazier. John Wesley and William Law. London:
      Epworth Press, 1945. 224p.

699. Green, Richard. The Conversion of John Wesley. Primers for
      Bible Students, no. 1. London: Francis Griffiths, 1909. 40p.

700. _____. An Itinerary in Which Are Traced the Rev. John
      Wesley's Journeys from October 14, 1735, to October 24, 1790.
      Proceedings of the Wesley Historical Society, vol. 6. Burnley:
      B. Moore, 1907-08. 134p.

701. _____. John Wesley. London: Cassell, Potter, Galpin and
      Co., 1881. 192p.

702. _____. John Wesley, Evangelist. London: Religious Tract
      Society, 1905. 542p.

703. _____. Mission of Methodism: Being the Twentieth Fernley
      Lecture. London: Wesleyan Methodist Book-Room, 1890. 226p.

704. _____. "Mr. Wesley's Publications." In The Homes, Haunts
      and Friends of John Wesley, 113-20. See no. 319.

705. _____. "Wesley's Hymn-Books." In Wesley Studies, 151-55.
      See no. 190.

706. Green, Vivian Herbert Howard. From St. Augustine to Wil-
      liam Temple; Eight Studies in Christian Leadership. London:

Latimer House, 1948. 172p. John Wesley, pp. 126-47. "...
no exaggeration to say that Wesley was the most influential
and most significant figure in eighteenth-century England."
There is a brief summary of his life, the times he lived in,
and his contributions.

707. _____. John Wesley. London: Nelson, 1964. 168p.

708. _____. "John Wesley and the Oxford Methodists." Chap. 7
in Religion at Oxford and Cambridge, 178-201. London: SCM
Press, 1964. 392p.

709. _____. "John Wesley at Lincoln." Chap. 13 in The Common-
wealth of Lincoln College 1427-1977, 325-50. Oxford: Oxford
University Press, 1979.

710. _____. Some New Letters of John Wesley. [Oxford: Lincoln College, 1969?]. pp. 12-19. Offprint from Lincoln College Record, 1968-69.

711. _____. The Young Mr. Wesley: A Study of John Wesley
and Oxford. London: E. Arnold; New York: St. Martin's
Press, 1961. 342p.

712. Greenfield, John. Methodists and Moravians. Nazareth, Pa.,
n.d. [4 p.]. GtBLMor

713. Gregory, Arthur Edwin. "Hymns of the Methodist Revival."
In The Hymn Book of the Modern Church: Brief Studies of
Hymns and Hymn-Writers, 155-223. London: C. H. Kelly,
1904. 350p.

714. Gregory, Arthur S. "Hymns of the Evangelical Revival:
Charles Wesley and the Methodist Hymn-Book." In Praises
with Understanding; Illustrated from the Words and Music of
the Methodist Hymn-Book, 61-69. London: Epworth Press,
1936. 348p.

715. Gregory, Benjamin. "Charles Wesley." In Champions of the
Truth: Short Lives of Christian Leaders in Thought and Ac-
tion, edited by A. R. Buckland. London: Religious Tract
Society, 1903. 464p.

716. _____. A Handbook of Wesleyan-Methodist Polity and His-
tory. London: Wesleyan Methodist Bookroom, 1888. 278p.
Pp. 1-110 deal largely with Wesley and the development of
Methodism.

717. _____. Three Great Methodists: John Wesley, Francis Asbury and Thomas Coke. Heroes of the Free Churches, no. 1.
London: Epworth Press, 1935. 44p.

718. Gregory, John Robinson. A History of Methodism Chiefly for
      the Use of Students. 2 vols. London: C. H. Kelly, 1911.

719. Gregory, John Robinson and Arthur E. Gregory. "Wesleyan
      Methodism--the Middle Period, 1791-1849." In vol. 1 of A New
      History of Methodism, 379-433. Parts of this chapter contain
      comments on Wesley and those who were concerned with his
      affairs after his death. See no. 229.

720. Gregory, T. S. According to Your Faith. London: Epworth
      Press, 1966. 110p. "An essay in prayer and meditation based
      on Charles Wesley's hymns."

721. Griffin, Ernest W. Watchers of a Beacon: The Story of the
      Keswick and Cockermouth Methodist Circuit. Cockermouth:
      West Cumberland Times, 1954. 24p. GtBLW

722. Gross, John Owen. John Wesley, Christian Educator. Nash-
      ville: Board of Education, The Methodist Church, 1954.
      30p.

723. _____. "John Wesley's Search for Religious Assurance,"
      and "Forward from Aldersgate." Chaps. 1 and 2 in The Be-
      ginnings of American Methodism, 11-34. New York: Abingdon
      Press, 1961. 142p.

724. Grubb, Arthur Page. Chelsea Centenary of Methodism, 1813-
      1913. London, 1913. 68p. NcD

725. H., E. G. John Wesley, His Principles and His Practice,
      Briefly Contrasted with Those of Modern-So-Called Wesleyans.
      London: Church Printing Co., 1874. 8p.

726. Haas, Alfred Burton. Charles Wesley. Papers of the Hymn
      Society, 22. New York: Hymn Society of America, 1957.
      22p.

727. Hack, Mary Pryor. "Susanna Wesley." Chap. 2 in Consecrated
      Women, 41-48. Philadelphia: H. Longstreth, 1882. 344p.

728. Haddall, Ingvar. John Wesley, a Biography. Translated from
      the original Norwegian. New York: Abingdon Press, 1961.
      175p.

729. Hadden, R. H. "The Methodists." In Church and Chapel:
      Sermons on the Church of England and Dissent, 64-80. London:
      Smith, Elder, 1881. 117p.

730. Haire, Robert. Jack of Lincoln Sails West Again; or, Tales of
      the Wesleyan Invasion of Ireland. Belfast: Nelson and Knox,
      Printers, 1960? 79p.

731. _____. Wesley's One-and-Twenty Visits to Ireland, a Short
Survey. London: Epworth Press, 1947. 186p.

732. Hale, Leonard. Highbury Methodism: Its Past, Its Present
and Its Future. N.p. 1924. 42p. The Wesleys never
preached at Highbury, but they did in Islington. GtBLW

733. Halévy, Elie. The Birth of Methodism in England. Translated
and edited by Bernard Semmel. Chicago: University of Chicago Press, 1971. 81p. Discusses the effect of the Evangelical
revival on the working class.

734. Halifax, Edward Frederick Lindley Wood. "John Wesley." In
American Speeches, 172-79. London: Oxford University Press,
1947. 449p. An address delivered at Wesleyan University,
1 June 1942.

735. Hall, Samuel Romilly. A Defence of John Wesley and Modern
Methodism; a Lecture of Mr. George Dawson's Opinion of John
Wesley; Delivered in the Music Hall, Birmingham, December 15,
1859.... London: Alexander Heylin, 1860. 44p.

736. _____. Illustrative Records of John Wesley and Early
Methodism; a Lecture Founded on Marshall Claxton's Painting
of the Death Bed of the Rev. J. Wesley; Delivered in the
Wesleyan School Room, Red Bank, Stocks, Manchester, July 3,
1856. London, 1856. 64p.

737. _____. John Wesley's Use of the Press. London, 1859.
72p. GtBBrP

738. Hall, Thomas Cuming. "The Methodist Movement." Lecture 2
in The Social Meaning of Modern Religious Movements in England, 40-74. Ely Lectures, 1899. New York: C. Scribner's
Sons, 1900. 283p.

739. Hamill, E. J. A Discussion on Methodist Episcopacy; between
Rev. E. J. Hamill and Samuel Henderson; Published at the
Mutual Request of Baptists and Methodists. Charleston:
Southern Baptist Publication Society, 1856. 380p.

740. Hamilton, J. Taylor. "The Beginnings of the Moravian Church
in England." Chap. 8 in A History of the Church Known as
the Moravian Church..., 78-83. Bethlehem, Pa.: Times Publishing Co., 1900. 631p.

741. Hamilton, John W. "John Wesley." In Lives of Methodist
Bishops, edited by Theodore Flood and John W. Hamilton,
21-38. New York: Phillips and Hunt, 1882. 792p. Deals
with Wesley's attitude to bishops.

742.   Hammond, Joseph. John Wesley "Being Dead, Yet Speaketh,"
        ... A Contribution to the Centenary of 1891. London: So-
        ciety for Promoting Christian Knowledge, 1891? 120p. The
        author sets forth his ideas of the message John Wesley would
        have for his followers 100 years after his death.

743.   Hampson, John. Memoirs of the Late Rev. John Wesley, A.M.,
        with a Review of His Life and Writings and a History of
        Methodism from Its Commencement in 1729 to the Present Time
        1791. 3 vols. Sunderland: James Graham, 1791.

744.   Hardcastle, Titus. John Wesley, His Life and Work. Bolton:
        J. Pendlebury and Sons, 1895. 24p. GEU-T, GtBMM

745.   _____. Methodism in Armley: With Stray Notes on Methodism
        in Leeds and Neighbourhood. London: Hamilton, Adam and
        Co., 1871. 68p.

746.   Hardesty, Nancy A. "The Wesleyan Movement and Women's
        Liberation." In Sanctification and Liberation, 164-73. See no.
        191.

747.   Harding, Frederick Alfred John. The Social Impact of the
        Evangelical Revival: A Brief Account of the Social Influences
        of the Teaching of John Wesley and His Followers. London:
        Epworth Press, 1947. 48p. (First published in the Historical
        Magazine of the Protestant Episcopal Church 15 (1946): 256-
        84.)

748.   Hardy, Robert Spence. Gleanings in Methodism: To Be Re-
        scattered in Scotland. Edinburgh: Robert Anderson, 1857.
        272p.

749.   Hare, Edward. Genuine Methodism Acquitted and Spurious
        Methodism Condemned.... Rochdale, Eng.: J. Hartley, 1807.
        88p. A rebuttal to J. Cooke, vindicating Wesley's doctrines
        as genuine Methodism.

750.   _____. A Refutation of the Charges against the Methodists
        Advanced by the Rev. Doctor Magee. London: Thomas
        Cordeux, 1810. 56p. Wesley's doctrines are examined and
        vindicated.

751.   Hargreaves, Thomas. The Rise and Progress of Wesleyan
        Methodism in Accrington and the Neighbourhood. Accrington,
        Eng.: T. M. Hepworth, 1883. 147p.

752.   Harkness, Georgia Elma. "Methodism in England," and "The
        Roots of Methodist Theology." Chaps. 1 and 6 in The Metho-
        dist Church in Social Thought and Action, 17-25, 89-98.
        Nashville: Abingdon Press, 1964. 172p. This is a study
        guide for Methodists.

Books   67

753. Harmer, E. G. "Contemporary Portraits of John Wesley."
      In The Homes, Haunts and Friends of John Wesley, 120-23.
      See no. 319.

754. _____. "The Hymns of Wesley's Boyhood." In The Homes,
      Haunts and Friends of John Wesley, 138-43. See no. 319.

755. _____. "The Judgement of His Peers." In The Homes,
      Haunts and Friends of John Wesley, 144-46. See no. 319.

756. Harmon, Nolan B. "How It Started." Chap. 1 in Understand-
      ing the Methodist Church, 11-24. Rev. ed. Nashville:
      Methodist Publishing House, 1961. 191p. Popular treatment
      written for Methodists.

757. _____. "Of Origins" and "Methodist Episcopacy; the First
      Period, 1784-1808." Chaps. 1 and 2 in The Organization of
      the Methodist Church; Historic Development and Present Work-
      ing Structure, 13-18, 21-28. Nashville: Methodist Publishing
      House, 1963. 288p.

758. _____. "The Sunday Service." In The Rites and Rituals
      of Episcopal Methodism..., 38-48. Nashville: Publishing
      House of the Methodist Episcopal Church, South, 1926. 417p.

759. Harmon, Rebecca Lamar. Susanna, Mother of the Wesleys.
      Nashville: Abingdon Press, 1968. 175p.

760. Harper, Charles George. "The Epworth Ghost." In Haunted
      Houses; Tales of the Supernatural, with Some Account of
      Hereditary Curses and Family Legends, 132-41. Philadelphia:
      Lippincott, 1907. 283p.

761. Harper, Howard V. "John Wesley." In Profiles of Protestant
      Saints, 29-41. New York: Fleet Press, 1968. 231p.

762. Harper, Steve. Devotional Life in the Wesleyan Tradition.
      Nashville: The Upper Room, 1983. 80p. The purpose of this
      book is "to show that the heart of Wesley's life and ministry
      was his all-encompassing commitment to the devotional life."

763. _____. John Wesley's Message for Today. Grand Rapids,
      Mich.: Zondervan Publishing House, 1983. 146p.

764. Harrison, Archibald H. W. "Eighteenth Century Methodism."
      Chap. 1 in The Methodist Church: Its Origin, Divisions and
      Reunion, 7-46. London: Methodist Publishing House, 1932.
      229p.

765. _____. "The Evangelical Revival." Chap. 7 in Arminianism,
      185-222. London: Duckworth, 1937. 246p.

766. _____. The Evangelical Revival and Christian Reunion.
Fernley-Hartley Lectures, 1942. London: Epworth Press,
1942. 207p. The major part of this book focuses on the
story of the Wesleys and the rise of Methodism in the eighteenth century, the influence of the Moravians, Wesley's relations with the Anglican Church, the societies, and his as-
sociates.

767. _____. The Separation of Methodism from the Church of
England. Wesley Historical Society Lectures, no. 11. London:
Epworth Press, 1945. 66p.

768. Harrison, Grace Elizabeth Simon. The Clue to the Brontës.
London: Methuen, 1948. 222p. Describes the influence of
John Wesley and Methodism on Patrick Brontë and his
children.

769. Haworth Parsonage: A Study of Wesley and the Brontës.
Wesley Historical Society Lectures, no. 3. London: Epworth
Press, 1937. 45p.

770. _____. Methodist Good Companions. London: Epworth
Press, 1935. 154p. Contains chapters on Grace Murray,
Jabez Bunting, Haworth Parsonage, Thomas Adams, John
Smith, with many references to John Wesley throughout.

771. _____. Son to Susanna: The Private Life of John Wesley.
London: I. Nicholson and Watson, 1937. 353p. (Rev. in
no. 2391.)

772. Hart, William John. Unfamiliar Stories of Familiar Hymns.
Boston: W. A. Wilde Co., 1940. 218p.

773. Harvey, Edmund George. John Wesley: His Principles and
His Practice, Briefly Contrasted with Those of Modern So-
called Wesleyans. London: Church Printing Co., 1874. 8p.

774. Harvey, J. D. The Wesleyan Way Today. Winona Lake, Ind.:
Light and Life Press, 1979. 72p.

775. Harwich Wesleyan Methodist Church. One Hundred Years and
More of Wesleyan Methodism at Harwich: the Centenary Handbook. Harwich: Wesleyan Methodist Church, 1929. 15p.

776. Harwood, George H. A History of Wesleyan Methodism. London: Whittaker and Co., 1854. 244p.

777. _____. The History of Wesleyan Methodism in Nottingham
and Its Vicinity. Nottingham: W. Bunny, 1859. 124p.

778. Harwood, H. W. History of Methodism in Midgley, Near Halifax. Halifax: Halifax Printing Works, 1933. 64p.

779. Harwood, Harry J. John Wesley, Pastor of a World Parish.
      Lucknow: Lucknow Publishing House, 1938. 36p. Issued by
      the committee on the bicentennial observance of Aldersgate
      day, for the Methodist Episcopal Church in Southern Asia.

780. Hassé, E. R. "Peter Böhler and John Wesley," and "The
      Moravian Share in the Great Revival--Doctrinally." Chaps.
      3 and 4 in The Moravians, 27-33, 34-48. 2d ed. London:
      National Council of Evangelical Free Churches, 1913. 142p.

781. Hastings, J. J. Misterton Methodism, Past and Present:
      Jubilee, 1928. Gainsborough: Newbold and Humphries,
      1928. 61p.

782. Hastling, Arthur Henry Lee, W. Addington Willis, and W. P.
      Workman. The History of Kingswood School: Together with
      Registers of Kingswood School and Woodhouse Grove School,
      and a List of Masters; by Three Old Boys. London: C. H.
      Kelly, 1898. 204p. The first nine chapters, pp. 13-81,
      describe the establishment of the school by John Wesley in
      1746 and its work under his guidance.

783. Hatch, Harold. Manchester Road Methodist Church, Hasling-
      den Centenary, 1857-1957. Manchester: C. Nicholls and Co.,
      1957. 16p. GtBLW

784. Hatfield, Edwin Francis. The Poets of the Church. 1884.
      Reprint. Boston: Milford House, 1972. 719p. Pp. 647-69
      discuss the Wesleys--Charles, John, and Samuel, the father.

785. Hatfield, Robert M. Wesley's Relations to the Methodist Epis-
      copal Church; a Sermon. New York: Nelson and Phillips,
      18--? 36p.

786. Haven, Erastus O. "Wesley as an Educator." In Wesley
      Memorial Volume, 300-309. See no. 257.

787. Haweis, Thomas. "Rise, Progress, and Present State of What
      Has Been Termed Methodism." In vol. 3 of An Impartial and
      Succinct History of the Rise and Declension and Revival of the
      Church of Christ, 221-82. 3 vols. London: J. Mawman,
      1800.

788. Hayes, Alan L. "John Wesley and Sophy Hopkey: A Case
      Study in Wesley's Attitude toward Women." In vol. 2 of
      Women in New Worlds: Historical Perspectives on the Wesleyan
      Tradition, edited by Rosemary Skinner Keller, Louise L. Queen,
      and Hilah F. Thomas, 29-44. 2 vols. Nashville: Abingdon
      Press, 1982.

789. Hayes, Ernest Henry. "John Wesley." Chap. 9 in Yarns on

Christian Pioneers. For Workers among Young Adolescents,
74-86. London: National Sunday School Union, 1928. 95p.

790. Hayman, John Gould. "The First Visits of the Wesleys."
Chap. 2 in History of Methodism in North Devon, 12-26.
London: Wesleyan Conference Office, 1871. 192p.

791. Head, Franklin Harvey. Studies in Early American History:
The Legends of Jekyll Island. Chicago, 18--? 37p.

792. Headley, Phineas Camp. Evangelists in the Church: From
Philip, A.D. 35, to Moody and Sankey, A.D. 1875. Boston:
Henry Hoyt, 1875. 456p. Brief section devoted to the
Wesleys.

793. Healing, C. Arnold. "History of Wesleyan Methodism in South
Shields." In South Shields Wesleyan Circuit Handbook of
Bazaar.... Newcastle-upon-Tyne: Andrew Reid and Co.,
1904. 91p. GtBLW

794. Heaton, Joseph. Two Lectures on the Wesleyan Hymn-Book....
8th ed. London: John Mason, 1872. 78p.

795. Hedley, George Percy. "Is Thy Heart Right?" In The
Christian Heritage in America, 101-15. New York: Macmillan
Co., 1947. 177p.

796. Heitzenrater, Richard P. John Wesley and the Road to Aldersgate: The Oxford Years. N.p.: Kentucky Methodist Heritage Center, 1973. 10p.

797. _____. John Wesley As Seen by Contemporaries and
Biographers. Vol. 2 of The Elusive Mr. Wesley. Nashville:
Abingdon Press, 1984. 224p.

798. _____. John Wesley His Own Biographer. Vol. 1 of The
Elusive Mr. Wesley. Nashville: Abingdon Press, 1984. 220p.

799. _____. "The Oxford Methodists." In Diary of an Oxford
Methodist, Benjamin Ingham, 1733-1734, 6-38. Durham: Duke
University Press, 1985. 304p.

800. Helmershausen, Adella. Memories for the Aldersgate Bi-
centenary. Chicago: Manz Corporation, Franklin Reporter
Print, 1938. 141p.

801. Hempton, David. "The Wesleyan Heritage." Chap. 2 in
Methodism and Politics in British Society 1750-1850, 20-54.
Stanford, Calif.: Stanford University Press, 1984. 276p.

802. Henderson, D. Michael. "Christian Education: Instructional

Theology; John Wesley and the Early Methodists." Chap. 19 in vol. 2 of A Contemporary Wesleyan Theology: Biblical, Systematic, and Practical, 868-70. See no. 279.

803. Henkle, Moses Montgomery. Primitive Episcopacy: An Attempt to Ascertain the Origins, Powers, and Duties of Christian Bishops, as Recognized by the Apostles, Primitive Church, and Protestant Reformers, and to Determine the Conformity of Methodist Episcopacy with the Primary Model. Nashville: E. Stevenson and F. A. Owen, 1857. 286p.

804. Henry, George W. Shouting, Genuine and Spurious ... History of the Outward Demonstrations ... Laughing, Screaming, Shouting, Leaping, Jerking.... Chicago: Metropolitan Church Association, 1903. 305p. Several chapters discuss John Wesley's writings.

805. Henry, Stuart C. "Early Contacts in America." Chap. 2 in vol. 1 of The History of American Methodism, 43-73. New York: Abingdon Press, 1964. This chapter includes sections entitled "Oglethorpe and the Colony of Georgia" and "The Work of the Wesleys."

806. Henschen, Walter G. "What Wesley Taught on Christian Perfection." Chap. 1 in Christian Perfection before Wesley; a Brief Historical Sketch of the Doctrine from the Early Church to the Days of Wesley, 11-18. Appollo, Pa.: West Publishing Co., n.d. 83p.

807. Henshaw, John Prentiss Kewley. The Apostolic Ministry: Views of Calvin and the Early Presbyterians, Wesley, Clarke, and Others, upon the Apostolic Succession. New York: Protestant Episcopal Tract Society, n.d. 28p.

808. Herbert, Chesley Carlisle. "Charles Wesley, the Poet-Theologian of Methodism." In The Theologians of Methodism, 48-59. See no. 422.

809. Herbert, Thomas Walter. Wesley As Editor and Author. Princeton Studies in English, no. 17. Princeton: Princeton University Press, 1940. His dissertation, Princeton University, 1935.

810. Herrick, Samuel Edward. "John Wesley." In Some Heretics of Yesterday, 291-314. Boston and New York: Houghton, Mifflin and Co., 1890. 320p.

811. Hervey, James W. "The Origin of Methodism and the Ministry of John Wesley." In Patterns in Church History: Essays on Comparative Religion, the Reformation, and John Wesley, 63-77. New York: Exposition Press, 1963. 96p.

72   John and Charles Wesley

812. Hicks, Cecil E. Early Methodism in Tavistock, 1746-1900, and
      Its Subsequent Development in the Wesleyan Connexion. Ply-
      mouth: Barnes Bros., 1948. 14p.

813. Higgins, Paul Lambourne. John Wesley: Spiritual Witness.
      Minneapolis: T. S. Denison, 1960. 134p.

814. High Wycombe Wesley Church. Souvenir Handbook Compiled
      for the Occasion of the Re-opening of Wesley Organ ... Sept.
      11th and 12th, 1948. High Wycombe: Freer and Hayter, 1948.
      12p. GtBLW

815. Hildebrandt, Franz. Christianity According to the Wesleys;
      the Harris Franklin Rall Lectures, 1954, Delivered at Garrett
      Biblical Institute, Evanston, Illinois. London: Epworth Press,
      1956. 80p.

816. _____. From Luther to Wesley. London: Lutterworth Press,
      1951. 224p.

817. _____. "The Meaning of Ordination in Methodism." Chap. 3
      in The Ministry in the Methodist Heritage, edited by Gerald O.
      McCulloh, 67-100. Nashville: Board of Education, The Metho-
      dist Church, 1960. 143p.

818. _____. "The Problem of Sacrifice in Wesley." Introduction to
      I Offered Christ; a Protestant Study of the Mass. Philadelphia:
      Fortress Press, 1967. 342p.

819. Hildebrandt, Franz, Oliver A. Beckerlegge, and James Dale.
      Introduction to A Collection of Hymns for the Use of the People
      Called Methodists, 1-69. Vol. 7 of The Oxford Edition of the
      Works of John Wesley, Frank Baker, Editor-in-Chief. Oxford:
      Clarendon Press, 1983. 848p.

820. Hill, A. Wesley. Introduction to John Wesley's Primitive Physic,
      3-20. London: Epworth Press, 1960. 127p.

821. _____. John Wesley among the Physicians; a Study of Eight-
      eenth Century Medicine. The Wesley Historical Lecture, no. 24.
      London: Epworth Press, 1953.

822. Hill, John. A Vindication of the Methodists in the Societies of
      the Late Rev. John Wesley, from Several Popular Accusations of
      the Present Day; Especially Those Contained in the Annual Re-
      view of Mr. Arthur Aiken: In Four Letters Addressed to Mr.
      Joseph Benson. London: Printed at the Conference Office,
      1806. GtBLW

823. Hill, Joseph. Memorials of Methodism in Bramley. Bramley: J.
      Dawson, 1859. 24p. NjMUM

Books   73

824. Hillis, Newell Dwight. "John Wesley and the Moral Awakening
     of the Common People." In Great Men As Prophets of a New
     Era, 143-65. New York: Fleming H. Revell Co., 1922. 221p.
     Also published as Ryerson Essays, no. 14, 1923.

825. Hillman, Robert John. "Grace in Calvin and Wesley." In Dig
     or Die..., 279-89. See no. 84.

826. Hilton, John Deane. The Master Preacher ... Being the
     Christmas Number of the Sunday Magazine 1904. London:
     Isbister and Co., 1904. 96p. "A history of the life and work
     of Mr. John Wesley ... told by passages extracted from the
     memoirs of ... Richard Ashton, gentleman, and Sir Anthony
     Pilgrim, bart., now printed for the first time, and edited by
     John Cleveland."

827. Hilton, Margeret. John Wesley in Scotland. N.p. 193-? 14p.

828. Hindmarsh, R. A Vindication of the Character and Writings of
     the Hon. Emmanuel Swedenborg: Against the Slanders and Mis-
     representations of the Rev. J. G. Pike, of Derby: Including
     a Refutation of the False Reports Propagated by the Late Rev.
     John Wesley.... Manchester: H. and R. Smith, 1822. 284p.

829. Hine, Gordon R. The Methodist Church Gloucester Circuit
     Records from the Time of John Wesley to 1970. [Gloucester:
     Southgate Printing Co., 1971.] 52p. NjMUM

830. Historical Notices of the Rev. John Wesley's Visit to Epworth,
     and a Sketch of the Life of the Rev. Charles Wesley, M.A.,
     Designed to Accompany the Engravings of the Rev. John Wesley,
     Preaching at Epworth, and the Rev. Charles Wesley Preaching
     to the North American Indians. Darlington, Eng.: Robert
     Swales, 1862. 8p. GtBMM

831. Historical Tablets--John Wesley's Chapel in Broadmead, Bristol,
     Called by Him the New Room in the Horsefair. London: Ep-
     worth Press, 1930. 91p.

832. History of John Wesley's Coat; Showing by Whom It Has Been
     Worn and by Whom It Has Been Trimmed. Derby: R. Keen,
     1851. 56p. John Wesley's coat is Methodism and the wearers
     are his followers.

833. Hitchman, Francis. "The Founder of Methodism." In Eighteenth
     Century Studies: Essays, 52-100. London: S. Low, Marston,
     Searle and Rivington, 1881. 386p.

834. Hobhouse, Stephen Henry. "John Wesley's Testimony." In
     William Law and Eighteenth Century Quakerism, 312-23. Lon-
     don: George Allen and Unwin, 1927. 342p. A discussion of
     Wesley's hostility to Law and his differences with Quakerism.

835. Hobrow, W. A Sermon, on the Death of the Rev. J. Wesley,
      A.M., Delivered at the New Chapel, in Edmund Street, Liverpool,
      Sunday, March 27, 1791.... Liverpool: H. Hodgson, 1791.
      40p.

836. Hocken, Joshua. A Brief History of Wesleyan Methodism in the
      Grimsby Circuit; Including References to the Horncastle, Boston,
      Barton, Louth, Spilsby, Alford and Rasen Circuits. London:
      John Mason, 1839. 67p.

837. Hockin, Frederick. John Wesley and Modern Methodism. 4th ed.
      London: Rivington, 1887. 218p.

838. _____. John Wesley and Modern Wesleyanism. 3d ed. London:
      J. T. Hayes, 1876. 86p.

839. Hodges, H. A., ed. Introduction to A Rapture of Praise: Hymns
      of John and Charles Wesley. London: Hodder and Stoughton,
      1966. 160p.

840. Hodgson, Francis. The Great Iron Wheel Reviewed; or, A De-
      fence of the Methodist Episcopal Church.... Philadelphia:
      T. Stokes, 1848. 113p. See nos. 248, 692.

841. Hodgson, Richard. Wesleyan Methodism Considered in Relation
      to the Church: To Which Is Subjoined a Plan for Their Union
      and More Effective Co-operation. London: J. Hatchard and
      Son, 1841. 83p.

842. Hodson, James Henry. Hymn Studies: Their Message in Biog-
      raphy and Devotion. London: H. R. Allenson, 1926. 269p.
      Five of Charles Wesley's hymns are considered.

843. Holden, Harrington William. John Wesley in Company with High
      Churchman. London: Church Press Co., 1869. 158p. A
      comparison of the doctrines of high churchmen and those of
      John Wesley.

844. Hole, Christina. "The Epworth Poltergeist." In Haunted Eng-
      land: A Survey of English Ghost-Lore. 166-69. London: B.
      T. Batsford, 1940. 183p.

845. Holland, Bernard G. Baptism in Early Methodism. London:
      Epworth Press, 1970. 200p. A revision of the author's thesis,
      University of London.

846. Holland, John. "Samuel Wesley" and "Charles Wesley." In vol.
      2 of The Psalmists of Britain..., 123-26, 247-51. 2 vols. Lon-
      don: R. Groombridge, 1843.

847. Holmes, David. The Wesley Offering; or, Wesley and His Times.
      Auburn, N.Y.: Derby and Miller, 1852. 308p.

Books   75

848. Holmes, John Haynes. John Wesley and the Methodist Revolt.
      Toronto: Ryerson Press, 1923. 27p.

849. Holsey, L. H. "Wesley and the Coloured Race." In Wesley
      Memorial Volume, 256-67. See no. 257.

850. Holt, Ivan Lee. "Aldersgate the Basis of Social Morality."
      Chap. 3 in What Happened at Aldersgate, 56-71. See no. 342.

851. Holy Ground; a Short History of Wesley's Chapel. London,
      n.d. 16p. TNMPH

852. Honest Munchin, and Other Sketches of Early Methodism in
      the Black Country, with the Romantic Story of the Leek-Seed
      Chapel. 3d ed. London: Hamilton, Adams, and Co., 1871.
      80p. These sketches appeared originally in the Methodist
      Recorder.

853. Hood, Edwin Paxton. Vignettes of the Great Revival of the
      Eighteenth Century. London: Religious Tract Society, 1880.
      224p.

854. _____. "Wesley and His Likeness." In World of Moral and
      Religious Anecdote, 127-31. London: Hodder and Stoughton,
      1897. 752p. Relates the story of Ceely's bust of John Wesley,
      and the use Wesley made of the ten guineas the artist paid him.
      Hood used Arvine's Cyclopaedia of Anecdote as his source of
      information.

855. Hook, Walter Farquhar. "John Wesley." In vol. 8 of An Ec-
      clesiastical Biography, Containing the Lives of Ancient Fathers
      and Modern Divines, 684-705. London: F. and J. Rivington;
      Leeds: T. Harrison, 1845-52. This volume also contains
      brief summary of Charles Wesley's life, p. 705-6.

856. Hooker, Edward Niles. Introduction to Epistle to a Friend
      Concerning Poetry and the Essay on Heroic Poetry, by Samuel
      Wesley, 1-6. Los Angeles: Augustan Reprint Society, 1947.

857. Hoole, Elijah. Byrom and the Wesleys. London: William
      Nichols, 1864. 48p. (First appeared in the Wesleyan Metho-
      dist Magazine 86 (1863): 597-601, 728-35, 789-98, 904-15,
      1011-17, 1101-12.

858. _____. Oglethorpe and the Wesleys in America. London:
      R. Needham, 1863. 20p.

859. Hooper, John Stirling Morley. The Story of Methodism in
      Stratford-upon-Avon. Stratford-upon-Avon, 1962. 36p.

860. Hore, A. H. "The Church of the Protestant Era, The

Methodists." Chap. 4 in Eighteen Centuries of the Church in England, 514-27. London: Parker and Co., 1881. 679p.

861. Horne, Charles Silvester. "The Great Revival." Chap. 12 in A Popular History of the Free Churches, 258-98. James Clarke and Co., 1903. 449p. This chapter discusses the great evangelists of the eighteenth century, Wesley being in the forefront.

862. Horner, Ralph C. Notes on Boland; or, Mr. Wesley and the Second Work of Grace. Chicago: McDonald and Gill; Toronto: W. Briggs, 1893. 230p. This is a rebuttal to J. M. Boland's The Problem of Methodism.

863. Hough, Lynn Harold. "Methodism's Recall to Aldersgate." Chap. 19 in What Happened at Aldersgate, 226-39. See no. 342.

864. Houlder, John Alden. "The Great Evangelical Revival." Chap. 8 in A Short History of the Free Churches, 97-112. London: R. D. Dickinson, 1899. 240p.

865. Houstoun, John Fleming. "Wesley, a Great Disciple." In Names of Renown. Glasgow: R. Gibson, 1954. 204p.

866. Howard, Harry Clay. "John Wesley." In Princes of the Christian Pulpit and Pastorate, 110-40. Nashville: Cokesbury Press, 1927. 392p.

867. Howard, Ivan. "The Doctrine of Assurance As Held and Taught by John Wesley." In Further Insights into Holiness: Nineteen Leading Wesleyan Scholars Present Various Phases of Holiness Thinking, edited by Kenneth Geiger, 231-46. Kansas City, Mo.: Beacon Hill Press, 1963. 349p.

868. Hubbard, Elbert. "John Wesley." In Great Reformers, 11-52. Vol. 9 of Little Journeys to the Homes of the Great. 14 vols. New York: W. H. Wise and Co., 1928.

869. Hubery, Douglas Stanley. "John Wesley's Visits to Mitcham." In Methodism in Mitcham, 1764-1944, 7-9. Mitcham: Acme Printers, 1944. 23p.

870. Hughes, Harry. St. Paul's Methodist Church: Jubilee Souvenir. Methodism at Brighouse. Brighouse, Eng., 1935. 47p.

871. Hughes, Henry Maldwyn. Wesley and Whitefield. London: C. H. Kelly, 1920. 160p.

872. _____. Wesley's Standards in the Light of Today. London: Epworth Press, 1921. 32p.

873. Hughes, Hugh Price. Introduction to The Journal of John Wesley, edited by Percy Livingstone Parker. The Tyndale Series of Great Biographies. Chicago: Moody Press, 1951. 438p.

874. Hulme, Thomas F. John Wesley and His Horse. London: Epworth Press, 1933. 130p. "Written to commemorate the gift of an equestrian statue of Wesley to the New Room at Bristol and to the Methodist Church"--preface.

875. _____. Voices of the New Room. Drew Lectureship in Biography, 1931. London: Epworth Press, 1933. 248p.

876. Humphrey, Grace. "The Man Who Wakened a Nation, John Benjamin Wesley." In The Story of the Johns, 176-96. Philadelphia: Penn Publishing Co., 1925. 214p.

877. Hunt, John. Wesley and Wesleyanism: Three Lectures. London: Hamilton, Adams, 1858. 77p.

878. Hunt, Ward W. Philosophy of Methodism. Watertown, N.Y.: Post Book and Job Printing Establishment, 1880. 71p.

879. Hunter, Frederick. John Wesley and the Coming Comprehensive Church. Wesley Historical Society Lecture, no. 33. London: Epworth Press, 1968. 112p. (Rev. in no. 2205.)

880. Hurley, Michael. Introduction to John Wesley's Letter to a Roman Catholic, edited by Michael Hurley, 22-47. London: G. Chapman, 1968. 64p.

881. _____. "Salvation Today and Wesley Today." Chap. 4 in The Place of Wesley in the Christian Tradition, 94-116. See no. 88.

882. Hurst, John Fletcher. The History of Methodism. 7 vols. New York: Eaton and Mains, 1902-04. Wesley's story is told in vols. 1-3. Popular treatment, with many illustrations.

883. _____. John Wesley, the Methodist: A Plain Account of His Life and Work, by a Methodist Preacher. New York: Eaton and Mains; Cincinnati: Jennings and Pye, 1903. 319p.

884. Husband, Edward. John Wesley: A Lecture. London: G. J. Palmer, 1873. 44p.

885. Hutchinson, Paul. "A Bit of History." Chap. 2 in The Next Step: A Study in Methodist Polity, 22-35. New York: Methodist Book Concern, 1922. 119p.

886. _____. "Wesley and the Methodists." In Men Who Made the Churches, 161-88. Nashville: Cokesbury Press, 1930. 212p.

887. Hutton, Joseph Edmund. "Moravians and Methodists." Chap.
      9, Book 2 of A History of the Moravian Church, 283-303. 2d
      ed. London: Moravian Publication Office, 1909. 520p.

888. Hutton, Laurence. Literary Landmarks of London. 4th ed.
      Boston: Ticknor, 1888. 363p. John Wesley, pp. 318-19.

889. Hutton, William Holden. "The Church in the Eighteenth Cen-
      tury." Chap. 5 in A Short History of the Church in Great
      Britain. Pages 246-56 are about Wesley and his movement.

890. _____. John Wesley. Great English Churchmen Series.
      London: Macmillan, 1927. 181p. (Rev. in no. 3842.)

891. Hyde, Ammi Bradford. The Story of Methodism throughout
      the World, from the Beginning to the Present Time; Tracing
      the Rise and Progress of That Wonderful Religious Movement
      .... Springfield, Mass.: Wiley and Co., 1889. 827p.
      Another popular rendition of Wesley's story and Methodism.

892. Hynson, Leon O. To Reform the Nation: Theological Founda-
      tions of Wesley's Ethics. Grand Rapids, Mich.: Zondervan
      Publishing House, 1984. 176p.

893. Inge, William Ralph. "John Wesley." In Our Present Dis-
      contents, 158-63. 1939. Reprint. Freeport, N.Y.: Books
      for Libraries Press, 1972. 351p.

894. Inskip, John Swanel. "John Wesley." Chap. 2 in Methodism
      Explained and Defended, 18-32. Cincinnati: H. S. and J.
      Applegate, 1851. 264p.

895. Is Modern Methodism Wesleyan Methodism? or, Wesleyan Metho-
      dism and the Church of England; Being a Sequel to "Was John
      Wesley a High Churchman?" A Dialogue for the Times. Lon-
      don: Wesleyan Methodist Book-room, 1882. Discusses Wesley's
      societies and their relationship to the Church of England.

896. Ives, Arthur Glendinning Loveless. Kingswood School in
      Wesley's Day and Since. London: Epworth Press, 1970.
      264p.

897- Jackson, Edward H. "John Wesley's Place in History." In
898. Wesley Studies, 227-32. See no. 190.

899. Jackson, George. Wesleyan Methodism in the Darlington Cir-
      cuit: With an Introduction and an Appendix, Containing
      Notices of Mr. Wesley's Earliest Visits to the Contiguous Cir-
      cuits, and Several of His Original Letters. Darlington: J.
      Manley; London: John Mason, 1850. 58p.

900. Jackson, George. The Old Methodism and the New. London: Hodder and Stoughton, 1903. 60p. An address delivered at the Wesleyan University, Middletown, Connecticut, June 28, 1903, on the occasion of the two hundred and fiftieth anniversary of John Wesley's birth.

901. Jackson, Thomas. Aids to Truth and Charity: A Letter Addressed to "William Fitzgerald, D.D., Bishop of Cork, Cloyne, and Ross;" Being a Vindication of John and Charles Wesley, George Whitefield and Their People.... London: John Mason, 1862. 78p.

902. _____. Centenary of Wesleyan Methodism: A Brief Sketch of the Rise, Progress, and Present State of the Wesleyan Methodist Societies throughout the World. New York: T. Mason and G. Lane, 1839. 240p.

903. _____. The Church and the Methodists. The Principles and Conduct of Mr. Wesley, and the Religious Connexion Founded by Him, in Regard to the Church of England, Being the Substance of a Speech Addressed to the Wesleyan Conference.... London: John Mason, 1834. 54p.

904. _____. Introduction to Journal of the Rev. Charles Wesley, with Selections from His Correspondence and Poetry. 2 vols. London: Wesleyan Methodist Bookroom, 1849.

905. _____. Introduction to Journal of the Rev. John Wesley, A.M., Sometime Fellow of the Lincoln College, Oxford. From October 14th, 1735 to October 24, 1790. 4 vols. London: Wesleyan Conference Office, 1895.

906. _____. Introductory Essay in vol. 1 of Lives of Early Methodist Preachers, Chiefly written by Themselves, v-xxxiv. 6 vols. London: Wesleyan Conference Office, 1865-66. (Rev. in no. 2235.)

907. _____. A Letter to the Rev. Edward B. Pusey, D.D...: Being a Vindication of the Tenets and Character of the Wesleyan Methodists, against His Misrepresentations and Censures. London: John Mason, 1842. 110p.

908. _____. The Life of the Rev. Charles Wesley, Some Time Student of Christ-Church, Oxford; Comprising a Review of His Poetry; Sketches of the Rise and Progress of Methodism; with Notices of Contemporary Events and Characters. 2 vols. London: John Mason, 1841.

909. _____. "Preface to the Third Edition." In vol. 1 of The Works of the Rev. John Wesley, A.M. Sometime Fellow of Lincoln-College, Oxford, i-xvi. 14 vols. London: John Mason, 1829-31.

910. _____. "Reminiscences of Preachers and Preaching during
     the Eighteenth and Nineteenth Centuries--Quaint American
     Preachers--Whitefield and the Two Wesleys." Chap. 7 in
     Curiosities of the Pulpit and Pulpit Literature: Memorabilia,
     Anecdotes, etc. of Celebrated Preachers from the Fourth
     Century of the Christian Era to the Present Time, 219-80.
     London: J. Hogg, 1868. 380p.

911. James, John Angell. "Wesleyan Methodists--Old Connexion."
     In Protestant Nonconformity: A Sketch of Its General History,
     with an Account of the Rise and Present State of Its Various
     Denominations in the Town of Birmingham, 196-209. London:
     Hamilton, Adams and Co., 1849. 279p.

912. Janion, J. Some Account of the Introduction of Methodism
     into the City, and Some Parts of the County, of Chester; To-
     gether with Brief Biographical Sketches of Several Eminent
     Characters Connected Therewith. Chester, Eng.: Evans
     and Son, 1833. 120p.

913. Jaques, J. R. "John and Charles Wesley." In Wesley Memo-
     rial Volume, 373-82. See no. 257.

914. Jefferson, Herbert Alfred Lewis. "For the Use of the People
     Called Methodists." Chap. 5 in Hymns in Christian Worship,
     59-75. New York: Macmillan, 1950. 282p.

915. Jeffery, Frederick. "John Wesley and Ireland." Chap. 1 in
     Irish Methodism: An Historical Account of Its Traditions,
     Theology, and Influence, 7-17. Belfast: Epworth House,
     1964. 104p.

916. Jeffery, Thomas Reed. John Wesley's Religious Quest. New
     York: Vantage Press, 1960. 439p.

917. Jessop, William. An Account of Methodism in Rossendale and
     the Neighbourhood: With Some Notices of the Rise and Pro-
     gress of the United Societies, and of Contemporary Events.
     Manchester: Tubbs, Brook and Chrystal; London: Simpkin,
     Marshall and Co., 1881. 403p.

918. "John Wesley." In vol. 1 of The Georgian Era: Memoirs of
     the Most Eminent Persons, Who Have Flourished in Great
     Britain, from the Accession of George the First to the Demise
     of George the Fourth..., 433-43. 4 vols. London: Vizetelly,
     Branston and Co., 1832-34. Also contains brief sketches of
     Charles and Samuel, the father.

919. "John Wesley." In vol. 3 of Historical Portraits ... the Lives
     by C. R. L. Fletcher ... the Portraits Chosen by Emery Wal-
     ker, 159-63. 4 vols. Oxford: Clarendon Press, 1909-19.

920. "John Wesley." In vol. 2 of Makers of Christianity, 241-53.
      3 vols. New York: H. Holt and Co., 1934-37.

921. John Wesley. Heroes of the Cross. London: Marshalls,
      1982. 94p. Popular treatment of Wesley and his movement.

922. John Wesley and Modern Wesleyanism. Hayle: Banfield Bros.,
      1873. 24p. This is a pamphlet which claims to demonstrate
      that Wesley through the last fifty years of his life held and
      recommended "popish" doctrines.

923. John Wesley and Usury. Sunderland, Eng.: B. Williams,
      1877. 29p. A series of articles taken from the Newcastle
      Weekly Chronicle.

924. "John Wesley As a Carthusian." In The Homes, Haunts and
      Friends of John Wesley, 151-54. See no. 319. This article
      was extracted from Greyfriar, the Charterhouse School
      magazine.

925. John Wesley, the Church of England, and Wesleyan Methodism;
      Their Relation to Each Other Clearly and Fully Explained in
      Two Dialogues. London: Wesleyan Methodist Book-Room,
      1883. 78p. Also published in two separate tracts: Was John
      Wesley a High Churchman? and Is Modern Methodism Wesleyan
      Methodism?

926. "John Wesley, the Man Who Revolutionised Britain in the 17th
      [sic] Century." In Faithful and Fearless: The Life Story of
      Mighty Men of Faith Who Moved the World by Their Labours of
      Love. London: Pickering and Inglis, 1927. 64p.

927. John Wesley Vindicated by Himself: An Allegory for the Wes-
      leyan Centenary. 2d ed. Leeds: T. Harrison, 1839. 24p.

928. John Wesley's Ghost, 1849. By Reflector. London: Arthur
      Hall, [1849]. 12p. NjMUM

929. John Wesley's Rooms in Lincoln College, Oxford, Being a Record
      of Their Reopening on the 10th September 1928 After Restora-
      tion by the American Committee. Oxford: Oxford University
      Press, 1929. 32p. Includes an account of Romney's portrait
      by J. W. Hamilton.

930. Johnson, Charles. "The Wesleys." In The History of Hymn
      Singing as Told through One Hundred and One Famous Hymns,
      38-46. Delavan, Wisc.: C. Hallberg, 1982. 231p.

931. Johnson, Pierce. "The Last Puritan and the First Pietist
      [John Wesley]." Chap. 4 in Dying into Life: A Study in
      Christian Life Styles, 87-110. New York: Abingdon Press,
      1972. 176p.

932. Johnson, R. Crawford. "Wesley and the Higher Christian
      Life." In Entire Sanctification, 301-16. See no. 304.

933. Johnson, Ronald. The Tunes of John Wesley's Hymns from
      the German. Edinburgh: Office Printing Services, 1976.
      22p. NjMUM

934. Johnson, Zachary Taylor. Methodism and Holiness; Authentic
      Answers to Present Day Questions, from John Wesley. Wil-
      more, Ky.: Asbury Press, 1942. 61p.

935. Jones, Dora M. Charles Wesley: A Study. London: Skef-
      fington, 1919. 284p.

936. Jones, Joseph. A Few Remarks on the "Life of Wesley" by
      R. Southey, Esq., Poet Laureate. In Two Letters to a Friend.
      London: Rivington; Edinburgh: Oliver and Boyd, 1822.
      176p. GtBLW

937. Jones, Mary Gwladys. The Charity School Movement: A Study
      of Eighteenth-Century Puritanism in Action. Cambridge: Cam-
      bridge University Press, 1938. 446p. Pp. 136-43 deal with
      John Wesley and Methodism.

938. Jowett, Benjamin. "John Wesley." In Sermons Biographical
      and Miscellaneous, 108-29, edited by W. H. Fremantle. Lon-
      don: John Murray, 1899. 370p.

939. Joy, James R. John Wesley's Awakening. New York: The
      Methodist Book Concern, 1937. 128p. Spanish edition pub-
      lished in 1938.

940. Judd, Walter D. The Record of Wesleyan Methodism in the
      Sevenoaks Circuit, 1746-1932, and John Wesley's Connection
      with the Early Days of Our Circuit. Bedford: Rush and
      Warwick, 1932. 140p. GtBMM

941. Judge, G. H. Bancroft. The Origin and Progress of Wes-
      leyan Methodism in Cheltenham and District. Cheltenham:
      S. R. Grove, 1912. 88p.

942. Julian, John. "The Wesley Family." In vol. 2 of A Dictionary
      of Hymnology, 1255-66. 2 vols. New York: Dover Publica-
      tion, Inc., 1957.

943. Jutsum, Humphrey. Jubilee Memorial: Being the Historical
      Sketch Read at the Celebration of the Jubilee of Tiviot Dale
      Wesleyan Chapel and Including a Brief History of Methodism
      in Stockport. Stockport: H. Foggitt, 1876. 104p.

944. Kalas, J. Ellsworth. Our First Song: Evangelism in the

Hymns of Charles Wesley. Nashville: Discipleship Resources, 1984. 55p.

945. Kay, J. Allan. "Charles Wesley." In Fifty Hymns by Charles Wesley, 9-13. London: Epworth Press, 1957. 72p.

946. _____. Introduction to Wesley's Prayers and Praises, vii-xviii. London: Epworth Press, 1958. 194p. This book includes none of Charles Wesley's hymns found in the Methodist Hymn-book.

947. Keeble, S. E. "John Wesley and Social Service." Chap. 3 in The Citizen of Tomorrow; a Handbook on Social Questions, 51-68. London: C. H. Kelly, 1906. 311p.

948. Keeler, W. T. "Jesu, Lover of My Soul." In The Romantic Origin of Some Favourite Hymns; Their Psychological Background and Modern Implications, 73-76. Letchworth Garden City, Eng.: Letchworth Printers, Ltd., 1947. 170p.

949. Keeling, Annie E. Susanna Wesley, and Other Eminent Methodist Women.... 3d ed. London: C. H. Kelly, 1897. 132p.

950. Kellogg, Amherst W. A Concise History of Methodism, in England and America, of Its Origin, Founders, Development and Institutions.... Milwaukee: H. O. Brown and Co., 1893. 409p.

951. Kelly, Charles H. "John Wesley as a Letter Writer." In Wesley Studies, 101-7. See no. 190.

952. _____. "The Man: His Teaching and His Work." In Wesley, the Man, His Teaching and His Work, 3-20. See no. 357.

953. Kennedy, Gerald Hamilton. Introduction to John Wesley's Journal, abridged by Nehemia Curnock, vii-xxii. New York: Capricorn Books, 1963. 433p.

954. _____. The Methodist Way of Life. Englewood Cliffs, N.J.: Prentice-Hall, 1958. 216p. The first five chapters of this book deal with John Wesley.

955. Kenyon, Edith C. The Centenary Life of Wesley. London: W. Scott, 1891. 404p.

956. Kepler, Thomas S., ed. Introduction to Christian Perfection: As Believed and Taught by John Wesley. New York: World Publishing Co., 1954. 144p.

957. _____. "John Wesley." In A Journey with the Saints, 86-88. Cleveland: World Publishing Co., 1951. 150p.

958. Kern, Paul B. "Aldersgate the Source of Missionary Passion."
      Chap. 12 in What Happened at Aldersgate, 165-174. See no.
      342.

959. Kershner, Frederick D. "Life of John Wesley." In Pioneers
      of Christian Thought, 311-15. Indianapolis: Bobbs-Merrill,
      1930. 373p.

960. Kewley, John. An Inquiry into the Validity of Episcopacy....
      Wilmington: Joseph Jones, 1807. An anti-Methodist publica-
      tion.

961. Keyes, Edwin Ruthven. Wesley and Swedenborg; a Fraternal
      Appeal to Methodist Ministers, Inviting Them to Consider the
      Relations of Methodism to the New Church. Philadelphia, 1872.
      72p.

962. Keys, Charles C. "A Succinct History of Class Meetings." In
      The Class Leader's Manual ... to Which is Prefixed an Intro-
      ductory Chapter on the History and Scriptural Basis of Class
      Meetings, 9-19. New York: Lane and Scott, 1851. 223p.

963. Kibble, John. Historical and Other Notes on Wychwood Forest
      and Many of Its Border Places. Charlburg, 1928. 121p.

964. Killpack, William Bennett. Preface to Opinions of the Late
      John Wesley upon Baptism, 3-6. London: Joseph Masters,
      1850. 24p.

965. King, James. Anglican Hymnology; Being an Account of the
      325 Standard Hymns of the Highest Merit According to the Ver-
      dict of the Whole Anglican Church. London: Hatchards, 1885.
      321p. This book divides the hymns into first, second, and
      third ranks. Charles Wesley had ten hymns in the first rank,
      the only hymnwriter with this many.

966. King, Willis Jefferson. Spiritual Pilgrimage of Two Christian
      Leaders--Saul of Tarsus and John Wesley. Maurovia, Liberia,
      W. Africa. N.p., n.d. NjMUM

967. Kirby, Ralph. The Methodist Bedside Book. London: Hulton
      Press, 1954. 384p. An anthology compiled from various
      sources, including Wesley's writings; it also contains inter-
      pretive notes by the author.

968. Kirk, John. Charles Wesley, the Poet of Methodism; a Lec-
      ture. London: Hamilton, Adams, 1860. 72p.

969. _____. Mother of the Wesleys, a Biography. London: H.
      J. Tresidder, 1864. 351p. (Rev. in no. 3796.)

Books   85

970. Kirsop, Joseph. "Wesley and Whitefield." In Wesley Memorial
     Volume, 350-60. See no. 257.

971. Kirton, John William. John Wesley, His Life and Work. Lon-
     don: Morgan and Scott, 1884. 128p.

972. _____. John Wesley, Methodism, and the Temperance Re-
     formation. London: J. Kempster and Co., 1873. 50p.

973. Kissack, Reginald. Introduction and Part One, Biographical,
     in Spotlight on John Wesley: An Anthology of His Own Writ-
     ings Arranged to Show How He Lived, Thought and Talked,
     8-55. London: Marshall, Morgan and Scott, 1962. 120p.

974. _____. "Self-Consciousness: Methodism under Wesley."
     In Church or No Church? A Study of the Development of the
     Concept of Church in British Methodism, 34-67. London: Ep-
     worth Press, 1964. 164p.

975. Kline, Donald L. Susanna Wesley: God's Catalyst for Revival.
     Lima, Ohio: C.S.S. Publishing Co., 1980. 79p. Includes
     writings and prayers of Susanna Wesley's, but also commentary
     by the compiler.

976. Knight, Lucian Lamar. A Sketch of the Work of John Wesley
     in Georgia. Atlanta: Tech High Press, n.d. 8p. Includes
     also "John Wesley," by C. T. Winchester.

977. Knox, R. B. "The Wesleys and Howell Harris." In Papers
     Read at the Third Winter and Summer Meetings of the Ec-
     clesiastical History Society, edited by G. J. Cuming, 267-76.
     Studies in Church History, vol. 1. Leiden: E. J. Brill,
     1966.

978. Knox, Roland Arbuthnott. Enthusiasm; a Chapter in the
     History of Religion, with Special Reference to the Seventeenth
     and Eighteenth Centuries. Oxford: Oxford University Press,
     1950. 622p. Chapters 18-21 deal with Wesley and his asso-
     ciates.

979. Koerber, Charles J. The Theology of Conversion According
     to John Wesley. Neo-Eboraci, 1967. 82p.

980. Kroll, Harry Harrison. The Long Quest; the Story of John
     Wesley. Philadelphia: Westminster Press, 1954. 192p.

981. Kronenberger, Louis. "The Wesleyans." Chap. 5 in Kings
     and Desperate Men; Life in Eighteenth Century England, 189-
     199. New York: A. A. Knopf, 1942. 323p.

982. Krummel, John W. "A Note on Wesley Materials Available in

Japanese." In Japanese Contributions to the Study of John
Wesley, 3-5. See no. 643.

983. Kuhn, Harold B. "Witness of the Spirit." In The Distinctive
      Emphases of Asbury Theological Seminary, 55-77. Salem,
      Ohio: Schmul Publishers, 1976. 100p.

984. Lainé, J. A. Methodism in and around Leicester: Two Days
      in John Wesley's Journal. Leicester, Eng.: W. Thronley and
      Sons, 1956. 15p.

985. Lambert, A. J. "The Beginnings of Methodism." In The
      Chapel on the Hill. Bristol: St. Stephens Press, 1929. 130p.
      This book is about Portland Chapel, which was built in Bristol
      in 1792, when the New Room in the Horsefair had become over-
      crowded and it was realized that a new chapel for Methodism in
      Bristol was needed.

986. "The Lament of a Collector." In Wesley Studies, 175-81. See
      no. 190. Describes the disastrous burning of many of Wesley's
      papers and books after his death.

987. Lamont, J. D. Historiette of Methodism in Cork: Wesley
      Chapel Centenary, 1805-1905. Cork: Guy and Co., 1905.
      54p.

988. Lancashire and Yorkshire Railway Company. Epworth, Lincoln-
      shire, England: The Birthplace of the Rev. John Wesley.
      What to See and How to Get There. [Manchester: H. Black
      and Co., 1905.] 44p.

989. Landon, John W. "John Wesley's Concept of the Ministry,"
      "John Wesley and Original Sin," and "Charles Wesley--the Man
      and the Message." Chaps. 1-3 in From These Men. Des
      Moines: Inspiration Press, 1966. 126p.

990. Langford, Laura Carter Holloway. "The Mother of the Wes-
      leys." In The Mothers of Great Men and Women, and Some
      Wives of Great Men, 146-68. New York: Funk and Wagnalls,
      1883. 647p.

991. Langford, Thomas A. Practical Divinity: Theology in the
      Wesleyan Tradition. Nashville: Abingdon Press, 1983. 303p.
      There are discussions of Wesley's theological doctrines through-
      out the book, and the author traces Wesley's influence on
      those who followed him.

992. Langton, Edward. "Methodists and Moravians," and "John
      Wesley's Visit to Herrnhut." Chaps. 13 and 14 in History of
      the Moravian Church, 98-105, 106-10. London: George Allen
      and Unwin, 1956. 173p.

993. Larrabee, William Clark. Wesley and His Coadjutors, edited
     by B. F. Tefft. 2 vols. Cincinnati: Swormstedt and Power,
     1851.

994. Lass, Alfred. Notes of the Rise and Progress of Methodism,
     Wandsworth and the Neighbourhood, the Formation of the
     Wandsworth Circuit in 1864, and Its History from That Date
     to 1902. London: C. H. Kelly, 1904. 127p.

995. _____. A Short History of the Rise and Progress of
     Methodism in the Wandsworth Circuit: Jubilee Souvenir.
     London: Kent and Matthews, 1914. 32p. GtBLW

996. The Last Days of Charles Wesley. New York: Tract So-
     ciety, 18--? 12p.

997. "The Last Illness, Death, and Character of the Rev. John
     Wesley, A.M." In The Journals of the Rev. John Wesley,
     xii-xix. See no. 542.

998. Laufer, Calvin Weiss. "Soldiers of Christ Arise." In
     Hymn Lore, 114-17. Philadelphia: Westminster Press, 1932.
     205p.

999. Laver, James. Wesley. London: Davies, 1932. 167p.

1000. Lawrence, Ralph. "The English Hymn." Chap. 5 in English
      Association, Essays and Studies, n.s. 7. London: John
      Murray, 1954. Pp. 118-21 deal with the Wesleys.

1001. Lawson, Albert Brown. John Wesley and the Christian
      Ministry; the Sources and Development of His Opinions and
      Practice. London: Society for the Promotion of Christian
      Knowledge, 1963. 210p.

1002. Lawson, John. "The People Called Methodists. Pt. 2. Our
      Discipline." Chap. 6 in vol. 1 of A History of the Methodist
      Church in Great Britain, 183-209. See no. 89.

1003. Lawson, John James. Notes on Wesley's Forty-four Sermons.
      London: Epworth Press, 1946. 291p.

1004. _____. Selections from John Wesley's 'Notes on the New
      Testament'; Systematically Arranged with Explanatory Com-
      ments. London: Epworth Press; Chicago: A. R. Allenson,
      1955. 219p.

1005. Lawson, McEwan. He Set Britain Aflame. Eagle Books, no.
      49. New York: Friendship Press, 1946. 24p.

1006. Lawton, George. John Wesley's English: A Study of His
      Literary Style. London: Allen and Unwin, 1962. 320p.

1007. Laycock, John William. Methodist Heroes in the Great Ha-
       worth Round, 1734 to 1784. Keighley: Wadsworth, 1909.
       380p.

1008. Lean, Garth. Strangely Warmed: The Amazing Life of John
       Wesley. Wheaton, Ill.: Tyndale House Publishers, 1964.
       144p. Originally published in England with the title John
       Wesley, Anglican.

1009. Leathem, William Harvey. John Wesley 1703-91: A Study in
       Sainthood and Genius. Great Churchmen, no. 7. London:
       Church Book Room Press, 1947. 34p.

1010. Le Cato Edwards, Wilfred. Epworth, the Home of the Wes-
       leys. Epworth Press, 1972. 34p., 12p.

1011. Lecky, William Edward Hartpole. "The Religious Revival."
       Chap. 9 in vol. 2 of A History of England in the Eighteenth
       Century. 8 vols. London: Longmans, Green, and Co.,
       1883-90. This Chapter has two sections: "Causes of the Undog-
       matic Character of English Theology in the Eighteenth Centu-
       ry," pp. 521-48, and "Methodism," pp. 549-642, which is
       essentially the Wesley story.

1012. Lee, B. F. "Wesley the Worker." In Wesley Memorial Volume,
       418-26. See no. 257.

1013. Lee, James Wideman, Naphtali Luccock, and James Main Dixon.
       The Illustrated History of Methodism; The Story of the Origin
       and Progress of the Methodist Church, from its Foundation by
       John Wesley to the Present Day.... St. Louis, Mo.: Metho-
       dist Magazine Publishing Co., 1900. Chaps. 2-6 tell the
       Wesley story, written in popular style.

1014. Lee, Jesse. "Of the Rise of the Methodists in 1729, and of
       the Beginnings of Methodism in the United States of America
       in 1766." Chap. 1 in A Short History of the Methodists in
       the United States of America ... to Which is Prefixed a Brief
       Account of Their Rise in England in the Year 1729..., 9-23.
       Baltimore: Magill and Clime, 1810. 366p.

1015. Lee, John David. The Evangelical Revival: A Re-Appraisal.
       Evanston, Ill.: Seabury-Western Theological Seminary, 1951.
       32p.

1016. Lee, Umphrey. "Freedom from Rigid Creed." In Methodism,
       128-38. See no. 287.

1017. _____. Historical Background of Early Methodist Enthusiasm.
       London: P. S. King and Son, 1931. 176p. His dissertation,
       Columbia University.

1018. _____. John Wesley and Modern Religion. Nashville: Cokesbury Press, 1936. 354p. (Rev. in nos. 2391, 3802.)

1019. _____. The Lord's Horseman: John Wesley the Man. Nashville: Abingdon Press, 1954. 220p.

1020. _____. Our Fathers and Us; the Heritage of the Methodists. Dallas: Southern Methodist University Press, 1958. 123p. A discussion of Wesley and Methodist doctrines and theology.

1021. _____. A Short History of Methodism. Nashville: Abingdon Press, 1956. 160p.

1022. _____. "The Significance of Savannah in the Spiritual Development of John Wesley." Chap. 2 in What Happened at Aldersgate, 43-55. See no. 342.

1023. Leech, Samuel Vanderlip. The Illustrious Methodist, John Wesley; an Address Delivered before the Biennial West Virginia Conference Epworth League, June 1899 at Grafton West Virginia, 1899. N.p. 18p.

1024. Leek Wesleyan Methodist Circuit. Year Book, 1887: Historical Notes. Leek: Clemesha and Clowes, 1888. 50p. GtBLM

1025. Leete, Frederick D. "The Significance of Aldersgate in History." Chap. 16 in What Happened at Aldersgate, 199-210. See no. 342.

1026. Léger, J. Augustin. John Wesley's Last Love. London: J. M. Dent and Sons, 1910. 300p. The first part is a reproduction of Narrative of a Remarkable Transaction in the Early Life of John Wesley. The second part is an assessment of Wesley's marriage and character.

1027. Lelièvre, Matthieu. John Wesley: His Life and His Work. London: Wesleyan Conference Office, 1871. 274p.

1028. _____. "Wesley as a Popular Preacher." In Wesley Memorial Volume, 294-99. See no. 257.

1029. Le Messurier, Brian. A History of the Mint Methodist Church, Exeter. Exeter, 1962. 40p. Published in connection with the 150th anniversary of the opening of the Mint Methodist Church.

1030. Leslie, Joseph Blackburn. Incidents in the Life and Times of the Rev. John Wesley, M.A.. Manchester: J. F. Wilkinson, 1876. 56p.

1031. Lester, George. Grimsby Methodism (1743-1889) and the

Wesleys in Lincolnshire. London: Wesleyan-Methodist Book-
Room, 1890. 164p.

1032. _____. "John Wesley and His Native County." In The
Homes, Haunts and Friends of John Wesley, 60-79. See no.
319.

1033. Lewin, Thomas Herbert. Life and Death: Being an Authentic Account of the Deaths of One Hundred Celebrated Men and
Women, with Their Portraits. London: Constable and Co.,
1910. 231p. Wesley, pp. 131-32. The information here was
taken form Southey's Life of Wesley.

1034. Lewis, Edwin. "Aldersgate the Motive Power of the Church."
Chap. 4 in What Happened at Aldersgate, 72-83. See no.
342.

1035. "The Life of John Wesley." In Christian Biography; Com-
prising Memoirs of the Revs. John Wesley, John Nelson,
Richard Burdsall, and Mrs. Rogers, 5-74. London: J. S.
Pratt, 1843. 72p. IEG

1036. Life of John Wesley; Fellow of Lincoln College, Oxford and
Founder of the Society of Methodists. London: Seeley Jackson and Halliday, 1856. 277p.

1037. Life of the Rev. John Wesley. London: Religious Tract
Society, [18--]. 144p.

1038. Life of the Rev. John Wesley, Compiled from Authentic
Sources; with an Appendix, Shewing the Real Character of
the Methodist Priesthood. Newcastle: D. France and Co.,
1842. 20p.

1039. "Life of the Rev. Samuel Wesley, M.A. [1691-1739]." In
Tales, Instructive and Entertaining, with a Sketch of His
Life, 3-12. London: W. Suttaby, B. Crosby and Co. and
Scatcherd and Letterman, 1808. 48p.

1040. Lightwood, James T. Methodist Music in the Eighteenth
Century. London: Epworth Press, 1927. 56p.

1041. _____. "Music of the Methodist Revival." Chap. 5 in
Hymn Tunes and Their Story, 118-45. London: C. H.
Kelly, 1905. 402p.

1042. Lindström, Harald G. A. Wesley and Sanctification; a Study
in the Doctrine of Salvation. Translated by H. S. Harvey.
Stockholm: Nya Bakforlags Aktiebolaget, 1946. 228p. His
dissertation, Uppsala University.

1043. Lipscomb, Andrew A. "Providence of God in Methodism." In Wesley Memorial Volume, 383-403. See no. 257.

1044. Lipsky, Abram. John Wesley; a Portrait. New York: AMS Press, 1971. 305p.

1045. Little, Arthur Wilde. The Times and Teaching of John Wesley. Milwaukee: Young Churchman Co., 1897. 68p. Describes Wesley as an Anglo-Catholic.

1046. Little, C. Deane. A Goodly Heritage: A Brief History of 150 Years of Blackrod Methodism. Wigan: E. Sidebotham, 1950. 44p. GtBLW

1047. _____. The History and Romance of Our Mother Sunday School: 150 Years of Bolton Methodism. Bolton, Eng.: Coop. Hunt and Co., 193- . 76p.

1048. _____. Our Old Sunday School (and Day School). 150 Years of Wigan Methodism. Wigan: E. Sidebotham, 1933. 68p.

1049. Little, Charles Joseph. John Wesley, Preacher of Scriptural Christianity. Evanston, Ill., 1903. 24p.

1050. _____. "The Social Activities of John Wesley." Chap. 3 in Social Ministry; an Introduction to the Study and Practice of Social Service, 57-75, edited by Harry F. Ward. New York: Eaton and Mains; Cincinnati: Jennings and Graham, 1910. 318p.

1051. Lloyd-George, David. Mr. Lloyd George's Tribute to Wesley and Methodism, Delivered at the Victoria Hotel, on June 20th, on Behalf of the Restoration Fund of Wesley's Chapel. London: Epworth Press, 1922. 14p.

1052. Lloyd-Jones, David Martyn. "The Conversion of John Wesley." In Conversions: Psychological and Spiritual, 22-26. Chicago and London: Inter-Varsity Press, 1959. 40p.

1053. Lockyer, Thomas F. Paul, Luther, Wesley: A Study in Religious Experience as Illustrative of the Ethic of Christianity. London: Epworth Press, 1922. 359p.

1054. Lofthouse, William F. "Charles Wesley." Chap. 4 in vol. 1 of A History of the Methodist Church in Great Britain, 113-44. See no. 89.

1055. London. Wesley's Chapel, City Road. Statement Concerning Death Watch Beetle Trouble in Chapel Roof. f800 Urgently Needed. London, 1927. 20p. Pamphlet describing the

discovery of an infestation of the Chapel's roof timber by
"beetles" and a plea for funds. Does contain some information about John Wesley. GtBMM

1056. Long, Edwin McKean. Illustrated History of Hymns and Their
Authors: Facts and Incidents of the Origin, Authors, Sentiments and Singing of Hymns.... Philadelphia: J. L. Landis
and Co., 1882. The Wesleys--Charles, John, and Susannah
are discussed on pp. 475-85.

1057. Lorkin, William. A Concise History of the First Establishment
of Wesleyan Methodism in the City of Norwich in the Year
1754, with Its Progress from That Period to Its Present State.
Norfolk and Norwich: Matchett and Stevenson, 1825. 63p.

1058. Lucas, Eric P. Methodism in Witheridge, 1809-1959. Win-
gate: E. P. Lucas, 1959. 40p.

1059. Luccock, Halford E. and Paul Hutchinson. The Story of
Methodism. New York: Methodist Book Concern, 1926.
508p. Popular telling of the Methodist story, with pages
13-212 devoted to Wesley.

1060. Luccock, Halford E. and Webb Garrison. Endless Line of
Splendor. Illustrated by Lynd Ward. 2d ed. Evanston,
Ill.: United Methodist Communications, 1975. 112p. Brief
stories about events and personalities in Methodism--many
of them concerning the Wesleys.

1061. Luckock, Herbert Mortimer. John Wesley's Churchmanship.
London: Longman's and Co., 1891. 55p. Luckock gives
the Anglican view of Wesley and Methodism, answered by E.
Theodore Carrier as a Methodist.

1062. _____. Who Are Wesley's Heirs? A Reply to the Challenge
of Rev. E. T. Carrier, Wesleyan Minister. London: Longmans, Green, 1891. 40p.

1063. Ludwig, Charles. Susanna Wesley, Mother of John and
Charles. Milford, Mich.: Mott Media, 1984. 190p.

1064. Lumley, William Benjamin. Methodist Church, Stephen's
Green, Dublin: A Jubilee Memorial, 1843-1893. London:
Wesleyan Methodist Book Room, 1893? 135p.

1065. Lunn, Arnold H. M. John Wesley. New York: Dial Press,
1929. 371p.

1066. Lunn, Henry S. John Wesley: The President's Prize Essay, Delivered in the Front Examination Hall of Trinity
College, November 16, 1885. Dublin: W. McGee, 1885.
39p.

1067. _____. Reunion and Lambeth: John Wesley's Message to the Bishops in Conference, July, 1920. London: Epworth Press, 1920. 103p.

1068. Lycoming College, Williamsport, Pa. John Wesley and Lycoming College: Celebrating the 250th Anniversary of John Wesley's Graduation from Christ Church College, Oxford University. Williamsport, Pa.: The College, 1976. 3 folders. NjMUM

1069. Lyles, Albert M. Methodism Mocked: The Satiric Reaction to Methodism in the Eighteenth Century. London: Epworth Press, 1960. 191p. The author has attempted to examine the satiric reaction to Methodism within the years 1732-1800, including the burlesque, the lampoon, the mock heroic, the parody, and ironic statements.

1070. Lynn, Surgeon-Major. A History of Wesleyan Methodism in the Armagh Circuit. Belfast: McBride, 1887. AUSVMQ

1071. Lyth, John. Glimpses of Early Methodism in York, and the Surrounding District. York: William Sessions, 1885. 320p.

1072. M, J. A. Two Death Scenes. London: Wesleyan Conference Office, 18--? 8p. Describes the death scene of Robert Darwin, persecutor of Samuel Wesley, the father, and the death of Samuel.

1073. McArthur, Kathleen Walker. The Economic Ethics of Wesley. New York: Abingdon Press, 1936. 166p.

1074. Macbrair, Robert Maxwell. An Apology for Wesley and Methodism, in Reply to the Misrepresentations of Isaac Taylor, and the "North British Review." Edinburgh: James Nichol, 1852. 54p.

1075. M'Caine, Alexander. The History and Mystery of Methodist Episcopacy. Baltimore, Md.: Richard J. Matchett, 1827. 76p.

1076. McClintock, John. "John Wesley." In Sketches of Imminent Methodist Ministers, 9-67. New York: Carlton and Phillips, 1854. 370p.

1077. _____. "Wesley, Charles." In vol. 10 of Cyclopedia of Biblical, Theological and Ecclesiastical Literature, 907-11. 12 vols. New York: Harper and Bros., 1886.

1078. _____. "Wesley, John." In vol. 10 of Cyclopedia of Biblical, Theological and Ecclesiastical Literature, 912-17. See previous entry.

1079. McConnell, Dorothy Frances. Guide to Three Spiritual Clas-
       sics: "Christian Perfection," by François Fénelon. "Christian
       Perfection," by John Wesley. "The Spiritual Life," by Evelyn
       Underhill. New York: Woman's Division of Christian Service,
       Board of Missions, Methodist Church, 1963. 68p. This
       guide is for use with the text Teachings toward Christian
       Perfection, by Olive Wyon.

1080. McConnell, Francis J. John Wesley. New York: Abingdon
       Press, 1939. 355p.

1081. _____. "John Wesley." In Evangelicals, Revolutionists
       and Idealists; Six English Contributors to American Thought
       and Action, 41-68. Drew Lectureship in Biography. New
       York: Abingdon-Cokesbury Press, 1942. 184p.

1082. McCown, Wayne G. "Wesley's Suggestions for Study [of the
       Bible]." In A Contemporary Wesleyan Theology: Biblical,
       Systematic, and Practical, 750-54. See no. 279.

1083. McCullagh, Thomas. "Wesley and the Moravians." In The
       Homes, Haunts and Friends of John Wesley, 88-94. See
       no. 319.

1084. _____. "Wesley's Many Discouragements." In Wesley
       Studies, 119-26. See no. 190.

1085. _____. "Wesley's Wife." In Wesley Studies, 112-18. See
       no. 190.

1086. McCulloh, Gerald O. "The Discipline of Life in Early Method-
       ism through Preaching and Other Means of Grace." Chap. 9
       in The Doctrine of the Church, 161-81. London: Epworth
       Press, 1964. 215p. Reviews the personal discipline of John
       Wesley and his rules for the societies.

1087. McCutchan, Robert Guy. "England's Development of the
       Hymn." In Hymns in the Lives of Men, 138-54. Nashville:
       Abingdon-Cokesbury Press, 1945. 208p.

1088. _____. Our Hymnody: A Manual of the Methodist Hymnal.
       2d ed. New York: Methodist Book Concern, 1937. 619p.
       Includes discussions on the hymns and hymnists included in
       the Methodist hymnals.

1089. _____. "A Singing Church." In Methodism, 148-64. See
       no. 287.

1090. Macdonald, Frederick W. "Bishop Butler and John Wesley:
       A Comparison and Contrast." In Recreations of a Book-Lover.
       London: Hodder and Stoughton, 1911. 216p.

1091. _____. "Divine Service." In Wesley, the Man, His Teaching and His Work, 126-37. See no. 357.

1092. _____. Introduction to The Journal of the Rev. John Wesley, A.M. 4 vols. London and Toronto: J. M. Dent and Sons; New York: E. P. Dutton and Co., 1907.

1093. McDonald, Hugh Dermot. "The Doctrine of a Leader [John Wesley]." Chap. 9 in Ideas of Revelation: An Historical Study, A.D. 1700 to A.D. 1860, 245-65. London: Macmillan, 1959. 300p.

1094. MacDonald, James. An Address to the Preachers Late in Connection with the Rev. J. Wesley on the Necessity and Utility of Establishing a Plan for Securing to All Children of the Methodists a Regular Christian Education. Rochdale: J. Hartley, 1821. 39p.

1095. _____. Strictures on Methodism. By a Careful Observer. London: Richard Edwards, 1804. 128p.

1096. Macdonald, James A. Wesley and the Neussers. London: Wesleyan Conference Office, n.d. 8p. IEG

1097. Macdonald, James Alexander. Wesley's Revision of the Shorter Catechism with Notes. Cincinnati: Jennings and Graham, 1906. 161p.

1098. MacDonald, Michael. "Religion, Social Change, and Psychological Healing in England, 1600-1800." In The Church and Healing; Papers Read at the Twentieth Summer Meeting and the Twenty-first Winter Meeting of the Ecclesiastical History Society, edited by W. J. Sheils, 101-25. Studies in Church History, vol. 19. Oxford: B. Blackwell, 1982. 440p.

1099. McDonald, William. Christian Perfection. [N.Y.? 1893]. 16p. NjMUM

1100. _____. John Wesley. New York: Methodist Book Concern, 1899. 119p.

1101. _____. John Wesley and His Doctrine. Boston: McDonald and Gill, 1893. 149p.

1102. _____. The People's Wesley. New York: Eaton and Mains; Cincinnati: Curts and Jennings, 1899. 62p.

1103. McDowell, William Fraser. "The Significance of Wesley and the Methodist Movement." In Wesley Bicentennial, Wesleyan University, 44-59. See no. 52.

1104. McGee, James. The March of Methodism from Epworth
       Around the Globe.... New York: Hunt and Eaton, 1893.
       147p.

1105. McGiffert, Arthur Cushman. "English Evangelicalism." In
       Protestant Thought Before Kant, 162-75. New York: Harper,
       1962. 265p. A discussion of Wesley and his Evangelical doc-
       trine. The author describes the effects of Evangelicalism on
       English religious life.

1106. McGinley, Phyllis. "Heroes without Halos." In Saint-
       Watching. New York: Viking Press, 1969. 243p.

1107. McGraw, James. "John Wesley." Chap. 9 in Great Evangeli-
       cal Preachers of Yesterday, 56-62. Nashville: Abingdon-
       Cokesbury Press, 1961. 159p.

1108. MacLennan, David A. "John Wesley and Christian Perfec-
       tion." In Christian Perfection: Selections, edited by David
       A. MacLennan, 5-9. New York: World Publishing Co.,
       1969. 63p. This is a collection of John Wesley's writings.

1109. MacMunn, George F. "John Wesley." In Leadership through
       the Ages, 172-81. 1935. Reprint. Freeport, N.Y.: Books
       for Libraries Press, 1968. 354p.

1110. McNeal, George H. In the Footsteps of Wesley in London:
       Pilgrimage to Methodist Shrines. London: Epworth Press,
       [193-]. 11p.

1111. McNeill, John T. Books of Faith and Power. New York:
       Harper, 1947. 183p. Contains a discussion of John Wesley's
       journal, pp. 155-83.

1112. _____. "John Wesley." In Makers of the Christian Tradi-
       tion; from Alfred the Great to Schleirmacher, 241-53. New
       York: Harper and Row, 1964. 279p.

1113. Macphail, Andrew. "John Wesley." Chap. 5 in Essays in
       Puritanism, 275-339. Boston and New York: Houghton,
       Mifflin and Co., 1905. 339p.

1114. McPheeters, Julian Claudius. John Wesley's Heart-Warming
       Religion. Louisville, Ky.: Pentecostal Pub. Co., [194-?]
       64p.

1115. McTyeire, Holland Nimmons. A History of Methodism: Com-
       prising a View of the Rise of This Revival of Spiritual Re-
       ligion in the First Half of the Eighteenth Century, and of
       the Principal Agents by Whom It Was Promoted in Europe and
       America.... Nashville: Southern Methodist Publishing
       House, 1884. 688p.

1116. _____. "Wesley the Founder of Methodism." In The Wesley Memorial Volume, 164-67. See no. 257.

1117. Madron, Thomas W. "John Wesley on Economics." In Sanctification and Liberation, 102-15. See no. 191.

1118. Major, Henry. A Vindication of the Episcopal Succession.... Harrisburg: Theo Fenn, Printer, 1844. 100p.

1119. Maker, Lawrence. Cob and Moorstone: The Curious History of Some Cornish Methodist Churches. London: Epworth Press, 1935. 94p.

1120. Mallalieu, W. F. Introduction to Christian Perfection As Taught by John Wesley, compiled by J. A. Wood, 5-8. Chicago and Boston: Christian Witness, 1885. 288p.

1121. Mallinson, Joel. History of Methodism in Huddersfield, Holmfirth and Denby Dale. London: C. H. Kelly, 1898. 224p.

1122. Manning, Bernard L. The Hymns of Wesley and Watts; Five Informal Papers. London: Epworth Press, 1942. 143p.

1123. Manwell, Reginald Dickinson, and Sophia Blanche Fahs. "John Wesley, 1703-1791." Chap. 10 in Church Across the Street, 192-213. Boston: Beacon Press, 1947. 258p.

1124. Marks, Harvey Blair. "Charles Wesley." In The Rise and Growth of English Hymnody, 98-103. New York: Fleming H. Revell Co., 1937. 288p.

1125. Marshall, Dorothy. "The Impact of John Wesley," in Eighteenth Century England, 244-51. London: Longmans, Green and Co., 1962. 537p.

1126. _____. John Wesley. London: Oxford University Press, 1965. 64p.

1127. Marshall, Madeleine Forell. "Self, Sense, and the Revival." Chap. 3 in English Congregational Hymns in the Eighteenth Century, 60-88. Lexington, Ky.: University of Kentucky Press, 1982. 181p.

1128. Marston, Leslie Ray. From Age to Age A Living Witness; a Historical Interpretation of Free Methodism's First Century. Winona Lake, Ind.: Light and Life Press, 1960. 608p.

1129. Martin, George Currie. "English Hymns from the Wesleys to Heber." Chap. 8 in The Church and the Hymn Writers, 166-80. London: James Clarke and Co., 1928. 255p.

1130. Martin, James Henry. John Wesley's London Chapels. Wes-
       ley Historical Society Lectures, no. 12. London: Epworth
       Press, 1946. 56p.

1131. Martin, Margaret Maxwell. "Susanna Wesley." In Heroines
       of Early Methodism, 7-55. Nashville: Publishing House,
       Methodist Episcopal Church, South, 189-? 224p.

1132. Maser, Frederic E. The Dramatic Story of Early American
       Methodism. New York: Abingdon Press, 1965. 109p. A
       brief account of the early years of Methodism in America
       prepared for the celebration in 1966 of the 200th anniversary
       of the beginnings of American Methodism.

1133. _____. "The Eighteenth Century." Part 1 in Proclaiming
       Grace and Freedom: The Story of United Methodism in Ameri-
       ca, edited by John G. McEllhenney, 9-45. Nashville:
       Abingdon Press, 1982. 141p.

1134. _____. Second Thoughts on John Wesley. Madison, N.J.:
       Drew Theological School, 1978. 58p. First published in Drew
       Gateway 49, no. 2, 1978.

1135. _____. The Story of John Wesley's New Testament: In
       Celebration of the Two Hundreth Anniversary of "Explanatory
       Notes upon the New Testament" by John Wesley. Philadelphia:
       Printed for the Historical Society of the Philadelphia Confer-
       ence of the Methodist Church, 1955. 18p.

1136. _____. Susanna Wesley. Lake Junaluska, N.C.: Associa-
       tion of Methodist Historical Societies, 1967. 31p.

1137. _____. Tales of a Wesleyana Collector.... Philadelphia:
       Stephenson-Brothers, 1977. 20p. This is an essay written
       for the presentation of the Maser Wesleyana and Prayerbook
       collections to Drew University.

1138. Mason, Arthur James. John Wesley: A Lecture. Church
       Historical Society Publications, 47. London: Society for the
       Promotion of Christian Knowledge, 1898. 55p.

1139. Mason, J. A. An Earnest Appeal to the People Called
       Methodists, and to the Nation at Large. London: W. E.
       Andrews, 1827. 52p. An anti-Methodist publication, re-
       futing Wesley and his doctrines. Mason was a Methodist
       preacher who became a Catholic.

1140. _____. Strictures on Wesley's Pretended Roman Catechism,
       Pointing Out Its Numerous Misrepresentations, False Glosses,
       and Gross Falsehoods. 3 vols. London: W. E. Andrews,
       1828-29.

1141. Massingberd, Francis Charles. "John Wesley; His Life and Times." In Sermons on Unity, with an Essay on Religious Societies, and a Lecture on the Life and Times of Wesley, 71-97. London: Rivingtons, 1868. 110p.

1142. Mathews, Horace Frederick. Methodism and the Education of the People, 1791-1851. London: Epworth Press, 1949. 215p.

1143. Matsumoto, Hiroaki. "John Wesley's Understanding of Man." In Japanese Contributions to the Study of John Wesley, 79-96. See no. 643.

1144. Mavis, W. Curry. "Aldersgate Answers Man's Needs." Chap. 8 in Methodism's Aldersgate Heritage, 55-62. See no. 62.

1145. May, George L. John Wesley. Little Books on Religion, no. 105. London: Society for the Promotion of Christian Knowledge, 1936. 32p.

1146. _____. "John Wesley." In Some Eighteenth Century Churchmen: Glimpses of English Church Life in the Eighteenth Century, 63-91. London: Society for the Promotion of Christian Knowledge, 1920. 224p.

1147. Meacham, Albert Gallatin. A Compendious History of the Rise and Progress of the Methodist Church, Both in Europe and America, Consisting Principally of Selections from Various Approved and Authentic Documents. New York: Knowlton and Rice, 1835. 503p. The first part of this book contains the rise and establishment of Methodism in England, with pp. 7-262 devoted to the Wesley family, John and Charles, and their activities in the revival of religion in England. The author indicates some of the incidents were related to him by John Wesley.

1148. Mee, F. Gordon, and John Oddie. The History of Wesleyan Methodism in Bamford, Heywood Circuit, 1789-1933. Heywood, Eng.: Atkinson and Co., 1933. 32p.

1149. Meeks, M. Douglas. "The Future of the Methodist Theological Traditions." Chap. 1 in The Future of the Methodist Theological Traditions, 13-33. See no. 57.

1150. Mees, James H. The Story of a Hundred Years: Handbook of the Wesleyan Methodist Church, Stourbridge Circuit. Stourbridge: Mark and Moody, 1928. 148p. GtBLW

1151. Meredith, W. H. Pilgrimages to Methodist Shrines. Cincinnati: Jennings and Pye; New York: Eaton and Mains, 1903.

335p. Among the many places described are Epworth, Kingswood, the New Room in the Horse Fair, London Chapel, John
Wesley's House.

1152.   . The Real John Wesley. Cincinnati: Jennings and
Pye; New York: Eaton and Mains, 1903. 425p.

1153. Messiter, Arthur Frederick. Notes on Epworth Parish Life
in the Eighteenth Century. London: Elliott Stock, 1912.
81p.

1154. Methodism As Held by Wesley, by D. S. P. 2d ed. Tracts
for the People, no. 4. Sketches of Sectarianism, no. 2. New
York? 1843. 36p.

1155. Methodism Unmasked. Wesley's Doctrine Proved to Be False
and Pernicious ... Answered and Refuted by the Rev. J. L.
Scarborough: J. Cole, 1828. 131p.

1156. The Methodist, a Historical and Biographical Sketch of the
Pioneers, Bishops, and Representative Men of American
Methodism ... Containing Portraits of the Pioneers and
Bishops of the Methodist Church.... Cincinnati: H. F.
Brown, 1867. 198p.

1157. Methodist Episcopal Church Conferences, New England. John
Wesley Bi-centenial Commission. John Wesley Bi-centenial;
People's Temple, Boston, June 29-30, '03.... Boston: Taylor
Press, 1903. 4p.

1158. Methodist Social Union, Toronto. Services on the Occasion of
the Unveiling of the Wesley Portrait in the Metropolitan
Church, Toronto, under the Auspices of the Methodist Social Union. Toronto: Miln-Bingham, 1901. 12p. NjMUM

1159. Meyler, L. J. John Wesley and Pembrokeshire. Haverfordwest, Wales: Western Telegraph, 1956? 20p. Contains articles originally published in the Western Telegraph on the
occasion of the bicentenary of Methodism in 1938. NcD

1160. Michalson, Carl. "The Hermeneutics of Holiness in Wesley."
In The Heritage of Christian Thought; Essays in Honor of
Robert Lowry Calhoun, edited by Robert E. Cushman and Egil
Grislis, 127-41. New York: Harper and Row, 1965. 243p.

1161. Mickey, Paul A. Essentials of Wesleyan Theology: A Contemporary Affirmation. Contemporary Evangelical Perspectives.
Grand Rapids, Mich.: Zondervan Publishing House, 1980.
185p. This book attempts "the monumental task of presenting
Wesleyan/Arminian theology in the form of a systematic that
communicates the essence of evangelical truth from a sound
biblical base"--foreword.

1162. Miley, John. "Sanctification." Chap. 8 in vol. 2 of Systematic Theology, 254-84. Library of Biblical and Theological Literature, vols. 5 and 6. New York: Hunt and Eaton; Cincinnati: Cranston and Stowe, 1892-94.

1163. _____. "The Work of the Christmas Conference of 1784." In Methodist Episcopal Church in the U.S. Proceedings, Sermon, Essays and Addresses of the Centennial Methodist Conference, 107-18. New York: Phillips and Hunt; Cincinnati: Cranston and Stowe, 1885. Includes an interpretation of John Wesley's part in the organization of Methodism in America, discussing his approval of establishing an independent church, with episcopacy as the best form of church government. Discusses also the ordination of Coke.

1164. Miller, Basil William. John Wesley, the World His Parish. Grand Rapids, Mich.: Zondervan Publishing House, 1943. 140p.

1165. _____. "Susannah Wesley, Famous Mother." Chap. 1 in Ten Girls Who Became Famous, 7-13. Grand Rapids, Mich.: Zondervan Publishing House, 1946. 72p.

1166. Miller, C. W. "John Wesley." In The Conflict of Centuries, 117-26. Nashville: Methodist Publishing House, 1884. 308p.

1167. Miller, Edward. John Wesley: The Hero of the Second Reformation. Splendid Lives Series. London: Sunday School Union, 1906. 120p.

1168. Miller, Josiah. Singers and Songs of the Church: Being Biographical Sketches of the Hymn-Writers in All the Principal Collections; with Notes on Their Psalms and Hymns. 2d ed. London: Longmans, Green, 1869. 617p. Includes the Wesleys.

1169. Mitchell, T. Crichton. Meet Mr. Wesley: An Intimate Sketch of John Wesley. Christian Service Training, 137b. Kansas City, Mo.: Beacon Hill, 1981. 206p.

1170. _____. Mr. Wesley; an Intimate Sketch of John Wesley. Kansas City, Mo.: Beacon Hill, 1957. 96p.

1171. Mitton, Charles Leslie. A Clue to Wesley's Sermons. London: Epworth Press, 1951. 44p.

1172. Modern Methodism Not in Accordance with the Principles and Plans of the Rev. John Wesley During Any Period of His Life: A Dialogue between a Clergyman and One of His Methodist Parishioners. London: James Burns, 1842. 36p.

102   John and Charles Wesley

1173. Modern Wesleyanism Compared with the Teaching of Mr.
       Wesley.... London: J. Leslie, 1844. 47p.

1174. Moede, Gerald F. The Office of Bishop in Methodism, Its
       History and Development. New York: Abingdon Press,
       1964. 277p.

1175. Monk, Robert C. John Wesley: His Puritan Heritage; a
       Study of the Christian Life. Nashville: Abingdon Press,
       1966. 286p. Based on his dissertation, Princeton Univer-
       sity, 1963.

1176. Moore, Benjamin. History of Wesleyan Methodism in Burnley
       and East Lancashire: Burnley, Colne, Padiham, Nelson,
       Barnoldswick. Burnley: Burnley Gazette, 1899. 268p.

1177. Moore, Henry. The Life of the Rev. John Wesley: in Which
       are Included, the Life of His Brother, the Rev. Charles
       Wesley ... and Memoirs of Their Family: Comprehending an
       Account of the Great Revival of Religion, in Which They were
       the First and Chief Instruments.... 2 vols. New York:
       Published by N. Bangs and J. Emory for the Methodist Epis-
       copal Church, J and J Harper, Printers, 1824-25. (Rev. in
       no. 3172.)

1178. _____. A Sermon Preached at Bristol, on Occasion of the
       Death of the Rev. John Wesley. Bristol: W. Pine, 1791.
       27p. NcD

1179. Moore, John M. "The Theology of Aldersgate." Chap. 11
       in What Happened at Aldersgate, 158-64. See no. 342.

1180. Moore, Richard Douglas. Methodism in the Channel Islands.
       London: Epworth Press, 1952. 175p.

1181. Moore, Robert L. John Wesley and Authority: A Psychologi-
       cal Perspective. American Academy of Religion Dissertation
       Series, no. 29. Missoula, Mont.: Scholars Press, 1979.
       245p. (Rev. in no. 2846.)

1182. Moorman, John Richard Humpidge. "The Age of Wesley
       (1738-1791)." Chap. 17 in A History of the Church in Eng-
       land, 293-314. 2d ed. New York: Morehouse-Barlow, 1967.
       460p.

1183. Morgan, Irvonwy. 'Twixt the Mount and the Multitude; the
       Relevance of John Wesley to His Age. London: Epworth
       Press, 1957. 63p.

1184. Morgan, Robert. "Old Gravel Walk": A Chapter in the
       History of the Blackhall Place Methodist Church, Dublin.
       Belfast, 1898. 21p. GtBLW

Books   103

1185. Morley, J. A. Wesleyan Chapel, Union Street, Rochdale: A
       Record of the Society, 1746-1926. Rochdale: E. Wrigley and
       Sons, 1926. 62p. GtBLW

1186. Morrell, William Wilberforce. Notices of Wesleyan Methodism
       in Selby, 1744-1892. Selby: W. B. Bellerby and Son, 1892.
       40p. GtBLW

1187. Morris, A. Clifford. A Brief Historical Sketch of Zion,
       Countess of Huntingdon's Connexion Congregational Church,
       St. Ives. St. Ives: W. and J. Jacobs, 1947. 20p. GtBLW

1188. Morrison, Duncan. The Great Hymns of the Church: Their
       Origin and Authorship. London: Simpkin, Marshall, Hamil-
       ton, Kent and Co., 1890. 250p. Twenty-eight hymns are
       discussed in this book. Three are by Charles Wesley: "Oh,
       for a Thousand Tongues to Sing," "Jesus, Lover of My Soul,"
       and "Hark, the Herald Angels Sing!"

1189. Morton, Harold Christopherson. Messages That Made the Re-
       vival: Being a Presentation of the Main Teachings of Wesley
       and His Helpers. London: Epworth Press, 1920. 108p.

1190. Moss, R. Waddy. "Wesley and the Moravians." In Wesley
       Studies, 88-95. See no. 190.

1191. Mossner, Ernest Campbell. "Enthusiasm: John Wesley."
       In Bishop Butler and the Age of Reason, 165-76. New York:
       Macmillan Co., 1936. 271p.

1192. Moulton, W. Fiddian. "The Influence of Wesley upon Eng-
       land." In Wesley As a World Force, 23-30. See no. 49.

1193. Mouzon, Edwin Du Bose. Fundamentals of Methodism. Nash-
       ville: Lamar and Barton, Agents, Publishing House, Method-
       ist Episcopal Church, South, 1923. 85p.

1194. Mowat, Robert Balmain. "John Wesley." Chap. 12 in vol. 2
       of Makers of British History, 150-62. 3 vols. London: Ed-
       ward Arnold, 1926.

1195. Moyer, Elgin Sylvester. Great Leaders of the Christian
       Church. Chicago: Moody Press, 1951. 490p.

1196. Mudge, James. Heart Religion, As Described by John Wesley,
       Selected from His Works. New York and Cincinnati: Method-
       ist Book Concern, 1913. 123p. Includes extracts of his
       writings from the Standard American edition, 1831.

1197. _____. History of Methodism. Lucknow: American Method-
       ist Press, 1878. 400p. The first three chapters deal with the
       Wesleys.

1198. _____. "John Wesley." In The Saintly Calling, 37-46.
Cincinnati: Jennings and Graham; New York: Eaton and
Mains, 1905. 260p.

1199. Mudge, Zachariah Atwell. Wesley and His Friends: Illustrat-
ing the Religious Spirit of Their Times. Philadelphia: American Sunday-school Union, 1856. 196p.

1200. Muir, Pearson M'Adam. "John Wesley." In Religious Writers
of England, 183-91. London: A. and C. Black, 1901.
213p.

1201. Muldoon, Sylvan Joseph. "John Wesley's Home Was Haunted."
In Psychic Experiences of Famous People, 130-35. Chicago:
Aries Press, 1947. 200p.

1202. Munro, William Fraser. "John Wesley." In Men Like Moun-
tains: Studies in Dynamic Discipleship, 49-55. Nashville:
Tidings, 1960. 72p.

1203. Murray, Robert Henry. "The Methodists--with a Reference
to the Evangelicals." In Group Movements throughout the
Ages, 231-84. New York and London: Harper and Bros.,
1935. 377p.

1204. Murrell, F. J. "Wesley and the Children." In Wesley, the
Man, His Teaching and His Work, 138-48. See no. 357.

1205. Musgrave, George Washington. "Methodist Episcopacy."
Chap. 1 in The Polity of the Methodist Episcopal Church
in the United States, 27-56. Baltimore: Richard J. Matchett,
1843. 344p.

1206. Musgrave, John. Origin of Methodism in Bolton. Bolton: H.
Bradbury, 1865. 52p. Relates Wesley's association with
Bolton, which started with his first visit there on Sunday,
August 28, 1748. Based largely on Wesley's journals.

1207. Myles, William. Chronological History of the People Called
Methodists, Containing an Account of Their Rise and Progress
from the Year 1729 to the Year 1799; ... Also Short Accounts
of Some of the Most Eminent Men Who Have Laboured among
Them. Liverpool: J. Nuttall, 1799. 223p.

1208. Nagler, Arthur Wilford. "The Doctrinal Position of Wesley,"
and "The Practical Religious Reforms of Wesley." Chaps. 7
and 8 in Pietism and Methodism; or, The Significance of
German Pietism in the Origin and Early Development of Methodism, 82-119. Nashville: Publishing House of the Methodist
Episcopal Church, South, 1918. 200p.

Books 105

1209. Neely, Thomas Benjamin. "The Beginnings of the Wesleyan System," "Wesley's Headship," and "Wesley's Supervisional Methods." Chaps. 2-4 in The Bishops and the Supervisional System of the Methodist Episcopal Church, 15-40. Cincinnati: Jennings and Graham; New York: Eaton and Mains, 1912. 350p.

1210. _____. A History of the Origin and Development of the Governing Conference in Methodism, and Especially of the General Conference of the Methodist Episcopal Church. New York: Hunt and Eaton, 1892. 452p. "... trace the Conference idea from the first Conference, held by the Rev. John Wesley in 1744, down to the Conferences of the present time"--preface.

1211. _____. "John Wesley and Doctrine." Chap. 5 in Doctrinal Standards of Methodism, 72-94. New York: Fleming H. Revell Co., 1918. 355p.

1212. _____. "Wesley's Views of Episcopacy, Ordination, and Church Government," and "Wesley's Relation to the Episcopate of American Methodism." Chaps. 3 and 4 in The Evolution of Episcopacy and Organic Methodism, 86-234. New York: Phillips and Hunt, 1888. 448p.

1213. The New Room in the Horsefair: The Story of John Wesley's Chapel, Bristol. Bristol, n.d. 8p. GtBLW

1214. Newman, J. P. "Wesley and Clarke." In Wesley Memorial Volume, 435-51. See no. 257.

1215. Newton, John Anthony. Methodism and the Puritans. Friends of Dr. William's Library, 18th Lecture. London: Dr. William's Library, 1964. 19p. The author gives evidence of Puritan influence on Wesley and Methodism, beginning with his parents.

1216. _____. Susanna Wesley and the Puritan Tradition in Methodism. London: Epworth Press, 1968. 216p.

1217. Newton, Joseph Fort. Wesley and Woolman; an Appraisal and Comparison. New York and Cincinnati: Abingdon Press, 1914. 80p.

1218. Nichols, William. "Life of Samuel Wesley, A.M. [1691-1739]." In Poems on Several Occasions...., 1-25. London: Simpkin, Marshall and Co., 1862. 660p.

1219. Nicolson, Harold George. "Religious Revival: John Wesley, 1703-1791." Chap. 20 in The Age of Reason, 1700-89, 368-86. London: Constable, 1960. 424p.

1220. Nightingale, Joseph. Portraiture of Methodism: Being an
       Impartial View of the Rise, Progress, Doctrines, Discipline,
       and Manners of the Wesleyan Methodists.... London: Long-
       man, Hurst, Rees, and Orme, 1807. 496p.

1221. Nix, James. "John Wesley at Oxford." In The Homes,
       Haunts and Friends of John Wesley, 79-86. See no. 319.

1222. Noro, Yoshio. "The Character of John Wesley's Faith."
       In Japanese Contributions to the Study of John Wesley, 6-22.
       See no. 643.

1223. _____. "Wesley's Understanding of Christian Perfection."
       In Japanese Contributions to the Study of John Wesley, 23-38.
       See no. 643.

1224. Norris, William Herbert. The Life of the Rev. John Wesley,
       A.M., Abridged from Authentic Sources. Rev. ed. New
       York: Lane and Scott, 1850. 143p.

1225. North, Eric McCoy. Early Methodist Philanthropy. New
       York: Methodist Book Concern, 1914. 181p. His disserta-
       tion, Columbia University.

1226. Northcott, William Cecil. Hymns We Love; Stories of the
       Hundred Most Popular Hymns. Philadelphia: Westminster
       Press, 1955. 168p. Includes discussions of three of
       Charles Wesley's hymns: "Rejoice, the Lord is King," "Je-
       sus, Lover of My Soul," and "Soldiers of Christ Arise."

1227. Northwich Methodist Church. Jubilee Year--a Wesley Calen-
       dar 1939; with Incidents from His Life for Every Day of the
       Year. N.p. 1939. 28p. GtBLW

1228. Norwood, Frederick Abbott. "The Age of Enlightenment."
       In The Development of Modern Christianity, 121-30. Nashville:
       Abingdon Press, 1962. 256p. The author discusses the Wes-
       leyan movement in England, giving a brief synopsis of Wes-
       ley's conversion, theology, and the economic and social in-
       fluence Methodism had on its members.

1229. _____. "The Wesleys," "The Wesleyan Movement," and
       "Roots and Structure of Wesley's Theology." Chaps. 1, 2,
       and 3 in The Story of American Methodism; a History of the
       United Methodists and Their Relations, 23-60. Nashville:
       Abingdon Press, 1974. 448p.

1230. Nott, George Frederick. Religious Enthusiasm Considered,
       in Eight Sermons Preached before the University of Oxford
       in the Year MDCCCII.... Oxford: Oxford University Press,
       1803. 502p. It was the author's hope "that these sermons

may contribute, in some degree, towards the repressing of
that restless spirit of Enthusiasm, the fatal tendency of
which has always been to unsettle the religious opinions of
mankind, and to destroy the peace of the church."

1231. Nottingham, Elizabeth Kristine. The Making of an Evangelist.
Gettysburg, Pa.: Times and News Publishing Co., 1938.
178p. Her dissertation, Columbia University.

1232. Nowell, Thomas W. ... John Wesley an Unconscious Ro-
manist.... London: Basil Montague Pickering, 1876. ScoE

1233. Nuelsen, John L. "Methodism in Germany." In Wesley As a
World Force, 117-31. See no. 49.

1234. Nuelsen, John Louis. John Wesley and the German Hymn:
A Detailed Study of John Wesley's Translations of Thirty-
three German Hymns. Translated by Theo Perry, Sydney H.
Moore, and Arthur Holbrook. Calverley, Eng.: A. S. Holbrook, 1972. 171p.

1235. Nutter, Charles S. and Wilbur F. Tillett. The Hymns and
Hymn Writers of the Church: An Annotated Edition of the
Methodist Hymnal. New York: Eaton and Mains, 1911.
567p. Contains criticism and historical notes on the hymns
included in the Methodist Hymnal, with brief biographical section on the hymn writers.

1236. Observations on Methodism, and on "The Sunday Service of
the Methodists".... Leeds: T. Harrison, 1840? 8p.

1237. Oden, Thomas C. Introduction to The New Birth, vii-xiv.
San Francisco: Harper and Row, 1984. 113p. This is a
modern edition of five of John Wesley's meditations.

1238. Odgers, J. F. Early Methodism in Camborne: Wesley Chapel,
1828-1958. Camborne: J. F. Odgers, 1960. 151p.

1239. Okely, William. A Letter to Robert Southey, Esq., Poet-
Laureate, etc., on His Life of the Late Mr. John Wesley, and
Especially That Part in Which He Treats of the Moravians.
Bristol, 1820. 55p.

1240. Oliphant, Margaret Oliphant Wilson. "The Reformer [John
Wesley]." In vol. 2 of Historical Sketches of the Reign of
George Second, 3-74. 2 vols. Edinburgh and London: Wil-
liam Blackwood and Sons, 1869. First published in Black-
wood's Magazine 104 (1868): 428-56 and reprinted in
Littell's Living Age 99 (1868): 323-44.

1241. Olmsted, Miles Newell. "John Wesley, the Founder of

Methodism." In Methodism; Its Origin, Progress and Hope; a Centennial Offering, 1-22. Mount Vernon, N.Y., 1884. 32p.

1242. Openshaw, Hannah Cottrell. Gate Pike: The Story of 80 Years' Methodism, 1843-1923. Bolton: Tillotsons, 1924. 303p.

1243. Orcibal, Jean. "The Theological Originality of John Wesley and Continental Spirituality." Chap. 3 in vol. 1 of A History of the Methodist Church in Great Britain, 81-111. See no. 89. First published in Revue Historique, 222 (1959): 51-80.

1244. Ormond, Richard, and Malcolm Rogers, eds. Dictionary of British Portraiture. 4 vols. New York: Oxford University Press, 1979. Vol. 2, p. 220 locates and describes portraits of Charles and John Wesley in museums and art galleries of England.

1245. Osbeck, Kenneth W. Singing with Understanding, Including 101 Favorite Hymn Backgrounds. Grand Rapids, Mich.: Kregel Publications, 1979. 323p. Includes discussions of Charles Wesley's "Jesus, Lover of My Soul," "Christ the Lord Is Risen Today," and "O for a Thousand Tongues."

1246. Osborn, G. Preface to John Wesley's Collection of Psalms and Hymns ... A Collection of Tunes, Set to Music, as They are Commonly Sung at the Foundery.... London: T. Woolmer, 1882. 74p. These are facsimile reprints of the 1727 and 1742 editions.

1247. Osgood, Samuel. "John Wesley and Methodism." In Studies in Christian Biography; or, Hours with Theologians and Reformers, 319-47. New York: C. S. Francis and Co.; Boston: J. H. Francis, 1850. 395p.

1248. Outler, Albert C. "Do Methodists Have a Doctrine of the Church?" Chap. 1 in The Doctrine of the Church, 11-28. See no. 1086.

1249. _____. Evangelism in the Wesleyan Spirit. Nashville: Tidings, 1971. 109p.

1250. _____. Introduction to John Wesley; a Representative Collection of His Writings, 3-39. New York: Oxford University Press, 1964. 516p. (Rev. in no. 2075.)

1251. _____. Introduction to Sermons I 1-33, 1-100. Vol. 1 of The Bicentennial Edition of the Works of John Wesley, Frank Baker, Editor in Chief. Nashville: Abingdon Press, 1984. 722p.

Books

1252. _____. "Methodism's Theological Heritage: A Study in Perspective." In Methodism's Destiny in the Ecumenical Age, edited by Paul Minus, Jr., 44-70. NY: Abingdon, 1969. 208p.

1253. _____. "A New Future for Wesley Studies: An Agenda for 'Phase III.'" Chap. 2 in The Future of the Methodist Theological Traditions, 34-52. See no. 57.

1254. _____. "The Place of Wesley in the Christian Tradition." Chap. 1 in The Place of Wesley in the Christian Tradition, 11-38. See no. 88.

1255. _____. Preface to John and Charles Wesley: Selected Prayers, Hymns, Journal Notes, Sermons, Letters and Treatises, edited with an Introduction by Frank Whaling, xiii-xvii. Classics of Western Spirituality. New York: Paulist Press, 1981. 412p. "This volume shows how their [i.e., the Wesleys'] spiritual roots lay in Orthodox and Roman Catholic as well as Lutheran, Moravian, Church of England, and Puritan sources"--preface.

1256. _____. Theology in the Wesleyan Spirit. Nashville: Tidings, 1975. 101p.

1257. Overton, John Henry. The Church in England. 2 vols. London: Gardner, Darton and Co., 1897. Wesley is discussed in vol. 1, pp. 231-38, 261-65.

1258. _____. The English Church, from the Accession of George I to the End of the 18th Century (1714-1800). Vol. 7 of A History of the English Church, edited by W. R. W. Stevens and William Hunt. London: Macmillan and Co., 1906. 374p. Several chapters in this volume deal almost exclusively with the Wesleys and the Wesleyan movement, but there are references throughout the entire volume to Methodism and Wesley's relationship with the Church of England and the English clergy.

1259. _____. "John Wesley." Chap. 2 in The Evangelical Revival in the Eighteenth Century, 9-29. London: Longmans, Green and Co., 1882. 208p. The rest of the book deals with Methodism and Evangelicalism, delineating the differences in the two groups, and includes brief descriptions of the Evangelical clergy and laity.

1260. _____. John Wesley. Boston and New York: Houghton, Mifflin and Co., 1891. 216p.

1261. _____. John Wesley's Relation to the Church of England.... London: Society for Promoting Christian Knowledge, 18--? 12p.

1262. _____. "Wesley and Fletcher." In Wesley Memorial Volume, 427-34. See no. 257.

1263. Owen, W. R. Methodism in the Hartlepools and Whitby and
       Darlington District, Including the Dales, Yarm, Stockton,
       Darlington, Middlesbrough, Whitby, etc. West Hartlepool:
       Alexander Salton: 1913. 120p.

1264. Page, Isaac E. and John Brash. Scriptural Holiness: As
       Taught by John Wesley. London: C. H. Kelly, 1891. 222p.

1265. Parker, Thomas L. Methodism in Scotland. Knottingley:
       W. S. Hepworth, 1867. 32p.

1266. Parkinson, George Anthony. The People Called Methodists:
       A Short Survey of the History of the Methodist Church.
       London: Methodist Publications, 193- . 128p.

1267. Parlby, William. A Brief Sketch of the Rise of Methodism in
       the County and City of Hereford. Hereford: Adam and
       Sons, 1929. 64p. GtBLW

1268. Parris, John R. John Wesley's Doctrine of the Sacraments.
       London: Epworth Press, 1963. 119p.

1269. Parry, Kenneth Lloyd. Christian Hymns. London: SCM
       Press, 1956. 124p. Includes some discussions on the Wes-
       ley hymns.

1270. Patrick, Millar. "The Great Revival: The Wesleys and
       Their New Song." Chap. 18 in The Story of the Church's
       Song. Richmond, Va.: John Knox Press, 1962. 208p.

1271. Patten, Simon N. "The Moralists." Chap. 4 in The Develop-
       ment of English Thought: A Study in the Economic Interpre-
       tation of History, 191-274. New York and London: Macmil-
       lan Co., 1899. 415p. A discussion of Wesley is included in
       this chapter.

1272. Pattison, Thomas Harwood. "John Wesley." The History of
       Christian Preaching, 255-64. Philadelphia: American Baptist
       Publication Society, 1916. 412p.

1273. Paulson, Ross. "On the Meaning of Faith in the Great
       Awakening and the Methodist Revival." In The Immigration
       of Ideas: Studies in the North Atlantic Community, 1-13.
       Augustana Historical Society Publications, no. 21. Rock Is-
       land, Ill.: The Society, 1968. 214p.

1274. Pawlyn, John S. Bristol Methodism in John Wesley's Day,
       with Monographs of the Early Methodist Preachers. Bristol:
       W. C. Hemmons, 1877. 144p.

1275. Payne, Ernest Alexander. "Revival: Wesley and His

Books   111

Contemporaries." Chap. 5 in The Free Church Tradition in
the Life of England, 72-87. London: SCM Press, 1946.
159p.

1276. Pearce, John. Introduction and Preface to The Wesleys in
Cornwall; Extracts from the Journals of John and Charles
Wesley and John Nelson. Truro, Eng.: D. B. Barton, 1964.
172p.

1277. Peaston, Alexander Elliott. "The Methodists." Chap. 3 in
The Prayer Book Tradition in the Free Churches, 35-65.
London: James Clarke and Co., 1964. 201p.

1278. Peck, George. An Examination of a Tract Entitled "Tracts
for the People, no. 4--Methodism as Held by Wesley. By
D.S.P." New York: Tract Society of the Methodist Episcopal
Church, n.d. 48p. NjMUM

1279. _____. "Theories on the Doctrine of Perfection--Wesleyan
Theories." Lecture 3 in The Scripture Doctrine of Christian
Perfection..., 59-83. New York: Lane and Sandford, 1843.
474p.

1280. Peebles, Isaac Lockhart. "John Wesley's Treatise on the
Meaning and Mode of Water Baptism." Chap. 10 in Water Bap-
tism: Its History, Meaning, Purpose..., 85-90. Nashville:
Methodist Episcopal Church, South, 1901. 128p.

1281. Peet, John B. Station Road Methodist Chapel, Biddulph,
1856-1956. Congleton, 1956. 14p. GtBLW

1282. Peirce, Bradford Kinney. "John Wesley." In The Eminent
Dead: or, The Triumphs of Faith in the Dying Hour, 161-85.
Rev. ed. Louisville: Morton and Griswald, 1850. 512p.

1283. Peirce, William. "The Founder of Methodism," and "The Rise
of Methodism." Chaps. 1 and 2 in The Ecclesiastical Principles and Polity of the Wesleyan Methodists; Comprising a
Full and Impartial Account of All Their Ordinances, Institutions, Laws, Regulations, and General Economy, 1-36. London: Hamilton, Adams, 1854. 668p.

1284. Pellowe, William C. S. "An Appraisal of John Wesley's Sermons." In Three Sermons That Gave Birth to Methodism;
Being Three Representative Sermons..., by John Wesley, 16-
26. Albion, Mich.: Golden Rule Book House, 192-? 55p.

1285. _____. John Wesley, Master in Religion; a Study in
Methods and Attitudes. Nashville: Methodist Episcopal
Church, South, 1939. 151p.

1286. Pelton, Samuel. Absurdities of Methodism. New York:
       E. Bliss and E. White, 1822. 268p.

1287. Penman, George. "Class Meetings." In I Remember, 140-
       48. London: C. H. Kelly, 1916. 186p.

1288. Perkins, E. Benson. Charles Wesley; a Short Life. Lon-
       don: Epworth Press, 1957. [6p.]

1289. _____. Methodist Preaching Houses and the Law; the
       Story of the Model Deed. Wesley Historical Society Lectures,
       no. 18. London: Epworth Press, 1952. 94p.

1290. Perkins, Harold William. "The Attitude of John Wesley."
       In The Doctrine of Christian or Evangelical Perfection, 206-
       11. London: Epworth Press, 1927. 298p. Originally pre-
       sented as the author's thesis, University of London.

1291. Perry, George Gresley. "The Revival Movement, 1727-1772."
       Chap. 4 in vol. 3 of A History of the English Church, 60-
       124. 2d ed. 3 vols. London: John Murray, 1890.

1292. Persons Who Are Ignorant of John Wesley's Real Opinion of
       the Church, May Gather It from This Methodist Remembrancer.
       2d ed. Leeds: T. Harrison, 1844. 4p.

1293. Peters, John Leland. Christian Perfection and American
       Methodism. New York: Abingdon Press, 1956. 252p. "This
       study is the result of a desire to discover certain facts about
       John Wesley's doctrine of Christian Perfection and in particular
       to learn what happened to it in the years following Wesley's
       death"--preface.

1294. Pfatteicher, Helen Emma. "Charles Wesley." In Every Cor-
       ner Sing, 98-101. Philadelphia: Muhlenberg Press, 1954.
       214p.

1295. Philalethes. [Pseud.]. A Character of the Late Rev. John
       Wesley ... with Various Other Essays.... Otley: W. Walker,
       1822. 36p.

1296. Phillips, Charles Stanley. "The Methodist and Evangelical
       Movements." Chap. 8 in Hymnody Past and Present, 171-
       97. London: Society for Promoting Christian Knowledge;
       New York: Macmillan Co., 1937. 300p.

1297. Phillips, Randall C. Irish Methodism. London: C. H. Kelly,
       1897. 107p.

1298. Pierce, George F. "Wesley as an Itinerant." In Wesley Me-
       morial Volume, 285-93. See no. 257.

1299. Pierce, Lorne Albert. Primitive Methodism and the New
       Catholicism. Ryerson Essays, no. 26. Toronto: Methodist
       Book and Publishing House, 1923. 70p. Has tried to show
       how "Methodism brings religion back to the primitive sim-
       plicity of the first Church by its emphasis upon practical
       spiritual values"--the promise of John Wesley.

1300. Pierce, T. R. The Intellectual Side of John Wesley. Nash-
       ville: Methodist Episcopal Church Publishing House, 1897?
       19p. NcD

1301. Piette, Maximin. John Wesley in the Evolution of Protestant-
       ism. Translated by J. B. Howard. New York: Sheed and
       Ward, 1937. 569p.

1302. Pike, Godfrey Holden. John Wesley: The Man and His Mis-
       sion. London: The Religious Tract Society, 1904. 190p.

1303. _____. Wesley and His Preachers, Their Conquest of
       Britain. London: T. F. Unwin, 1903. 309p.

1304. Pilkington, James Penn. The Methodist Publishing House;
       a History. Nashville, Abingdon Press, 1968. The first part
       of this book is devoted to John Wesley and publishing.

1305. Pilkington, W. Flashes of Preston Methodism: In Celebration
       of the Jubilee of Wesley Circuit, Preston, 1916. Preston:
       Lambert Bros., 1916. 63p.

1306. _____. The Makers of Wesleyan Methodism in Preston; and
       the Relation of Methodism to the Temperance and Teetotal
       Movements, Adventure, Enterprise, and Noble Deeds of Pres-
       ton Methodist Celebrities. London, 1890. 275p.

1307. Pinfold, James T. "Wesley's Influence in New Zealand."
       In Wesley As a World Force, 109-16. See no. 49.

1308. The Pious Life and the Heavenly Death of the Late Rev. John
       Wesley. London, 1791.

1309. Platt, Frederic. The Theology of the "Warmed Heart," a
       Meditation. Wesley Bi-Centenary Manuals, no. 8. London:
       Epworth Press, 1938. 27p.

1310. Plumb, John Harold. "John Wesley and the Road to Salvation."
       Part 2, Chap. 3 in England in the Eighteenth Century, 91-97.
       Harmondsworth, Middlesex: Penguin Books, 1950. 224p.

1311. Plummer, Alfred. The Church of England in the Eighteenth
       Century. Handbook of English Church History, 6. London:
       Methuen and Co., 1910. 248p.

1312. Pocock, W. W. A Sketch of the History of Wesleyan-Method-
       ism in Some of the Southern Counties of England. London:
       Wesleyan-Methodist Book-Room, 1885. 79p.
       Brief notes on
       Wesley's visits to Hants, Surray, Berks, Isle of Wight, Wilts,
       and Sussex counties.

1313. Podmore, Frank. "John Wesley and the Epworth Poltergeist."
       In vol. 1 of Modern Spiritualism: A History and a Criticism,
       32-39. 2 vols. London: Methuen and Co., 1902.

1314. Poling, David. "About John Wesley." Chap. 3 in The Wis-
       dom of Martin Luther. The Wisdom of John Calvin. The
       Wisdom of John Wesley, 89-100. New Canaan, Conn.: Keats
       Publishing, 1973. 145p. The book contains a chapter about
       each man, followed by brief extracts from his writings.

1315. Pollard, Hazel. John Wesley in Northumberland. Theological
       Occasional Papers, n.s., no. 12. London: Society for
       Promoting Christian Knowledge, 1949. 23p.

1316. Ponsonby, Arthur. "John Wesley." In English Diaries; a
       Review of English Diaries from the Sixteenth to the Twentieth
       Century, 156-63. London: Methuen, 1923. A description of
       Wesley's diaries and journals. It is the author's opinion that
       they are of interest to Methodists but lack appeal for the
       ordinary reader.

1317. The Popery of Methodism; or, The Enthusiasm of Papists and
       Wesleyans Compared.... Leeds: T. Harrison, 1839. 24p.
       Extracts of Wesley's writings are compared with Catholic doc-
       trine.

1318. Porter, James. A Compendium of Methodism.... New York:
       Phillips and Hunt, 1875. 506p.

1319. _____. A Comprehensive History of Methodism, Embracing
       Origin, Progress, and Present Spiritual, Educational, and
       Benevolent Status in All Lands. Cincinnati: Hitchcock and
       Walden, 1876. 601p. Chaps. 1-8 tell the Wesley story.

1320. Potter, Charles Francis. "Wesley (1703-1791) Who Revived
       Religion in England." Chap. 16 in The Story of Religion As
       Told in the Lives of Its Leaders, 471-90. Garden City, N.Y.:
       Garden City Publishing Co., 1929. 627p.

1321. Potts, James Henry. "The Principal Founder." In Back to
       Oxford, a Search for the Essentials of Methodism, 19-31.
       New York: Eaton and Mains; Cincinnati: Jennings and Pye,
       1903. 243p.

1322. Potts, John. "John Wesley and His Mother." In Wesley
       Memorial Volume, 361-72. See no. 257.

1323   Powell, Jessie. John Wesley. London: Lutterworth Press, 1947. 32p.

1324. Powell, Lyman Pierson. "John Wesley." In Heavenly Heretics, 31-56. New York and London: G. P. Putnam's Sons, 1909. 139p. "The chapters which make up this little volume, after finding expression in the pulpit, appeared at weekly intervals in the pages of the Hampshire Gazette"--preface.

1325. Pratt, Alfred Camden. Black Country Methodism. London: C. H. Kelly, 1891. 174p.

1326. Prescott, C. J. John Wesley, a Lecture Delivered before the Lincoln Guild, Sydney. Sydney, Australia: Epworth Printing and Publishing House, 1898. 39p. NjMUM

1327. Pressly, I. P. "John Wesley." In A York Miscellany, Compiled from Records of the Past Four Centuries, 213-19. London and Hull: A. Brown, 1938. 269p.

1328. Price, Carl Fowler. "Charles Wesley's Brogue." Curiosities of the Hymnal, 44-49. New York and Cincinnati: Methodist Book Concern, 1926. 84p.

1329. _____. More Hymn Stories. New York: Abingdon Press, 1929. 115p. Many of Charles Wesley's hymns are discussed.

1330. _____. The Music and Hymnody of the Methodist Hymnal. New York: Eaton and Mains; Cincinnati: Jennings and Graham, 1911. 296p. Contains many references to both Wesleys.

1331. _____. One Hundred and One Hymn Stories. New York: Abingdon Press, 1923. 112p. Six of the hymn stories are about hymns by Charles Wesley; one by Samuel, his father.

1332. _____. One Hundred and One Methodist Stories. New York and Cincinnati: Methodist Book Concern, 1938. 111p. Seventeen of the brief stories are about the Wesleys.

1333. Priestly, Joseph. The History and Present State of Electricity, with Other Original Experiments. 5th ed. London: J. Johnson, 1794. 641p. Contains a brief discussion of Wesley's use of electricity in healing, pp. 356-57.

1334. Prince, Henry Herbert. The Romance of Early Methodism in and around West Bromwich and Wednesbury. West Bromwich, 1925. 92p.

1335. Prince, John Wesley. "John Wesley, Founder of Methodism." In Founders of Christian Movements, edited by Philip Henry Lotz. New York: Association Press, 1941. 160p.

1336. _____. "Susannah Wesley, Noble Mother." In Women
Leaders, edited by Philip Henry Lotz, 118-26. New York:
Association Press, 1940. 149p.

1337. _____. Wesley on Religious Education; a Study of John
Wesley's Theories and Methods of the Education of Children
in Religion. New York and Cincinnati: Methodist Book
Concern, 1926. 164p. His dissertation, Yale University,
1924.

1338. Pritchard, Frank Cyril. "John Wesley's Education Theory,"
and "John Wesley's Own Contribution." Chaps. 1 and 2 in
Methodist Secondary Education, 11-58. London: Epworth
Press, 1949. 351p.

1339. Probert, John Charles Cripps. Methodism in Redruth until
the Death of John Wesley. [Redruth, Eng., 1965.] 33p.

1340. _____. The Sociology of Cornish Methodism to the Present
Day. Occasional Publication of the Cornish Methodist Historical Association, no. 17. Redruth: Cornish Methodist Historical Association, 1971. 86p. A revision of the author's earlier
book entitled An Introduction to the Sociology of Cornish
Methodism, 1964.

1341. Programme of the Celebration of the Bi-centenary of the Birth
of John Wesley, at Epworth, on June 17, 1903. Epworth:
Barnes and Breeze; Lincoln, J. W. Ruddoch, 1903. Contains
some excerpts from John Wesley's Journal, pictures of the Epworth Church and rectory, and other Wesleyana. NjMUM

1342. Pudney, John. John Wesley and His World. New York:
Scribner, 1978. 128p. See also no. 4563.

1343. Punshon, William Morley. "Wesley and His Literature." In
Wesley Memorial Volume, 310-28. See no. 257.

1344. _____. Wesley and His Times. London: T. Woolmer,
1884. 48p. Translated into Swedish (1891) and Italian
(1881).

1345. Purefoy, George Washington. History of Episcopal Methodism
.... Chapel Hill, 1858. 47p.

1346. Pyke, Richard. John Wesley Came This Way. London: Epworth Press, 1938. 159p.

1347. _____. "John Wesley in America." Chap. 2 in The Dawn
of American Methodism, 21-32. London: Epworth Press,
1933. 184p.

1348. Quick, William Abraham. Methodism; a Parallel. London:
       T. Woolmer, 1889. 200p. The author's purpose is to show
       that the Methodist Church is truly apostolic. He compares
       England to Palestine, the early Methodist preachers to the
       Apostles, the persecution of the Methodists to that of the
       early Christians.

1349. Rack, Henry D. "Doctors, Demons and Early Methodist His-
       tory." In The Church and Healing..., 137-52. See no.
       1098.

1350. _____. The Future of John Wesley's Methodism. Ecumenical
       Studies in History, no. 2. London: Lutterworth, 1965. 80p.

1351. Railton, George Scott. The Story of John Wesley, the Saved
       Clergyman, Who Was Turned Out of Church.... London:
       Salvation Army Headquarters, 1882. 32p.

1352. Rainy, Principal. "Characteristics of Wesley and His Teach-
       ing." In Wesley, the Man, His Teaching and His Work, 91-
       107. See no. 357.

1353. Rall, Harris Franklin. "The Search for Perfection." In
       Methodism, 139-47. See no. 287.

1354. _____. Was John Wesley a Premillennialist? Toronto:
       Methodist Book and Publishing House, 1921. 12p. IEG

1355. Ramage, Ian. Battle for the Free Mind. London: Allen
       and Unwin, 1967. 269p. A rejection of William Sargant's
       interpretation of John Wesley's work as a form of brainwash-
       ing.

1356. Ratcliff, Nora. Preface to The Journal of John Wesley,
       7-22. Abridged ed. London and New York: Thomas Nelson
       and Sons, Ltd., 1940. 463p.

1357. Ratnayaka, Shanta. Two Ways of Perfection: Buddhist and
       Christian. Colombo: Lake House Investments, 1978. 180p.

1358. Rattenbury, John Ernest. "Balanced Worship." Chap. 3 in
       Vital Elements of Public Worship, 68-89. London: Epworth
       Press, 1954. 176p. The author states that Wesley's was an
       example of balanced worship--balance between institutional
       worship and worship by the individual. He comments on Wes-
       ley's sacramental and corporate worship.

1359. _____. The Conversion of the Wesleys; a Critical Study.
       London: Epworth Press, 1938. 243p.

1360. _____. The Eucharistic Hymns of John and Charles Wesley

to Which is Appended Wesley's Preface Extracted from
Brevint's "Christian Sacrament and Sacrifice," Together with
Hymns on the Lord's Supper. London: Epworth Press,
1948.   253p.

1361.   _____. The Evangelical Doctrines of Charles Wesley's
Hymns. London: Epworth Press, 1941.   365p.

1362.   _____. "The Evangelical Sacrament."   Chap. 8 in Thoughts
on Holy Communion, 84-96. London: Epworth Press, 1958.
108p.

1363.   _____. John Wesley and Social Service.   Social Tracts for
the Times, n.s., no. 2. London: C. H. Kelly, n.d.   19p.

1364.   _____. Wesley's Legacy to the World: Six Studies in the
Permanent Values of the Evangelical Revival. Nashville:
Cokesbury Press, 1928.   309p.

1365. Ray, George H.   A Sermon on the Influence of the Teachings
and Work of John Wesley.   [Richmond, Va.:   Hasker and
Marcuse, 1891.]   18p.

1366. Rayner, Edward C.   The Story of the Christian Community
1685-1909; a Notable Record of Christian Labour in London
Workhouses and Lodging Houses. London: Memorial Hall,
1909.   127p.

1367. Read, William.   "Family of Wesley."   In Read's History of the
Isle of Axholme; Its Manors and Parishes: Biographical
Notices of Eminent Men, edited by Thomas C. Fletcher, 153-
225. Epworth: Read and Co., Printers, 1858.   452p.
GtBMM

1368. A Recall to Methodism. London and Southampton: Camelot
Press, 1938.   15p.

1368a. Redd, Alexander.   Problem of Methodism Reviewed; or, John
Wesley and the Methodist Standards Defended.   Mt. Sterling,
Ky.:   Advocate Publishing Co., 1893.   99p.

1369. Reddish, Robert O.   John Wesley, His Way of Knowing God.
Evergreen, Colo.:   Rorge Publishing Co., [1972].   123p.
NjMUM

1370. Reed, Charles.   "Wesley and Sunday Schools."   In Wesley
Memorial Volume, 329-34. See no. 257.

1371. Rees, Allen.   The Burning of "Old City Road"; a Sermon
Preached ... in the Canning Town Wesleyan Chapel, ...
December 14, 1879. London: Wesleyan Conference Office,
18--?   27p.

1372. Reese, Edward. The Life and Ministry of John Wesley, 1703-
       1791. Christian Hall of Fame Series, no. 21. Glenwood, Ill.:
       Fundamental Publishers, 1975. 15p.

1373. Reeves, Jeremiah Bascom. "The Period of the Wesleys."
       Chap. 6 in The Hymn as Literature, 161-214. New York and
       London: Century Co., 1924. 369p.

1374. Remarks on Several Passages in the Works of the Late Rev.
       John Wesley: Being a Brief Description of What Is Called
       "The Old Plan"; and of Mr. Wesley's Sentiments Concerning
       a Christian Church. Bristol: R. Edwards, 1794. 12p.

1375. Remsburg, John Eleazer. Paine and Wesley. The Image
       Breaker, no. 5. New York: Truth Seeker Co., 1900? 12p.

1376. The Rev. John Wesley and His Friends at Oxford; the Origin
       of the Great Revival in the Last Century, Painted by Mar-
       shall Claxton. Manchester: Thomas Agnew, 1860. 14p.
       Describes the painting by Marshall Claxton. IEG

1377. Reverand Doctor Wesley's Dream, Being an Apology for His
       Fall, and His Late Pamphlet, etc. Also His Disciples Address
       in Consequence of His Dream, and Admonitions. N.p. 1792.
       23p. NN

1378. Reynolds, Arthur. "The Wesleys." In English Sects: An
       Historical Handbook, 68-95. London: A. R. Mowbray, 1921.
       244p.

1379. Reynolds, John. Anecdotes of the Rev. John Wesley. Leeds:
       H. Cullingworth, 1828. 57p. Contains 77 brief anecdotes
       about Wesley, a few taken from his own writings, a few from
       the author's own friends, but most of them the author heard
       from Wesley himself or was himself acquainted with the cir-
       cumstances. IEG

1380. Reynolds, John Stewart. "The Awakening, 1735-1744," and
       "The Revival, 1744-1768." Chaps. 1 and 2 in The Evangeli-
       cals at Oxford, 1735-1871; a Record of an Unchronicled Move-
       ment, 5-21, 22-42. Oxford: Basil Blackwell, 1953. 212p.

1381. Rice, Merton S. "The Aldersgate Evangel." Chap. 7 in What
       Happened at Aldersgate, 103-14. See no. 342.

1382. Richardson, Harry V. "The Beginnings of Methodism."
       Chap. 1 in Dark Salvation: The Story of Methodism as It
       Developed among Blacks in America, 1-13. Garden City,
       N.Y.: Doubleday, 1976. 324p.

1383. Rigg, James H. The Churchmanship of John Wesley, and the

Relations of Wesleyan Methodism to the Church of England.
London: Wesleyan Conference Office, 1878. 120p.

1384. _____. "John Wesley." In Champions of the Truth: Short
Lives of Christian Leaders in Thought and Action. See no.
715.

1385. _____. John Wesley, the Church of England and Wesleyan
Methodism. Their Relation to Each Other Clearly and Fully
Explained....New ed. London: Wesleyan Methodist Bookroom,
1893. 43p.

1386. _____. The Living Wesley, As He Was in His Youth and in
His Prime. New York: Nelson and Phillips, 1874. 269p.

1387. _____. "The Puritan Ancestors and High-Church Parents
of the Wesleys: A Sketch and Study, 1630-1750." In Essays
for the Times: On Ecclesiastical and Social Subjects, 106-69.
London: E. Stock, 1866. 532p.

1388. _____. The Relations of John Wesley and Wesleyan Methodism to the Church of England, Investigated and Determined.
London: Longmans, Green and Co., 1868. 63p.

1389. _____. "Wesley and the Church of England." In Wesley
Memorial Volume, 76-97. See no. 257.

1390. _____. "Wesley the Preacher." In Wesley Memorial Volume,
268-84. See no. 257.

1391. _____. "The Wesleyan Controversy:" Correspondence between James H. Rigg ... and H. W. Holden.... London:
Church Press Co., 1869. 30p.

1392. _____. "Wesleyan Methodism." Part 5 of A Comparative
View of Church Organizations, Primitive and Protestant,
205-36. 2d ed. London: C. H. Kelly, 1891. 348p.

1393. Riggin, John H. Lectures on the Origin and History of
Methodism and What Methodism Stands for. Warren, Ark.:
Democrat News, [1907]. 29p.

1394. Ritchie, Elizabeth. Authentic Narrative of the Life, Together
with the Circumstances Relative to the Departure of the Late
Rev. John Wesley. Birmingham: T. P. Trimer, 1791. 23p.
Numerous accounts of Wesley's death were published by this
author.

1395. Ritson, Joseph. "Of Its Revival." Chap. 12 in The Romance
of Non-Conformity, 145-59. London: W. A. Hammond, 1910.
352p. Tells the story of Wesley and the Methodist movement.

1396. Ritson, Thomas Nicholson. The Story of a Century: The
       History of Wesleyan Methodism in the Ipswich Circuit: A
       Romance of Progress. London: Wyman and Sons, 1908.
       166p. GtBLW

1397. Rivers, Isabel. "Dissenting and Methodist Books of Practical
       Divinity." Chap. 6 in Books and Their Readers in Eighteenth
       Century England, edited by Isabel Rivers, 127-64. New York:
       St. Martins Press, 1982. 267p.

1398. _____. "'Strangers and Pilgrims': Sources and Patterns of
       Methodist Narrative." In Augustan Worlds, edited by J. C.
       Hilson, M. M. B. Jones and J. R. Watson, 189-203. Leices-
       ter: Leicester University Press; New York: Harper and
       Rowe, 1978. 311p. Discusses the early Methodist preachers,
       and the demands made by Wesley on their intellectual de-
       velopment and personal lives.

1399. Roberts, Edward Whitford. John Wesley in Monmouthshire.
       Free Churches in Monmouthshire. Abersychan, 1965. 12p.

1400. Roberts, Herbert E. Dudley Hill Wesleyan Chapel Centenary.
       1823-1923. Kirkgate, Bradford, Eng.: William Byles and
       Son, 1923. 61p.

1401. Roberts, Richard. History of Methodism in Almondbury.
       London: H. J. Tresidder, 1864. 40p.

1402. Roberts, Richard Ellis. "John Wesley." In Reading for
       Pleasure and Other Essays, 148-57. London: Methuen,
       1928. 245p.

1403. Robinson, David. The Priest, Calvin and Wesley, an Inquiry
       into the Present State of Religion in America.... New York:
       Lange, Little and Hillman, 1872. 443p.

1404. Robinson, John Ryley. Notes on Early Methodism in Dews-
       bury, Birstal, and Neighbourhood. Batley: J. Fearnsides,
       1900. 171p.

1405. Rockledge, J. Memorials of Early Methodism in the Easing-
       wold Circuit. London: Hayman Bros., and Lilly, 1872.
       99p. Preface signed J. R. Authorship ascribed by Dr.
       Frank Baker.

1406. Rodda, Richard. A Discourse Delivered at the Chapel in
       Oldham-Street, Manchester, March 13th, 1791, on Occasion
       of the Death of the Rev. John Wesley, A.M. Manchester:
       J. Radford, 1791. 28p.

1407. _____. A Reply [by R. Rodda, J. Bakewell, etc.] to a

Hand-Bill, Said to Be Written by Dr. Whitehead [Justifying His "True Narrative" of the Circumstances Connected with His Undertaking the Publishing of a Life of Wesley]: Signed by G. Cussens, J. Milburne, etc. London, 1792. 11p.

1408. Rogal, Samuel J. John and Charles Wesley. Twayne's English Authors Series, TEAS 368. Boston: Twayne Publishers, 1983. 178p.

1409. Rogers, James. Some Account of the Last Sickness and Death of the Rev. John Wesley.... Philadelphia: P. Hall, 1791.

1410. Rogers, James A. John Wesley and Congregational Singing. Evanston, 1968. 46p.

1411. Roosevelt, Franklin Delano. "Two hundredth Anniversary of Wesley's Birth." In Wesley Studies, 233-37. See no. 257.

1412. Rose, Delbert R. "Aldersgate and Wesley's Inner Life," "Aldersgate Made Wesley an Evangelist," and "Aldersgate Set Wesley on Fire for God." Chaps. 3-5 in Methodism's Aldersgate Heritage, 23-42. See no. 62.

1413. _____. "Christian Perfection--Not Sinless Perfection." In Insights into Holiness..., 107-28. See no. 61.

1414. _____. "The Wesleyan Understanding of Sin." In The Distinctive Emphases of Asbury Theological Seminary, 7-30. See no. 983.

1415. Rose, Edward Alan. Methodism in Ashton-under-Lyne. Ashton-under-Lyne: E. A. Rose, 1967. 43p.

1416. Rose, Samuel P. The Genius of Methodism. Ryerson Essays, no. 12. Toronto: Ryerson Press, 1923. 15p. A discussion of John Wesley's role in the contribution of Methodism to the doctrinal and spiritual development of the Christian Church.

1417. Ross, Frederick Augustus. The Doctrine of the Direct Witness of the Spirit as Taught by the Rev. John Wesley Shown to be Unscriptural, False, Fanatical and of Mischievous Tendency. Philadelphia: Perkins and Purves, 1846. 108p.

1418. Rosser, James. A History of Wesleyan Methodism in the Isle of Man: With Some Account of the Island.... London: Mary A. Quiggin, 1849. 207p.

1419. Rosser, Leonidas. "Origin of Class Meetings." Part 1, Chap. 1 in Class Meetings: Embracing Their Origin, Nature, Obligation and Benefit..., 37-46. 2d ed. Richmond, Va.: L. Johnson Co., 1855. 365p.

1420. Routley, Erik. "Charles Wesley and His Family." In A Pano-
       rama of Christian Hymnody, 25-32. Collegeville, Mn.: Litur-
       gical Press, 1979. 259p.

1421. _____. "Evangelical Revival and Methodism." In English
       Religious Dissent, 145-52. Cambridge: Cambridge University
       Press, 1960. 213p.

1422. _____. Hymns and the Faith. Greenwich, Conn.: Sea-
       bury Press, 1956. 311p. Contains essays on five of the best
       known Wesley hymns.

1423. _____. Hymns Today and Tomorrow. New York and Nash-
       ville: Abingdon Press, 1964. 205p. Includes discussion of
       two of Charles Wesley's hymns--"Come, O Thou Traveler,"
       and "Love Divine."

1424. _____. "John Wesley." In The Gift of Conversion, 23-27.
       Philadelphia: Muhlenberg Press, 1958. 144p.

1425. _____. The Musical Wesleys. New York: Oxford Univer-
       sity Press, 1968. 272p. (Rev. in no. 3667.)

1426. _____. "Watts and Wesley." In Hymns and Human Life,
       63-74. London: J. Murray, 1952. 346p.

1427. Rowe, G. Stringer. "Wesley's Dilemma." In Wesley Studies,
       127-30. See no. 190.

1428. Rowe, Gilbert Theodore. The Meaning of Methodism; a Study
       in Christian Religion. Nashville: Cokesbury Press, 1926.
       234p.

1429. Rowe, Henry Kalloch. "John Wesley." In Modern Pathfinders
       of Christianity; the Lives and Deeds of Seven Centuries of
       Christian Leaders, 114-25. New York and Chicago: Fleming
       H. Revell Co., 1928. 253p.

1430. Rowe, Kenneth E. "Editor's Introduction: The Search for
       the Historical Wesley." In The Place of Wesley in the Chris-
       tian Tradition, 1-10. See no. 88.

1431. Roy, James. Catholicity and Methodism; or, The Relation of
       John Wesley to Modern Thought. Montreal: Burland-
       Desbarats Lithographic Co., 1877. 109p.

1432. Runyon, Theodore. "Introduction: Wesley and the Theologies
       of Liberation." In Sanctification and Liberation, 9-48. See
       no. 191.

1433. Rupp, Ernest Gordon. "The Holy Communion in the Methodist

Church." In The Holy Communion: A Symposium, edited
by Hugh Martin, 113-26. London: SCM Press, Ltd., 1947.
127p.

1434.   . Introductory Essay in vol. 1 of A History of the
Methodist Church in Great Britain, xi-xl. See no. 89.

1435.   . "John Wesley: Christian Prophet." In Prophets
in the Church, edited by Roger Aubert, 45-56. Concilium,
vol. 37. New York: Paulist Press, 1968. 152p.

1436.   . "Methodists, Anglicans and Orthodox." In We
Belong to One Another: Methodists, Anglicans and Orthodox
Essays, edited by A. M. Allchin, 13-29. See no. 43.

1436a.   . "Paul and Wesley." In De Dertiende apostel en
het elfde gebod, edited by G. C. Berkouwer and H. A. Ober-
man, 102-10. Kampen: J. H. Kok, 1971. 200p.

1437.   . The Plant of Salvation [with Particular Reference
to the Doctrine of John Wesley]. N.p. 1982. A lecture to
the Friends of Wesley's Chapel, given on May 27, 1982, at
Wesley's Chapel.

1438.   . "Son of Samuel: John Wesley, Church of England
Man." Chap. 2 in The Place of Wesley in the Christian
Tradition, 11-38. See no. 88.

1439. Rusling, James Fowler. John Wesley and Methodism ... an
Address at State Street M.E. Church, Trenton, N.J., June
28, 1903. Trenton, N.J.: MacCrellish and Quigley, 1903.
14p. NcD

1440. Russell, Phillips. "Death of Certainty." In Glittering Century, 113-34. New York and London: Scribner, 1936.
326p. Describes John Wesley's activities and influence in the
eighteenth century.

1441. Russell, Samuel J. Historical Notes of Wesleyan Methodism in
the Rotherham Circuit. Rotherham: H. Garnett, 1910. 138p.

1442. Rutledge, Edward. "... Containing Some Account of the
Methodists." In History of the Church of England, from the
Earliest Periods to the Present Time, 288-94. Middletown,
Conn.: E. and H. Clark, 1825. 310p.

1443. Ryle, John Charles. "John Wesley and His Ministry." In
The Christian Leaders of the Last Century; or, England a
Hundred Years Ago, 64-105. London and New York: T.
Nelson and Sons, 1869. 432p.

1444. Sack, K. H. "John Wesley." In Lives of the Leaders of Our
       Church Universal, from the Days of the Successors of the
       Apostles to the Present Time..., 516-25. Pittsburgh: United
       Presbyterian Board of Publication, 1879. An abridged version
       appeared in the Wesleyan Methodist Magazine 103 (1880):
       739-44.

1445. Sackett, A. Barrett. Kingswood School and John Wesley,
       Educator. Nashville: Board of Education, The Methodist
       Church, 1960. 8p. NjMUM

1446. Sakakibara, Gan. "A Study of John Wesley's Economic
       Ethics." In Japanese Contributions to the Study of John
       Wesley, 56-68. See no. 643.

1447. Sampson, George. The Century of Divine Songs. Proceed-
       ings of the British Academy, vol. 29. London: H. Milford,
       1943? 28p. Discusses the great English hymn writers of the
       eighteenth century.

1448. Sangster, Paul. "Toleration, Decline and Revival." Chap. 6
       in A History of the Free Churches, 110-40. London: Heine-
       mann, 1983. 216p.

1449. Sangster, Paul Edwin. Pity My Simplicity: The Evangelical
       Revival and the Religious Education of Children, 1738-1800.
       London: Epworth Press, 1963. 200p. Revision of thesis,
       University of Oxford.

1450. Sangster, W. E. Path of Perfection: An Examination and Re-
       statement of John Wesley's Doctrine of Christian Perfection.
       London: Hodder and Stoughton, 1943. 211p. His disserta-
       tion, University of London, 1942.

1451. Sargant, William Walter. The Battle of the Mind: A Physi-
       ology of Conversion and Brainwashing. Garden City, N.Y.:
       Doubleday, 1957. 263p. The author equates evangelism and
       conversion with brainwashing--manipulation of susceptible men
       through fear and excitement. Sargant says "Wesley changed
       the religious and social life of England for the better with the
       help of such methods." States it is the ordinary man who is
       most susceptible to this reconditioning process.

1452. Sargent, George Etell. The Oxford Methodist; or, The Early
       Life of John Wesley. London: Benjamin L. Green, 1850.

1453. Sauer, Charles A. A Pocket Story of John Wesley. Nash-
       ville: Tidings, 1967. 104p.

1454. Scharpff, Paulus. "Evangelistic Movements of the Eighteenth
       Century." Chap. 3 in History of Evangelism: Three Hundred

Years of Evangelism in Germany, Great Britain, and the
United States of America, 32-84. Grand Rapids, Mich.:
William B. Eerdmans Publishing Co., 1966. 373p.

1455. Schilling, Sylvester Paul. "John Wesley's Theology of Salvation." Pt. 1, Chap. 2 in Methodism and Society in Theological Perspective, 44-64. Methodism and Society, vol. 3.
Nashville: Abingdon Press, 1960. 318p.

1456. Schmidt, Martin. John Wesley; a Theological Biography.
Translated by Norman P. Goldhawk. 2 vols. N.Y.: Abingdon Press, 1963-73.

1457. _____. "Wesley's Place in Church History." Chap. 3 in
The Place of Wesley in the Christian Tradition, 67-93. See
no. 88.

1458. _____. The Young Wesley; Missionary and Theologican of
Missions. Translated by L. A. Fletcher. London: Epworth
Press, 1958. 48p.

1459. Schofield, Charles Edwin. Aldersgate and After. New York
and Cincinnati: Methodist Book Concern, 1937. 52p.

1460. _____. "The Fruit of the Evangelical Revival." Chap. 1
in We Methodists, 7-20. New York: Methodist Publishing
House, 1939. 135p.

1461. Scholes, Lilian Lelean. "John Wesley Gives the Shoe Buckles."
Chap. 3 in John Wesley's Silver Buckles: a Cornish Saga, 9-
13. Melbourne: Aldersgate Press, 1967. 31p. NjMUM

1462. Schwab, Ralph Kendall. Christian Perfection in the Evangelical Association. Menasha, Wis.: George Banta Publishing
Co., 1922. 153p. His dissertation, University of Chicago,
1920.

1463. Scott, Abraham. The Results of an Inquiry, Instituted with
a View to Ascertain, How Far the Late Rev. R. Watson Agrees
with the Scriptures, in His Notion of Justification by Faith
Alone: and Likewise, Whether He Has Properly Stated the
Rev. J. Wesley's Opinion on This Subject. London: R.
Groombridge, 1836. 76p.

1464. Scott, Orange. The Grounds of Secession from the Methodist
Episcopal Church. 1851. Reprint. New York: Arno Press
and The New York Times, 1969. 229p. In addition to Wesley's Thoughts upon Slavery, it includes discussions on Wesley's attitudes toward episcopacy and slavery.

1465. Scrutator [pseud.] The Third Appearance of Wesley's Ghost.
London: Grattan, 1849. RPB

1466. _____. Wesley's Ghost and Whitfield's [sic] Apparition.
London: James Gilbert, 1846. 12p.

1467. Scudder, Moses Lewis. "The True Origin of Methodism,"
"Wesley and His Assistants," and "How Wesleyan Methodism
Was Constructed." Chaps. 2-4 in American Methodism, 23-
121. Hartford, Conn.: S. S. Scranton and Co., 1867.
592p. Another telling of the Wesley story and the introduction of Methodism to America.

1468. Seed, Thomas Alexander. Norfolk Street Wesleyan Chapel,
Sheffield; Being a History of This Famous Sanctuary, Together with an Account of the Earlier and Later History of
Methodism in the Town and Neighborhood. London: Jarrold
and Sons, 1907. 327p.

1469. [Seeley, Robert Benton.] The Life of John Wesley, Fellow
of Lincoln College, Oxford, and Founder of the Society of
Methodists. London: Seeley, Jackson, and Halliday, 1856.
277p.

1470. Selbie, W. B. Non-conformity: Its Origin and Progress,
174-88. Home University Library of Modern Knowledge.
London: Williams and Norgate, 1912. 256p. A brief discussion of Wesley's work in the Revival.

1471. _____. "The Revival." Chap. 10 in English Sects: A
History of Nonconformity, 171-98. London: Williams and
Norgate; New York: Henry Holt, 1912. 256p. Much of
this chapter is about John Wesley.

1472. _____. "What We May Learn from Wesley." Chap. 1 in
Wesley As a World Force..., 9-18. See no. 49.

1473. Selecman, Charles Claude. The Methodist Primer. Nashville:
Tidings Press, 1944. 55p. A concise account of the story of
Methodism written for Methodists.

1474. _____. "The Need of Aldersgate in Modern Life." Chap.
10 in What Happened at Aldersgate, 145-57. See no. 342.

1475. Sell, Alan P. F. The Great Debate: Calvinism, Arminianism
and Salvation. Grand Rapids, Mich.: Baker Book House,
1983. 141p.

1476. Semmel, Bernard. The Methodist Revolution. New York:
Basic Books, 1973. 273p. Semmel argues that the Methodist
Revival was a revolution itself, and was probably a decisive
force in shaping nineteenth century England. Wesley's role
in this process is defined.

1477. Semmens, Bernard L. "John Wesley, 1744-1791," and "Wesley and the National Church." Chaps. 1 and 2 in The Conferences After Wesley: An Attempt to Keep the Record Straight; a Study of the Basic Documents of Early Methodism, 15-26. Melbourne: National Press, 1971. 106p.

1478. Senior, Maud Mary. John Wesley. The African Home Library, no. 78. London: Sheldon Press, 1946. 16p.

1479. Shantz, Ward M. "John Wesley's Teaching on Christian Perfection." In Insights into Holiness..., 131-42. See no. 61.

1480. Sharp, Douglas S. A Brief Sketch of Methodism in Heptonstall, to Commemorate the 150th Anniversary of the Chapel, July 4th, 1914, Hebden Bridge, Waddingtons, 1914. N.p., n.d. 20p. GtBLW

1481. Shaw, George. "Methodism." In Old Grimsby, 231-38. London: William Andrews and Co., 1897. 261p. Brief account of Wesley's contacts with Grimsby.

1482. _____. "Rev. Samuel Wesley (1666-1735)." In Our Religious Humourists, with Anecdotes and Illustrations, 90-100. London: Simpkin, Marshall and Co., 1880. 256p.

1483. Shaw, Thomas. A History of Cornish Methodism. Truro: Barton, 1967. 145p.

1484. _____. John Wesley and Methodism: A Guide for Schools. Broxton, Chester: Alfred A. Taberer, Bankhead Press, 1971. 24p.

1485. _____. Methodism in Illogan, 1743-1958. N.p. [1958?]. 50p.

1486. _____. Methodism in the Camelford and Wadebridge Circuit, 1743-1963. [Camelford, Eng.], 1963. 239p.

1487. _____. St. Petroc and John Wesley: Apostles in Cornwall; An Examination of the Celtic Background of Cornish Methodism. Redruth: Cornish Methodist Historical Association, 1962. 40p.

1488. Shawcross, John Peter. "John Wesley and Bengeworth." Chap. 8 in Bengeworth: Being Some Account of the History of the Church and Parish of Bengeworth in Evesham Co. Worcester. Evesham: Journal Press, 1927. 155p.

1489. Sheardown, William. Wesleyan Methodism: Its Introduction into Doncaster. Doncaster: Brooke, White and Hatfield, 1868. 29p.

1490. Sheldon, W. C. Early Methodism in Birmingham: A Histori-
       cal Sketch. Birmingham, Eng.: Buckler and Webb, 1903.
       54p.

1491. _____. Early Methodism in Hill and Its Neighbourhood:
       A Historical Sketch. Birmingham, Eng.: Buckler and Webb,
       1903. 16p. GtBLW

1492. Shelton, E. Stanley. The Centenary Volume of the Wesleyan
       Methodist Church, Clayton Street, Blackburn, 1885. Black-
       burn: J. Bennett and Son, 1886. 96p.

1493. Shepherd, Thomas Boswell. Methodism and the Literature of
       the Eighteenth Century. New York: Haskell House, 1966.
       286p. Shortened form of his dissertation, University of Lon-
       don.

1494. Sheppard, Nathan. "John Wesley." In Heroic Stature; Five
       Addresses, 59-108. Philadelphia: American Baptist Publica-
       tion Society, 1897. 226p.

1495. Sheppard, William John Limmer. Great Hymns and Their
       Stories. London: Religious Tract Society, 1923. 186p.

1496. Sherwin, Oscar. John Wesley, Friend of the People. New
       York: Twayne Publishers, 1961. 234p.

1497. Shields, James Kurtz. Fifty Years in Buckles and Saddle;
       Dramatic Story of John Wesley, Founder of Methodism.
       Newark, N.J.: Chronicle Press, 1937. 64p.

1498. Shipley, David C. "The European Heritage." Chap. 1 in
       vol. 1 of The History of American Methodism, 9-42. See no.
       805. This chapter includes 'The Rise of Wesleyan Methodism,'
       and 'Wesleyan Theology.'

1499. _____. "The Ministry in Methodism in the Eighteenth Cen-
       tury." In The Ministry in the Methodist Heritage, 11-31.
       See no. 817.

1500. Short, Roy Hunter. My Great Redeemer's Praise: The
       Methodist Witness in the Wesley Hymns. Nashville, Tenn.:
       Tidings, 197-? 32p.

1501. Short, Ruth Gordon. Affectionately Yours, John Wesley.
       Nashville: Southern Publishing Association, 1963. 298p.

1502. A Short Account of the Life and Death of the Rev. John
       Wesley.... London and York, n.d. 68p.

1503. Shrimpton, Joseph. A Brief History of Bedford St. Paul's

Wesleyan Methodist Church: Published in Connection with
the Centenary Celebrations, 1832-1932.   Bedford: Rush and
Warwick, 1932.   20p.   GtBLW

1504.   Sigourney, Lydia Howard Huntley.   "John Wesley."   In
Examples from the Eighteenth and Nineteenth Centuries,
7-26.   New York: Scribner, 1857.   349p.

1505.   Sigsworth, John Wilkins.   World-Changers: Karl Marx and
John Wesley.   Stirling, Ont., Canada: Easingwold Publications, 1982.   404p.

1506.   Simon, John Smith.   "The Associations of Wesley's House."
In Wesley's House: Sermons and Addresses, 99-109.   See
no. 358.

1507.   _____.   "Historic Background."   In Wesley Studies, 30-40.
See no. 190.

1508.   _____.   John Wesley and the Advance of Methodism.   London: Epworth Press, 1925.   352p.

1509.   _____.   John Wesley and the Methodist Societies.   London:
Epworth Press, 1923.   381p.   A continuation of the author's
John Wesley and the Religious Societies.

1510.   _____.   John Wesley and the Religious Societies.   London:
Epworth Press, 1921.   363p.

1511.   _____.   John Wesley, the Last Phase.   London: Epworth
Press, 1934.   355p.

1512.   _____.   John Wesley, the Master Builder, 1757-72.   London: Epworth Press, 1927.   344p.

1513.   _____.   Methodism in Dorset: A Sketch.   Weymouth:
James Sherren, 1870.   103p.

1514.   _____.   The Revival of Religion in England in the Eighteenth Century.   Fernley Lectures, 37.   London: C. H. Kelly,
n.d.   331p.

1515.   _____.   Wesley or Voltaire?...   London: C. H. Kelly,
1904.   24p.

1516.   Simpson, Matthew.   A Hundred Years of Methodism.   New
York: Hunt and Eaton, 1876.   369p.   Tells the Wesley story
and the development of the Methodist Church in Great Britain
and America.

1517.   _____.   "Wesley."   In Cyclopaedia of Methodism, Embracing

Sketches of Its Rise, Progress, and Present Condition; with
Biographical Notes, 911-16. Philadelphia: Everts and
Stewart, 1878. 1027p.

1518. Simpson, William John Sparrow. John Wesley and the Church
of England. London: Society for Promoting Christian
Knowledge, 1934. 100p.

1519. Sinclair, William MacDonald. "John Wesley, the Evangelist of
the Masses." Chap. 7 in Leaders of Thought in the English
Church, 162-89. London: Hodder and Stoughton, 1896.
378p.

1520. Sis, Martin. The Life of John Wesley. Showing How He
Sowed Some Wild Oats in His Youth, and Preached at the
Same Time.... Leeds: J. Johnson, [1870?]. 31p. GtBLU

1521. Skeats, Herbert S. "John Wesley." In A History of the
Free Churches of England, 348-91. London: Arthur Miall,
1868. 638p.

1522. Skewes, Joseph Henry. A Complete and Popular Digest of
the Polity of Methodism, Each Subject Alphabetically Arranged. London: E. Stock, 1869. 224p.

1523. Skinner, Raymond Frank. "Early Methodism in Shropshire."
Chap. 6 in Nonconformity in Shropshire, 1662-1816: A Study
in the Rise and Progress of Baptist, Congregational, Presbyterian, Quaker and Methodist Societies, 57-67. Shrewsbury:
Wilding, 1965. 143p.

1524. Slaatte, Howard Alexander. Fire in the Brand: An Introduction to the Creative Work and Theology of John Wesley.
New York: Exposition Press, 1963. 157p.

1525. Slater, William Fletcher. Methodism in the Light of the Early
Church. Fernley lectures, no. 15. London: T. Woolmer,
1885. 166p. Includes mention of Wesley and his doctrines
in the chapters "Apostolicity" and "The Work of the Spirit."

1526. _____. Wesley and Church History. London: C. H.
Kelly, 1891. 23p. GtBLMor, NjMUM

1527. Smart, Ninian. "John Wesley and Methodism." In The
Religious Experience of Mankind, 473-78. New York: Charles
Scribner's Sons, 1969. 574p.

1528. Smith, A. Frank. "The Recurrence of Aldersgate." Chap.
17 in What Happened at Aldersgate, 211-21. See no. 342.

1529. Smith, Alan. "The Impact of Methodism." In Part 2, Chap.

6 of The Established Church and Popular Religion, 1750-1850, 33-40. London: Longman Group Ltd., 1970. 120p.

1530. Smith, Benjamin. Methodism in Macclesfield. London: Wesleyan Conference Office, 1875. 382p.

1531. Smith, Charles Merrill. "John Wesley." In When the Saints Go Marching Out, 192-225. A light-hearted rendition of some lives of the saints and "stalwart Christians."

1532. Smith, David L. "Wesley's Concept of the Church." In A Contemporary Wesleyan Theology: Biblical, Systematic, and Practical, 588-90. See no. 279.

1533. Smith, George. Wesley and His Times. Vol. 1 in History of Wesleyan Methodism. 3 vols. London: Longman, Brown, Green, Longman and Roberts, 1857-61. (Rev. in no. 3292.)

1534. Smith, George Gilman. History of Methodism in Georgia and Florida. Macon, Ga.: J. W. Burke and Co., 1877. 530p. The first chapter deals with the Wesleys in Georgia.

1535. Smith, Henry, and Alfred H. Beard. Bethesda Chapel, Hanley. Hanley: New Press Printing Co., 1899. 68p. GtBLW

1536. Smith, J. T. Entire Sanctification (Heart Purity) and Regeneration, as Defined by Mr. Wesley, One and the Same.... Marshall, Texas: Howard Hamments, 1895. 36p. TxDaM-P

1537. Smith, Nicholas. "Jesus, Lover of My Soul." Chap. 9 in Hymns Historically Famous, 69-83. Chicago: Advance Publishing Co., 1901. 275p.

1538. Smith, Robert Elmer. "Jesus, Lover of My Soul." Chap. 1 in Modern Messages from Great Hymns, 17-36. New York: Abingdon Press, 1916. 283p.

1539. Smith, Thornley. "Biographical Sketch of the Rev. John Wesley, A.M." In Christian Theology: A Selection of the Most Important Passages in the Writings of John Wesley, 1-74. London: William Tegg, 18--. 422p.

1540. _____. What Hath God Wrought? A Memorial of Wesleyan Methodism in Oakworth, Near Keighley, Yorkshire. London: John Mason, 1858. 36p.

1541. Smith, Timothy L. "A Historical and Contemporary Appraisal of Wesleyan Theology." Chap. 3 in A Contemporary Wesleyan Theology: Biblical, Systematic, and Practical, 73-101. See no. 279.

1542. _____. Introduction to The Pentecost Hymns of John and

Books   133

Charles Wesley..., 7-15. Kansas City, Mo.: Beacon Hill
Press, 1982. 85p. Also includes commentary on the hymns.

1543. Smith, Timothy L., Roy S. Nicholson, Sr., and T. Crichton
Mitchell. "Hymnology: The Theology of the Wesleys' Hymns."
Chap. 22 in A Contemporary Wesleyan Theology: Biblical,
Systematic, and Practical, 1007-42. See no. 279.

1544. Smith, Warren Thomas. John Wesley and Slavery. Nashville:
Abingdon Press, 1986. 160p.

1545. Smith, William. A Consecutive History of the Rise, Progress
and Present State of Wesleyan Methodism in Ireland. Dublin:
T. W. Doolittle, 1830. 320p.

1546. Smyth, Charles Hugh Egerton. "Berridge of Everton." Chap.
4 in Simeon and Church Order; a Study of the Origins of the
Evangelical Revival in Cambridge in the Eighteenth Century....
Cambridge, Eng.: Cambridge University Press, 1940. 315p.

1547. Smyth, James. John Wesley and the Episcopal Church. Belfast: Irish Methodist Publishing Co., 1911. 32p.

1548. Snell, Frederick John. Wesley and Methodism. The World's
Epoch-Makers, 21. New York: C. Scribner's Sons, 1900.
243p.

1549. Snowden, Rita Frances. Such a Woman; the Story of Susanna
Wesley. Nashville: Upper Room, 1962. 55p.

1550. Snyder, Henry Nelson. "Aldersgate and the Transformation
of Character." Chap. 8 in What Happened at Aldersgate,
115-25. See no. 342.

1551. Snyder, Howard A. The Radical Wesley and Patterns for
Church Renewal. Downers Grove, Ill.: InterVarsity Press,
1980. 189p. Based in part on the author's thesis, Notre
Dame.

1552. Somervell, David Churchill. "Methodists and Evangelicals."
Chap. 19 in A Short History of Our Religion, from Moses to
the Present Day, 252-64. London: G. Bell, 1928. 356p.

1553. Southey, Robert. Life of Wesley; and Rise and Progress of
Methodism, edited by Charles Cuthbert Southey. 3d ed.
2 vols. London: Longman, Brown, Green, and Longmans,
1846. (Rev. in nos. 2490, 2605, 3172, 3512.)

1554. Sowton, Stanley. John Wesley. Grand Rapids, Mich.:
Zondervan, 1953. 94p.

1555.   Spencer, Allan. The History of Methodism in Davyhulme:
        Together with an Introductory Chapter on the Origin of
        Methodism in Manchester. Manchester: W. H. Landless,
        1898. 70p.

1556.   Spilman, Mrs. James H. Susanna Wesley: The Mother of
        Methodism, a Story of a Woman Whose Influence As a Mother
        Gave John Wesley to the Ages. Harrodsburg, Ky.: Har-
        rodsburg Herald Press, 1938. 16p. This is an address de-
        livered at the annual conference at Corbin, Kentucky,
        September 1, 1938.

1557.   Spinka, Matthew. "John Wesley and the Evangelical Awaken-
        ing." In Christian Thought from Erasmus to Berdyaev,
        89-95. Englewood Cliffs, N.J.: Prentice Hall, 1962. 246p.

1558.   Spivey, Ronald Vincent. The Pictorial History of Wesley's
        Chapel and Its Founder. London: Pitkin Pictorials, 1957.
        24p.

1559.   Spooner, John Alden. Methodism as Held by Wesley. Tracts
        for the People, no. 4. N.p. 1841. 26p. An anti-methodist
        publication.

1560.   Spoor, Ralph H. Illustrated Hand-Book to City Road Chapel,
        Burying Ground, and Wesley's House; with Notices of the
        Foundry and Bunhill Fields Burying-ground. London: Wes-
        leyan Conference Office, 1881. 71p.

1561.   Spurgeon, Charles Haddon. The Two Wesleys: A Lecture
        Delivered in the Metropolitan Tabernacle Lecture Hall, on
        December 6th, 1861. Pasadena, Tex.: Pilgrim Publications,
        1975. 64p.

1562.   Staley, Sue Reynolds. "John Wesley." In Great Soul Win-
        ners, 9-29. Harrisburg, Pa.: Evangelical Press, 1926. 362p.

1563.   Stamp, William Wood. Historical Notes of Wesleyan Methodism
        in Bradford and Its Vicinity. Bradford: Wardman, [1841].
        123p.

1564.   _____. The Orphan-House of Wesley; with Notices of Early
        Methodism in Newcastle-Upon-Tyne, and Its Vicinity. London:
        John Mason, 1863. 299p.

1565.   Stampe, George. "An Oxford Wesley Relic." In Wesley
        Studies, 62-70. See no. 190.

1566.   _____. "A Peep into a Methodist Museum." In The Homes,
        Haunts and Friends of John Wesley, 133-38. See no. 319.

1567. Stanley, A. P. "John and Charles Wesley." In Addison to
       Blake, 254-59. Vol. 3 of The English Poets; Selections with
       Critical Introductions. 5 vols. New York: Macmillan, 1903.

1568. _____. "Wesley's Liberality and Catholicity." In Wesley
       Memorial Volume, 452-63. See no. 257.

1569. Stanley, Jacob. The Increase, Influence, and Stability, of
       Unestablished Religion, No Cause of Alarm to Established
       Christians.... Wednesbury: J. Booth, 1813. 63p.

1570. Starkey, Lycurgus M. The Work of the Holy Spirit, a Study
       in Wesleyan Theology. New York: Abingdon Press, 1962.
       176p.

1571. Stead, W. T. Hymns That Have Helped.... New York:
       Doubleday and McClure Co., 1897. 276p. Nine of Charles'
       and three of John's hymns are included in this collection,
       with brief commentary on them.

1572. Steele, Anthony. History of Methodism in Barnard Castle
       and the Principal Places in the Dales Circuit. London:
       Vickers, 1857. 239p.

1573. Stephen, Leslie. History of English Thought in the Eight-
       eenth Century. 2 vols. London: Smith, Elder and Co.,
       1876. vol. 2, pp. 409-35 are concerned with Wesley and
       Methodism.

1574. Stephens, David Stubert. Wesley and Episcopacy.... Pitts-
       burg: Methodist Protestant Publishing House, 1892. 90p.
       Reprinted from the Methodist Recorder.

1575. Stephenson, George Malcolm. "The Rise of Methodism." In
       The Puritan Heritage, 62-71. New York: Macmillan, 1952.
       282p.

1576. Stephenson, W. H. "The Orphan House, Newcastle-upon-
       Tyne." In The Homes, Haunts and Friends of John Wesley,
       109-13. See no. 319.

1577. Sterling, Edward [Vetus, pseud.]. Wesley's Ghost. 5th ed.
       Manchester: J. Gadsby; London: R. Groombridge and Sons,
       1846. 12p.

1578. Stevens, Abel. The Centenary of American Methodism: A
       Sketch of Its History, Theology, Practical System and Suc-
       cess. New York: Carlton and Porter, 1865. 287p.

1579. _____. An Essay on Church Polity: Comprehending an
       Outline of the Controversy on Ecclesiastical Government, and

136   John and Charles Wesley

a Vindication of the Ecclesiastical System of the Methodist
Episcopal Church, 83-112. New York: Lane and Tippett,
1847. 206p. Concerned with church government, Wesley,
and other early leaders of the Methodist Episcopal Church.

1580. _____. History of the Life and Times of John Wesley, Embracing the History of Methodism, from Its Rise to His Death:
and Including Biographical Notices and Anecdotes of His Contemporaries and Coadjutors. New ed. London: W. Tegg,
1864. 826p.

1581. _____. History of the Methodist Episcopal Church. 4
vols. New York: Carlton and Porter, 1864-67. Volumes one
and two contain considerable Wesley material.

1582. _____. History of the Religious Movement of the Eighteenth
Century, Called Methodism, Considered in Its Different Denominational Forms, and Its Relations to British and American
Protestantism. 3 vols. New York: Phillips and Hunt, 1858-
1861. (Rev. in nos. 2993, 3292.)

1583. _____. The Illustrated History of Methodism; Being an
Account of the Wesleys, Their Contemporaries and Their
Times.... 2 vols. Nottingham: J. R. Haslam, [1882?].

1584. _____. Introduction to Sermons, Chiefly on the Spiritual
Life, by John Wesley, 5-16. New York: N. Tibbals, 1875.
384p.

1585. _____. "Mrs. Susanna Wesley." In Our Excellent Women
of the Methodist Church, in England and America, edited by
Gabriel Poillon Disoway, 9-29. New York: J. C. Buttre,
1861. 286p.

1586. _____. "Susanna Wesley." In Women of Methodism; Its
Three Foundresses, Susanna Wesley, the Countess of
Huntingdon, and Barbara Heck, 23-55. New York: Carlton
and Porter, 1866. 304p.

1587. _____. "Wesley--Apostleship." Chap. 8 in Character
Sketches, 352-97. New York: Phillips and Hunt, 1882.
397p.

1588. _____. "Wesleyan Lyric Poetry." In Wesley Memorial
Volume, 464-72. See no. 257.

1589. Stevens, William Oliver. "The Epworth Rectory." In Un-
bidden Guests: A Book of Real Ghosts, 50-57. New York:
Dodd, Mead and Co., 1945. 322p.

1590. Stevenson, Daniel. "The History of Methodism." Chap. 21

in Elements of Methodism in a Series of Short Lectures...,
168-95. Claremont, N.H., 1879. 212p.

1591. Stevenson, George John. City Road Chapel, London and Its
Associations: Historical, Biographical, and Memorial. London: Stevenson, 1872. 624p. The first half of this volume
is concerned with the Foundery--Wesley's headquarters for the
Methodist movement until 1778--and the City Road Chapel
which he built to replace the Foundery. The City Road Chapel
is considered the Mother Church of Methodism. The second
half of the volume deals with the graveyards associated with
Wesley's chapel and those who are buried there.

1592. _____. "John Wesley, A.M., Founder of Methodism," and
"Charles Wesley, A.M., the Poet of Methodism." In Vol. 1,
Methodist Worthies; Characteristic Sketches of Methodist
Preachers of the Several Denominations, with Historical Sketch
of Each Connexion, 91-127. 6 vols. London: T. C. Jack,
1884-86.

1593. _____. Memorials of the Wesley Family: Including Bio-
graphical and Historical Sketches of All the Members of the
Family for Two Hundred and Fifty Years; Together with a
Genealogical Table of the Wesleys, with Historical Notes, for
More Than Nine Hundred Years. London: S. W. Partridge
and Co.; New York: Nelson and Phillips, 1876. 562p.

1594. _____. The Methodist Hymn Book and Its Associations....
London: Hamilton, Adams, 1870. 420p. Gives historical
and biographical explanations for each hymn in the Methodist
Hymn-Book.

1595. _____. "The Wesley Family." In Wesley Memorial Volume,
27-50. See no. 257.

1596. Stevenson, Robert M. "John Wesley's First Hymnbook."
Chap. 9 in Patterns of Protestant Church Music, 112-30.
Durham, N.C.: Duke University Press, 1953. 219p. Re-
printed in John Wesley's First Hymn-Book; a Collection of
Psalms and Hymns; a Facsimile with Additional Material,
edited by Frank Baker and George Walton Williams, v-xxiii.

1597. Stevenson, Robert M., and Thomas F. Wright. "The Eight-
eenth-Century Hymn Tune." In English Hymnology in the
Eighteenth Century; Papers Read at Clark Library Seminar,
5 March 1977, 21-66. Los Angeles: Clark Memorial Library,
University of California, 1980. 76p. First appeared in
Inter-American Music Review 2, no. 1 (1979): 6-26.

1598. Stock, Robert D. "Religious Love and Fear in Late-Century
Poetry: Smart, Wesley, Cowper, and Blake." Chap. 8 in

The Holy and the Daemonic from Sir Thomas Browne to William
Blake, 314-73. Princeton: Princeton University Press, 1982.
395p.

1599. Stocker, S. Wilcox. "Methodism in Scotland." In Wesley As
a World Force, 44-52. See no. 49.

1600. Stoeffler, F. Ernest. "Tradition and Renewal in the Eccle-
siology of John Wesley." In Traditio-Krisis-Renovatio aus
theogischer Sicht: Festschrift Winfried Zeller zum 65. Geburtstag, edited by Bernd Jaspert and Rudolf Mohr, 298-316.
Marburg: N. G. Elwert, 1976. 676p.

1601. Stokes, Mack B. The Bible in the Wesleyan Heritage. Nashville, Tenn.: Abingdon Press, 1979. 95p.

1602. _____. Our Methodist Heritage. Nashville: Graded Press,
1963. 128p. The purpose of this book is to assist Methodists
in their understanding of their church. John Wesley is the
subject of much of the book.

1603. Stonehouse, William Brocklehurst. "Family of Wesley." in
The History and Topography of the Isle of Axholme: Being
That Part of Lincolnshire Which Is West of Trent, 175-222.
London: Longman, Rees, Orme, 1839. 463p. Begins in 1650
with Bartholomew Wesley, grandfather of Samuel, John Wes-
ley's father.

1604. Stott, John. Notices of Methodism in Haslingden. London:
Hayman, Christy and Lilly, 1898. 132p.

1605. Stoughton, John. The Church in the Georgian Era. Vol. 6
of History of Religion in England, from the Opening of the
Long Parliament to the End of the Eighteenth Century. 6
vols. London: Hodder and Stoughton, 1881. Significant
portions of chaps. 5 and 12 are concerned with Wesley and
Methodism.

1606. _____. Religion in England Under Queen Anne and the
Georges, 1702-1800. 2 vols. London: Hodder and Stoughton,
1878. Chapters in both volumes discuss Wesley and his movement.

1607. Straughn, James H. "Aldersgate the Basis of Methodist Doctrine." Chap. 9 in What Happened at Aldersgate, 126-44.
See no. 342.

1608. Sturm, Roy A. Sociological Reflections on John Wesley and
Methodism. Indianapolis: Central Publishing Co., 1982.
166p.

Books

1609. Sugden, Edward H. Introduction to Wesley's Standard Sermons; Consisting of Forty-Four Discourses.... London: Epworth Press, 1921.

1610. _____. John Wesley's London: Scenes of Methodist and World-Wide Interest, with Their Historical Associations. London: Epworth Press, 1932. 249p.

1611. _____. "Wesley's Influence upon Australia." In Wesley As a World Force..., 89-108. See no. 49.

1612. Summers, Thomas O. "Wesley and Asbury." In Wesley Memorial Volume, 497-528. See no. 257.

1613. "Susanna Wesley." In Mothers: 100 Mothers of the Famous and the Infamous, 256-58. New York: Paddington Press, 1976. 267p.

1614. Sutcliffe, Joseph. A Review of Methodism in a Discourse Delivered on Laying the Foundation-Stone of New-Street Chapel, York, January 1, 1805. York: T. Wilson and R. Spence, 1805. 46p.

1615. Swallow, J. Albert. Methodism in the Light of English Literature of the Last Century. Münchener Beiträge zur Romanischen und Englischen Philologie, 9. Erlangen and Leipzig: A. Deichert'sche Verlagsbuchh Nachf, (Georg Böhme), 1895. 160p. The major portion of this work "endeavoured to collect and collate all the references about Methodism that are to be found in the literary writers who were contemporary with John Wesley."

1616. Swallow, Thomas. Disruptions and Secessions in Methodism: Their Causes, Consequences and Lessons. London: Ralph Fenwick, Primitive Methodist Conference, 1880. 215p.

1617. Swan, James W., and John Hampson. Methodism at Fletcher Street. Bolton: Coop, 1911. 57p.

1618. Sweet, William W. "The Message of Wesley to His Time." In Methodism in American History, 27-46. New York: Methodist Book Concern, 1933. 434p.

1619. _____. "Methodism's Debt to the Church of England." In Methodism, 38-50. See no. 287.

1620. _____. The Methodists, a Collection of Source Materials. Religion in the American Frontier, 1783-1840, vol. 4. Chicago: University of Chicago Press, 1946. 800p.

1621. _____. "Wesley's Missionaries to America," and "Thomas

Coke and John Wesley's Last Embassy to America." Chaps. 3
and 5 in Men of Zeal; the Romance of American Methodist
Beginnings, 85-118, 150-78. Drew Lectureship in Biography.
New York and Cincinnati: Abingdon Press, 1935. 208p.

1622. Swift, Rowland C. Lively People: Methodism in Nottingham
1740-1979. Nottingham: University of Nottingham, Dept.
of Adult Education, 1982. 189p.

1623. _____. Methodism in Cropwell Bishop. Nottingham: H.
Jones, 1952. 24p.

1624. Swift, Wesley F. "John Wesley in Scotland." Chap. 1 in
Methodism in Scotland, the First Hundred Years, 17-24.
Wesley Historical Society Lectures, no. 13. London: Ep-
worth Press, 1947. 96p.

1625. _____. The Romance of Banffshire Methodism. Banff:
Banffshire Journal, 1927. 64p.

1626. Swindells, William. A Short History of Trinity Methodist
Church, Stockport in Commemoration of the Diamond Jubilee
of the Building, 1946. Stockport: Cloister Press, 1946.
22p.

1627. Symons, R. The Rev. John Wesley's Ministerial Itineraries
in Cornwall: Commenced in 1743, and Concluded in 1789....
Truro: Symons, 1879. 147p.

1628. "Synopsis of the Life and Death of the Rev. John Wesley,
A.M." In Interesting Extracts from the Journals of the Rev.
John Wesley, A.M., with a Synopsis of His Life and Death,
7-17. Boston: William S. Spear, 1819. 300p.

1629. Tamez, Elsa. "Wesley As Read by the Poor." Chap. 3 in
The Future of the Methodist Theological Traditions, 67-84.
See no. 57.

1630. Tavard, George H. Justification: An Ecumenical Study.
New York: Paulist Press, 1983. 137p. Contains a discussion
of John Wesley, pp. 83-92.

1631. Taylor, Blaine. A Blueprint for Church Renewal: John Wesley's Relevance in the Twenty-First Century. Champaign,
Ill.: C-4 Resources, 1984. 221p.

1632. Taylor, Ernest Richard. "The Father of Methodism: John
Wesley and the Position of Methodism in the Church." Chap.
2 in Methodism and Politics, 1791-1851, 18-53. Cambridge,
Eng.: Cambridge University Press, 1935. 226p.

Books

141

1633. Taylor, Gertrude W. John Wesley and the Anglo-Catholic
Revival. London: Christian Knowledge Society, 1905. 32p.
GtBLU

1634. Taylor, Gordon Rattray. "The Raptur'd Soul." Chap. 8 in
The Angel-Makers: A Study in the Psychological Origins of
Historical Change, 1750-1850, 127-47. London: Heinemann,
1958. 388p. This chapter discusses religious conversion in
the eighteenth century, especially Wesley's own experience
as well as his methods with others. Also discusses Wesley's
relationship with his parents.

1635. Taylor, Isaac. Wesley and Methodism. London: Longman,
Brown, Green, and Longmans, 1851. 366p. (Rev. in nos.
3172, 3436, 3995, 3996.)

1636. Taylor, Richard S. "Historical and Modern Significance of
Wesleyan Theology." Chap. 2 in A Contemporary Wesleyan
Theology: Biblical, Systematic, and Practical, 51-71. See
no. 279.

1637. Taylor, Samuel. Echoes in Glossop Dale: Being Sketches of
the Rise and Spread of Methodism in the Glossop Circuit.
Glossop: D. Woodhead, 1874. 192p.

1638. Taylor, Thomas. A Defence of the Methodists Who Do Not
Attend the National Church.... Liverpool: Hodgson, 1793.
72p.

1639. _____. A Funeral Sermon Occasioned by the Death of That
Eminent Servant of God, the Rev. John Wesley Who Departed
This Life March 2, 1791, in the 88th Year of His Age; Preached
in the Methodist Chapel at Hull, March 10, 1791. Hull: J.
Ferraby, 1791. 39p.

1640. Taylor, Vincent. "Sanctification." Chap. 5 in Forgiveness
and Reconciliation: A Study of New Testament Theology,
144-88. London: Macmillan and Co., 1941. Wesley is brought
into this discussion of sanctification only briefly.

1641. Tearle, John Douglas. Our Heritage: Luton Methodist Church
Centenary, 1852-1952. London: J. D. Tearle, 1952. 40p.

1642. Tees, Francis Harrison. The Beginnings of Methodism in England and America. Nashville: Parthenon Press, 1940. 225p.

1643. _____. Methodist Origins. Nashville: Parthenon Press,
1948. 223p. Discusses many aspects of early Methodism--so-
cieties, love feasts, meeting places, itinerant preaching, class
meetings, Sunday schools.

1644. Tefft, Benjamin Franklin. Character of Wesley; a Centenary
       Discourse. [n.p. 186-?] NjMUM

1645. Telford, John, ed. Introduction in vol. 1 of The Letters of
       the Rev. John Wesley, vii-xxviii. 8 vols. London: Ep-
       worth Press, 1931. (Rev. in no. 3440.)

1646. _____. John Wesley, 1703-1791. Little Books of the Kindly
       Light, no. 4. London: Epworth Press, 1936. 16p.

1647. _____. "John Wesley's Executors." In The Homes, Haunts
       and Friends of John Wesley, 31-33. See no. 319. The execu-
       tors were John Horton, George Wolff, and William Marriott.

1648. _____. Life of the Rev. Charles Wesley. London: Reli-
       gious Tract Society, 1886. 224p.

1649. _____. Life of Wesley. London: Hodder and Stoughton,
       1886. 363p.

1650. _____. Life-Story of John Wesley. London: Epworth
       Press, 1930. 92p.

1651. _____. Memorable Scenes in the Life of John Wesley; a
       Lecture to Accompany a Set of Lantern Slides. London:
       Kempsall and Briginshaw, n.d. 16p. NjMUM

1652. _____. The Methodist Hymn-Book Illustrated. 2d ed.
       London: Robert Culley, 1909. 533p. In addition to the
       discussion of each hymn, many by the Wesleys, there is a
       section entitled "Wesley Hymns and Hymn Books," pp. 1-17.

1653. _____. The New Methodist Hymn-Book Illustrated in His-
       tory and Experience. London: Epworth Press, [1934].
       485p.

1654. _____. Notes to The Treasure House of Charles Wesley;
       a Short Anthology of the Evangelical Revival. London: Ep-
       worth Press, 1933. 136p.

1655. _____. Popular History of Methodism. London: C. H.
       Kelly, 1896. 64p.

1656. _____. Sayings and Portraits of Charles Wesley with
       Family Portraits, Historic Scenes, and Additional Portraits of
       John Wesley, edited by John Telford. London: Epworth
       Press, 1924. 267p.

1657. _____. "Some of Wesley's Great Sayings." In Wesley
       Studies, 191-200. See no. 190.

1658.   . "A Tour in Methodist London." In The Homes,
Haunts and Friends of John Wesley, 33-59. See no. 319.

1659.   . Two West-End Chapels; or, Sketches of London
Methodism from Wesley's Day (1740-1886). London: Wesleyan Methodist Book-Room, 1886. 292p.

1660.   . Wesley Anecdotes. London: Religious Tract Society, 1885. 159p.

1661.   . "The Wesleyan Methodist Church." Chap. 4 in
Our Churches and Why We Belong to Them, 115-53. London:
Service and Paton, 1898. 381p.

1662.   . Wesley's Chapel and Wesley's House. London:
C. H. Kelly, 1906. 128p.

1663.   . "Wesley's First 'Plan' for London." In Wesley
Studies, 96-100. See no. 190.

1664. Tell Me the Story of John Wesley: A Pictorial Account of
Methodist Beginnings. Nashville: Tidings, 197-? 24p. Brief
pamphlet highlighting Wesley's life and Methodism's development.

1665. Temperley, Harold William Vazeille. "The Age of Walpole and
the Pelhams." Chap. 2 in The Eighteenth Century, 82-89.
Cambridge Modern History, vol. 6. Cambridge: Cambridge
University Press, 1909. A Discussion of Wesley, Whitefield,
and Methodism.

1666. Temple, Arthur. Hymns We Love: Stories of the Hundred
Most Popular Hymns. London: Lutterworth Press, 1954.
168p. Contains brief discussions of Charles Wesley's "Rejoice, the Lord is King," "Jesus, Lover of My Soul," and
"Soldiers of Christ Arise."

1667. Tenney, Mary Alice. Blueprint for a Christian World; an
Analysis of the Wesleyan Way. Winona Lake, Ind.: Light
and Life Press, 1953. 292p.

1668.   . "The Origin and History of the Methodist Class
Meeting." Chap. 1 in Spiritual Renewal for Methodism,
edited by Samuel Emerick, 11-19. Nashville: Methodist
Evangelistic Materials, 1958. 77p.

1669.   . "The Wesleyan Doctrine of Christian Perfection."
Chap. 6 in The Wesleyan Message, Its Scriptures and His-
torical Bases, 163-93. Winona Lake, Ind.: Light and Life
Press, 1940. 220p.

1670. Theobald, Charles H. The Story of Methodism in Fenwick.
       Doncaster, n.d. 8p. GtBLW

1671. Thomas, George Ernest. Abundant Life through Aldersgate.
       Nashville: Methodist Evangelistic Materials, 1962. 62p.

1672. Thomas, Gilbert Oliver. "The Evangelical Revival." Chap.
       7 in William Cowper and the Eighteenth Century, 158-92.
       London: I. Nicholson and Watson, 1935. 395p. The author
       states that Cowper found in Methodism the most joyful and
       vital influence of his life. There are numerous references in
       this chapter to the Wesleys.

1673. _____. "John Wesley," and "Brother Charles." Chaps.
       10 and 11 in Builders and Makers: Occasional Studies, 78-
       103. London: Epworth Press, 1944. 219p.

1674. Thomas, Henry, [pseud.] and Dana Lee Thomas [pseud.].
       "John Wesley." In Living Biographies of Religious Leaders,
       237-50. Garden City, N.Y.: Garden City Publishing Co.,
       1942. 297p.

1675. Thomas, Ivor. Methodism in Cury with List of Methodist
       Ministers in the Helston Circuits, 1799-1950. Cury, 1950.
       24p. GtBLW

1676. _____. Methodism in Mullion. Mullion: Mullion Methodist
       Church, Centenary Publication Committee, 1978. 104p.

1677. Thomas, John Edward, and Mazelle Wildes Thomas. Susannah's
       Sanctuary: A Book for Christian Mothers Containing Inspira-
       tion and Practical Suggestions for a Spiritual Fellowship of
       Mother and Child. Minneapolis: Voyageur Press, 1939. 84p.

1678. Thomas, Lowell. "John Wesley." In The Vital Spark: 101
       Outstanding Lives, 332-34. Garden City, N.Y.: Doubleday,
       1959. 480p.

1679. Thompson, David Decamp. John Wesley As a Social Reformer.
       The Black Heritage Library Collection. Freeport, N.Y.:
       Books for Libraries Press, 1971. 111p.

1680. Thompson, Edgar W. "The Methodist Movement and Its
       Churchmanship." Chap. 4 in The Methodist Doctrine of the
       Church, 27-38. London: Epworth Press, 1939. 48p.

1681. _____. Wesley, Apostolic Man; Some Reflections on Wes-
       ley's Consecration of Dr. Thomas Coke. London: Epworth
       Press, 1957. 84p.

1682. _____. Wesley at Charterhouse. Wesley Bi-Centenary
       Manuals, no. 4. London: Epworth Press, 1938. 17p.

1683. Thompson, Edward Palmer. "The Transforming Power of the
       Cross." Chap. 11 in The Making of the English Working
       Class, 350-400. London: Gollancz, 1963. 848p. Many
       references to Wesley in this chapter.

1684. Thompson, Ernest Trice. The Religious Development of John
       Wesley; a Series of Chapel Talks. Union Seminary Bulletin,
       25, no. 4. Richmond, Va.: Union Theological Seminary,
       1938. 15p.

1685. Thompson, Francis. "John Wesley: Manifest Hard Work."
       In The Real Robert Louis Stevenson, and Other Critical
       Essays, edited by Terence L. Connolly, 47-51. New York:
       Published for Boston College by University Pubs., 1959. 409p.

1686. Thompson, Henry Lewis. Four Biographical Sermons on John
       Wesley and Others, Preached at St. Mary the Virgin, Oxford.
       London: Henry Frowde, 1905. 96p.

1687. Thompson, R. Duane. "The Practices and Views of John
       Wesley." In A Contemporary Wesleyan Theology: Biblical,
       Systematic, and Practical, 705-12. See no. 279. Discusses
       Wesley's impact on social concerns, stating that his life and
       theology cannot be understood without also understanding his
       ideas on social ethics.

1688. Thompson, W. H. Early Chapters in Hull Methodism, 1746-
       1800. London: C. H. Kelly, 1895. 76p.

1689. Thornhill, Albert. "John Wesley." Chap. 15 in Heroes of
       the Faith, from Wiclif to Priestley, 117-25. London: The
       Sunday-School Association, 1913. 150p.

1690. Thwaites, William. Wesleyan Methodism in Durham City:
       Notes on Its Beginnings and Development. Durham: H.
       Procter, 1909. 63p.

1691. Tice, Frank. "Wesleyan Methodism." In History of Method-
       ism in Cambridge, 3-50. London: Epworth Press, 1966.
       143p. Contains some references to Wesley.

1692. Tigert, John James. "Shall Wesley's Powers Descend to the
       Conference or to a Designated Successor?" and "The Christ-
       mas Conference and Wesley's Final Settlement of Episcopal
       Methodism." Chaps. 2 and 11 in A Constitutional History of
       American Episcopal Methodism, 25-35, 161-207. Nashville,
       Tenn.: Publishing House of the Methodist Episcopal Church,
       South, 1894. 414p.

1693. Timpson, Thomas. "Rise of the Methodists." Chap. 9 in
       British Ecclesiastical History, Including ... the Rise,

Progress, and Present State of Every Denomination of Christians in the British Empire, 398-429, 2d ed. London: Aylott and Jones, 1847.

1694. Tipple, Ezra S. "The Beginnings of American Methodism." In Vol. 2 of A New History of Methodism, 53-152. See no. 229.

1695. Todd, John M. John Wesley and the Catholic Church. London: Hodder and Stoughton, 1958. 195p.

1696. Towlson, Clifford W. "Methodism in Yorkshire." Chap. 9 in A History of Christianity in Yorkshire, edited by F. S. Popham, 133-49. Wallington: Religious Education Press, 1954. 160p.

1697. _____. "Wesley the Pupil." Chap. 3 in Moravian and Methodists; Relationships and Influences in the Eighteenth Century, 35-67. London: Epworth Press, 1957. 265p. Shortened version of his dissertation, University of London. In addition there is much discussion of Wesley in other chapters. The author concludes that every English Moravian leader of note came under the influences of John and Charles Wesley in the eighteenth century. He has tried to show how closely the two churches were once linked, and to explain what each church owes the other.

1698. Towns, Elmer L. "John Wesley." Chap. 17 in A History of Religious Educators, 212-25. Grand Rapids, Mich.: Baker Book House, 1975. 330p.

1699. Townsend, James. History of Darwen Wesleyan Methodism. Darwen: J. J. Riley, 95p. GtBLW

1700. Townsend, William John. "English Life and Society, and the Condition of Methodism at the Death of Wesley." Chap. 7 in vol. 1 of A New History of Methodism, 333-78. See no. 229.

1701. Treen, William E. Methodism in East Leeds, Richmond Hill. Leeds: Wildblood and Ward, 1947. 51p. Published in commemoration of the centenary of the chapel, 1849-1949.

1702. Treffry, Richard. Memoirs of Mr. John Edwards Trezise of St. Just, Cornwall: Consisting Principally of Extracts from His Diary, with Some Account of Methodism in St. Just. London: John Mason, 1837. 224p.

1703. _____. Memoirs of Mr. Richard Trewavas ... to Which Is Prefixed an Account of Methodism in Mousehole. London: John Mason, 1839. 196p. GtBLW

1704.   Tripp, David. "The Sources of the Covenant Service," and
        "The Observance and Its Regulation until the Death of Wes-
        ley." Chaps. 1 and 2 in The Renewal of the Covenant in the
        Methodist Tradition, 5-35. London: Epworth Press, 1969.
        220p. His M.A. thesis, University of Leeds.

1705.   A True Narrative of the Origin and Progress of the Difference
        between Dr. Coke, Mr. Moore, Mr. Rogers and Dr. Whitehead,
        concerning the Publication of the Life of the Late Rev. John
        Wesley ... to Which Is Added an Abstract from the Minutes
        of the Committee Showing Their Endeavours to Promote Peace
        in the Society. London: C. Paramore, 1792. 27p.

1706.   Truesdale, Albert. "Theism: The Eternal, Personal, Creative
        God." Chap. 4 in A Contemporary Wesleyan Theology: Bib-
        lical, Systematic, and Practical, 103-43. See no. 279.

1707.   Trusty, J. B. Historical Catechism of the Methodist, from
        the Origin of Methodism by John Wesley. Philadelphia: J.
        H. Johnson, 1875. 15p. DLC

1708.   Tsanoff, Radoslav A. "John Wesley." Chap. 5 in Autobiog-
        raphies of Ten Religious Leaders: Alternatives in Christian
        Experience, 105-35. San Antonio: Trinity University Press,
        1968. 304p. "The purpose of this book is to examine prin-
        cipal varieties of Christian experience as they have been ex-
        pressed in the intimate autobiographies of great religious
        leaders"--foreword.

1709.   Tuck, Stephen. Wesleyan Methodism in Frome, Somerset-
        shire. Frome: S. Tuck; London: John Mason, 1837. 126p.

1710.   Turner, George. Justification by Faith Alone, the Doctrine
        of the Scriptures: or, The Sentiments of the Revs. John Wes-
        ley and R. Watson on This Subject, Vindicated: In Reply to
        Rev. Abraham Scott. London: J. Mason, 1836. 68p.
        GtBLW

1711.   _____. "Mr. Wesley the Annotator": Harmonized and
        Identified With "Mr. Wesley the Polemic", on the Scriptural
        Mode of Baptism: In Reply to Rev. John Craps.... London:
        John Mason and F. W. Calder, 1844. 24p.

1712.   _____. The Old Protestant Doctrine of Justification by
        Faith Asserted...: The Sentiments of the Revs. J. Wesley
        and R. Watson Further Vindicated. In Reply to Rev. Abra-
        ham Scott. London: J. Mason, 1838. 56p. GtBLW

1713.   Turner, George Allen. "John Wesley As an Interpreter of
        Scripture." In Inspiration and Interpretation, edited by
        John F. Walvoord, 156-78. Grand Rapids, Mich.: Eerdmans,
        1957. 280p.

1714.   . The Vision Which Transforms; Is Christian Perfection Scriptural? Kansas City, Mo.: Beacon Hill Press,
1964. 348p. A revision of the author's thesis, M.S., Harvard University, first published in 1952 under the title
The More Excellent Way.

1715. Turner, Joseph Horsfall. "Methodism." In Haworth-Past
and Present: A History of Haworth, Stanbury and Oxen-
hope, 101-13. Brighouse: J. S. Jowett, 1879. 184p.

1716. Turrell, W. J. John Wesley, Physician and Electrotherapist.
Oxford: B. Blackwell, 1938. 24p.

1717. Tuttle, Robert G. John Wesley: His Life and Theology.
Grand Rapids: Zondervan Publishing House, 1978. 368p.

1718. Twentieth Century Aldersgate, by Ten Methodist Bishops.
Nashville: Methodist Evangelistic Materials, 1962. 64p.

1719. Two-hundred-and-fiftieth Anniversary of the Birth of Charles
Wesley, 1707-1957: Souvenir Programme. Belfast: Nelson
and Knox, 1957. Programme for the musical festival of Wesley hymns held under the auspices of the Wesley Historical
Society, Irish Branch, Belfast, December 18, 1957. IEG

1720. Tydings, Richard. A Refutation of the Doctrine of Uninter-
rupted Apostolic Succession, with a Correction of Errors
concerning Rev. John Wesley and Dr. Coke.... Louisville,
1844. 364p.

1721. Tyerman, Luke. Life and Times of the Rev. John Wesley,
Founder of the Methodists. 3 vols. London: Hodder and
Stoughton, 1871. (Rev. in nos. 2729, 4001.)

1722.   . Life and Times of the Rev. Samuel Wesley, M.A.,
Rector of Epworth, and Father of the Revs. John and Charles
Wesley, the Founders of the Methodists. London: Simpkin,
1866. 472p.

1723.   . "Wesley's Death and Character." In Wesley
Memorial Volume, 548-93. See no. 257.

1724.   . Wesley's Designated Successor: The Life, Letters
and Literary Labours of the Rev. John Fletcher. London:
Hodder and Stoughton, 1882. 581p.

1725. Underwood, Elinor. John Wesley the Methodist; a Photo Drama
by Fortuna Films, Inc. New York: Ruffin North and Co.,
1922. 32p. This booklet describes the film to be produced entitled "John Wesley; the Methodist." IEG

Books   149

1726. Underwood, Peter. "Epworth." In A Gazeteer of British
       Ghosts, 65-67. London: Souvenir, 1971. 256p.

1727. Urlin, Richard Denny. The Churchman's Life of Wesley.
       London: Society for Promoting Christian Knowledge, 1880.
       352p. (Rev. in no. 2729.)

1728. _____. John Wesley's Place in Church History, Determined
       with the Aid of Facts and Documents Unknown to, or Un-
       noticed by His Biographers. London: Rivingtons, 1870.
       272p.

1729. Urwin, Evelyn Clifford and Douglas Wollen. John Wesley--
       Christian Citizen; Selections from His Social Teaching. Lon-
       don: Epworth Press, 1937. 127p. Includes an introductory
       essay and notes on the extracts from Wesley's writings.

1730. Vallins, George Henry. The Wesleys and the English Lan-
       guage. London: Epworth Press, 1957. 88p.

1731. Verhalen, Philippo A. The Proclamation of the Word in the
       Writings of John Wesley. Rome: Pontificia Universitas Gre-
       goriana, 1969. 89p. A printed excerpt of the author's
       thesis.

1732. Vevers, William. An Essay on the National Importance of
       Methodism. London: John Mason, 1831. 138p.

1733. Vickers, John A. The Story of Canterbury Methodism.
       Canterbury: Gibbs and Son, 1961. 32p.

1734. Vickers, John A., and Betty Young. A Methodist Guide to
       London and the South-East. Bognor Regis, West Sussex:
       World Methodist Historical Society (British Section), 1980.
       44p.

1735. A View of the Economy of Methodism, from the Most Approved
       Authorities. New Haven, Conn.: Hezekiah Howe, 1830.
       24p. First published in the Quarterly Christian Spectator,
       vol. 1, pp. 509-26. Begins with a brief but sympathetic re-
       view of the pamphlet by John W. Barber, Thoughts on Some
       Parts of the Discipline of the Methodist Episcopal Church,
       1829, but most of the article is a diatribe against Wesley and
       Methodism.

1736. Vinter, Dorothy. Trapped in the Pit and Other Kingswood
       Stories. Kingswood, Eng.: Central Press, 1951. 20p.
       NjMUM

1737. Vranch, W. J. Coleford Wesley Church, 1745-1945: Bicen-

tenary Souvenir. Paulton: Durham West and Sons, 1945.
31p. GtBLW

1738. Vulliamy, Colwyn Edward. John Wesley. 3d ed. London:
       Epworth Press, 1954. 370p. (Rev. in no. 3440.)

1739. Waddy, Edith. Father of Methodism: A Sketch of the Life
       and Labours of the Rev. J. Wesley, M.A. London: Wes-
       leyan Conference Office, 1872. 120p.

1740. Waddy, J. Leonard. The Bitter Sacred Cup: The Wednes-
       bury Riots, 1743-44. Wesley Historical Society Lectures, no.
       36. London: World Methodist Historical Society, 1976. 46p.

1741. Waddy, John T. "Wesley As an Aphorist." In Wesley
       Studies, 201-6. See no. 190.

1742. Wade, John Donald. John Wesley. New York: Coward-
       McCann, 1930. 301p.

1743. Wainwright, Geoffrey. "Ecclesial Location and Ecumenical
       Vocation." Chap. 4 in The Future of the Methodist Theolog-
       ical Traditions, 93-129. See no. 57.

1744. Wakefield, Gordon S. "John Wesley." In Fire of Love; the
       Spirituality of John Wesley, 9-28. London: Darton, Long-
       man and Todd, 1976. 80p. The remainder of the book con-
       tains excerpts from the writings of John Wesley.

1745. _____. "The Legacy from the First Days." Chap. 1 in
       Methodist Devotion; the Spiritual Life in the Methodist Tra-
       dition, 1791-1945, 13-43. London: Epworth Press, 1966.
       120p.

1746. Wakeley, Joseph Beaumont. Anecdotes of the Wesleys: Il-
       lustrative of Their Character and Personal History. New
       York: Carlton and Lanahan, 1869. 391p.

1747. Wakeman, Henry Offley. "Methodism and the Evangelical Re-
       vival." Chap. 19 in An Introduction to the History of the
       Church of England from the Earliest Times to the Present Day,
       428-47. 12th ed. London: Rivingtons, 1938. 519p.

1748. Wakinshaw, William. John Wesley. Rev. ed. London: Ep-
       worth Press, 1954. 87p.

1749. Walker, James Uriah. A History of Wesleyan Methodism in
       Halifax and Its Vicinity from Its Commencement to the Present
       Period. Halifax: Hartley and Walker; London: Simpkin,
       Marshall and Co., 1836. 279p.

1750.   Walker, John. An Expostulatory Address to the Members of
        the Methodist Society in Ireland. Hittsburgh: Butler and
        Lambdin, 1820. 39p. Accuses the Methodists of following
        Wesley and Fletcher instead of Christ, and supplanting Scrip-
        ture with their writings.

1751.   Walker, Williston. "John Wesley." In Great Men of the
        Christian Church, 319-38. Chicago: University of Chicago
        Press, 1908. 378p.

1752.   _____. "Wesley and Methodism." In A History of the
        Christian Church, 507-18. New York: C. Scribner's Sons,
        1924. 624p.

1753.   Wallace, Archer. "The Mother of John Wesley." In Mothers
        of Famous Men, 7-14. New York: Richard R. Smith, 1931.
        105p.

1754.   Wallace, David Duncan. John Wesley.... Spartanburg, S.C.?
        19- . 15p. Wallace was professor of history and economics
        at Wofford College. NcD

1755.   Wallace, Williard M. "John Wesley and the American Revolu-
        tion." In Essays in Honor of Conyers Read, edited by Nor-
        ton Downs, 52-64. Chicago: Chicago University Press,
        1953. 304p.

1756.   Walmsley, Luke S. "John Wesley." In Fighters and Martyrs
        for the Freedom of Faith, 294-363. London: James Clarke,
        1912. 508p.

1757.   Walsh, John D. "Methodism and the Mob in the Eighteenth
        Century." In Popular Belief and Practice; Papers Read at
        the Ninth Summer Meeting and the Tenth Winter Meeting of
        the Ecclesiastical History Society, edited by G. J. Cuming
        and Derek Baker, 213-27. Studies in Church History, vol.
        8. Cambridge, Eng.: Cambridge University Press, 1972.
        330p.

1758.   _____. "Origins of the Evangelical Revival." In Essays
        in Modern English Church History, in Memory of Norman
        Sykes, edited by Gareth Vaughan Bennett and John Dixon
        Walsh, 132-62. London: Black, 1966.

1759.   Walters, Arthur. John Wesley. London: S. W. Partridge,
        1909. 159p.

1760.   Ward, Arthur. The Scene of Wesley's Last Sermon. Leather-
        head, Eng.: Dyer, 1929. 15p. Wesley preached his last
        sermon in Leatherhead.

1761. Ward, John.   Historical Sketches of the Rise and Pro-
       gress of Methodism in Bingley, with Brief Notices of Other
       Places in the Circuit. Bingley: John Harrison and Sons,
       1863. 115p.

1762. _____. Methodism in the Thirsk Circuit. Thirsk: David
       Peat, 1860. 122p.

1763. _____. The Rise and Progress of Wesleyan Methodism in
       Blackburn and the Neighbourhood. Blackburn: B. T. Bar-
       ton, 1871. 80p.

1764. _____. Round and through the Wesleyan Hymn Book.
       Leeds: B. W. Sharp, 1868. 132p.

1765. Ward, Jonathan.   A Vindication of A Brief Statement and Exami-
       nation of the Sentiments of the Wesleyan Methodists": In Re-
       ply to Rev. Joshua Taylor's Answer. To Which Is Subjoined,
       a Letter from Rev. Mr. Whitefield, to Rev. Mr. Wesley, in
       Answer to His Sermon Entitled Free Grace. Hallowell: Peter
       Edes, 1801. 120p.

1766. Ward, Valentine.   A Miniature of Methodism; or, A Brief Ac-
       count of the History, Doctrines, Discipline, and Character of
       the Methodists. 5th ed. London: John Mason, 1829. 152p.

1767. Ward, W. R.   "The Legacy of John Wesley: The Pastoral Of-
       fice in Britain and America." In Statesmen, Scholars and
       Merchants: Essays in Eighteenth-Century History Presented
       to Dame Lucy Sutherland, edited by Anne Whiteman, J. S.
       Bromley, and P. G. M. Dickson, 323-50. Oxford: Claren-
       don Press, 1973. 375p.

1768. Wardle, Addie Grace.   "English Antecedents of the American
       Methodist Sunday School Movement." Chap. 1 in History of
       the Sunday School Movement in the Methodist Episcopal Church,
       11-42. New York: Methodist Book Concern, 1918. 232p.

1769. Wardle, John W.   Sketches of Methodist History in Leek and
       the Moorlands, 1753 to 1943. [Leek, Eng., 1943.] 64p.

1770. Warfield, Donald Arthur.   A Lively People: The Story of A
       Village Methodist Society. Paulton and London: Purnell,
       1960. 175p.

1771. Warne, Arthur.   "Methodism and the Church." Chap. 8 in
       Church and Society in Eighteenth-Century Devon, 106-28.
       New York: A. M. Kelley, 1969. 184p.

1772. Warner, Stephen Alfred.   Lincoln College, Oxford. London:
       Fairbairns and Co., 1908. 107p.

1773. Warner, Wellman Joel. The Wesleyan Movement in the Indus-
       trial Revolution. London: Longmans, Green and Co., 1930.
       299p. A study of Wesley's economic ethics.

1774. Warren, Samuel. "Statement of the Principal Doctrines of
       Wesleyan Methodism." In vol. 1 of Chronicles of Wesleyan
       Methodism, 3-30. 2 vols. London: John Stephens, 1827.

1775. Was John Wesley a High Churchman? A Dialogue for the
       Times. London: Wesleyan-Methodist Book-Room, 1882. 31p.

1776. Washburn, Charles Campbell. Hymn Interpretations. Nash-
       ville: Cokesbury Press, 1938. 119p.

1777. _____. Hymn Stories. Nashville: Publishing House,
       Methodist Episcopal Church, South, Whitmore and Smith,
       Agents. 1935. 80p.

1778. Waterhouse, John Walters. The Bible in Charles Wesley's
       Hymns. Manual of Fellowship. 3d ser., no. 5. London:
       Epworth Press, 1954. 32p.

1779. Watkin-Jones, Howard. The Holy Spirit from Arminius to
       Wesley: A Study of Christian Teaching concerning the Holy
       Spirit and His Place in the Trinity in the Seventeenth and
       Eighteenth Centuries. London: Epworth Press, n.d. 335p.
       His dissertation, Cambridge University.

1780. Watkins, Owen Spencer. Soldiers and Preachers Too; Being
       the Romantic Story of Methodism in the British Army....
       London: C. H. Kelly, 1906. 267p.

1781. Watkins, William Turner. Out of Aldersgate. Nashville:
       Methodist Episcopal Church, South, 1937. 160p.

1782. _____. "Wesley's Message to His Own Age." In Methodism,
       21-27. See no. 287.

1783. Watkinson, John M. "Wesley and South Africa." In Wesley
       As a World Force..., 80-88. See no. 49.

1784. Watkinson, W. L. "The Calibre of Wesley." In Wesley
       Studies, 9-15. See no. 190.

1785. _____. Introduction to The Journal of John Wesley...,
       ix-xii. 2 vols. London: C. H. Kelly, 1903.

1786. Watmough, Abraham. A History of Methodism in the Neigh-
       bourhood and City of Lincoln; Including a Sketch of Early
       Methodism in the County of Lincoln. London: R. E. Leary,
       1829. 155p.

1787. _____. A History of Methodism in the Town and Neighbourhood of Great Yarmouth, Including Biographical Sketches
of Some of the Leading Characters Who Have Been among the
Methodists at That Place. London: John Kershaw, 1826.
228p.

1788. Watson, David Lowes. The Early Methodist Class Meeting:
Its Origins and Significance. Nashville: Discipleship Resources, 1985. 273p.

1789. Watson, Philip S. Introduction to The Message of the Wesleys: A Reader of Instruction and Devotion. New York:
Macmillan, 1964. 263p.

1790. Watson, Richard. The Life of the Rev. John Wesley to Which
are Subjoined Observations on Southey's Life of Wesley: Be-
ing a Defense of the Characters, Labors and Opinions of the
Founder of Methodism, against the Misrepresentations of That
Publication. New ed. with notes by Thomas O. Summers.
Nashville: Southern Methodist Publishing House, 1880. 345p.
(Rev. in no. 3172.)

1791. Watson, Wright, and J. Horsfall Turner. Idle Thorpe Wesleyan Methodist Chapel, 1810-1910: A Centenary Memorial.
Bradford: Fanciers' Newspaper, 1910. 199p.

1792. Watt, Hugh. "John Wesley." Representative Churchmen of
Twenty Centuries, 227-42. London: James Clarke, 1927.
255p.

1793. Watters, Philip S. A Hymn Festival Service Commemorating
the 250th Anniversary of the Birth of Charles Wesley. New
York: Hymn Society of America, 1957. 4p. IEG

1794. Watts, Michael R. "The Evangelical Revival." In The Dissenters, 394-482. Oxford: Clarendon Press, 1978. 543p.

1795. Weakley, Clare. Happiness Unlimited: John Wesley's Commentary on the Sermon on the Mount. Plainfield, N.J.:
Logos International, 1979. 297p.

1796. _____. Preface to John Wesley: The Holy Spirit and
Power, v-viii. Plainfield, N.J.: Logos International, 1977.
189p. This is a collection of John Wesley's writings, para-
phrased.

1797. Wearmouth, Robert F. Methodism and the Common People of
the Eighteenth Century. London: Epworth Press, 1945.
276p. Describes the condition of the common people in Great
Britain in the eighteenth century, the growth of Methodism,
and the contribution Methodism made to the common people.

The author states that Methodism made religion come alive,
gave the people opportunity to engage in social and economic
ventures, and to develop responsibility, discipline, and
loyalty, both to the state and to Methodism.

1798. Weatherill, George W. The Story of Darlington Methodism,
1753-1953. Darlington, Eng.: Dresser, 1953. 84p.

1799. Webber, Frederick Roth. "The Evangelical Awakening."
Chap. 8 in vol. 1 of A History of Preaching in Britain and
America, 319-76. 3 vols. Milwaukee, Wisc.: Northwestern
Publishing House, 1952.

1800. Webster, Thomas. "Wesley and Church Polity." In Wesley
Memorial Volume, 245-55. See no. 257.

1801. Wedgwood, Julia. John Wesley and the Evangelical Reaction
of the Eighteenth Century. London: Macmillan and Co.,
1870. 412p. (Rev. in nos. 2586, 2729, 4001.)

1802. Wedley, John F. A History of Methodism in the Stourport
Circuit from A.D. 1781 to A.D. 1899. Stourport: Stourport
Printing Co., 1899. 119p.

1803. Weems, Lovett Hayes. The Gospel According to Wesley: A
Summary of John Wesley's Message. Nashville: Discipleship
Resources, 1982. 63p.

1804. Welch, Herbert. "John Wesley." In Men of the Outposts;
the Romance of the Modern Christian Movement, 61-82. Drew
Lectureship in Biography. New York: Abingdon Press, 1937.
261p.

1805. _____. Preface to Selections from the Writings of the Rev.
John Wesley, M.A., 5-12. New York and Cincinnati: Methodist Book Concern, 1918. 405p.

1806. Wells, Amos Russel. A Treasure of Hymns; Brief Biographies
of One Hundred and Twenty Leading Hymn Writers with Their
Best Hymns. Freeport, N.Y.: Books for Libraries Press,
1945. 392p. Includes a brief discussion of Charles Wesley's
hymn, "Jesus, Lover of My Soul." It is the author's opinion
that this is the best of his hymns.

1807. Welsh, Robert E. "William Law's Serious Call: Jacob Behmen
and John Wesley." Chap. 11 in Classics of the Soul's Quest,
195-227. London: Hodder and Stoughton, 1922. 342p.

1808. Wesley, Eliza. "Wesleyan Hymn Music." In Wesley Memorial
Volume, 473-80. See no. 257.

1809. Wesley, John. A Compend of Wesley's Theology, edited by
       Robert W. Burtner and Robert E. Chiles. Nashville:
       Abingdon Press, 1954. 302p. This book contains a sys-
       tematic arrangement of selected passages from Wesley's the-
       ological writings with brief introductions by the editors.

1810. _____. Wesley's First Sermon and Other First Things in
       the Life of the Father of Methodism; in Remembrance, June
       17, 1703. London: C. H. Kelly, 1903. 63p. A collection
       of John Wesley's writing with brief introductions to each
       piece. "The Wesleyan Methodist Conference Office is in-
       debted to Mr. Russell J. Colman, of Norwich, for permission
       to photograph and reproduce the manuscripts in this sou-
       venir. Mr. Colman inherited them from his father, the late
       Mr. J. J. Colman, into whose possession they came, many
       years ago, through Mr. Gandy, from the Rev. Henry Moore,
       one of the executors under the will of John Wesley"--note.
       IEG

1811. Wesley, Sarah. Introduction to Sermons by the Late ...
       Charles Wesley..., iii-xxxiv. London: Baldwin, Cradock,
       and Joy, 1816. 244p. This introduction was written by
       Charles' widow.

1812. Wesley and His Successors; a Centenary Memorial of the Death
       of John Wesley. London: C. H. Kelly, 1891. 257p.

1813. Wesley Bi-centennial Celebration by Charleston Methodist
       Churches, June 24-28, 1903.... N.p. [1903?]

1814. "The Wesley Family." In The Journals of the Rev. John Wes-
       ley, xx. See no. 542.

1815. "Wesley in America." In AmeriChristendom, 172-84. Port-
       land, Or.: Printed at Graphic Arts Center, for A Garrett,
       1967. 250p.

1816. Wesleyan Methodism Defended, and the Apostolical Succes-
       sion Shown to Be a Broken Chain.... Truro: G. Clyma,
       1842. 16p.

1817. Wesleyan Methodist Church. A Handbook of Wesleyan Method-
       ist Polity and History. London: Wesleyan Methodist Book
       Room, 1888. 278p.

1818- Wesleyan Takings: or, Centenary Sketches of Ministerial
1819. Character, As Exhibited in the Wesleyan Connexion During
       the First Hundred Years of Its Existence. 2 vols. London:
       Hamilton, Adams and Co., 1851. 364p. Contains biographical
       sketches of John and Charles Wesley.

1820. Wesleyana: A Selection of the Most Important Passages in the
       Writings of the Late Rev. J. Wesley, A.M.:   Arranged to Form
       a Complete Body of Divinity: With a Portrait and Biographical
       Sketch. London: W. Booth, 1825. 457p. Biographical sketch
       on pp. 9-53.

1821- Wesley's England. Drawings by Geoffrey Fletcher; photo-
1822. graphs by John Ray, Kathleen Stevens and E. W. Tattersall.
       London: Methodist Recorder, 1966. 82p.

1823. Wesley's Interpretation of the Bible. Wesley and Methodism,
       no. 6. Tokyo: Japan Wesley Association, 1972. 67, 43p.
       Text in Japanese with synopses in English.

1824. West, Anson. "The Doctrinal Unity of Methodism." In
       Methodist Episcopal Church in the U.S., 245-55. See no. 1163.
       A discussion of the unity of Methodist doctrine as formulated
       and defended by John Wesley.

1825. West, George. Methodism in Marshland. London: Wesleyan
       Conference Office, 1886. 105p.

1826. [West, Nathaniel]. John Wesley and Premillenialism. Louis-
       ville, Ky.: Pentecostal Publishing Co., 1894. 47p.

1827. West, W. R. Nonconformity in a Village. The Story of
       Methodism in the Village of Silverton, Devon, etc. Silverton:
       Rockwell Printers, 1964. 31p.

1828. Westbrook, Francis B. Some Early Methodist Tune Books.
       Wesley Historical Society Lectures, no. 4. Penzance, Corn-
       wall: Headland Print Co., 1974. 24p. A lecture on three
       tune books issued by Wesley: the Foundery Tune Book
       (1742), Select Hymns with Tunes Annext (1761), and Sacred
       Harmony (1780).

1829. Weston, Frank. The Teaching of John Wesley As Gathered
       from His Writings. London: Society for Promoting Christian
       Knowledge, 1912. 31p.

1830. Whaling, Frank. Introduction to John and Charles Wesley;
       Selected Prayers, Hymns, Journal Notes, Sermons, Letters
       and Treatises, 1-64. See no. 1255.

1831. Whedon, D. A. Entire Sanctification. John Wesley's View.
       Noblesville, Ind.: Newby Books, n.d. 40p.

1832. Whedon, Daniel Denison. "Methodist Episcopacy." In Es-
       says, Reviews and Discourses, 157-97. New York: Phillips
       and Hunt; Cincinnati: Cranston and Stowe, 1887. 352p.

158   John and Charles Wesley

1833. Wheeler, Alfred. "The Relation of Mr. Wesley to American
       Methodism." In Methodist Episcopal Church in the U.S.,
       143-51. See no. 1163.

1834. Wheeler, Henry. "Wesley's Abridgement Compared with the
       Original Thirty-nine Articles." In History and Exposition of
       the 25 Articles of Religion of the Methodist Episcopal Church,
       14-46. New York: Eaton and Mains, 1908. 382p.

1835. When God Came. Chapters on S. Francis of Assisi, Johann
       Tauler, and John Wesley. Preface by Cyril C. B. Bardsley.
       London: Church Missionary Society, 1915. 78p.

1836. White, James F. Introduction with Notes to John Wesley's
       Sunday Service of the Methodists in North America, 9-37.
       Nashville: United Methodist Publishing House, 1984. 87p.

1837. White, William. An Essay, Containing Objections against the
       Position of a Personal Assurance of the Pardon of Sin....
       Philadelphia: Moses Thomas, 1817. 67p. An anti-methodist
       publication.

1838. _____. "Of Mr. Wesley." Section 16 in A Review of the
       Question of a Personal Assurance of Pardon of Sin, by a
       Direct Communication of the Holy Spirit..., 54-63. Phila-
       delphia: Moses Thomas, 1818. 79p.

1839. Whitehead, John. A Discourse Delivered at the New Chapel,
       in the City-Road, on the Ninth of March, 1791, at the Fune-
       ral of the Late Rev. Mr. John Wesley. London: G. Paramore,
       1791. 71p.

1840. _____. The Life of the Rev. John Wesley, M.A. Collected
       from His Private Papers and Printed Works; and Written at
       the Request of His Executors. To Which Is Prefixed, Some
       Account of His Ancestors and Relations; with the Life of the
       Rev. Charles Wesley, M.A. Collected from His Private Jour-
       nal, and Never Before Published.... 2 vols. London: S.
       Couchman, 1793-96.

1841. _____. Proposals for Printing, by Subscription, the Life
       of the Late Rev. J. Wesley. 1791.

1842. Whiteley, J. H. Wesley's Anglican Contemporaries: Their
       Trials and Triumphs. Wesley Historical Society Lectures, no.
       5. London: Epworth Press, 1939. 67p.

1843. _____. Wesley's England; a Survey of Eighteenth Century
       Social and Cultural Conditions. London: Epworth Press,
       1945. 332p.

Books 159

1844. Whitford-Roberts, Edward. John Wesley in Monmouthshire. Free Churches in Monmouthshire. Newport, Eng.: R. H. Jones, 1965. 12p.

1845. Who Shall Be Saved? The Twenty Years Conflict between John Wesley and William Law, the Mystic; Studied from Their Work and Correspondence, by T. O. Beachcroft. London: British Broadcasting Corporation, 1956. InU-Lilly

1846. Whyte, Alexander. "John Wesley." In Thirteen Apprecia- tions, 361-80. Edinburgh: Oliphant, Anderson, and Fer- rier, 1913. 380p.

1847. Wickham, Edward Ralph. "The Birth and Growth of Method- ism," and "The Social Composition of Methodism." In Church and People in an Industrial City, 49-58. London: Lutter- worth Press, 1957. 292p. Describes the activities of the Wesleys in Sheffield.

1848. Wightman, William M. "Wesley and Coke." In Wesley Memo- rial Volume, 481-96. See no. 257.

1849. Wilcox, Leslie D. "The Wesleyan Revival," and "Wesley and His Contemporaries." Chaps. 17 and 22 in Be Ye Holy; a Study of the Teaching of Scripture Relative to Entire Sanc- tification with a Sketch of the History and the Literature of the Holiness Movement, 139-64, 247-302. Cincinnati: Revi- valist Press, 1965. 407p.

1850. Wilder, Franklin. Father of the Wesleys; a Biography. Hicksville, N.Y.: Exposition Press, 1971. 220p.

1851. _____. Immortal Mother. New York: Vantage Press, 1967. 230p.

1852. _____. Martha Wesley. Hicksville, N.Y.: Exposition Press, 1976. 136p.

1853. _____. The Methodist Riots: The Testing of Charles Wesley. Great Neck, N.Y.: Todd and Honeywell, 1981. 160p.

1854. _____. The Remarkable World of John Wesley, Pioneer in Mental Health. Hicksville, N.Y.: Exposition Press, 1978. 192p.

1855. Wilkinson, John Thomas. "Revival: The Age of Wesley." Chap. 8 in 1662 and After: Three Centuries of English Non- conformity, 117-37. London: Epworth Press, 1962. 269p.

1856. Wilkinson, Wilfred R. "John Wesley." In Religious Experience:

The Methodist Fundamental, 54-64. Hartley Lectures, 28.
London: Holborn Publishing House, 1928. 248p.

1857. Williams, Albert Hughes. Introduction to John Wesley in
Wales, 1739-1790: Entries from His Journal and Diary Re-
lating to Wales. Cardiff: University of Wales Press, 1971.
141p. This volume contains all the accounts written by
John Wesley of his many visits to Wales. These accounts
were extracted from his journal, with references also to his
diary. In his introduction, Williams discusses Wesley's
visits to Wales, the development of the religious societies
with the two distinct Methodist movements--Howell Harris's
Welsh Calvinistic Methodism and Wesleyan Methodism.

1858. _____. "John Wesley and Welsh Wesleyan Methodism.
Chap. 1 in Welsh Wesleyan Methodism, 1800-1858; Its Origins,
Growth and Secessions, 15-43. Bangor, Wales: Cyhoeddwyd
gan Lyfrfa'r Methodistiaid, 1935. 378p.

1859. Williams, Charles. "John Wesley." In Stories of Great
Names, 165-92. London: Oxford University Press, 1937.
216p.

1860. Williams, Colin Wilbur. John Wesley's Theology Today. New
York: Abingdon Press, 1960. 252p.

1861. Williams, George Walton. "Bibliographical Notes." In John
Wesley's First Hymn-Book; a Collection of Psalms and Hymns;
a Facsimile with Additional Material, edited by Frank Baker
and George Walton Williams, xxxv-xxxvii. Charleston:
Dalcho Historical Society; London: Wesley Historical Society,
1964.

1862. Williams, Howard King. "Morning Star of Spirituality, John
Wesley, England." In Stars of the Morning, 143-58. New
York: George H. Doran Co., 1926. 200p.

1863. Williams, James R. "Primitive or Ancient Methodism." Chap.
1 in History of the Methodist Protestant Church, 13-29.
Baltimore: Book Committee of the Methodist Protestant Church,
1843. 401p.

1864. Williams, Robert R. Flames from the Altar: Howell Harris
and His Contemporaries. Caernarvon: Calvinistic Methodist
Book Agency, 1962. 99p.

1865. Williams, Thomas Grange. Methodism and Anglicanism in the
Light of Scripture and History. Toronto: W. Briggs, 1888.
282p. The first three chapters discuss Wesley's relationship
to the Church of England, his plan for the Methodist societies, and his high churchmanship.

1866. Williamson, A. Wallace. The Methodist Church. St. Giles'
       Lectures. 4th ser. Edinburgh: Macnivan and Wallace,
       1884. 35p.

1867. Wilson, Charles R. "John Wesley's Christology." In A Con-
       temporary Wesleyan Theology: Biblical, Systematic, and
       Practical, 342-50. See no. 279.

1868. Wilson, David. Methodism in Scotland; a Brief Sketch of the
       Rise, Progress and Present Position in That Country. Aber-
       deen: J. Ogilvie, A. Brown, 1850. 48p.

1869. Wilson, David Dunn. Many Waters Cannot Quench: A Study
       of Sufferings of Eighteenth Century Methodism and Their
       Significance for John Wesley and the First Methodists. Lon-
       don: Epworth Press, 1969. 213p.

1870. Wilson, James Hood. "John Wesley." In Evangelical Succes-
       sion: A Course of Lectures Delivered in Free St. George's
       Church, Edinburgh, 1883-84, 145-78. 3d ser. Edinburgh:
       Macnivan and Wallace, 1884.

1871. Wilson, Woodrow. John Wesley's Place in History. New York
       and Cincinnati: Abingdon Press, 1915. 48p. An address
       delivered at Wesleyan University on the occasion of the Wes-
       ley bicentennial. It is also contained in Frederick A. Nor-
       wood's Sourcebook of American Methodism, (1982) and Wesley
       Bicentennial, Wesleyan University, 157-70, no. 52. In addi-
       tion, it appears in Together, March 1964.

1872. Wimberly, Charles Franklin. "John Wesley." In Beacon
       Lights of Faith, 127-34. New York: Fleming H. Revell Co.,
       1929. 191p.

1873. Winchester, Caleb Thomas. "John Wesley, the Man." In
       Wesley Bicentennial, Wesleyan University, 97-124. See no.
       52.

1874. _____. Life of John Wesley. New York and London: Mac-
       millan, 1906. 301p.

1875. Winchester, Elhanan. A Funeral Sermon for the Reverend
       Mr. John Wesley, Who Departed This Life, March 2nd, 1791,
       in the Eighty-Eighth Year of His Age, Delivered March 10th,
       the Day After His Internment. London, 1791. 59p.

1876. Winters, William. An Account of the Remarkable Musical
       Talents of Several Members of the Wesley Family, Collected
       from Original Manuscripts.... London: F. Davis, 1874.
       91p.

1877. Wise, Daniel. The Ancestry of the Wesley Family. Oxford
       League Series, no. 1. New York: Phillips and Hunt, 18--?
       20p.

1878. _____. The Literary Work of the Wesleys. Oxford
       League Series, no. 5. New York: Phillips and Hunt,
       [188-?]. 16p. NjMUM

1879. Wiseman, Frederick Luke. Charles Wesley and His Hymns.
       London: Epworth Press, 1938. 30p. First appeared in A
       New History of Methodism, no. 229.

1880. _____. Charles Wesley, Evangelist and Poet. New York
       and Cincinnati: Abingdon Press, 1932. 231p.

1881. _____. "John Wesley As a Musician." In Wesley Studies,
       156-60. See no. 190.

1882. _____. "John Wesley's Tunes." In Wesley Studies, 161-
       69. See no. 190.

1883. Wiseman, Luke Holt. Agents in the Religious Revival of the
       Last Century: A Lecture. London: James Nisbet and Co.,
       1855. 36p.

1884. Witherow, J. M. Church Rebels and Pioneers. London:
       Religious Tract Society, 1927. 272p.

1885. Withrow, William Henry. Makers of Methodism. London:
       C. H. Kelly, 1903. 256p.

1886. Wolverhampton, Henry Hartley Fowler. A Lecture on the
       Institutions of Wesleyan Methodism. London: Hamilton,
       Adams and Co., 1858. 40p. Examines the origin of Method-
       ism and its institutions as established by Wesley.

1887. Wood, A. Harold. "Charles Wesley's Hymns on Holiness." In
       Dig or Die..., 67-76. See no. 84.

1888. _____. "Our Heritage in Charles Wesley's Hymns." In
       Dig or Die..., 48-66. See no. 84.

1889. Wood, A. Skevington. The Burning Heart: John Wesley,
       Evangelist. Exeter: Paternoster Press, 1967. 302p.

1890. _____. "The Contribution of John Wesley to the Theology
       of Grace." In Grace Unlimited, edited by Clark Pinnock,
       209-22. Minneapolis: Bethany Fellowship, 1975. 264p.

1891. _____. The Inextinguishable Blaze: Spiritual Renewal
       and Advance in the Eighteenth Century. London: Pater-
       noster Press, 1960. 256p.

1892. Wood, E. M. "John Wesley a Friend of the American
       Colonies," and "How Methodism in Great Britain Failed to Be-
       come Episcopal: Wesley's Desire and Efforts to Make It Such."
       Part 1, Chap. 1, and Part 2, Chap. 4 in Methodism and the
       Centennial of American Independence, 13-37, 163-74. New
       York: Nelson and Phillips, 1876. 414p.

1893. Wood, John Allen. Mistakes Respecting Christian Holiness.
       Chicago: Christian Witness, 1905. 136p.

1894. Wood, Wallace. "John Wesley." In Hundred Greatest Men;
       Portraits of the One Hundred Greatest Men of History Re-
       produced from Fine and Rare Steel Engravings, 191-94.
       Introduction by Ralph Waldo Emerson. New York: D. Ap-
       pleton and Co., 1885. 504p.

1895. Woodhead, Donald W. Buxton Wesley Chapel: The Story of
       a Hundred Years, 1849-1949. Buxton: Buxton Printing
       Co., 1949. 76p. GtBLW

1896. Woodward, E. "Of Methodist Episcopacy." Chap. 2 in A
       Brief View of Methodist Episcopacy, 9-12. Lexington, Mass.:
       Herndon and Savary, 1831. 40p.

1897. Woodward, Max W. One at London: Some Account of Mr.
       Wesley's Chapel and London House. London: Epworth
       Press, 1966. 140p.

1898. Workman, H. B. "John Wesley." Chap. 2 in Methodism,
       25-67. Cambridge: Cambridge University Press, 1912.
       133p.

1899. _____. The Place of Methodism in the Catholic Church.
       Rev. ed. London: Epworth Press, 1921. 104p. This is a
       "survey of the place of Methodism in the life-history of the
       Church...."

1900. _____. "The Place of Methodism in the Life and Thought
       of the Christian Church." In vol. 1, Chap. 1 of A New
       History of Methodism, 1-73. See no. 229.

1901. Wrangham, Digby Strangeways. "Rescue and Retire!" A Se-
       quel to "Modern Methodism," in a Correspondence between
       Rev. James H. Rigg and Digby S. Wrangham. Pontefract,
       [Eng.]: R. Holmes, 1884. 27p. NjMUM

1902. Wright, Arnold. Annesley of Surat and His Times: True
       Story of Mythical Wesley Fortune. London: A. Melrose,
       1918. 357p.

1903. Wright, Dudley. The Epworth Phenomena, to Which Are
       Appended Certain Psychic Experiences Recorded by John

164   John and Charles Wesley

Wesley in the Pages of His Journal, Collated. London: W.
Rider, 1917. 110p.

1904. Wright, Elliott. "The Wesleys--Susanna, John, Charles."
In Holy Company: Christian Heroes and Heroines, 187-92.
New York: Macmillan Publishing Co., 1980. 272p.

1905. Wright, Ernest H. A Story of Timperley Methodism, 1833-
1933. Altrincham: Mackie and Co., 1933. 44p. GtBLW

1906. Wright, Fred C. Wesleyan Methodism; a Defence. London:
C. H. Kelly, 1893. 32p.

1907. Wright, J. "Methodist Antiquities." In Wesley Studies, 170-
74. See no. 190. Describes collections of Wesleyana that
have been lost or destroyed.

1908. Wright, John. Early Methodism in Yarm. Billingham:
Billingham Press, 1949. 32p. GtBLW

1909. Wright, Louis B. "John Wesley: Scholar and Critic." In
Making of English History, edited by R. L. Schuyler and H.
Ausubel, 438-49. New York: Henry Holt, 1952. 686p.
Describes Wesley's literary activities, claiming that "he was
scarcely more concerned over the souls than over the minds
of his followers in Britain and America."

1910. Wright, Robert. A Memoir of General James Oglethorpe, One
of the Earliest Reformers of Prison Discipline in England, and
the Founder of Georgia, in America. London: Chapman and
Hall, 1867. 414p. Several chapters are devoted to the Wesley's experiences in Georgia.

1911. Wycherley, Richard Newman. The Methodist Class-Meeting.
London: Robert Culley, [1908]. 199p.

1912. _____. The Pageantry of Methodist Union.... London:
Epworth Press, 1936. 411p. Pages 11-63 deal with the Wesleys and Wesleyan Methodism.

1913. Wycliffe to Wesley; Heroes and Martyrs of the Church in
Britain. London: C. H. Kelly, 1902. 344p. Both John
Wesley and Charles Wesley are included.

1914. Wyman, Edward. Methodism in Robin Hood's Bay: Old and
New. Whitby: John Hudson, n.d. 7p. GtBLW

1915. Wynkoop, Mildred Bangs. Foundations of Wesleyan-Arminian
Theology. Kansas City, Mo.: Beacon Hill Press, 1967. 128p.

1916. _____. John Wesley: Christian Revolutionary. Kansas
City, Mo.: Beacon Hill Press, 1970. 53p.

1917. _____. A Theology of Love; the Dynamic of Wesleyanism. Kansas City, Mo.: Beacon Hill Press, 1972. 372p.

1918. Wynne-Jones, T. Wesleyan Methodism in the Brecon Circuit; and Introduction of English and Welsh Methodism into the Principality: A Historical and Biographical Sketch from 1750 to 1888. Brecon: Edwin Poole; London: Wesleyan Methodist Book Room, 1888. 128p.

1919. Wyon, Olive. Desire for God: A Study of Three Spiritual Classics: Frances Fénelon, "Christian Perfection"; John Wesley, "Christian Perfection"; Evelyn Underhill, "The Spiritual Life." London: Collins, 1966. 126p.

1920. Yates, Arthur S. The Doctrine of Assurance, with Special Reference to John Wesley. London: Epworth Press, 1952. 242p. His dissertation, Leeds University, 1949.

1921. Young, David. "John Wesley--His Great Work." Chap. 5 in The Origin and History of Methodism in Wales and the Borders. London: C. H. Kelly, 1893. 731p. There are many references to both Wesleys throughout the book.

1922. Young, Dinsdale T. "Wesley As a Popular Preacher." In Wesley Studies, 207-12. See no. 190.

1923. Young, Frank. Early History of Methodism around Houghton-Le-Spring [County Durham]. N.p. 1922. 35p. GtBLW

1924. Youngs, James. A History of the Most Interesting Events in the Rise and Progress of Methodism, in Europe and America. New Haven, Conn.: A. Daggett and Co., 1830. 443p. Pp. 13-199 deal with Wesley's life and work.

ARTICLES

1925. Abelove, Henry. "George Berkeley's Attitude to John Wesley: The Evidence of a Lost Letter." Harvard Theological Review 70 (1977): 175-76.

1926. Abraham, William J. "Response: The Perils of a Wesleyan Systematic Theologian." Wesleyan Theological Journal 17, no. 1 (1982): 23-29. Response to article no. 2551.

1927. "An Accident to John Wesley." Methodist People, 18 May 1889, 59. Relates an accident reported in the Belfast Newsletter, 7 May 1790. Wesley was thrown overboard while going from Egypt, Isle of Wight, to Portsmouth.

1928. "Account of the Opening of a New School-Room at Kingswood." Wesleyan Methodist Magazine 45 (1822): 661-65.

1929. Adam, James. "At 'The Tail of the Bark': The Growth of Our Church at Greenock." Methodist Recorder, 7 April 1910, 10.

1930. Adams, Charles. "Wesley the Catholic." Methodist Quarterly Review 32 (1850): 179-97.

1931. Adams, Edward Bradford. "Hymn-writing Families." Hymn 8 (1957): 57-59.

1932. Adams, Evyn M. "Wesley and Sören Kierkegaard on the 'New Birth.' Are There Similarities or Not?" Wesleyan Quarterly Review 4 (1967): 220-26.

1933. Adams, Morley. "An Historic City: Sketches of Methodism in Norwich." Methodist Recorder, 8 October 1903, 13-14.

1934. _____. "Methodism in Bedford: St. Mary's Circuit." Methodist Recorder, 12 February 1903, 13-14.

1935. _____. "Methodism in Bunyan Land: The St. Paul's Circuit, Bedford." Methodist Recorder, 5 February 1903, 17-18.

1936. _____. "Methodism in Oyster-land: The Colchester Circuit." Methodist Recorder, 27 November 1902, 15-16.

1937. Adlard, J. Cartwright. "Did Wesley Lack Charm?" Wesleyan Methodist Magazine 145 (1922): 751-52.

1938. Akerman, James. "Letter from the Salisbury Circuit." Wesleyan Methodist Magazine 59 (1836): 51-54.

1939. Akers, Milburn P. "John Wesley--a Man to Know." Together 7, no. 5 (1963): 32-34.

1939a. Albin, Thomas R. "Charles Wesley's Earliest Evangelical Sermons." Methodist History 21 (1982): 60-62. Describes six unpublished shorthand manuscript sermons by Charles Wesley discovered in the Methodist Archives in Great Britain.

1940. Alderfer, Owen H. "British Evangelical Response to the American Revolution: The Wesleyans." Fides et Historia 8, no. 2 (1976): 7-34.

1941. _____. "John Wesley on Aspects of Christian Experience After Justification." Asbury Seminarian 18, no. 2 (1964): 22-48.

1942. "Aldersgate and After." Methodist Recorder, 19 May 1949, 8.

1943. Aldridge, Alfred Owen. "Dryden Song and Wesley Hymn." Saturday Review of Literature 25, no. 22 (1942): 15.

1944. Alexander, Gross. "Two Chapters from the Early History of Methodism in the South." Methodist Quarterly Review (Nashville) 63 (1914): 419-37. Discusses the significance for Methodism of John Wesley's residence in Savannah and the early growth of Methodism in the South.

1945. Alger, B. A. M. "Methodism in Derby." Methodist Recorder, 2 October 1902, 13-15.

1946. Allbeck, Willard D. "Plenteous Grace with Thee Is Found." Religion in Life 29 (1960): 501-6.

1947. Allen, Mortimer. "Kingsley's Country: Bideford and Its Methodism, Past and Present." Methodist Recorder, 22 February 1906, 9.

1948. Allen, William. "Glimpses of Former Days - Dr. Beaumont on John Wesley." Methodist Recorder, Christmas Number, 1892, 12-13.

1949. Alnwick, Arthur B. "Wesley and Ourselves." Baptist Quarterly 9 (1939): 475-83.

168   John and Charles Wesley

1950.   Alsobrook, Aubrey. "John Wesley's 'Savannah-gate' Ex-
        perience." Christian Advocate 9, no. 10 (1965): 11-12.

1951.   "An Ancient Naval Station: Methodism in Sheerness-on-Sea."
        Methodist Recorder, 25 January 1912, 10.

1952.   Anderson, Kenneth N., and Richard Dunlap. "John Wesley:
        Man of Medicine, Too!" Together 8, no. 2 (1964): 22-25.

1953.   Andrews, C. F. "John Wesley and the East." Visva-Bharati
        Quarterly 6 (1928): 281-94.

1954.   Andrews, Stuart. "John Wesley and America." History To-
        day 26 (1976): 353-59. This article concerns early Methodism
        in the American colonies, and Wesley's Calm Address.

1955.   _____. "John Wesley and the Age of Reason." History
        Today 19 (1969): 25-32. Describes Wesley's interest in things
        intellectual, and claims that he was not out of tune with the
        age of reason.

1956.   "Anecdote of Early Methodism in Bristol." Wesleyan Methodist
        Magazine 85 (1862): 1111-13.

1957.   "Anecdotes of the Late Charles Wesley, Esq." Wesleyan
        Methodist Magazine 57 (1834): 514-19.

1958.   "Anniversary of Wesley's Death." Methodist Recorder, 3
        March 1865, 68-69.

1959.   Arnett, William M. "John Wesley and the Bible." Wesleyan
        Theological Journal 3 (1968): 3-9.

1960.   _____. "John Wesley and the Law." Asbury Seminarian
        34, no. 4 (1979): 22-31.

1961.   _____. "The Many-sidedness of John Wesley." Asbury
        Seminarian 24, no. 2 (1970): 3-6.

1962.   _____. "The Role of the Holy Spirit in Entire Sanctifica-
        tion in the Writings of John Wesley." Asbury Seminarian
        29, no. 2 (1974): 5-23. Reprinted in Wesleyan Theological
        Journal 14, no. 2 (1979): 15-30.

1963.   _____. "A Study in John Wesley's Explanatory Notes upon
        the Old Testament." Wesleyan Theological Journal 8 (1973):
        14-32.

1964.   _____. "What Happened to Wesley at Aldersgate?" Asbury
        Seminarian 18, no. 1 (1964): 6-17.

1965. "As John Wesley Was." Newsweek 56 (21 November 1960):
       78. An article on the announcement of the plan to publish
       the new edition of Wesley's works.

1966. Ashdown, Dulcie. "John Wesley: The Founder of Methodism
       Regarded Himself As a Loyal Priest of the Church of England
       to the Very End." British History Illustrated 4, no. 6 (1978):
       8-15.

1967. Ashley, John. "With Wesley in Holland." Methodist Magazine,
       October 1956, 448-51.

1968. Attwood, A. "The Life and Ministry of Wesley." Methodist
       Recorder, 30 July 1872, 406.

1969. Aukema, Richard L. "Dusting Off John Wesley." Christian
       Advocate 7, no. 9 (1963): 12.

1970. Aurand, Evelyn. "Voices of Reformation." Music Ministry 1,
       no. 3 (1968): 2-7. Discusses Luther's and Charles Wesley's
       hymns.

1971. Austen, Edmund. "John Wesley and His Sussex Friends."
       Sussex County Magazine 4 (1930): 586-94.

1972. _____. "John Wesley and the Magistrate at Rolvenden,
       Kent." Proceedings of the Wesley Historical Society 18
       (1932): 113-20.

1973. _____. "John Wesley, Dr. Stonestreet and Early Methodism
       in Northiam, East Sussex." Proceedings of the Wesley Histori-
       cal Society 15 (1926): 169-73. John Stonestreet was a medical
       practitioner. Wesley's keen interest in medicine may have in-
       fluenced his frequent visits to Dr. Stonestreet.

1974. _____. "John Wesley, the 'Haddocks', Early Methodism in
       Rye, and Wesley's Last Open-Air Service at Winchelsea."
       Proceedings of the Wesley Historical Society 16 (1928): 79-87.

1975. _____. "John Wesley, the 'Holmans' and Early Methodism in
       East Sussex." Proceedings of the Wesley Historical Society
       15 (1925): 1-8.

1976. _____. "John Wesley, the 'Pikes' and Early Methodism in
       Robertsbridge, East Sussex." Proceedings of the Wesley His-
       torical Society 15 (1926): 128-31.

1977. _____. "John Wesley's Special Visit to Ewhurst, East Sus-
       sex." Proceedings of the Wesley Historical Society 19 (1934):
       112-14.

1978. _____. "A Sussex Centenary: The Story of Methodism in Staplecross." Methodist Recorder, 9 January 1913, 10.

1979. _____. "Wesley's Tree at Winchelsea." Proceedings of the Wesley Historical Society 16 (1928): 107-10.

1980. B. "In the 'Shirley' Country: Gomersall and Its Methodism." Methodist Recorder, 11 October 1906, 9.

1981. _____. "A Memorable Jubilee: Pits-o'-Th'-Moor and Its Methodist History." Methodist Recorder, 31 December 1908, 1365.

1982. _____. "Methodism in Loughborough: A Typical Midland County Circuit." Methodist Recorder, 3 February 1910, 10.

1983. B., F. "The Orphan House." Methodist Recorder, 21 February 1946, 1.

1984. B., H. "A Book That Influenced the Wesleys." Methodist Recorder, 4 October 1906, 15.

1985. _____. "Methodism in Darlington: The Birthplace of the Locomotive." Methodist Recorder, 16 August 1906, 10.

1986. B., R. "Re-opening of Wesley's Rooms at Oxford: American Methodism's Acknowledgment of a Great Debt to Lincoln College." Methodist Recorder, 13 September 1928, 4.

1987. B., W. T. "John Dolman and the Wesleys." Musical Standard 11 (1918): 147-48.

1988. _____. "John Wesley's Charleston Hymn-Book." Musical Standard 9 (1917): 287-88.

1989. Backhouse, William. "Ancient Methodism in a Quiet Corner: Delph: In the Saddleworth Circuit." Methodist Recorder, 25 May 1911, 10.

1990. _____. "A Bit of Ancient Methodism, Beeston: In the Leeds (Hunslet) Circuit." Methodist Recorder, 1 April 1909, 10.

1991. Bacon, William. "Methodism in Newcastle-upon-Tyne." Wesleyan Methodist Magazine 62 (1839): 584-86.

1992. Baillie, A. S. "John Wesley's Last Sermon at Oxford." Christian Evangelist 64 (1927): 1099-1100, 1126.

1993. Bainbridge, T. A. "John Wesley's Travels in Westmorland and Lancashire North-of-the-Sands." Transactions of the

Articles   171

Cumberland and Westmorland Antiquarian and Archaeological
Society, n.s. 52 (1953): 106-13.

1994. Bainbridge, T. H. "John Wesley's Travels in Cumberland."
Transactions of the Cumberland and Westmorland Antiquarian
and Archaeological Society, n.s. 47 (1947): 183-98.

1995. Bainbridge, W., and Marmaduke Riggall. "Wesley and Dr.
John Taylor, of Norwich." Proceedings of the Wesley Historical Society 16 (1928): 69-71.

1996. Baker, Donald. "Charles Wesley and the American Loyalists."
Proceedings of the Wesley Historical Society 35 (1965): 5-9.
Discusses Charles Wesley's poetical treatment of the American
loyalists.

1997. _____. "Charles Wesley and the American War of Independence." Methodist History 5, no. 1 (1966): 5-37.

1998. _____. "Charles Wesley and the American War of Independence." Proceedings of the Wesley Historical Society 34
(1964): 159-64.

1999. _____. "Charles Wesley and the American War of Independence." Proceedings of the Wesley Historical Society 40
(1976): 125-34, 165-82.

2000. _____. "Patriots and Howe!" Contemporary Review 230
(1977): 15-23. This is an article on Charles Wesley's poem
"The American War under the Conduct of Sir William Howe."

2001. Baker, Ernest A., and W. M. Parker. "Sentimentalism."
Times Literary Supplement, 23 May, 1936, 440. Two letters
in response to Herbert's letter, no. 2853a.

2002. Baker, Frank. "'Aldersgate' and Wesley's Editors." London
Quarterly and Holborn Review 191 (1966): 310-19.

2003. _____. "Aldersgate 1738-1963; the Challenge of Aldersgate."
Duke Divinity School Bulletin 28 (1963): 67-80. An address
delivered at the "Aldersgate Around the World" gathering in
Winston-Salem, 24 May 1963.

2004. _____. "American Methodism: Beginnings and Ends."
Methodist History 6, no. 3 (1968): 3-15.

2005. _____. "The Beginnings of American Methodism." Methodist History 2, no. 1 (1963): 1-15.

2006. _____. "The Beginnings of the Methodist Covenant Service." London Quarterly and Holborn Review 180 (1955): 215-
20.

2007.   . "The Birth of Charles Wesley." Proceedings of the Wesley Historical Society 31 (1957): 25-26.

2008.   . "The Birth of John Wesley's Journal." Methodist History 8, no. 2 (1970): 25-32.

2009.   . "Charles Wesley to 'Varanese' [possibly Sally Kirkham]." Proceedings of the Wesley Historical Society 25 (1946): 97-104.

2010.   . "Charles Wesley's 'Hymns for Children.'" Proceedings of the Wesley Historical Society 31 (1957): 81-85.

2011.   . "Charles Wesley's Scripture Playing Cards." Proceedings of the Wesley Historical Society 29 (1954): 136-38.

2012.   . "Dr. Thomas Coke and Methodism in the Isle of Wight." Proceedings of the Wesley Historical Society 38 (1971): 56-59.

2013.   . "Early American Methodism: A Key Document." Methodist History 3, no. 2 (1965): 3-15. Discussion of a letter from Thomas Taylor in New York to John Wesley, 11 April 1768.

2014.   . "Edward Dromgoole and John Wesley." Proceedings of the Wesley Historical Society 26 (1947): 25-28. Discusses relations between English and American Methodists in 1783.

2015.   . "The Erskines and the Methodists." London Quarterly and Holborn Review 183 (1958): 36-45. Discusses relations between Ebenezer and Ralph Erskine, Scottish reformers, Wesley, and Whitefield.

2016.   . "The Field Bible." Proceedings of the Wesley Historical Society 24 (1944): 126-29.

2017.   . "The Frank Baker Collection: An Autobiographical Analysis." Library Notes, no. 36 (December 1962): 1-9.

2018.   . "Hugh Moore and John Wesley: Some Unpublished Correspondence." Proceedings of the Wesley Historical Society 29 (1954): 112-16.

2019.   . "It Was the Birth of an Epoch: On the Wesley Anniversary." Methodist Recorder, 25 June 1953, 9.

2020.   . "John Wesley and a Quaker Mystic." Proceedings of the Wesley Historical Society 26 (1948): 114-18. Concerns correspondence with Richard Freeman, 1779.

2021. _____. "John Wesley and America." Proceedings of the
Wesley Historical Society 44 (1984): 117-29.

2022. _____. "John Wesley and Ann Loxdale: Two Unpublished
Letters." Proceedings of the Wesley Historical Society 24
(1944): 107-13.

2023. _____. "John Wesley and Bishop Joseph Butler: A Fragment of John Wesley's Manuscript Journal, 16th to 24th August
1739." Proceedings of the Wesley Historical Society 42 (1980):
93-100.

2024. _____. "John Wesley and Cokesbury College's First President." Methodist History 11, no. 2 (1973): 54-59. Levi
Heath was the first president of Cokesbury College.

2025. _____. "John Wesley and John Bousell." Journal of the
Friends' Historical Society 40 (1948): 50-52.

2026. _____. "John Wesley and Lord George Gordon." Proceedings of the Wesley Historical Society 26 (1947): 45.

2027. _____. "John Wesley and Miss Mary Clark of Worcester."
Methodist History 10, no. 2 (1972): 45-51.

2028. _____. "John Wesley and Sarah Crosby." Proceedings of
the Wesley Historical Society 27 (1949): 76-82.

2029. _____. "John Wesley and the Imitatio Christi." London
Quarterly and Holborn Review 166 (1941): 74-87.

2030. _____. "John Wesley and the Moravians of Fulneck."
Proceedings of the Wesley Historical Society 36 (1968):
153-54.

2031. _____. "John Wesley and Thomas Hanson, the 'Brown-Bread
Preacher.'" Proceedings of the Wesley Historical Society 30
(1956): 127-31.

2032. _____. "John Wesley and William Law: A Reconsideration."
Proceedings of the Wesley Historical Society 37 (1970): 173-77.

2033. _____. "John Wesley, Literary Arbiter: An Introduction
to His Use of the Asterisk." Proceedings of the Wesley Historical Society 40 (1975): 25-33.

2034. _____. "John Wesley on Christian Perfection." Proceedings of the Wesley Historical Society 34 (1963): 53-57.

2035. _____. "John Wesley's Churchmanship." London Quarterly
and Holborn Review 185 (1960): 210-15, 269-74.

2036. _____. "John Wesley's First Marriage." London Quarterly and Holborn Review 192 (1967): 305-15. Discusses Wesley's relationship with Grace Murray.

2037. _____. "John Wesley's Introduction to William Law." Proceedings of the Wesley Historical Society 37 (1969): 78-82.

2038. _____. "John Wesley's Last Visit to Charleston." South Carolina Historical Magazine 78 (1977): 265-71.

2039. _____. "Jonathan Swift and the Wesleys." London Quarterly and Holborn Review 179 (1954): 290-300.

2040. _____. "Methodism and Literature in the Eighteenth Century." Proceedings of the Wesley Historical Society 22 (1940): 174-83. Reviews John Wesley as Editor and Author by T. W. Herbert, and Methodism and the Literature of the Eighteenth Century by T. B. Shepherd. See nos. 809, 1493.

2041. _____. "Methodism and the '45 Rebellion." London Quarterly and Holborn Review 172 (1947): 325-33. Describes Wesley's movement during the rebellion and the accusations of papist which were made against him.

2042. _____. "Methodist Archives." Amateur Historian 3 (1957): 143-49. Discusses the value of Methodist records for family research.

2043. _____. "New Light on John Wesley's Evangelical Conversion." Methodist Recorder, 15 December 1949, 4.

2044. _____. "The Origins, Character, and Influence of John Wesley's Thoughts upon Slavery." Methodist History 22, no. 2 (1984): 75-86.

2045. _____. "The Oxford Edition of Wesley's Works." Duke Divinity School Review 36 (Spring 1971): 87-99.

2046. _____. "The Oxford Edition of Wesley's Works." Methodist History 8, no. 4 (1970): 41-48.

2047. _____. "Prose Writings of Charles Wesley." London Quarterly and Holborn Review 182 (1957): 268-74.

2048. _____. "The Real John Wesley." Methodist History 12, no. 4 (1974): 183-97.

2049. _____. "The Relations between the Society of Friends and Early Methodism." London Quarterly and Holborn Review 174 (1948): 312-23; 175 (1949): 239-48.

2050. _____ . "The Re-printing of Wesley's Publications." Proceedings of the Wesley Historical Society 22 (1939): 57-61.

2051. _____ . "Richard Ireland and John Wesley." Proceedings
of the Wesley Historical Society 28 (1952): 85-88.

2052. _____ . "Riding the Rounds with John Wesley." Methodist
History 23 (1984): 163-67.

2053. _____ . "The Shaping of Wesley's 'Calm Address.'"
Methodist History 14, no. 1 (1975): 3-12.

2054. _____ . "Some Observations on John Wesley's Relationship
with Grace Murray." Methodist History 16, (1977): 42-45.

2055. _____ . "The Sources of John Wesley's Collection of Psalms
and Hymns, Charleston, 1737." Proceedings of the Wesley
Historical Society 31 (1958): 186-93. (Also published in John
Wesley's First Hymn-book; a Collection of Psalms and Hymns;
a Facsimile with Additional Material, edited by Frank Baker
and George Walton Williams, xxvii-xxxiv, no. 1861.)

2056. _____ . "A Strange Wesley Pedigree." Proceedings of the
Wesley Historical Society 26 (1948): 102-4. Gives the pedigree
published in the Reliquary, 8 (1867-68): 188. See no. 3689.

2057. _____ . "A Study of John Wesley's Readings." London
Quarterly and Holborn Review 168 (1943): 140-45, 234-41.

2058. _____ . "Susanna Wesley, Apologist for Methodism." Proceedings of the Wesley Historical Society 35 (1965): 68-71.

2059. _____ . "Thomas Maxfield's First Sermon." Proceedings of
the Wesley Historical Society 27 (1949): 7-15.

2060. _____ . "The Trans-Atlantic Triangle: Relations between
British, Canadian and American Methodism during Wesley's
Lifetime." Bulletin of the Committee on Archives of the United
Church of Canada 28 (1979): 5-21.

2061. _____ . "Wesley and Arminius." Proceedings of the Wesley
Historical Society 22 (1939): 118-19.

2062. _____ . "Wesley and John King: Three Little-Known Letters." Proceedings of the Wesley Historical Society 25 (1945):
50-52.

2063. _____ . "Wesleyana at Keighley." Proceedings of the Wesley
Historical Society 23 (1942): 111-15, 135-39.

2064. _____ . "Wesleyana in Headingley College Library [Leeds]."

176   John and Charles Wesley

Proceedings of the Wesley Historical Society 23 (1941): 64-68,
85-89, 104-8.

2065. _____. "The Wesleys and The Song of the Three Children." Proceedings of the Wesley Historical Society 23
(1942): 167-71.

2066. _____. "Wesley's Ordinations." Proceedings of the Wesley Historical Society 24 (1944): 76-80, 101-2.

2067. _____. "Wesley's Printers and Booksellers." Proceedings
of the Wesley Historical Society 22 (1939): 61-65, 97-101, 131-
40, 164-68.

2068. _____. "Wesley's Puritan Ancestry." London Quarterly
and Holborn Review 187 (1962): 180-86.

2069. _____. "Wesley's Sermons." Methodist Recorder, 20 September 1945, 9.

2070. _____. "When Did Methodism Begin? Sparked in 1729 by
the Holy Club, Societies Sprang Up in Many Places." Together 7, no. 7 (1963): 27-29.

2071. _____. "Whitefield's Break with the Wesleys." Church
Quarterly 3 (1970): 103-13.

2072. Balch, A. E. "The Centenary of Methodism in Luton."
Wesleyan Methodist Magazine 131 (1908): 725-32.

2073. Ball-Kilbourne, Gary L. "The Christian As Steward in John
Wesley's Theological Ethics." Quarterly Review (Nashville)
4, no. 1 (1984): 43-54. Stewardship was the way of life for
John Wesley, not only in matters of money but in all other
aspects of life. This article describes Wesley's concept of
stewardship.

2074. Bangs, Carl O. "Historical Theology in the Wesleyan Mode."
Wesleyan Theological Journal 17, no. 1 (1982): 85-92. See
also no. 2938.

2075. _____. "John Wesley." Church History 35 (1966): 245-46.
This is a review of Outler's John Wesley, 1964. See no. 1250.

2076. Banks, J. Dinsdale. "Methodism in Three Centuries: The
Story of Rotherham." Methodist Recorder, 30 January 1902,
11-13.

2077. Banks, Louis Albert. "The Love-Affairs of John Wesley."
Everybody's Magazine 9 (1903): 45-50. Sophia Hopkey, Grace
Murray, Mrs. Vazeille.

2078. Banks, Stanley. "Our Wesleyan Heritage: Christian Perfection." Asbury Seminarian 14, no. 2 (1960): 33-51.

2079. _____. "Our Wesleyan Heritage: The Witness of the Spirit." Asbury Seminarian 14, no. 1 (1960): 48-60.

2080. Baragar, C. A. "John Wesley and Medicine." Annals of Medical History 10 (1928): 59-65. A discussion of the remedies suggested in Wesley's Primitive Physic.

2081. Barber, F. Louis. "John Wesley Edits a Novel [Henry Brooke, The Fool of Quality]." London Quarterly and Holborn Review 171 (1946): 50-54. Discusses Wesley's abridgement and publication of Brooke's novel without mentioning the author's name on the title page.

2082. _____. "Wesley's Philosophy." Biblical World, n.s. 54 (1920): 142-49.

2083. Bardell, Eunice Bonow. "Primitive Physick: John Wesley's Receipts." Pharmacy in History 21 (1979): 111-21.

2084. Baring-Gould, Sabine. "The Fool of Quality." Bookman 9 (1895): 55-58. Charges John Wesley with plagiarism. See also nos. 2748, 3007.

2085. Barley, B. A. Hurd. "Early Methodism in Sunderland." Proceedings of the Wesley Historical Society 7 (1909): 13.

2086. _____. "Methodist Beginnings in Barton-on-Humber Circuit." Proceedings of the Wesley Historical Society 8 (1912): 129-40.

2087. _____. "Sunderland Methodism in the Eighteenth Century." Wesleyan Methodist Magazine 133 (1910): 165-71.

2088. _____. "Wesley's Visits to Otley." Proceedings of the Wesley Historical Society 7 (1910): 158-61.

2089. Barnabas. "How Wesley Became an Extempore Preacher." Methodist Recorder, 3 June 1926, 12.

2090. Barnes, A. M. "Americana: the South Carolina Gazette, 1733-1737." Proceedings of the Wesley Historical Society 16 (1927): 58-62.

2091. Baron, Ruth Smith. "John Wesley's Folly." Together 13, no. 5 (1969): 66. Gives a brief discussion of Wesley's disastrous marriage.

2092. Barr, D. William. "Woolwich and Its Methodism." Methodist Recorder, 28 December 1911, 9.

2093. Barr-Brown. "Wesley's Memorials." Wesleyan Methodist
       Church Record 12 (1903): 133-34.

2094. Barraclough, Alfred. "Beverley Chimes: Methodism in the
       East Riding of Yorkshire." Methodist Recorder, 6 October
       1904, 9-10.

2095. _____. "A Story of Methodist Evolution." Methodist Re-
       corder, 19 December 1901, 11-12.

2096. Barratt, Thomas H. "The Place of the Lord's Supper in
       Early Methodism." London Quarterly Review 140 (1923):
       56-73. Wesley demanded "constant" communion, believing
       one should receive it as often as possible.

2097. Barton, J. Hamby. "A Double Letter: John Wesley and
       Thomas Coke to Freeborn Garrettson." Methodist History
       17, no. 1 (1978): 59-63.

2098. _____. "Thomas Coke and American Methodism, 1784-92."
       Proceedings of the Wesley Historical Society 34 (1964): 104-8.

2099. _____. "The Two Versions of the First Edition of John
       Wesley's The Sunday Service of the Methodists in North
       America." Methodist History 23 (1984): 153-62.

2100. Bashford, Joseph Whitford. "John Wesley's Conversion."
       Methodist Review 85 (1903): 775-89.

2101. Bate, A. G. "Quaint Records of Liverpool Methodism,
       1765-1791." Proceedings of the Wesley Historical Society 14
       (1924): 172-76.

2102. Bates, E. Ralph. "John Wesley's First Preaching Sunday."
       Proceedings of the Wesley Historical Society 40 (1975): 7-16.
       Considers the problems involved in determining with certainty
       the details of Wesley's first sermon.

2103. _____. "The Methodist Legend of South Leigh, an Article
       in Celebration of the 250th Anniversary of the Ordination of
       John Wesley, Sunday, September 19, 1725." Methodist His-
       tory 13, no. 4 (1975): 18-24.

2104. _____. "Sarah Ryan and Kingswood School." Proceedings
       of the Wesley Historical Society 38 (1972): 110-14. The author
       claims that Sarah Ryan was housekeeper at the New Room, not
       Kingswood School.

2105. _____. "Wesley's Property Deed for Bath." Proceedings of
       the Wesley Historical Society 44 (1983): 25-35.

2106. Beals, J. Duane. "Doing Christian Education in a Wesleyan
       Mode: A Response to Wesley Tracy." Wesleyan Theological
       Journal 17, no. 1 (1982): 54-57. See no. 3883.

2107. _____. "John Wesley's Concept of the Church." Wesleyan
       Theological Journal 9 (1974): 28-37.

2108. Bebb, Evelyn Douglas. "John Wesley at Ouston." Proceed-
       ings of the Wesley Historical Society 28 (1951): 45-46.

2109. _____. "An Unpublished Wesley Letter to Lancelot Harri-
       son." Proceedings of the Wesley Historical Society 28 (1951):
       17-18.

2110. Beckerlegge, Oliver A. "An Attempt at a Classification of
       Charles Wesley's Metres: A Contribution to the Study of
       English Prosody." London Quarterly and Holborn Review
       169 (1944): 219-27.

2111. _____. "Charles Wesley's Politics." London Quarterly and
       Holborn Review 182 (1957): 280-91.

2112. _____. "Charles Wesley's Vocabulary." London Quarterly
       and Holborn Review 193 (1968): 152-61. An examination of
       some of the rarer words used by Charles Wesley in his
       hymns.

2113. _____. "Early Methodism in Greenock and Port Glasgow."
       Proceedings of the Wesley Historical Society 29 (1953): 37-
       42.

2114. _____. "'Hymns of Eternal Truth.'" Hymn Society of
       Great Britain and Ireland Bulletin 8 (1977): 246-49. Reviews
       a new collection of 120 hymns of the Wesleys, published by
       the Horton Trust of Bradford.

2115. _____. "John Wesley and the German Hymns." London
       Quarterly and Holborn Review 165 (1940): 430-39.

2116. _____. "Wesley Prints on Pottery." Proceedings of the
       Wesley Historical Society 38 (1972): 103-5.

2117. Beckerlegge, Oliver A., and Frank Baker. "Humorous Ver-
       ses by Samuel Wesley." Proceedings of the Wesley Historical
       Society 39 (1973): 6-11.

2118. Beckett, Arthur. "Wesley's Word to a Smuggler." Sussex
       County Magazine 15 (1941): 284-87.

2119. Beecham, H. A. "Samuel Wesley Senior: New Biographical
       Evidence." Renaissance and Modern Studies 7 (1963): 78-109.

2120. Beecham, John. "Memoir of the Rev. William Myles." Wesleyan Methodist Magazine 54 (1831): 289-307.

2121. Beecroft, Joseph J. "In the Upper Thames Valley: Reading and Its Methodism." Methodist Recorder, 6 April 1905, 12.

2121a. Beesor, Trevor. "Reopening of Wesley's Chapel: An Act of Faith." Christian Century 95 (1978): 1124-26.

2122. Beet, Joseph Agar. "John Wesley's Conversion." Proceedings of the Wesley Historical Society 8 (1911): 3-6.

2123. _____. "Methodist Revival." London Quarterly Review 133 (1920): 54-69. Discusses Wesley's conversion and the Moravian influence on him.

2124. _____. "Wesley and Luther." Proceedings of the Wesley Historical Society 8 (1911): 2-3.

2125. Bell, H. I. "New Letters of John Wesley." British Museum Quarterly 8 (1933-34): 135-37. Contains a description of 36 letters of John Wesley to Ann Tindall of Scarborough, in the years 1774-90, given to the British Library, Department of Manuscripts.

2126. Bellwood, Norman A. "John Wesley in Newcastle-upon-Tyne." Wesleyan Methodist Magazine 142 (1919): 361-63.

2127. Belshaw, Harry. "Eighteenth Century Wit and Methodism." London Quarterly Review 156 (1931): 50-60.

2128. _____. "The Influence of John Wesley on Dr. Johnson's Religion." London Quarterly and Holborn Review 169 (1943): 226-34.

2129. Bence, Clarence L. "Advice for the Not Yet Perfect." Preacher's Magazine 58, no. 2 (1982-83): 38-39.

2130. _____. "Experimental Religion." Preacher's Magazine 56, no. 2 (1980-81): 50-51. This is a discussion of the meaning of Wesley's concept of experimental religion.

2131. _____. "In the Middle Is Not Good Enough." Preacher's Magazine 59, no. 2 (1983-84): 42, 60. Claims Wesley chose a middle course between Pelagius and Augustine.

2132. _____. "Not Worth Contending for." Preacher's Magazine 57, no. 2 (1981-82): 57-58. Concerns Wesley's use of "sinless perfection."

2133. _____. "The Wesleyan Syndrome." Preacher's Magazine

55, no. 2 (1979-80): 54-55. Describes Wesley's compulsive
spirituality coupled with his compulsive drive for perfection.

2134. Benger, F. B. "John Wesley's Visit to Leatherhead." Proceedings of the Leatherhead and District Local History Society 2 (1965): 265-69. Wesley died one week following the
visit.

2135. Bennetts, George Armstrong. "Chelsea Methodism." Wesleyan Methodist Magazine 131 (1908): 595-600.

2136. _____. "In John Wesley's Footsteps: An Ancient Preaching
Place in East Cornwall." Methodist Recorder, 16 January
1913, 9.

2137. Benson, Frederick H. "John Wesley and the Madans." Proceedings of the Wesley Historical Society 5 (1906): 141-46.

2138. Benson, George. "Wesley Souvenirs." Connoisseur 24 (1909):
238-40. Describes several Charles Wesley musical manuscripts.

2139. Beresford, John. "Wesley and Judith Beresford, 1734-1756."
London Quarterly Review 147 (1927): 35-50.

2140. Bernhardt, William H. "Was John Wesley a Pacifist?" Methodist Review 108 (1925): 551-60.

2141. Bett, Henry. "The Alleged Illiteracy of the Early Methodist
Preachers." Proceedings of the Wesley Historical Society 15
(1925): 85-92.

2142. _____. "Archaisms in Wesley's Hymns." Proceedings of the
Wesley Historical Society 8 (1911): 85-90.

2143. _____. "A Detail of Pronunciation in Wesley's Hymns."
Proceedings of the Wesley Historical Society 14 (1923): 78-80.

2144. _____. "Dr. Robert Gell and the Wesleys." Proceedings
of the Wesley Historical Society 24 (1943): 4-8. Discusses the
Wesleys' views on Gell's Essay toward the Amendment of the
Last English Translation of the Bible, 1659.

2145. _____. "A French Marquis and the Class Meeting." Proceedings of the Wesley Historical Society 18 (1931): 43-45.
The French marquis was Baron de Renty.

2146. _____. "John Wesley and Charterhouse: The Tercentenary
of a Famous Foundation." Methodist Recorder, 7 December
1911, 9.

2147. _____. "John Wesley's Translations of German Hymns."

Proceedings of the Wesley Historical Society 8 (1912): 141-
46.

2148.   . "John Wesley's Translations of German Hymns in
Reference to Metre and Rhyme." London Quarterly and Holborn Review 165 (1940): 288-94.

2149.   . "Pepys and Wesley." Methodist Recorder, 5 July
1951, 9.

2150.   . "Some Classical Allusions in Hymns of the Wesleys."
Proceedings of the Wesley Historical Society 9 (1914): 116-20.

2151.   . "Some Latinisms in the Wesleys' Hymns." London
Quarterly and Holborn Review 163 (1938): 308-19.

2152.   . "An Unpublished Latin Letter to Zinzendorf by
Charles Wesley." Proceedings of the Wesley Historical Society
15 (1926): 166-68.

2153.   . "Wesley and Dante." Methodist Recorder, 14 May
1908, 9.

2154.   . "Wesley and Luther." London Quarterly and Holborn Review 171 (1946): 250-52.

2155.   . "Wesley As a Preacher." Methodist Recorder, 2
June 1949, 9.

2156.   . "The Wesleys and the English Bible." Methodist
Recorder, 16 March 1911, 12-13.

2157. Bibby, G. "John Wesley and Vegetarianism." Methodist
Magazine, May 1958, 221-23.

2158. Bible, Ken. "The Wesleys' Hymns on Full Redemption and
Pentecost: A Brief Comparison." Wesleyan Theological Journal 17, no. 2 (1982): 79-87.

2159. "The Bicentenary of the Birth of John Wesley." Methodist
Weekly (Manchester), 18 June 1903, 3.

2160. "The Bi-centenary of Wesley's Birth, June 17, 1703." Wesleyan Methodist Church Record 12 (1903): 131-32. Reprints
one of Wesley's early letters--23 September 1723--to his
mother.

2161. Bicknell, Percy F. "A Neglected English Classic." Dial 34
(1903): 393-95. The author considers John Wesley's Journal
an English classic.

2162. Bird, Frederick M. "Charles Wesley and Methodist Hymns." Bibliotheca Sacra 21 (1864): 127-62, 284-318.

2163. Bird, Isabella L. "The Wesleys and Their Hymns." Littell's Living Age 100 (1869): 112-17; 101 (1869): 368-75.

2164. Bird, Lewis Penhall. "John Wesley--Unlucky in Love." Eternity 27, no. 11 (1976): 74-79.

2165. _____. "Wesley and the Women in His Family." Eternity 27, no. 12 (1976): 59-61.

2166. Birley, Robert. "Charterhouse Notes." Proceedings of the Wesley Historical Society 26 (1947): 7-9.

2167. Birrell, Augustine. "John Wesley, 1703-1791." Empire Review 42 (1925): 555-62.

2168. Bishop, John. "John Wesley As a Preacher." Religion in Life 26 (1957): 264-73.

2169. "Bishop Kip versus John Wesley." Southern Review 10 (1872): 226-38, 421-45.

2170. "The Bishop of Manchester and John Wesley's Policy." Methodist Recorder, 12 September 1873, 526.

2171. Black, Bob. "John Wesley and Social Holiness." Preacher's Magazine 58, no. 4 (1983): 42-43. Discusses Wesley's concerns and efforts in social reform.

2172. Bland, James C. "What Christmas Meant to the Wesleys." Presbyterian Journal 39, no. 33 (1980): 8-9.

2173. Blankenship, Paul F. "The Significance of John Wesley's Abridgement of the Thirty-Nine Articles As Seen from his Deletions." Methodist History 2, no. 3 (1964): 35-47.

2174. Blundell, Henry. "Early Methodism in Luton." Wesleyan Methodist Magazine 124 (1901): 921-25.

2175. Bodgener, J. Henry. "Methodism in Oxford District." Methodist Magazine 151 (1928): 270-76.

2176. Body, Alfred Harris. "John Wesley As an Educationist." Religion in Education, a Quarterly Review 5 (1938): 143-48.

2177. Bolster, George R. "Wesley's Doctrine of Justification." Evangelical Quarterly 24 (1952): 144-55.

2178. Bond, Robert. "Cardiff: The Conference City of 1911." Methodist Recorder, 13 July 1911, 9-11.

2179. _____. "The Image of the 'Warmed Heart.'" London Quarterly and Holborn Review 163 (1938): 168-71.

2180. Bone, Florence. "The Early Methodists in York." Wesleyan Methodist Magazine 129 (1906): 931-36.

2181. _____. "The Mistress of the Mersey: Growth and Greatness of England's Premier Seaport." Methodist Recorder, 11 July 1912, 9. Contains a little about Wesley's first impressions of Liverpool.

2182. _____. "The Wesleys in Lincolnshire: Highways and Byways of the Conference County." Methodist Recorder, 29 April 1909, 9.

2183. _____. "The Yorkshire Round: A District Beloved of Our Founder." Methodist Recorder, 9 July 1908, 9.

2184. Bonino, José Miguez. "Conversion, New Creature, and Commitment." International Review of Missions 72 (1983): 324-32.

2185. Boscher, Professor. "John Wesley As a Solar Myth." Methodist Recorder, 3 September 1886, 595.

2186. Boshears, Onva K., Jr. "The Books in John Wesley's Life." Wesleyan Theological Journal 3 (1968): 48-56. This article is concerned only with the books Wesley read, not those written by him.

2187. Bosward, Samuel T. "The Literary Contemporaries of Wesley." Wesleyan Methodist Magazine 127 (1904): 94-100, 259-63. The writers mentioned are Alexander Pope, Matthew Prior, Thomas Gray, William Cowper, Joseph Addison, Samuel Butler, Daniel Defoe, David Hume, Samuel Johnson, and Smollett.

2188. Boulton, David J. "Women and Early Methodism." Proceedings of the Wesley Historical Society 43 (1981): 13-17.

2189. Bowling, John C. "The Witness of the Spirit." Herald of Holiness 69, no. 18 (1980): 10-11. After Aldersgate, Wesley emphasized the doctrine of Assurance--the Witness of the Spirit. It became one of the great themes in his preaching.

2190. Bowmer, John C. "Catchwords of 'The Conversations.' 1. 'A Converting Ordinance and the Open Table.'" Proceedings of the Wesley Historical Society 34 (1964): 109-113. Discusses the questions, "Did early Methodism practice, and John Wesley advocate, an absolutely open Table?" The writer believes the answer is negative.

2191. _____. "The Churchmanship of Charles Wesley." Proceedings of the Wesley Historical Society 31 (1957): 78-80.

2192. _____. "The Diaries of R. Bennett Dugdale." Proceedings of the Wesley Historical Society 38 (1971): 89-92. Dugdale was a respected layman in Irish Methodism. His diaries contain references to John Wesley.

2193. _____. "Dr. Johnson and John Wesley." New Rambler 8 (January 1970): 12-25.

2194. _____. "Early Methodism and the Quakers." Religion in Life 23 (1954): 418-29.

2195. _____. "John Wesley and Ireland." London Quarterly and Holborn Review 178 (1953): 252-62; 179 (1954): 38-45.

2196. _____. "John Wesley and William Green." Proceedings of the Wesley Historical Society 36 (1968): 132-33.

2197. _____. "John Wesley's First Marriage." Proceedings of the Wesley Historical Society 36 (1968): 110-11. See also no. 2036.

2198. _____. "John Wesley's Philosophy of Suffering." London Quarterly and Holborn Review 184 (1959): 60-66. A discussion of Wesley's ventures into medicine, his attitude toward suffering, and his faith, which required him to serve the sick.

2199. _____. "Memorable Christmasses with the Wesleyan Stress on the Season's Essential Significance." Methodist Recorder, 10 December 1953, 5.

2200. _____. "The Relations between the Society of Friends and Early Methodism." London Quarterly and Holborn Review 175 (1950): 148-53, 222-27. A discussion of Wesley and George Fox.

2201. _____. "Two Wesley Letters." Proceedings of the Wesley Historical Society 34 (1963): 76-78. Letters to George Whitefield and William Seward.

2202. _____. "The Wesleyan Conception of the Ministry." Religion in Life 40 (1971): 85-96.

2203. _____. "Wesley's Last Days." Proceedings of the Wesley Historical Society 36 (1968): 155-56.

2204. _____. "Wesley's Revision of the Communion Service in The Sunday Service of the Methodists." London Quarterly and Holborn Review 176 (1951): 230-37.

2205. _____. "Wesley's Vision." Methodist Recorder, 31 October 1968, 12. Reviews Hunter's John Wesley and the Coming Comprehensive Church. See no. 879.

2206. Boyling, Percy J. "Aftermath: What Next, John Wesley?" London Quarterly and Holborn Review 163 (1938): 302-7.

2207. _____. "In Love with John Wesley." Methodist Magazine 161 (1938): 205-7. Concerns John Wesley's biographers.

2208. _____. "John Wesley Comes to Westminster." Methodist Magazine 156 (1933): 391-95.

2209. _____. "John Wesley's Holiday." Methodist Magazine 159 (1936): 463-67. Describes him in his old age, according to the diary of Sophie v. La Roche.

2210. _____. "Portraits and Pictures of John Wesley." Methodist Recorder, Wesley Bicentennial Supplement, 19 May 1938, xiv.

2211. _____. "Wesley's Oracle." London Quarterly and Holborn Review 164 (1939): 218-21. A discussion of William Law and Wesley.

2212. Brackenbury, Thomas. "Methodism in Trowbridge: A Wiltshire Story." Methodist Recorder, 6 March 1902, 13-14.

2213. _____. "Wesley's Visits to Salisbury." Proceedings of the Wesley Historical Society 2 (1899): 54.

2214. Bradford, A. "Tolstoy and Wesley." Methodist Recorder, 12 April 1945, 7.

2215. Bradford, C. A. "Wesley: Portraits or Statues on Horseback." Notes and Queries 176 (1939): 49.

2216. Bradshaw, David B. "Dublin Methodist Notes." Proceedings of the Wesley Historical Society 5 (1905): 67-80.

2217. _____. "John Wesley in Belfast." Proceedings of the Wesley Historical Society 22 (1939): 25-28.

2218. _____. "John Wesley's Belfast." Proceedings of the Wesley Historical Society 17 (1929): 57-63.

2219. _____. "John Wesley's Preaching Plans for Ulster." Proceedings of the Wesley Historical Society 16 (1927): 35-37.

2220. _____. "A Link with John Wesley." Proceedings of the Wesley Historical Society 18 (1931): 53-54. Concerns Alexander Gordon and John Wesley.

2221.   _____. "A Sidelight on the Dublin (Whitefriar Street)
Preaching House in 1789." Proceedings of the Wesley Historical Society 9 (1914): 188-91.

2222.   _____. "A Statuette of John Wesley." Proceedings of the
Wesley Historical Society 21 (1938): 137-38.

2223.   _____. "A Wesley Statuette in Ireland." Proceedings of
the Wesley Historical Society 21 (1938): 137-38.

2224.   Brantley, Richard E. "Johnson's Wesleyan Connection."
Eighteenth-Century Studies 10 (1976-77): 143-68.

2225.   _____. "Keats' Method." Studies in Romanticism 22 (1983):
389-405. Discusses Wesleyan elements in the poetry of Keats.

2226.   Brash, W. Bardsley. "Characteristics That Made a National
Figure: The Real Wesley." Methodist Recorder, Wesley Bicentennial Supplement, 19 May 1938, iii.

2227.   _____. "Great Wesley Celebration at Oxford: Bicentenary
of Wesley's Election to a Fellowship." Methodist Recorder, 1
April 1926, 4.

2228.   _____. "John Wesley and Literature." London Quarterly
and Holborn Review 163 (1938): 203-7.

2229.   _____. "John Wesley's Conversion, What It Meant." Manchester Guardian, 21 May 1938, 13-14.

2230.   _____. "Three Carthusians." Methodist Recorder, 1 June
1944, 7.

2231.   _____. "Wesley's Wit and Humour." London Quarterly Review 135 (1921): 53-67.

2232.   Bray, James B. "Father Hardon's Methodists." Homiletic
and Pastoral Review 57 (1957): 686-94. This article takes issue with some of the statements regarding Wesley in John A.
Hardon's book The Protestant Churches of America (1956).

2233.   Bretherton, Francis Fletcher. "The Christian Community."
Proceedings of the Wesley Historical Society 20 (1936): 98-100.
The Christian Community was a society established by the
Huguenots in 1685 and reorganized under the patronage of
John Wesley in 1772. This article includes brief description
of Wesley's relationship to this group.

2234.   _____. "The Colman Wesleyana." Proceedings of the Wesley Historical Society 21 (1937): 93-97.

188   John and Charles Wesley

2235. _____. "Early Methodist Preachers and Wesley's Veterans."
Proceedings of the Wesley Historical Society 22 (1940): 102-5.
Discusses these two books by Thomas Jackson and John Tel-
ford. See no. 906.

2236. _____. "The Epworth Fire--Who Was the Rescuer?" Proceedings of the Wesley Historical Society 22 (1939): 6-12.

2237. _____. "Exhibition of Wesleyana." Proceedings of the Wesley Historical Society 21 (1938): 163-68.

2238. _____. "John Wesley and John Vatton." Proceedings of
the Wesley Historical Society 20 (1935): 14-16.

2239. _____. "John Wesley and Margate." Proceedings of the
Wesley Historical Society 7 (1910): 102-5.

2240. _____. "John Wesley and Philip Thicknesse." Proceedings of the Wesley Historical Society 23 (1941): 15-20.
Thicknesse was in Georgia during Wesley's time there.

2241. _____. "John Wesley and Professor Liden, 1769." Proceedings of the Wesley Historical Society 17 (1929): 1-2.
Johan Henrik Liden was a professor at Uppsala University.

2242. _____. "John Wesley and the Gilberts of Antigua." Proceedings of the Wesley Historical Society 13 (1921): 7-8.

2243. _____. "John Wesley's Field Bible." Proceedings of the
Wesley Historical Society 24 (1943): 13-15. Wesley's Field
Bible was printed in 1653. In 1788 he gave it to Henry
Moore. Since 1844 it has been passed from president to
president of the British Methodist Conference.

2244. _____. "John Wesley's Letter to Miss P. Newman, with
Notes." Proceedings of the Wesley Historical Society 25
(1946): 86-88. The letter was dated 1775.

2245. _____. "John Wesley's Visit to Holland in 1783: A Side-
Light." Proceedings of the Wesley Historical Society 24
(1944): 80-82.

2246. _____. "John Wesley's Visit to Mr. Hampson's Church,
Sunderland." Proceedings of the Wesley Historical Society
20 (1936): 131-35.

2247. _____. "John Wesley's Visit to St. John's Church, Sunderland." Proceedings of the Wesley Historical Society 14
(1923): 73-77.

2248. _____. "John Wesley's Visits to Monkwearmouth." Antiquities of Sunderland 21 (1954): 1-4.

2249.   _____. "John Wesley's Visits to Sunderland." Antiquities of Sunderland 20 (1951): 129-41.

2250.   _____. "John Wesley's Visits to Thorne." Proceedings of the Wesley Historical Society 10 (1916): 164.

2251.   _____. "John Wesley's Visits to Tunbridge Wells." Proceedings of the Wesley Historical Society 10 (1916): 197-99.

2252.   _____. "The Kingswood of the North." Proceedings of the Wesley Historical Society 20 (1936): 121-27. Describes Wesley's activities at Gateshead Fell.

2253.   _____. "Letters from John Wesley to Ann Tindall." Proceedings of the Wesley Historical Society 19 (1934): 188-93.

2254.   _____. "Letters from Wesley to Daniel Bumstead." Proceedings of the Wesley Historical Society 20 (1935): 10-13.

2255.   _____. "Methodism in Haverford West and Neighbourhood." Proceedings of the Wesley Historical Society 15 (1925): 61-67.

2256.   _____. "Methodism in Tunbridge Wells: Its Origin and Progress." Methodist Recorder, 18 December 1913, 10.

2257.   _____. "Miss Boone of Tunbridge Wells." Proceedings of the Wesley Historical Society 21 (1937): 14-21.

2258.   _____. "Portrait of John Wesley by Thomas Horsley of Sunderland." Proceedings of the Wesley Historical Society 23 (1941): 31-37.

2259.   _____. "A Portrait of John Wesley Recently Presented to the Mission House." Proceedings of the Wesley Historical Society 16 (1928): 107. The portrait reproduced here is by an unknown artist.

2260.   _____. "The Rev. William Duck, Incumbent of Danby (1781-1825) and Stipendiary Curate of Westerdale. Sidelights on Wesley's Journal." Proceedings of the Wesley Historical Society 23 (1941): 38-39.

2261.   _____. "Saugh House." Proceedings of the Wesley Historical Society 23 (1942): 117. This article tells of a thorn tree planted at the Saugh House, near Scots Gap, Northumberland, to commemorate Wesley's service there June 17, 1782.

2262.   _____. "An Unpublished Wesley Letter [to Joseph Taylor]." Proceedings of the Wesley Historical Society 25 (1945): 49-50.

2263. _____. "An Unrecorded Visit of Wesley to Margate."
Proceedings of the Wesley Historical Society 17 (1929): 72-75.

2264. _____. "A Visit to Jersey." Proceedings of the Wesley
Historical Society 21 (1937): 81-88, 127-28. Discusses John
Wesley's visit there in 1787.

2265. _____. "Wesley and Miss Whateley's Poems." Proceedings
of the Wesley Historical Society 20 (1935): 93-95.

2266. _____. "Wesley at Blanchland." Proceedings of the Wesley Historical Society 23 (1941): 91-93.

2267. _____. "Wesley Day - 1938." Proceedings of the Wesley
Historical Society 21 (1938): 144-51.

2268. _____. "Wesley Window and Desk at Sheffield Cathedral."
Proceedings of the Wesley Historical Society 22 (1940): 122-23

2269. _____. "Wesley's Last Visit to Chester." Proceedings of
the Wesley Historical Society 26 (1948): 76-79. His last
visit was in 1790.

2270. _____. "Wesley's Visit to Holland in 1783: A Side-Light."
Proceedings of the Wesley Historical Society 24 (1944): 80-82.

2271. _____. "Wesley's Visits to Holland." Proceedings of the
Wesley Historical Society 19 (1934): 106-12.

2272. _____. "Wesley's Visits to Monkwearmouth." Proceedings
of the Wesley Historical Society 15 (1925): 29-33.

2273. Brigden, Thomas E. "The Ancestry and Arms of the Wesleys." Proceedings of the Wesley Historical Society 12
(1919): 25-27.

2274. _____. "Charles Wesley (1762) and Dr. Robert Bridges."
Proceedings of the Wesley Historical Society 12 (1920): 171-
74.

2275. _____. "The Christmas Pilgrimages and Songs of the Wesleys, 1737-1790." Proceedings of the Wesley Historical Society 16 (1928): 156-59. A discussion of some Wesley hymns.

2276. _____. "George-Yard Chapel, Hull." Proceedings of the
Wesley Historical Society 12 (1920): 121-24.

2277. _____. "Haslingden." Proceedings of the Wesley Historical Society 3 (1902): 199-201.

Articles   191

2278. _____. "Isabella Johnson and the Wesleys." Proceedings
of the Wesley Historical Society 13 (1921): 36-39.

2279. _____. "The Life and Letters of Robert Leighton, by Rev.
D. Butler." Proceedings of the Wesley Historical Society 6
(1907): 12-13. Review of Butler's book, in which he compares Wesley and Leighton.

2280. _____. "The Methodist Pilgrim in London." Wesleyan
Methodist Magazine 130 (1907): 503-11, 615-21.

2281. _____. "Pascal and the Wesleys." Proceedings of the
Wesley Historical Society 7 (1909): 60-63, 84-88.

2282. _____. Review of The Life and Letters of Robert Leighton, by Rev. D. Butler. Proceedings of the Wesley Historical
Society 6 (1907): 12-13.

2283. _____. "Smith House, Lightcliffe." Proceedings of the.
Wesley Historical Society 7 (1910): 169-73.

2284. _____. "Wesley and Joseph Galloway, Member of the First
American Continental Congress." Proceedings of the Wesley
Historical Society 9 (1913): 5-9.

2285. _____. "Wesley and Politics: Oxford, Exeter, St. Ives,
Bristol." Proceedings of the Wesley Historical Society 15
(1926): 133-37.

2286. _____. "Wesley and the Conference on Wigs, Hair-Powder,
Curls and Barbers." Proceedings of the Wesley Historical
Society 13 (1922): 138-41. Wesley recommended abstaining
from the use of wigs and hair powder.

2287. _____. "Wesley and the 'Dry Bones of Aldrich': Logic
at Oxford." Proceedings of the Wesley Historical Society 7
(1910): 124-25.

2288. _____. "Wesley and the Homilies of Macarius." Proceedings of the Wesley Historical Society 8 (1911): 6-7. Wesley
abridged Macarius for his The Christian Library.

2289. _____. "Wesley and the Slave Trade: Benezet and Clarkson." Proceedings of the Wesley Historical Society 12 (1920):
132-34.

2290. _____. "Wesley Cottage, Swanage." Proceedings of the
Wesley Historical Society 13 (1921): 52-54.

2291. _____. "Wesley on the Ethics of Dress." Wesleyan Methodist Magazine 127 (1904): 41-45, 128-34, 190-95.

2292.   . "The Wesleys and Islam." Proceedings of the Wesley Historical Society 8 (1911): 91-95.

2293.   . "Wesley's 'Field Bible' of 1653." Proceedings of the Wesley Historical Society 13 (1922): 121-23.

2294.   . "Wesley's London 'Retreats.'" Proceedings of the Wesley Historical Society 10 (1915): 84-86.

2295.   . "Wesley's Ordination at Bristol." Proceedings of the Wesley Historical Society 7 (1909): 8-11.

2296.   . "Wesley's Ordinations: Another Certificate Found in America. John Harper, 1787." Proceedings of the Wesley Historical Society 15 (1925): 34-35.

2297.   . "Wesley's Peril on the Sands of Furness." Wesleyan Methodist Magazine 135 (1912): 47-50.

2298.   . "Wesley's References to China and the Chinese." Proceedings of the Wesley Historical Society 9 (1914): 130-33.

2299.   . "The Wesleys, the Metrical Psalms, and a Stray Trevecca College M.S." Proceedings of the Wesley Historical Society 12 (1919): 59-62.

2300. Brimmell, W. Langdon. "Portsmouth Methodism: Our Church History in the Great Naval Station." Methodist Recorder, 1 January 1903, 15-17.

2301. "Bristol, 1790: Wesley's Last Conference." Proceedings of the Wesley Historical Society 15 (1925): 57-60.

2302. Britton, William J. "The Cornish County Town: Bodmin and Its Methodist History." Methodist Recorder, 30 August 1906, 9.

2303. Broadbent, James H. "Methodism in Alnwick from 1744 to 1791." Proceedings of the Wesley Historical Society 7 (1909): 63-69, 88-96.

2304. Broadley, A. M. "The Dorset Wesleys." Proceedings of the Wesley Historical Society 6 (1907): 1-4.

2305. Brockwell, Charles W., Jr. "John Wesley's Doctrine of Justification." Wesleyan Theological Journal 18, no. 2 (1983): 18-32.

2306. Broholm, Richard R. "The Evangelizing Community and Social Transformation." Foundations 20 (1977): 352-61. Discussion of John Wesley's class meetings.

2306a.   _____.   "Personal Piety and Social Transformation: Learning from the Past."   Other Side 18, no. 4 (1982): 14.

2307. Bromfield, Richard F.   "Leeds and the Making of Methodism."
Wesleyan Methodist Magazine 137 (1914): 549-54.

2308. Broughton, R. J.   "Davyhulme Methodism: An Historical
Chapel."   Methodist Recorder, 1 June 1905, 12.

2309. _____.   "The Story of Blackley Methodism."   Methodist
Weekly (Manchester), 27 February 1902, 262; 6 March 1902,
275.

2310. Brown, H. Miles.   "Early Days of Cornish Methodism.   Opposition."   Proceedings of the Wesley Historical Society 26
(1947): 49-56, 69-76, 89-96, 137-40.

2311. _____.   "The Rise of Methodism in Cornwall."   Church
Quarterly Review 142 (1946): 78-91.

2312. Brown, Samuel G.   "Life, Character, and Works of John
Wesley."   American Biblical Repository, n.s. 9 (1843): 388-
423.

2313. Broxap, E. A.   "Methodism in Manchester: First Beginnings."   Methodist Weekly (Manchester), 17 July 1902, 3,
24 July 1902, 13.

2314. Broxap, Ernest.   "Gerard Groot and John Wesley."   Wesleyan Methodist Magazine 133 (1910): 133-35.

2315. Buchanan, C. Barron.   "Holiness and the Christian Year in
the Hymns of Charles Wesley."   Asbury Seminarian 32 (1977):
11-16.

2316. Buckley, J. M.   "Wesley and the Wesleyan Movement."   Review of Reviews 27 (1903): 714-23.   Popular treatment of
Wesley's life and Methodism.

2317. Bundy, David D.   "Wesleyan Perspectives on the Holy Spirit."
Asbury Seminarian 30, no. 2 (1975): 31-41.

2318. Bunnett, Arthur W.   "The Conference Town: Methodism in
Sheffield."   Wesleyan Methodist Church Record 13 (1904):
195-97.

2319. _____.   "Methodism in Doncaster; from Roman Camp to
Railway Centre."   Methodist Recorder, 28 April 1904, 9-10.

2320. Burgess, Harold.   "Wesleyan Theology of Ministry."   Wesleyan Theological Journal 18, no. 1 (1983): 30-43.

2321. Burnett, Ivan, Jr. "Methodist Origins: John Wesley and
       Alcohol." Methodist History 13, no. 4 (1975): 3-17. Wesley
       had complex views regarding alcohol, which did not support
       total abstention.

2322. Burnham, Elizabeth. "Susanna Wesley's Influence upon the
       Hymnody of Her Sons." Methodist Review 112 (1929): 540-
       50.

2323. Burrows, Thomas. "Methodism in Holyhead." Wesleyan Meth-
       odist Magazine 61 (1838): 623-24.

2324. Burtner, Robert W. "John Wesley in Switzerland." Quarter-
       ly Review (Nashville) 4, no. 1 (1984): 22-30. Describes the
       meeting of 35 pastors and theologians in Zurich, Switzerland
       in 1982, to discuss Wesleyan theology.

2325. Burtt, Percy E. "Comparison of Charles Wesley and Isaac
       Watts." Pittsburgh Christian Advocate 77, no. 17 (1910):
       21.

2326. Butcher, J. Williams. "Glasgow: Its Methodism and Its Ex-
       hibition." Methodist Recorder, 13 June 1901, 8-10.

2327. Butler, John F. "John Wesley's Defence before Bishop But-
       ler." Proceedings of the Wesley Historical Society 20 (1935):
       63-67, 193-94.

2328. Butterworth, Richard. "Dryden and the Methodist Hymn
       Book." Proceedings of the Wesley Historical Society 10
       (1916): 159-62.

2329. _____. "Dummer and the Oxford Methodists." Proceed-
       ings of the Wesley Historical Society 12 (1919): 49-53.

2330. _____. "John Wesley's Health." Proceedings of the Wes-
       ley Historical Society 14 (1924): 162-65.

2331. _____. "Milton and the Methodist Hymn Book." Proceed-
       ings of the Wesley Historical Society 10 (1915): 97-102.

2332. _____. "The Mutual Friends of Wesley and Goldsmith."
       Proceedings of the Wesley Historical Society 8 (1912): 148-50.

2333. _____. "Prior and the Methodist Hymn Book." Proceed-
       ings of the Wesley Historical Society 10 (1916): 184-87.

2334. _____. "Repetitions in Wesley's Hymns." Proceedings of
       the Wesley Historical Society 10 (1915): 63-65. Discusses
       favorite expressions, lines, and couplets repeated in the
       hymns.

2335. _____. "The Rev. Edward Phillips, of Maesmynis, and the Wesleys." Proceedings of the Wesley Historical Society 12 (1920): 174-76.

2336. _____. "Shakespeare and the Methodist Hymn Book." Proceedings of the Wesley Historical Society 10 (1915): 75-80.

2337. _____. "A Voyage to Georgia: Begun in the Year 1735." Proceedings of the Wesley Historical Society 11 (1918): 108-11.

2338. _____. "Wesley and His Father at Wentworth House in 1733." Proceedings of the Wesley Historical Society 6 (1907): 11.

2339. _____. "Wesley and the Dissenters." Proceedings of the Wesley Historical Society 8 (1911): 25-29.

2340. _____. "Wesley As the Agent of the S.P.G." Proceedings of the Wesley Historical Society 7 (1910): 99-102.

2341. _____. "Wesley's Journal; a Few Notes on the Journals of Wesley and Visits to Cardiff and the Neighbourhood." Proceedings of the Wesley Historical Society 3 (1902): 81-84, 175-77.

2342. _____. "The Wesleys of the Principality." Proceedings of the Wesley Historical Society 3 (1902): 131-32. This article is about the Wesleys of Wales.

2343. _____. "Wesley's Visits to Llandaff Court." Wesleyan Methodist Magazine 129 (1906): 469-72.

2344. _____. "William Pritchard of Bodlewfawr." Proceedings of the Wesley Historical Society 7 (1910): 111-14.

2345. _____. "Young and the Methodist Hymn Book." Proceedings of the Wesley Historical Society 11 (1917): 63-66.

2346. Byrnside, Ron. "Toward a History of Music in Georgia." Georgia Historical Quarterly 65 (1981): 16-21. Discusses John Wesley's Collection of Psalms and Hymns, compiled while in Georgia but published in South Carolina, now known as the Charlestown Collection and the Foundery Collection, published in London in 1742.

2347. C. "Centenary of Wardle Methodism; John Wesley at a Wardle Cottage." Methodist Recorder, 17 February 1910, 10.

2348. C., G. H. "Our Greatest Naval Port: A Methodist Centenary in Portsmouth." Methodist Recorder, 27 April 1911, 9.

2349. C., H. "The Conference Town of Wesley's Day and There-
        abouts." Methodist Recorder, 13 July 1911, 11-12.

2350. C., S. F. "John Wesley in Lancashire." Manchester Guard-
        ian, 23 May 1938, 6.

2351. C., T. C. "A John Wesley Find." Notes and Queries 179
        (1940): 7. Describes two letters of John Wesley's, concern-
        ing a visit of his to Sheffield. See no. 3909 for additional
        comments.

2352. C., W. "Historical Notices of the Origin and Progress of
        Methodism in Belfast and Its Neighbourhood." Wesleyan
        Methodist Magazine 91 (1868): 914-23.

2353. C., W. L. "A Typical Methodist Circuit, Burngreave Rd.,
        Sheffield." Methodist Recorder, 18 August 1910, 9.

2354. Cadman, S. Parkes. "Wesley's Influence upon the United
        States of America." Methodist Magazine (London) 150 (1927):
        67-73; 131-38.

2355. Cahall, W. C. "John Wesley As a Scientist." Methodist Re-
        view 74 (1892): 77-88.

2356. Callaway, C. Wayne. "John Wesley's Primitive Physick. An
        Essay in Appreciation." Proceedings of the Mayo Clinic 49
        (1974): 318-24. This paper was a prizewinning essay in the
        1973 Annual Essay Award Contest of the Mayo Foundation
        History of Medicine Society and of the Section of the History
        of Medicine.

2357. Callister, Christopher. "Jottings from Knaresborough: How
        an Unknown Man Scattered the Methodist Seed." Methodist
        Recorder, 23 February 1905, 10.

2358. Cameron, Richard M. "John Wesley's Aldersgate Street Ex-
        perience." Drew Gateway 25 (1955): 210-19.

2359. _____. "The Little Flowers of John Wesley." Religion in
        Life 23 (1954): 267-78. Despite the differences between Wes-
        ley and St. Francis, there were striking similarities. The
        spiritual experiences described in the writings of early
        Methodism are likened to those contained in the Little Flower
        and other legends of St. Francis.

2360. Candler, Mark Allen. "John Wesley's Love Affair." Magazine
        of History (N.Y.) 13 (1911): 289-95. This is another account
        of Wesley and Sophia Hopkey.

2361. Canney, W. R. Ladd. "In the Fens: A Sketch of Methodism
        in the Ely Circuit." Methodist Recorder, 16 April 1908, 12.

2362. Cannon, William R. "The Holy Spirit in Vatican II and in
       the Writings of John Wesley." Religion in Life 37 (1968):
       440-53. Describes differences in interpretation of the Holy
       Spirit in Roman Catholicism and in the writings of John Wes-
       ley.

2363. _____. "John Wesley: He Laid Methodism's Cornerstone."
       Together 7, no. 2 (1963): 30-32.

2364. _____. "John Wesley's Doctrine of Sanctification and Per-
       fection." Mennonite Quarterly Review 35 (1961): 91-95.

2365. _____. "John Wesley's Years in Georgia." Methodist
       History 1, no. 4 (1963): 1-7.

2366. _____. "Methodism in a Philosophy of History." Methodist
       History 12, no. 4 (1974): 27-43. Discusses the meaning of
       history for John Wesley.

2367. _____. "Perfection." London Quarterly and Holborn Re-
       view 184 (1959): 213-17.

2368. _____. "Salvation in the Theology of John Wesley." Bul-
       letin of the Committee on Archives of the United Church of
       Canada 27 (1978): 42-54.

2369. Capey, A. C. "Charles Wesley and His Literary Relations."
       Gadfly 6, no. 1 (1983): 17-26. Discusses the use Charles
       Wesley made of his literary sources--the Bible, Milton's
       Paradise Lost, and George Herbert's work.

2370. "The Capital of the Cotswolds: What a Country Town Guild
       Is Like." Methodist Recorder, 10 May 1906, 9.

2371. Carlton, William J. "The Wesleys and the Winged Art."
       Wesleyan Methodist Magazine 138 (1915): 470-74.

2372. Carpenter, Edmund Snow. "The Role of Archaeology in the
       Nineteenth Century Controversy between Developmentalism
       and Degeneration." Pennsylvania Archaeologist 20 (1950):
       5-18. Includes a discussion of John Wesley's attitude toward
       the American Indian.

2373. Carrier, E. Theodore. "Wesley's Views on Prayers for the
       Dead." Proceedings of the Wesley Historical Society 1
       (1898): 123-25. Discusses Wesley's views on Dean Luckock's
       After Death (1879).

2374. Carter, Charles. "Evangelical Religion and Art." London
       Quarterly Review. 159 (1934): 337-44. Discusses the lack
       of artistic expression during the development of Methodism
       in the eighteenth century.

2375.   _____. "The Pottery of John Wesley." Hobbies 55, no.
8 (1950): 85, 93. Contains a discussion of the pottery busts
of John Wesley. Nearly all of them are based on the bust
modeled in 1781 by Enoch Wood.

2376.   _____. "Wesley's Mark on Old English Pottery." Hobbies
55, no. 12 (1951): 101. John Wesley's portrait has been used
to decorate jugs, teapots, mugs, wall plaques, and glasses.

2377. Carter, Thomas. "The Wesley Bicentenary at Vanderbilt."
Vanderbilt University Quarterly 3 (1903): 225-36. Describes
the series of lectures given at Vanderbilt during the bicentenary celebration of Wesley's birth.

2378. Cell, George Croft. "Decay of Religion." Methodist Review
107 (1924): 64-78, 207-19. A discussion of Wesley's attitude
toward secularism, philanthropy, and accumulation of wealth.

2379.   _____. "Influence of Religion upon Its Subjects As
Economic Agents." Methodist Review 107 (1924): 380-400.

2380. Centenary of John Wesley's Death; Special Supplement to the
Methodist Times (London). 26 February 1891. Contains
biographical sketch of John Wesley with a page of his portraits, facsimiles of the handwriting of the Wesley family.
Also contains an article on John and Charles Wesley's use of
shorthand.

2381. "The Centenary of Portland Chapel, Bristol." Methodist Recorder, 10 September 1891, 727.

2382. "A Century of Methodism in Bury." Bury Guardian 13 November 1886, 6; 20 November 1886, 8; 27 November 1886, 8.

2383. Chamberlayne, John H. "From Sect to Church in British
Methodism." British Journal of Sociology 15 (1964): 139-49.

2384.   _____. "Methodism--Society or Church." London Quarterly and Holborn Review 189 (1964): 104-9.

2385. Chandler, Douglas R. "John Wesley and His Preachers."
Religion in Life 24 (1955): 241-48.

2386. "The Character of John Wesley." Methodist Magazine 23
(1800): 90-94, 138-42.

2387. "Character of the Late Mr. Wesley." Gentleman's Magazine
69 (1791): 428-29.

2388. "Charles and Sarah Wesley." Quiver 13 (1878): 171-73, 310-
12, 374-78.

2389. Chilcote, Paul Wesley. "John Wesley as Revealed by the
       Journal of Hester Ann Rogers, July 1775-October 1784."
       Methodist History 20, no. 3 (1982): 111-23.

2390. Cho, J. C. "John Wesley's View on Baptism." Wesleyan
       Theological Journal 7 (1972): 60-73.

2391. Chorley, E. Clowes. Review of Son to Susanna, by G. Elsie
       Harrison, no. 771, John Wesley and Modern Religion, by
       Umphrey Lee, no. 1018, and John Wesley in the Evolution of
       Protestantism, by Maximin Piette, no. 1301. Historical
       Magazine of the Protestant Episcopal Church 7 (1938): 178-
       98.

2392. The Christian Advocate. Aldersgate Unification Edition,
       May 19, 1938. 98p. Commemoration of the 200th anniver-
       sary of John Wesley's experience in Aldersgate Street, May
       24, 1738.

2393. "The Christian Observer and the Methodists." Wesleyan
       Methodist Magazine 56 (1833): 32-43, 106-12. A response to
       charges against Wesley and Methodism which appeared in the
       Christian Observer.

2394. Church, Leslie Frederic. "Charles Wesley: The Man."
       London Quarterly and Holborn Review 182 (1957): 247-53.

2395. _____. "John Wesley: A Very Human Evangelist: A Man
       God Commissioned to Change the Heart of England."
       Methodist Recorder, 25 June 1953, 1.

2396. _____. "A Letter from John Wesley." London Quarterly
       and Holborn Review 176 (1951): 193-94. The text of a re-
       cently discovered letter is reprinted with comment.

2397. _____. "The Pastor in the Eighteenth Century." London
       Quarterly and Holborn Review 181 (1956): 19-23.

2398. _____. "Port Royal and John Wesley." London Quarterly
       and Holborn Review 175 (1950): 291-93. Discusses Wesley's
       use of and agreement with many of the doctrines of the Port-
       Royalists.

2399. "The Churchmanship of John Wesley." London Quarterly Re-
       view 30 (1868): 265-316. This article reviews numerous pub-
       lications on John Wesley.

2400. "City Road's World Witness; Importance of Wesley's Chapel."
       Methodist Recorder, 24 January 1963, 1.

2401. Clapper, Gregory S. "'True Religion' and the Affections: A

200   John and Charles Wesley

Study of John Wesley's Abridgement of Jonathan Edwards'
Treatise on Religious Affections." Wesleyan Theological Journal 19, no. 12 (1984): 77-89.

2402. Clarkson, George E. "John Wesley and William Law's Mysticism." Religion in Life 42 (1973): 537-44.

2403. _____. "William Law, John Wesley, and Quakerism."
Friends Journal 17 (1971): 488-89.

2404. Cleeve, John. "Methodism in 'Merrie' Wakefield." Methodist
Recorder 11 January 1900, 11-12.

2405. Cleland, James T. "A Presbyterian Looks at John Wesley."
Duke Divinity School Bulletin 28 (1963): 81-87.

2406. Clemons, James T. "John Wesley--Biblical Literalist?" Religion in Life 46 (1977): 332-42.

2407. Clifford, Alan C. "Philip Doddridge and the Oxford Methodists." Proceedings of the Wesley Historical Society 42
(1979): 75-80.

2408. Clifford, John. "The Prophet of the Eighteenth Century:
Sermon." Methodist Recorder, 12 March 1891, 196-97.

2409. Close, Charles. "Wesley and Whitby: The Passing of an
Historic Sanctuary." Wesleyan Methodist Magazine 146
(1923): 135-37.

2410. "Closing Scenes of John Wesley's Life." United Methodist
Free Churches' Magazine 34 (1891): 124-26.

2411. Cobleigh, Dr. "Wesley's Preaching." Methodist Recorder,
29 August 1861, 198. Brief comparison of Wesley's and
Whitefield's preaching.

2412. Codling, Henry. "Wesley's House." Methodist Monthly 13
(1904): 199-203.

2413. Cole, F. J. "The Belshaw Papers and Wesley." Proceedings
of the Wesley Historical Society 23 (1942): 101-4, 133-35. Includes extracts from the Freeman family papers.

2414. _____. "John Wesley and His Ulster Contacts." Proceedings and Reports of the Belfast Natural History and Philosophy
Society 2d ser., pt. 5 (1946): 199-215.

2415. _____. "Wesley at Newtownards." Proceedings of the Wesley Historical Society 25 (1945): 30-32.

2416. _____. "Wesley's Visits to Co. Antrim and Co. Down."
Proceedings of the Wesley Historical Society 21 (1938): 141-
43.

2417. Cole, F. J., and David B. Bradshaw. "John Wesley at Car-
rickfergus." Proceedings of the Wesley Historical Society
16 (1928): 122-25.

2418. Cole, Richard Lee. "Skinner's Alley, Dublin: Some Wesley
Letters [to John Cennick and others], 1748." Proceedings
of the Wesley Historical Society 17 (1929): 36-50.

2419. _____. "Some Wesley Letters." Proceedings of the Wesley
Historical Society 25 (1945): 1-3.

2420. _____. "The Wesleys and James Erskine (Lord Grange)."
Proceedings of the Wesley Historical Society 23 (1942): 164-66.

2421. _____. "Wesley's Handwriting." London Quarterly and
Holborn Review 178 (1953): 145-47.

2422. _____. "The Widow's Home, Dublin." Proceedings of the
Wesley Historical Society 24 (1943): 73-75.

2423. Coleman, Robert E. "Why Wesleyan Evangelism Worked."
Moody Monthly 84, no. 7 (1984): 76-78.

2424. Coley, Hilda M. "John Wesley Prescribes for Bodily Ailments."
Bookman 85 (1934): 446-47.

2424a. Collier, John. "Wesley's Christian Perfection in Light of
Luther and Niebuhr." Church Divinity (1981): 12-22.

2425. Collingwood, Peter J. "Prison Visitation in the Methodist Revival." London Quarterly and Holborn Review 180 (1955):
285-92. Relates the Wesleys' work with prisoners.

2426. Collins, Edward M., Jr. "John Wesley's Congregations."
Wesleyan Quarterly Review 4 (1967): 227-36.

2427. Colquhoun, Frank. "Charles Wesley's Eucharistic Hymns."
Churchman, n.s. 63 (1949): 103-7.

2428. "Commemoration of the Centenary of the Late Rev. John Wesley's Ordination to the Office of the Christian Ministry."
Methodist Magazine 7 (1824): 455-66.

2429. "Completion of the Epworth Memorial." Methodist Recorder,
4 June 1891, 426-27.

2430. "The Conversion of John Wesley: A Date in English History."
Times Literary Supplement, 21 May 1938, 348.

2431.   Cooke, Arthur W.   "Edinburgh's Little Sister: The Story of
        Methodism in Leith."   Methodist Recorder, 9 March 1911, 10.

2432.   Coomer, Duncan.   "The Local Preachers in Early Methodism."
        Proceedings of the Wesley Historical Society 25 (1945): 33-42.

2433.   Cooper, W. Hargreaves.   "The Golden Valley: How Method-
        ism Came to Bacup in 1744."   Methodist Recorder, 24 April
        1902, 13-14.

2434.   _____.   "Historic Tiviot Dale: A Fragmentary Record of
        Stockport Methodism."   Methodist Recorder, 12 January 1905,
        9.

2435.   Copeland, Arthur.   "Woodrow Wilson's Opinion of John Wes-
        ley."   Methodist Review (N.Y.) 97 (1915): 728-30.

2436.   Copestake, R. H.   "John Wesley and Moral Re-armament."
        Methodist Magazine 162 (1939):   664-66.   Discussion of Wes-
        ley's doctrine of holiness.

2437.   Coppedge, Allan.   "John Wesley and the Issue of Authority
        in Theological Pluralism."   Wesleyan Theological Journal 19,
        no. 2 (1984): 62-76.

2438.   Copplestone, J. Tremayne.   "John Wesley and the American
        Revolution."   Religion in Life 45 (1976): 89-105.

2439.   Coradine, W. H.   "Wesley and the Colonies."   Proceedings of
        the Wesley Historical Society 2 (1900): 201-2.

2440.   Coulson, John E.   "Mr. Wesley at Bolton."   Methodist Re-
        corder, 5 December 1861, 308.

2441.   Coulter, Ellis Merton.   "When John Wesley Preached in Geor-
        gia."   Georgia Historical Quarterly 9 (1925): 317-51.

2442.   Court, Lewis H.   "John Wesley and the Quakers of Dartmoor."
        Wesleyan Methodist Magazine 131 (1908): 520-25.

2443.   Cowell, Henry J.   "John Wesley and America."   Landmark 6
        (1924): 653-56.

2444.   Cowell, R. Corlett.   "The North Cornwall Mission: A New
        Harvest in an Old Field, Newquay and St. Columb Section."
        Methodist Recorder, 4 July 1907, 9.

2445.   _____.   "The North Cornwall Mission: A New Harvest in
        an Old Field, the St. Agnes Section."   Methodist Recorder,
        5 December 1907, 14.

2446. Cox, Leo George. "John Wesley's Concept of Sin." Bulletin
       of the Evangelical Theological Society 5 (1962): 18-24.

2447. _____. "John Wesley's View of Martin Luther." Bulletin
       of the Evangelical Theological Society 7 (1964): 83-90.

2448. Crabtree, J. H. "A Century of Methodism at Bagslate."
       Methodist Recorder, 10 March 1910, 11.

2449. Crane, Denis. "A Trip Round Methodist London." Methodist
       Recorder, 18 July 1907, 5-8.

2450. Crawford, George H. "Three Mountmellick Quakers and Wes-
       ley." Proceedings of the Wesley Historical Society 22 (1940):
       107-9.

2451. Crawford, Robert C. "John Wesley and the Weather."
       Methodist Magazine 157 (1934): 508-10.

2452. _____. "John Wesley and Waterford." Methodist Magazine
       161 (1938): 109-12.

2453. _____. "John Wesley's Humour." Methodist Magazine 157
       (1934): 313-15.

2454. _____. "Wesley and Boswell." Methodist Magazine 158
       (1935): 509-10.

2455. _____. "Wesley and Leisure." Wesleyan Methodist Maga-
       zine 156 (1933): 111-12.

2456. _____. "Wesley and Voltaire." Methodist Magazine 158
       (1935): 677-79.

2457. Crawshaw, E. "A Bust of John Wesley." Proceedings of the
       Wesley Historical Society 2 (1900): 119-20.

2458. Croft, E. Whitfield. "Some Cornish Sketches: Before Wesley
       and After." Wesleyan Methodist Church Record 12 (1903):
       92-94.

2459. Crooks, G. R. "Charles Wesley and His Poetry." Methodist
       Quarterly Review 31 (1849): 378-87.

2460. Crookshank, Charles H. "The Early History of Methodism in
       the City of Waterford." Wesleyan Methodist Magazine 102
       (1879): 151-55, 433-41.

2461. _____. "Was Wesley a Freemason?" Proceedings of the
       Wesley Historical Society 7 (1910): 163-64.

2462. Cross, Colin. "John Wesley, Organization Man." Observer
      Magazine, 6 July 1969, 11-20.

2463. _____. "Mr. Wesley's Parish." Observer Magazine, 13
      July 1969, 26-31.

2464. Cross, William C. "Wesley and Medicine: Primitive Physic
      and Its Critics." Wesleyan Methodist Magazine 137 (1914):
      613-18.

2465. Crossland, George H. "The Wesleys and the Cotswolds."
      Methodist Recorder, 24 September 1953, 15.

2466. Cubie, D. L. "Perfection in Wesley and Fletcher: Inaugural
      or Teleological?" Wesleyan Theological Journal 11 (1976):
      22-37.

2467. Cullwick, William E. "The Conference at Plymouth: The Life
      and Methodism of Three Towns." Methodist Recorder, 17 July
      1913, 13-15.

2468. Cumbers, Frank Henry. "The Methodist Magazine, 1778-
      1969." Proceedings of the Wesley Historical Society 37
      (1969): 72-76.

2469. Curnock, Nehemiah. "John Wesley's Journal." Spectator
      103 (1909): 596-97.

2470. _____. "The Recent Discoveries of Wesley MSS at the
      Book Room." Proceedings of the Wesley Historical Society
      9 (1913): 1-4.

2471. _____. "Wesley's House." Wesleyan Methodist Church
      Record 7 (1898): 99-100.

2472. Curnow, A. Garfield. "Wesley and Bunyan: A Criticism
      Criticized." Methodist Magazine 160 (1937): 461-64.

2473. Curteis, George H. "Dissent in Its Relation to the Church
      of England." The Bampton Lecture for 1871. Wesleyan
      Methodist Magazine 96 (1873): 115-23, 216-25, 302-11.

2474. Cushman, Robert E. "Theological Landmarks in the Revival
      under Wesley." Religion in Life 27 (1957): 105-18. (Also
      contained in his Faith Seeking Understanding..., 51-62, no.
      438.)

2475. Cuttell, John. "The Three Great Parallels--Paul, Luther and
      Wesley." Methodist Monthly 12 (1903): 49-51, 76-78, 106-8,
      173-75.

2476. D., C. J. "A Church Diary, June 24th-30th: Wesley's
First Conference." Methodist Recorder, 24 June 1937, 18.

2477. Dale, J. "Some Echoes of Charles Wesley's Hymns in His
Journal." London Quarterly and Holborn Review 184 (1959):
336-44.

2478. Dale, R. W. "The Theology of John Wesley." Methodist
Recorder, 5 March 1891, 173-74.

2479. Dale, T. P. "Kingswood, Bristol and Methodism." United
Methodist Magazine 25 (1932): 201-7.

2480. Dando, Norman E. "When Wesley Went to Plymouth." Methodist Recorder, 11 July 1929, 16.

2481. Daniels, W. M. "Mispraise of John Wesley." Nation 77
(1903): 25-26. The author of this article believed it was
wrong to say that Wesley saved English society.

2482. Davey, Cyril J. "Easter with Wesley." Methodist Magazine
158 (1935): 219-21.

2483. "David Simpson and John Wesley." Wesleyan Methodist Magazine 80 (1857): 896-98.

2484. Davies, D. Darley. "Towyn, Merionethshire: Where the
Welsh Assembly Meets." Methodist Recorder, 1 June 1911, 9.

2485. Davies, Frank. "William Norris of Lincoln." Musical Times
114 (1973): 738-41. Norris used a poem of Samuel Wesley's
for his ode, composed probably in the mid-1690s.

2486. Davies, G. C. B. "Early Evangelicals." Church Quarterly
Review 155 (1954): 121-30. A discussion of Elliott-Binns'
The Early Evangelicals: A Religious and Social Study, no.
570.

2487. Davies, J. Llewelyn. "Wesleyan Methodism, in Wesley's Lifetime and After." Contemporary Review 27 (1875-76): 114-39,
171-98.

2488. Davies, Rupert E. "The People of God." London Quarterly
and Holborn Review 184 (1959): 223-30. This article considers the doctrines of the Methodist Church by discussing
them from a historical viewpoint.

2489. Davis, H. Francis. "The Spirit in Nonconformist Spirituality."
Blackfriars 31 (1950): 220-29.

2490. Davis, Samuel. "A Centenary Appreciation of Southey's Life

of John Wesley." London Quarterly and Holborn Review 168
(1943): 319-23.

2491. Davison, W. T. "Wesley and Present-Day Preaching." London Quarterly Review 137 (1922): 1-15.

2492. Daw, A. R. "John Wesley in Scotland: The Bicentenary of
Methodism." Scots Magazine 29 (1938): 127-32.

2493. Daw, Charles. "Early Birmingham Methodism." Methodist
Recorder, 12 July 1894, 452-53.

2494. Daw, Leslie T. "New Light on Later Relationships between
Wesley and the Moravians." Proceedings of the Wesley Historical Society 18 (1932): 155-60, 185-88.

2495. _____. "Two Polemical Pamphlets. Did Wesley Write
Them?" Proceedings of the Wesley Historical Society 16
(1928): 98-104.

2496. Day, James Roscoe. "The Gospel of John Wesley: Bi-
centenary of John Wesley's Birth--Inaugural Celebration in
America." Methodist Recorder, 12 March 1903, 5-6.

2497. Dayton, Lucille Sider, and Donald W. Dayton. "'Your Daugh-
ters Shall Prophesy': Feminism in the Holiness Movement."
Methodist History 14, no. 2 (1976): 67-92. Beginning with
Susanna Wesley, treats the place of women in the Holiness
Movement.

2498. "A Defence of Mr. Wesley and of His Doctrines, against the
Reflections Cast upon Them by the Right Rev. William Van
Mildert, D.D. Lord Bishop of Llandaff." Methodist Magazine
47 (1824): 437-51.

2499. Denman, Harry. "What Aldersgate Means to Me." Together
7, no. 5 (1963): 23-24.

2500. Dent, William. "Methodism: A Retrospect and a Comparison."
Primitive Methodist Quarterly Review, n.s. 5 (1883): 16-25.
Compares Wesleyan Methodism with primitive Methodism.

2501. DeRemusat, Charles. "Wesley and Methodism." Methodist
Quarterly Review 53 (1871): 217-34, 384-99. This article
was translated from the Revue des Deux Mondes. Ser. 2,
85 (1870): 350-86.

2502. "Description of the Monuments, Erected in the City Road
Chapel, London." Wesleyan Methodist Magazine 46 (1823):
25-28.

2503. Devis, P. Addison. "John Wesley As Field Preacher: England

Changed by Open-Air Witness." Methodist Recorder; Open-
Air Preaching Supplement, 30 March 1939, ii.

2504.   . "The Road to Aldersgate Street; a Narrative of
John Wesley's Spiritual Pilgrimage." Methodist Recorder,
Wesley Bicentennial Supplement, 19 May 1938, ii.

2505. Dieter, Melvin E. "John Wesley and Creative Synthesis."
Asbury Seminarian 39, no. 3 (1984): 3-7. A discussion of
Wesley's theological development.

2506. Dilks, T. Bruce. "The Wesleys and Others; Letters Found
in Salvage." Times Literary Supplement, 11 December 1943,
600; 8 January 1944, 19. See also no. 3859.

2506a. Dillman, Charles N. "Wesley's Approach to the Law in Discourse XXV, on the Sermon on the Mount." Wesleyan
Theological Journal 12 (Spring 1977): 60-65.

2507. Dimond, Sidney George. "The Genius of Methodism: A
Psychological Study. Pt. 3, The Human Wesley." Methodist
Magazine 154 (1931): 139-43.

2508.   . "William Blake and Methodism." Methodist Magazine
150 (1927): 459-65.

2509. Dinwiddie, Richard D. "Two Brothers ... Who Changed the
Course of Church Singing." Christianity Today 28, no. 13
(1984): 30-34.

2510. Dixon, Neil. "A 'New' Wesley Hymn." Hymn Society of Great
Britain and Ireland Bulletin 10 (1984): 204-6.

2511.   . "The Wesleys' Conversion Hymn." Proceedings of
the Wesley Historical Society 37 (1969): 43-47.

2512. Dobbin, Orlando T. "John Wesley and the Principles Developed in His Character." Journal of Sacred Literature 3
(1849): 1-49.

2513. Dock, George. "The Primitive Physic of John Wesley; a Picture of Eighteenth Century Medicine." Journal of the American Medical Association 64 (1915): 629-38. A lengthy discussion of Wesley's medical remedies as outlined in Primitive
Physic, indicating that it contains much good sense as well
as superstition.

2514. Dodsley, Charles E. "John Wesley As Physician." Pharma-
ceutical Journal and Pharmacist 104 (1920): 26-27.

2515. Doidge, Reginald J. "John Wesley's Message for Today."

Methodist Magazine 157 (1934): 25-28, 119-21, 180-82, 237-40, 265-66, 343-45, 413-15.

2516. Dooley, Allan C. "An Echo of Wesley in 'The Bishop Orders His Tomb.'" Studies in Browning and His Circle: A Journal of Criticism, History and Bibliography 8, no. 1 (1980): 54-55. The author believes Browning echoes Wesley's Earnest Appeal to Men of Reason and Religion in his "The Bishop Orders His Tomb."

2517. Dorr, Donal J. "Total Corruption and the Wesleyan Tradition; Prevenient Grace." Irish Theological Quarterly 31 (1964): 303-21.

2518. _____. "Wesley's Teaching on the Nature of Holiness." London Quarterly and Holborn Review 190 (1965): 234-39.

2519. Dorsett, Cyril. "How the Wesleys Helped Children to Sing." Music Ministry 5, no. 2 (1964): 2-5.

2520. Doughty, William Lamplough. "Bicentenary of the First Methodist Conference: John Wesley's Early Aims and Rules." Methodist Recorder, 22 June 1944, 3.

2521. _____. "Charles Wesley, Preacher." London Quarterly and Holborn Review 182 (1957): 263-67.

2522. _____. "John Wesley in the Pew." Methodist Magazine, July 1961, 254-56.

2523. _____. "John Wesley Writes His Own Epitaph: Illness That Enabled Him to Begin Notes on the New Testament." Methodist Recorder, 3 December 1953, 9.

2524. _____. "John Wesley's Letter to Mr. Berington, 1780." Proceedings of the Wesley Historical Society 26 (1947): 38-44.

2525. _____. "Joseph Bradford: Wesley's Traveling Companion." Methodist Recorder, 29 May 1958, 9.

2526. _____. "Kingswood School, 1748-1948." Methodist Recorder, 27 May 1948, 7.

2527. _____. "New Year's Day with John Wesley." Methodist Magazine, January 1948, 5-9. Reviews some of John Wesley's New Year's Days.

2528. _____. "Notes on Duplicate Wesley Letters." Proceedings of the Wesley Historical Society 32 (1959): 40-41.

Articles   209

2529. _____. "Records of Some Christmas Days Two Centuries
Ago: John Wesley among Friends." Methodist Recorder, 20
December 1945, 17.

2530. _____. "Thomas Fuller and the Wesleys." London Quarterly and Holborn Review 180 (1955): 42-47.

2531. _____. "Three Letters of John Wesley [to John Valton
and Richard Rodda]." Proceedings of the Wesley Historical
Society 31 (1958): 178-81.

2532. _____. "Wesley and English Modernism." Modern Churchman 28, no. 2 (1938): 70-80.

2533. _____. "Wesley and Lyttleton." Methodist Recorder, 27
March 1947, 9.

2534. _____. "Wesley's Fourth Conference." Methodist Recorder,
26 June 1947, 9.

2535. Doughty, William Lamplough and Francis Fletcher Bretherton. "Changed Names in Wesley Letters." Proceedings of
the Wesley Historical Society 26 (1948): 125-27.

2536. Dowling, William C. "Wesley and Social Care." Proceedings
of the Wesley Historical Society 36 (1968): 129-31.

2537. Downey, James. "Barnabas and Boanerges: Archtypes of
Eighteenth Century Preaching." University of Toronto Quarterly 51 (1981): 36-46. This article discusses two types of
preachers: Barnabas, the casual, cheerful and exhortive
one, and Boanerges, the direct, exuberant, vituperative type.
Wesley could be both kinds of preachers, letting the occasion
decide for him the proper role to take.

2538. Draper, H. Mudie. "Douglas Methodism: The Leading Manx
Circuit." Methodist Recorder, 23 October 1902, 13-14.

2539. _____. "Manxland's Ancient Capital: The Story of Castle-
town and Its Methodism." Methodist Recorder, 26 March 1903,
15-17.

2540. _____. "Methodism in Ramsey: Some Manx Methodist
Worthies and Their Work." Methodist Recorder, 19 February
1903, 13-16.

2541. Dreyer, Frederick. "Faith and Experience in the Thought of
John Wesley." American Historical Review 88, no. 1 (1983):
12-30. Discusses Wesley in relation to philosophy--claims he
was a thinker, not just an enthusiast.

2542. Drury, B. C. "John Wesley, Hymnologist." Proceedings of the Wesley Historical Society 32 (1960): 102-8, 132-35.

2543. DuBois, Patterson. "John Wesley's Journal." Book News 21 (1903): 480-81.

2544. Dugan, C. C. "A Wesley Letter in Tasmania [to Alexander McNab]." Proceedings of the Wesley Historical Society 18 (1932): 166-69.

2545. Duke, John A. "The 'Cork Stewards' Book: A Relic of the Days of Wesley." Proceedings of the Wesley Historical Society 9 (1913): 58-66.

2546. _____. "Irish Methodism and the House of Rosse." Wesleyan Methodist Magazine 132 (1909): 772-77.

2547. _____. "Irish Methodist Notes - Cork." Proceedings of the Wesley Historical Society 9 (1914): 159-63.

2548. "Duke Gets Wesley Papers." Christian Advocate 5, no. 25 (1961): 21-22.

2549. Dunlap, E. Dale and Kenneth E. Rowe. "George Croft Cell's 1935 Rediscovery of John Wesley and Assessment of American Methodist Theology." Methodist History 19, no. 4 (1981): 238-41. See no. 308.

2550. Dunlop, Richard. "John Wesley: Medical Missionary in the New World." Today's Health 42, no. 12 (1964): 20-23, 70-72. Popular account of Wesley's Georgian experiences with medicine.

2551. Dunning, H. Ray. "Systematic Theology in a Wesleyan Mode." Wesleyan Theological Journal 17, no. 1 (1982): 15-22.

2552. Durbin, Linda M. "The Nature of Ordination in Wesley's View of the Ministry." Methodist History 9, no. 3 (1971): 3-20.

2553. E., T. H. "The Approaching Conference at Newcastle-upon-Tyne." Wesleyan Methodist Magazine 96 (1873): 626-32.

2554. _____. "London Conferences." Wesleyan Methodist Magazine 95 (1872): 630-36.

2555. Earle, Ralph. "John Wesley's New Testament." Asbury Seminarian 14, no. 1 (1960): 61-67.

2556. "Early Methodism in Bristol." Methodist Monthly 15 (1906): 218-20.

Articles   211

2557. "The Early Methodist Conferences." Wesleyan Methodist
Magazine 86 (1863): 55-67, 121-33.

2558. East, James T. "Carn Brea: The Cornish Pisgah." Methodist Recorder, 17 October 1901, 11.

2559. Eayrs, George. "The New John Wesley." Holborn Review
59 (1917): 349-57.

2560. _____. "Sidelights on Methodist History--Wesley's New
Room in the Horsefair, Bristol." United Methodist Magazine
3 (1910): 65-69.

2561. _____. "Wesley and Asbury: New Estimates As World
Leaders." Methodist Review 107 (1924): 20-34.

2562. _____. "Wesley's Newcastle Work and Romance." Methodist Recorder, 17 July 1919, 6.

2563. Eckhart, Ruth Alma. "Wesley and the Philosophers."
Methodist Review 112 (1929): 330-45.

2564. Edwards, Maldwyn L. "'Aldersgate' and the Three Freedoms."
Methodist Recorder, 9 May 1963, 4.

2565. _____. "Charles Wesley's Engagement: Light from Unpublished Letters." Proceedings of the Wesley Historical Society
36 (1967): 33-35.

2566. _____. "Charles Wesley's Poetical Version of the Psalms."
Proceedings of the Wesley Historical Society 31 (1957): 62-
64.

2567. _____. "Did Wesley's Political Activities Interfere with His
Spiritual Appeal?" Methodist Magazine, June 1948, 259-61.

2568. _____. "Early Methodism in Birmingham." Methodist Recorder, 9 July 1953, 3.

2569. _____. "Early Methodism on Tyneside." Methodist Recorder, 3 July 1958, 7.

2570. _____. "Historic Turning Point in Bradford Methodism:
The Witness of John Nelson." Methodist Recorder, 13 July
1950, 7.

2571. _____. "The Reluctant Lover: John Wesley As Suitor."
Methodist History 12, no. 2 (1974): 46-62. Discusses Sophia
Hopkey, Grace Murray, and Mrs. Vazeille.

2572. _____. "Significance of Aldersgate for the Present Day."
Methodist Recorder, 2 May 1963, 7.

212   John and Charles Wesley

2573. _____. "Two Master Builders: The Relation of John Wesley and Francis Asbury." Proceedings of the Wesley Historical Society 38 (1971): 42-45.

2574. _____. "The Years of Unrest: 1790-1800." London Quarterly and Holborn Review 166 (1941): 451-58; 167 (1942): 84-
93. Describes the age of Wesley as an age of benevolent des-
potism.

2575. Edwards, R. A. "Needless Schism: A Comment on the Bi-
centenary of Wesley's Conversion." Hibbert Journal 36
(1938): 545-56.

2576. Edwards, T. J. "Military Aspects of John Wesley's Life:
John Wesley and the Young Pretender." Methodist Magazine
151 (1928): 308-14.

2577. _____. "Military Aspects of John Wesley's Life: Wesley
and the British Soldier." Methodist Magazine 151 (1928):
34-38.

2578. _____. "Military Aspects of John Wesley's Life: Wesley
and the Press-Gangs." Methodist Magazine 151 (1928): 470-
72.

2579. _____. "Military Aspects of John Wesley's Life: Wesley's
Soldier Preachers." Methodist Magazine 151 (1928): 550-54.

2580. _____. "Wesley, the Army Recruiter." Methodist Magazine 152 (1929): 56-58.

2581. "An 18th Century Emmanuel Movement." Albany Medical Annals 34 (1913): 672-81. This is largely a reprinting of the
preface to Wesley's Primitive Physic, 21st edition, 1789.

2582. Elderkin, Henry. "The Bi-centenary of John Wesley." Experience 12 (1903): 81-87.

2583. Elias, Edward Alfred. "The Wesleys and Their Circle."
Methodist Monthly 16 (1907): 78-81. Discusses the hymn-
writing of John and Charles Wesley.

2584. Ellingworth, Paul. "'I' and 'We' in Charles Wesley's Hymns."
London Quarterly and Holborn Review 188 (1963): 153-64.

2585. Ellinwood, Leonard. "Wesley's First Hymnal Was Never Of-
ficially Condemned." Hymn (New York) 12 (1961): 56-59.

2586. Ellis, G. A. "John Wesley." Atlantic Monthly 27 (1871):
321-31.

2587. Elmen, Paul. "The Fame of Jeremy Taylor." Anglican Theo-
       logical Review 44 (1962): 389-403.

2588. England, John. "The Conference Town and Its Methodism."
       Supplement to the Methodist Recorder, 18 July 1895, 477-79.

2589. England, Martha Winburn. "Blake and the Hymns of Charles
       Wesley." Bulletin of the New York Public Library 70
       (1966): 7-26, 93-112, 153-68, 251-64.

2590. _____. "The First Wesley Hymn Book." Bulletin of the
       New York Public Library 68 (1964): 225-38. Discusses A
       Collection of Psalms and Hymns, compiled by John Wesley
       while in Georgia and published in Charleston, South Carolina
       in 1737.

2591. English, John C. "The Cambridge Platonists in Wesley's
       Christian Library." Proceedings of the Wesley Historical
       Society 8 (1968): 161-68.

2592. _____. "The Heart Renewed: John Wesley's Doctrine of
       Christian Initiation." Wesleyan Quarterly Review 4 (1967):
       115-92.

2593. _____. "John Norris and John Wesley on the 'Conduct of
       the Understanding.'" Proceedings of the Wesley Historical
       Society 37 (1970): 101-4.

2594. _____. "John Wesley and Francis Rous." Methodist His-
       tory 6, no. 4 (1968): 28-35.

2595. _____. "John Wesley and the Anglican Moderates of the
       Seventeenth Century." Anglican Theological Review 51 (July
       1969): 203-20.

2596. _____. "John Wesley and the Principle of Ministerial Suc-
       cession." Methodist History 2, no. 2 (1964): 31-36.

2597. _____. "The Sacrament of Baptism According to the Sun-
       day Service of 1784." Methodist History 5, no. 2 (1967):
       10-16.

2598. "Epitaph on a Tomb-stone in the Burying Ground in the City
       Road." Gentleman's Magazine 70 (1791): 1144.

2599. Esdaile, Mrs. Arundell. "Wesley's Bust: Sculptor Identi-
       fied." Times, 5 March 1928, 17. This author claims the only
       known marble bust of Wesley was by a sculptor named Silves-
       ter.

2600. Eustis, W. T. "John Wesley." New Englander 12 (1854):
       82-93.

2601. "The Evangelistic Mission of Methodism." United Methodist
      Free Churches' Magazine 34 (1891): 605-7.

2602. Evans, Charles. "The Ancestry of the Wesleys." Notes
      and Queries 193 (1948): 255-59.

2603. Evans, Seth. "Methodism about Whaley Bridge on John Wes-
      ley's Favorite Ground." Methodist Recorder, 25 September
      1902, 13-15.

2604. _____. "A Pilgrimage in Peak Land." Methodist Recorder,
      10 April 1902, 13-14.

2605. Everett, James. "Remarks on Southey's Character of John
      Wesley." Methodist Magazine 41 (1818): 260-80, 340-53, 419-
      34.

2606. Everson, F. Howell. "John Wesley and Sophy Hopkey."
      Proceedings of the Wesley Historical Society 32 (1960): 119.

2607. Ewens, J. Baird. "Henry Carey, John Wesley and 'Namby
      Pamby'." London Quarterly Review 161 (1936): 40-51.

2608. "Extension of Methodism on Historic Ground: Tantobie."
      Methodist Recorder, 13 August 1891, 542.

2609. Failing, George E. "God Taught Me Better." Preacher's
      Magazine 53, no. 3 (1978): 10-11.

2610. _____. "Sent to Raise the Dead." Preacher's Magazine
      55, no. 3 (1980): 45-46.

2611. _____. "Wesley's Suggestions to Preachers." Preacher's
      Magazine 54, no. 3 (1979): 35.

2612. Fairbour, Joshua M. "A Typical Cornish Town: Redruth
      and Its Methodism." Methodist Recorder, 23 February 1905,
      9.

2613. Fallaw, H. F. "John Wesley's First Visit to Gateshead."
      Proceedings of the Wesley Historical Society 12 (1920): 112-
      14.

2614. Fallaw, H. F. and Francis Fletcher Bretherton. "Two Johns:
      John Glas, 1695-1773; John Wesley, 1703-1791." Proceedings
      of the Wesley Historical Society 20 (1935): 83-87.

2615. Fallon, George O. "John Wesley--Get Off Your Horse."
      Methodist Story 11, no. 4 (1967): 9-12. Projects Wesley and
      his methods into the twentieth century.

2616. Fallows, W. G. "The Wesleys and Methodism." Methodist Magazine, November 1952, 486-88.

2617. "Falmouth and Its Methodism: A Sunny Corner of Cornwall." Methodist Recorder, 20 November 1902, 15-16.

2618. Farrar, F. W. "John Wesley." Contemporary Review, 59 (1891): 343-53.

2619. Faulkner, John Alfred. "John Wesley As a Student and Author." Methodist Review 85 (1903): 579-88.

2620. _____. "Wesley As a Churchman." Papers of the American Society of Church History 8 (1897): 163-77.

2621. _____. "Wesley the Mystic." London Quarterly Review 153 (1930): 145-60.

2622. _____. "Wesley's Attitude toward Luther." Lutheran Quarterly 36 (1906): 155-78.

2623. _____. "Wesley's Sociological Views." London Quarterly Review 109 (1908): 226-40.

2624. Feather, James. "Wesley at Charterhouse School." Methodist Weekly (Manchester), 18 June 1903, 4.

2625. _____. "A Yorkshire Centenary: The Memories of a Crosshills Boy." Methodist Recorder, 7 January 1909, 11.

2626. Federer, Charles A. "John Wesley and the Quakers in Ireland." Proceedings of the Wesley Historical Society 1 (1898): 59-62.

2627. _____. "Parkgate, near Guiseley, Yorkshire." Proceedings of the Wesley Historical Society 5 (1906): 240-44.

2628. _____. "Wesley and the North Shields Chapel Case." Proceedings of the Wesley Historical Society 4 (1904): 223-30.

2629. _____. "Wesley's Visit to Leeds in 1775." Proceedings of the Wesley Historical Society 2 (1899): 115-18.

2630. Ferguson, Charles W. "He Made Methodists Sing!" Together 1, no. 12 (1957): 23-25.

2631. Ferguson, Duncan S. "John Wesley on Scripture: The Hermeneutics of Pietism." Methodist History 22, no. 4 (1984): 234-45.

2632. Fick, Edward W. H. "John Wesley's Teaching concerning

Perfection." <u>Andrews University Seminar Studies</u> 4 (1966):
201-17.

2633. Fiddick, Harold G. "The Care of Souls: John Wesley on
the Preacher's Work and Ways." <u>Methodist Recorder</u>, 28
January 1932, 9.

2634. Fillingham, Albert L. "The Coming Conference: Third Visit
to the Potteries: Homes; Hives; History." <u>Methodist Re-
corder</u>, 19 July 1900, 11-12.

2635. Findlay, George H. "Father of Boundless Grace." <u>London
Quarterly and Holborn Review</u> 169 (1944): 157-60. Discusses
this hymn written by Charles Wesley.

2636. _____. "First and Last Words: A Study of Some Wesley
Metres." <u>London Quarterly and Holborn Review</u> 21 (1952):
123-28.

2637. _____. "A Study in Wesley Six-Eights." <u>London Quarterly and Holborn Review</u> 180 (1955): 138-42.

2638. "The First Minister of Health." <u>Economist</u> 131 (1938): 468-
69. Praises John Wesley for his efforts on behalf of social
service to the poor of England.

2639. "The First Principles of Early Methodism." <u>London Quarterly
Review</u> 61 (1884): 267-90. Discusses the philosophic base of
early Methodism--the salvation of souls.

2640. Fisk, Dr. "Anecdote of John Wesley." <u>Wesleyan Methodist
Association Magazine</u> 2 (1839): 149-51.

2641. Fisk, Everett O., and Stuart P. Sherman. "Wesley or Sa-
tan?" <u>Nation</u> 98 (1914): 207-8. This is a discussion of the
quotation "Better to rule in hell than serve in heaven," which
had been attributed to John Wesley.

2642. Fitch, Donald. "John Fletcher's Letter to Wesley on Settling
at Madeley." <u>Soundings</u> (Santa Barbara) 6 (1974): 41-45.

2643. Fitch, Robert E. "Character Education à la mode; Christianity: Spiritual Personality." <u>Religion in Life</u> 23 (1954): 534-
36. A discussion of Wesley's experience and teachings. This
author describes Wesley as a Puritan romantic, an Evangelical
materialist, and a warrior for Christ, transcending denominational lines.

2644. Flanigan, Alex. "'Jesu, Lover of My Soul'." <u>Hymn Society
of Great Britain and Ireland Bulletin</u> 10 (1984): 194. Claims
this hymn was inspired by Kempis's <u>The Imitation of Christ</u>,
Book 3, Chap. 20.

Articles   217

2645. Fletcher, G. Arthur. "Derby - The Old Chapel in St.
       Michael's Lane." Proceedings of the Wesley Historical So-
       ciety 15 (1925): 109-12.

2646. _____. "A 'Wesley Tree' at Belper, Derbyshire." Pro-
       ceedings of the Wesley Historical Society 16 (1928): 111-13.

2647. Foakes-Jackson, F. J. "The Wesleys." American Church
       Monthly 14, no. 1 (1923): 22-30.

2648. Foley, G. P. "John Wesley's Dental Therapeutics." Journal
       of the American Dental Association 85 (1972): 249-50.

2649. Ford, C. Lawrence. "An Examination of Quotations, Latin,
       Greek and English in the Journal of John Wesley." Pro-
       ceedings of the Wesley Historical Society 5 (1905-1906):
       24-31, 47-53, 87-91, 110-21, 152-59, 174-84, 214-22.

2650. Ford, Ernest. "The Wesleys." Monthly Musical Record 47
       (1917): 152-53. This article is primarily concerned with the
       musical genius demonstrated in the Wesley family, and the fact
       that it was "steeped in the traditions and prejudices of Puri-
       tanism" which, the article claims, "wrecked English music."

2651. Forde, P. A. "Conversion and Revivals." Ecclesiastical
       Review 55 (1916): 28-48.

2652. Forsaith, Peter S. "Wesley's Designated Successor." Pro-
       ceedings of the Wesley Historical Society 42 (1979): 69-74.
       Explores the ambivalent relationship that existed between
       John Fletcher and John Wesley.

2653. Foss, Helen. "John Wesley's Thought Development."
       Methodist Review 85 (1903): 895-908.

2654. Foster, Henry J. "The House Where Dr. Coke Was Ordained
       for America." Proceedings of the Wesley Historical Society 2
       (1900): 99-109.

2655. _____. "In the Isle of Axholme." Proceedings of the Wes-
       ley Historical Society 5 (1906): 196-205.

2656. _____. "John Wesley at the Brickyard." Proceedings of
       the Wesley Historical Society 3 (1902): 25-41.

2657. _____. "Wesley's Humour." Wesleyan Methodist Magazine
       126 (1903): 446-49.

2658. _____. "Where Was John Wesley's First Open-Air Sermon
       in England Preached?" Proceedings of the Wesley Historical
       Society 2 (1900): 3-8.

2659. Fowler, James C. "Burslem." Wesleyan Methodist Magazine
       108 (1885): 340-50.

2660. Fox, Adam. "Hymns and Charles Wesley." Spectator 169
       (1942): 306-7.

2661. Fox, Harold G. "John Wesley and Natural Philosophy." Uni-
       versity of Dayton Review 7, no. 1 (1970): 31-39. Discusses
       Wesley's attitude toward science and his epistemology.

2662. Fraser, Bishop of Manchester. "The Bishop of Manchester
       and John Wesley's Policy." Methodist Recorder, 12 September
       1873, 526.

2663. Freeman, C. B. "Charles Wesley: The Poet and the Editors."
       Theology 61 (1958): 503-7.

2664. Freeman, David. "John Wesley's Journal." National Review
       97 (1931): 83-92. A discussion of John Wesley's belief in the
       supernatural and witchcraft.

2665. Freeman, T. E. "A Cheshire Centenary: The Ancient
       Borough of Congleton and Its Methodism." Methodist Record-
       er, 2 April 1908, 12.

2666. Freeman, T. W. "John Wesley in Ireland." Irish Geography
       8 (1975): 86-96.

2667. French, Alfred J. "The Three Year Term: John Wesley and
       Itinerancy." Methodist Recorder, 6 June 1895, 367-68.

2668. French, E. Aldom. "Wesley and Field Preaching." Methodist
       Magazine 162 (1939): 197-202.

2669. "A French View of Wesley." Methodist Recorder, 25 February
       1870, 95.

2670. Frost, Francis. "Biblical Imagery and Religious Experience in
       the Hymns of the Wesleys." Proceedings of the Wesley His-
       torical Society 42 (1980): 158-66.

2671. Frost, George. "A Wesley Letter in New Zealand." Proceed-
       ings of the Wesley Historical Society 23 (1941): 29-31.

2672. Frost, Maurice. "John Wesley's Hymn Tunes." Hymn Society
       of Great Britain and Ireland Bulletin 28 (July 1944): 5-7.
       Identifies the tunes in Wesley's first tune book, A Collection
       of Tunes, Set to Music As They Are Commonly Sung at the
       Foundery, 1742, and indicates which libraries own copies of
       the psalm books.

2673. _____. "The Tunes Associated with Hymn Singing in the Lifetime of the Wesleys." Hymn Society of Great Britain and Ireland Bulletin 4 (1957-58): 118-26.

2674. Frost, Stanley B. "John Wesley As Translator." Proceedings of the Wesley Historical Society 27 (1949): 5-6.

2675. "The 'Fruitful Hill' of Rye: Some Wesley Memories." Methodist Recorder, 5 October 1905, 12.

2676. Fry, Edward. "Earthquakes and John Wesley." Nature 79 (1908): 98.

2677. Fuhrman, Eldon R. "Speaking the Truth in Love: Dual Emphases in Wesleyan Thought." Wesleyan Theological Journal 11 (1976): 5-21.

2678. Fukamachi, Masanobu. "The Love-Feast." Wesleyan Quarterly Review 4 (1967): 73-82.

2679. Furniss, Harry. "Wesley's Tree, Winchelsea, Sussex." Wesleyan Methodist Magazine 140 (1917): 92-96.

2680. G., A. "Northwich and Early Methodism: A Great Cheshire Salt Town." Methodist Recorder, 22 October 1908, 9.

2681. _____. "Warrington and Wesley: An Ancient Town in Cheshire." Methodist Recorder, 5 July 1906, 10.

2682. Galliers, Brian J. N. "Baptism in the Writings of John Wesley." Proceedings of the Wesley Historical Society 32 (1960): 121-24, 153-57.

2683. Gamble, H. R. "John Wesley." Nineteenth Century and After 87 (1920): 668-77. This author claims that Wesley's movement has contributed to the "prosperous middle class-- keen in business, devoid of culture, narrow in his outlook on the world, a militant teetotaller and Sabbatarian...."

2684. Gambold, John. "The Character of Mr. John Wesley: In a Letter from Rev. Mr. Gambold to a Friend: Wrote about the Time When Mr. Wesley Was in America." Methodist Magazine 21 (1798): 117-21, 168-72.

2685. Garland, Thomas W. "Our Hymn Book." Wesleyan Methodist Magazine 84 (1861): 902-8.

2686. Garrison, Richard Benjamin. "Vital Interaction: Scripture and Experience: John Wesley's Doctrine of Authority." Religion in Life 25 (1956): 563-73.

2687. Gaulter, John. "Of the Introduction of Methodism into the
       Neighbourhood and City of Chester; in a Memoir of Mrs.
       Lowe, of That City." Methodist Magazine 32 (1809): 187-91,
       231-39.

2688. "General Oglethorpe and the Wesleys." Wesleyan Methodist
       Magazine 90 (1867): 805-9.

2689. Gentry, Peter W. "What Happened at Aldersgate."
       Preacher's Magazine 55, no. 1 (1979): 8, 59-60.

2690. George, A. Raymond. "Catchwords of 'The Conversations' -
       4. The Real Presence and the Lord's Supper." Proceedings
       of the Wesley Historical Society 34 (1964): 181-87.

2691. _____. "The Sunday Service." Proceedings of the Wesley
       Historical Society 40 (1976): 102-5.

2692. _____. "Wesley and Coke." Proceedings of the Wesley
       Historical Society 31 (1957): 27-31.

2693. _____. "Wesley Letters at Wesley College, Headingley."
       Proceedings of the Wesley Historical Society 26 (1948): 83-
       85; 27 (1950): 157-60, 181-84.

2694. "Georgia Museum: Wesley Items Added." Christian Advocate
       10, no. 12 (1966): 23. Items included are two busts of Wes-
       ley, a "silent clock," and a Currier and Ives print.

2695. Gering, William. "John Wesley on Preaching." Preaching 2,
       no. 3 (1967): 13-17.

2696. Gifford, George. "'Great Uncle John': A New Wesley Let-
       ter." Proceedings of the Wesley Historical Society 31 (1958):
       119-20.

2697. _____. "John Wesley in Liverpool." Methodist Recorder,
       30 June 1960, 10.

2698. _____. "Week by Week with Wesley, 1758." Methodist
       Recorder, 1958. Each week the author writes about Wesley's
       activities 200 years ago.

2699. _____. "Which Whitchurch [Visited by Wesley in 1742]?"
       Proceedings of the Wesley Historical Society 33 (1961): 4.

2700. _____. "With John Wesley in 1759." Methodist Recorder,
       1959. Each week the author writes about Wesley's activities
       200 years ago.

2701. Gilchrist, Agnes Addison. "The Greatest Traveller in

Eighteenth Century Ireland." Quarterly Bulletin of the Irish
Georgian Society 3 (1960): 4-9. Describes visits by John
Wesley during 1747-89.

2702. Gill, Frederick C. "Wesley and the Children; a Lesson for
Modern Methodism." Methodist Recorder, 15 October 1936,
7.

2703. _____. "Wesley As a Propagandist." Methodist Recorder,
21 October 1937, 11.

2704. Gill, Thomas H. "Charles Wesley." Congregationalist 6
(1877): 513-29.

2705. _____. "Watts and Charles Wesley Compared." Congregationalist 7 (1878): 129-44.

2706. Gillespie, Norman. "New Light on a Source of Charles Wesley and Thomas Morell." Notes and Queries 31 (1984): 10-11.

2707. Gillett, E. H. "John Wesley: His Character and Opinions."
Presbyterian Quarterly 1 (1872): 694-719.

2708. Gillies, Andrew. "Sidelights on John Wesley from Boswell's
Johnson." Methodist Review 103 (1920): 22-29.

2709. Girdler, Lew. "Defoe's Education at Newington Green
Academy." Studies in Philology 50 (1953): 573-91. Samuel
Wesley was a student at Newton Green Academy a generation
after Defoe. This article discusses books and authors studied
by Defoe based on a list made by Samuel Wesley.

2710. Gladding, Rosa E. "Great Horton and Thereabouts: Historic
West Riding Circuit." Methodist Recorder, 24 September
1908, 10.

2711. _____. "A Town of Varied Interests: When Wesley Came
to Warrington - and After." Methodist Recorder, 16 December
1909, 9.

2712. _____. "When Wesley Came to Macclesfield." Wesleyan
Methodist Magazine 136 (1913): 133-39.

2713. Glanville, Reginald. "A Link between Wesley and Donne."
Proceedings of the Wesley Historical Society 28 (1951): 13-14.

2714. Glasson, T. Francis. "Jeremy Taylor's Place in John Wesley's Life." Proceedings of the Wesley Historical Society 36
(1968): 105-7.

2715. _____. "John Wesley's Silver Buckles." Proceedings of
the Wesley Historical Society 33 (1962): 177-78.

2716. Gleckner, Robert F. "Blake and Wesley." Notes and Queries
       201 (1956): 522-24.

2717. "A Glimpse of Methodism in 'The Three Towns'; by a Bird of
       Passage." Methodist Recorder, 4 July 1889, 444; 11 July
       1889, 461.

2718. Godbold, Albea. "The Beginnings of Methodism in America."
       Proceedings of the Wesley Historical Society 35 (1966):
       106-9.

2719. _____. "Francis Asbury and His Difficulties with John Wes-
       ley and Thomas Rankin." Methodist History 3, no. 3 (1965):
       3-19.

2720. _____. "Methodist Episcopacy." Methodist History 11,
       no. 1 (1972): 15-29. Discusses the role of John Wesley,
       Francis Asbury, and William McKendree.

2721. Godsey, John D. "The Interpretation of Romans in the
       History of the Christian Faith." Interpretation: A Journal
       of Bible and Theology 34 (1980): 3-16.

2722. Godwin, Henry G. "John Wesley and Joseph Townsend."
       Proceedings of the Wesley Historical Society 25 (1946): 75-77.

2723. _____. "John Wesley's Visits to Banbury." Proceedings
       of the Wesley Historical Society 13 (1921): 81-84.

2724. Golden, James. "John Wesley on Rhetoric and Belles Lettres."
       Speech Monographs 28 (1961): 250-64. Discusses Wesley's
       taste and genius, his literary style, pulpit eloquence, and his
       role as a literary critic.

2725. Goldhawk, Norman. "Hymns for the Use of the People Called
       Methodists 1780." Hymn Society of Great Britain and Ireland
       Bulletin 9 (1980): 170-75. An address given at the Hymn
       Society Conference, Exeter, July 1980.

2726. Goldthorp, Leslie M. "John Wesley's Visits to the Upper Cal-
       der Valley." Transactions of the Halifax Antiquarian Society
       (1975): 55-74.

2727. Goodwin, Rowland. "Methodist Conference City: John Wesley
       in Bristol." Manchester Guardian, 2 July 1959, 6. This is
       an article concerning the Methodist Conference held in Bristol,
       July 6-16, 1959, with possible reunion with the Church of
       England being the important question of the day.

2728. Gordon, J. Wesley. "Methodist Beginnings." Methodist
       Magazine 160 (1937): 649-51, 719-21; 161 (1938): 47-49, 78-
       80, 140-43, 216-18.

2729. Gordon, John. "John Wesley." Theological Review 8 (1871):
       193-221, 374-406. Reviews the works of Tyerman, Wedgewood,
       and Urlin. See nos. 1721, 1801, 1727.

2730. Goss, W. A. "Early Methodism in Bristol. With Special
       Reference to John Wesley's Visits to the City." Proceedings
       of the Wesley Historical Society 19 (1933-1934): 30-37, 57-65,
       81-89, 101-6, 133-42, 161-68, 183-88; 20 (1935): 1-9, 25-30.

2731. Gough, Charles H. "The Methodism of the Fen Country."
       Methodist Recorder, 3 July 1902, 13-14.

2732. _____. "A Progressive Lincolnshire Circuit: Notes on
       Brigg and Scunthorpe." Methodist Recorder, 18 October
       1906, 10.

2733. _____. "Wordsworthshire: Wesley and the English Lake
       District." Methodist Recorder, 14 February 1901, 13-14.

2734. Grabo, Carl H. "Some Characteristics of John Wesley."
       Chautauguan 47 (1907): 184-203.

2735. Grant, Frank R. "The Revolution in Religious Rhetoric:
       John Wesley and the Evangelical Impact on England." His-
       torian 39 (1977): 439-54. This article attempts to "analyze
       the process through which the evangelical convictions were
       translated into moral attitudes and behavioral ideals."

2736. Grant, Peter W. "The Wesley's Conversion Hymn." Pro-
       ceedings of the Wesley Historical Society 35 (1966): 161-64.

2737. Graves, A. S. "Wesley's Variations in Belief, and the In-
       fluence of the same on Methodism." Methodist Review 69
       (1887): 192-211.

2738. Gray, Richard. "Moorfields and Methodism." United
       Methodist Free Churches' Magazine 20 (1877): 78-86.

2739. Gray, W. Forbes. "John Wesley and Scotland." Records of
       the Scottish Church History Society 8 (1944): 209-24.

2740. _____. "John Wesley in Edinburgh." Book of the Old
       Edinburgh Club 8 (1916): 159-203.

2741. Greathead, Thomas. "John Wesley and the Bull." Methodist
       Recorder, 22 November 1878, 699.

2742. Greathouse, William M. "Sanctification and the Christus Vic-
       tor Motif in Wesleyan Theology." Wesleyan Theological Jour-
       nal 7 (1972): 47-59. A discussion of Gustaf Aulen's Christus
       Victor and its relevance for Wesley's doctrine of sanctifica-
       tion.

2743. Greaves, Brian. "Eighteenth-Century Opposition to Method-
       ism." Proceedings of the Wesley Historical Society 31 (1957-
       1958): 93-98, 105-11.

2744. Greaves, J. George. "Methodism and 'the Faithful City,' the
       Growth of Our Church in Worcester." Methodist Recorder,
       15 January 1903, 13-15.

2745. Green, James. "Yarm and Methodism." Methodist Recorder,
       21 November 1901, 13-14.

2746. Green, Richard. "Enoch Wood's Busts of Wesley." Pro-
       ceedings of the Wesley Historical Society 6 (1907): 17-23.

2747. _____. "John Wesley and Grace Murray." Wesleyan
       Methodist Magazine 126 (1903): 431-36.

2748. _____. "John Wesley's Editorial Character Vindicated."
       Methodist Recorder, 7 November 1895, 801. See nos. 2084,
       3007.

2749. _____. "Roubiliac's Bust of Wesley." Proceedings of the
       Wesley Historical Society 5 (1906): 161-62.

2750. _____. "A True Portrait of Wesley." Proceedings of the
       Wesley Historical Society 4 (1904): 121-23.

2751. Greet, Kenneth. "The Wesleyan Spirit." Tablet 237 (1983):
       821-22.

2752. Greeves, Frederic. "John Wesley and Divine Guidance."
       London Quarterly and Holborn Review 162 (1937): 379-85.

2753. Gregory, Arthur S. "The Birthday Hymns." London Quar-
       terly and Holborn Review 163 (1938): 182-84.

2754. _____. "'Nearer While We Sing' 1780-1980: Methodist
       Hymnbooks." Proceedings of the Wesley Historical Society
       42 (1980): 125-31.

2755. Gregory, Benjamin. "Wanted, a Good History of Methodism in
       Hull." Methodist Recorder, 17 October 1895, 754.

2756. Gregory, T. S. "Beati Mundo Corde: John Wesley's Assize
       Sermon." Tablet (1958): 227-28.

2757. _____. "Charles Wesley's Hymns and Poems." London
       Quarterly and Holborn Review 182 (1957): 253-62.

2758. Grider, J. Kenneth. "Come Alive, Mr. Wesley." Preacher's
       Magazine 57, no. 3 (1982): 30-31.

Articles 225

2759. _____. "Evaluation of Timothy Smith's Interpretation of Wesley." Wesleyan Theological Journal 15, no. 2 (1980): 64-69.

2760. _____. "The Nature of Wesleyan Theology." Wesleyan Theological Journal 17, no. 2 (1982): 43-57.

2761. Grislis, Egil. "The Wesleyan Doctrine of the Lord's Supper." Duke Divinity School Bulletin 28 (1963): 99-110.

2762. Grubb, G. Watkins. "Cullompton in Devonshire: The Parish and the Parson." Notes and Queries 190 (1946): 28-31.

2763. Guerin, Basil C. de. "John Wesley in the 'French Islands.'" Methodist Magazine (1948): 358-61.

2764. Guernsey, Alfred H. "John Wesley." Galaxy 17 (1874): 200-15.

2765. H. "The Methodists at 'Cranford': Jubilee of Knutsford Church." Methodist Recorder, 28 May 1914, 9.

2766. H., J. E. "Herne Bay Methodism: A Minister's Benefit." Methodist Recorder, 7 July 1910, 10.

2767. H., J. M. "Methodism in Kent." Wesleyan Methodist Magazine 103 (1880): 37-46, 273-80, 446-56, 581-90, 837-47.

2768. H., W. M. "Early Methodism in Bristol." United Methodist Free Churches' Magazine 25 (1882): 385-92.

2769. Hackwood, Frederick William. "Two Notable Converts." Methodist Recorder, 29 January 1903, 16. Refers to "Honest Munchin" and the Earl of Dartmouth.

2770. Hagany, John B. "John Wesley." Harper's Magazine 19 (1859): 211-23.

2771. _____. "Mehetabel Wesley." Harper's Magazine 24 (1862): 218-23.

2772. Haines, Lee. "Susanna, Mother of the Wesleys." Wesleyan Advocate 135, no. 4 (1977): 6-7, 14.

2773. Hale, John G. "Charles Wesley and Methodist Hymns." Boston Review 5 (1865): 296-305.

2774. Hall, Albert F. "John Wesley's Tract Society." Proceedings of the Wesley Historical Society 12 (1920): 136-38. Describes Wesley's efforts at publishing and distributing religious tracts to members of his societies.

2775. _____. "Leeds, the Conference City of 1914." Methodist
      Recorder 16 July 1914, 13-14.

2776 _____. "An Unpublished Sermon of John Wesley." London
      Quarterly and Holborn Review 165 (1940): 139-46.

2777. Hall, Frank. "Town and Village Methodism: Contrast and
      Harmony in a Cheshire Circuit." Methodist Recorder, 1 July
      1909, 10.

2778. Hall, Thor. "The Christian Life: Wesley's Alternatives to
      Luther and Calvin." Duke Divinity School Bulletin 28 (1963):
      111-26.

2779. Hambrick, Charles H. "Lessons from an 'Unsuccessful Mis-
      sionary'." Practical Anthropology 8 (1961): 186-88, 192.
      An editorial, expressing his interpretation of Wesley's Georgia
      experience.

2780. Hannam, Wilfred L. "Johnson's Boswell: An Illusion Dis-
      pelled." Methodist Recorder, 12 January 1933, 21. Boswell
      visited Wesley about a Newcastle ghost.

2781. Hansford, F. E. "Links with Early Methodism: Wesley and
      Perronet." Methodist Recorder, 11 January 1962, 9.

2782. _____. "With the Wesleys in Dorset." Methodist Recorder,
      9 October 1952, 9.

2783. Hardcastle, Titus. "The Mother Church of Leeds: The Story
      of Armley Methodism." Methodist Recorder, 21 June 1906, 9.

2784. Hargitt, Charles W. "John Wesley and Science." Methodist
      Review 110 (1927): 383-93.

2785. Harkey, Simeon W. "The Conversion of John Wesley and His
      Indebtedness to Martin Luther." Lutheran Quarterly, n.s.
      14 (1884): 518-44.

2786. Harlan, Lowell B. "Theology of Eighteenth Century English
      Hymns." Historical Magazine of the Protestant Episcopal
      Church 48 (1979): 167-93.

2787. Harlow, J. Edward. "The Kingswood of the North." Method-
      ist Recorder, 1 June 1899, 11. Wesley called Gateshead Fell
      the Kingswood of the North.

2788. _____. "Methodism in Halifax." Methodist Recorder, 31
      August 1899, 9.

2789. Harmer, E. G. "John Wesley and the Newspapers of His Day."
      Methodist Monthly 5 (1896): 246-48.

2790. Harmer, H. A. "Methodism at Mitcham." Methodist Monthly
       5 (1896): 18-21.

2791. _____. "Methodism at Mitcham: Filling in the Gaps."
       Methodist Recorder, 25 February 1909, 9.

2792. Harmon, Nolan B. "John Wesley's Sunday Service and Its
       American Revisions." Proceedings of the Wesley Historical
       Society 39 (1974): 137-44.

2793. Harmon, Nolan B. and John W. Bardsley. "John Wesley and
       the Articles of Religion." Religion in Life 22 (1953): 280-91.
       A comparison of the Articles of Religion of the Church of
       England and Wesley's abridgement, The Sunday Service.

2794. Harper, Kenneth. "Law and Wesley." Church Quarterly
       Review 163 (1962): 61-71.

2795. Harries, John. "An Historic Chapel: The Story of Mankin-
       holes." Methodist Recorder, 18 April 1912, 10.

2796. Harrington, Susan F. "Friendship Under Fire: George
       Whitefield and John Wesley, 1739-1741." Andover Newton
       Quarterly 15 (1975): 167-81. Discusses their disagreement
       on free grace and universal redemption.

2797. Harris, H. Wilson. "Whitefield-Wesley-Johnson-Walpole."
       Proceedings of the Wesley Historical Society 13 (1921): 4-6.

2798. Harris, Rendel. "John Wesley and John Milton." Methodist
       Recorder 9 August 1934, 12.

2799. Harris, Thomas. "Methodism in Tunstall and Its Vicinity."
       Wesleyan Methodist Magazine 58 (1835): 518-20.

2800. Harrison, Archibald W. "The Arminian Magazine." Pro-
       ceedings of the Wesley Historical Society 12 (1920): 150-52.

2801. _____. "Bristol Methodism: Its Past and Present."
       Wesleyan Methodist Magazine 146 (1923): 502-7.

2802. _____. "The Greek Text of Wesley's Translation of the New
       Testament." Proceedings of the Wesley Historical Society 9
       (1914): 105-13.

2803. _____. "John Wesley's Last Sermon." Methodist Recorder,
       16 May 1935, 13.

2804. _____. "John Wesley's Visit to Ockbrook in June, 1741."
       Proceedings of the Wesley Historical Society 8 (1912): 108-
       12.

2805. _____. "Methodist Churchmanship." London Quarterly
and Holborn Review 163 (1938): 193-96.

2806. _____. "The Oldest Methodist Place of Worship [the New
Room in the Horse Fair]." Proceedings of the Wesley Historical Society 17 (1930): 101-2.

2807. _____. "One of Wesley's Science Note Books." Proceedings
of the Wesley Historical Society 18 (1931): 8-11.

2808. _____. "Present Day Faiths: Methodism." Expository
Times 38 (1927): 416-20.

2809. _____. "Restoration of Charles Wesley's Tomb." Proceedings of the Wesley Historical Society 17 (1930): 149-50.

2810. _____. "Romanticism in Religious Revivals." Hibbert
Journal 31 (1933): 582-94. The author of this article claims
that Charles Wesley is the earliest of the romantics, yet he
is not mentioned in the standard history of eighteenth-
century romanticism.

2811. _____. "St. Paul and Protestantism." London Quarterly
and Holborn Review 166 (1941): 425-35. Compares Wesley's
preaching with St. Paul's.

2812. _____. "Wesley's Reading at Oxford." Proceedings of the
Wesley Historical Society 15 (1926): 161-65. A discussion of
the books Wesley read while a student at Oxford.

2813. _____. "Wesley's Reading during the Voyage to Georgia."
Proceedings of the Wesley Historical Society 13 (1921): 25-29.

2814. _____. "Wesley's Reading in Georgia." Proceedings of the
Wesley Historical Society 15 (1926): 113-17.

2815. Harrison, Frank Mott. "Two Johns: Bunyan (1628-1688)--
Wesley (1703-1791)." London Quarterly and Holborn Review
164 (1939): 347-54.

2816. Harrison, Grace Elizabeth Simon. "Christmas Letters and
John Wesley: Greetings from the Eighteenth Century."
Methodist Recorder, 9 December 1937, 10.

2817. _____. "John Wesley, 24th May 1738." Lincolnshire
Magazine 3 (1938): 319-22.

2818. _____. "Modern Youth and Aldersgate Street." London
Quarterly and Holborn Review 163 (1938): 215-18.

2819. _____. "Susanna Wesley." Methodist Recorder, 21 May
1953, 9.

2820. _____. "A Wesley Letter." Proceedings of the Wesley
Historical Society 25 (1945): 17-23. Written on board the
Simmonds, off Georgia, 1736, to Varanese.

2821. Harvard, C. "The Wesley Bi-centenary: Wesley's Chapel,
Bristol." Methodist Weekly (Manchester), 18 June 1903, 10.

2822. Harvey, F. Brompton. "John Wesley at School: Charterhouse in the Eighteenth Century." Methodist Recorder, 7
January 1932, 8.

2823. _____. "Methodism and the Romantic Movement." London
Quarterly and Holborn Review 159 (1934): 289-302.

2824. _____. "The Three R's of Methodism." London Quarterly
and Holborn Review 166 (1941): 49-60. The three R's are
reality, rapture, and rule.

2825. "Has the 'Holy Club' of 1729 a Counterpart in 1949? Methodism
among Undergraduates Today." Methodist Recorder, 29 September 1949, 3.

2826. Hatfield, James Taft. "John Wesley's Translation of German
Hymns." Publications of the Modern Language Association 11
(1896): 171-99.

2827. Haven, G. "John Wesley and Modern Philosophy." Methodist
Quarterly Review 61 (1879): 5-20, 205-23.

2828. Havens, Raymond D. "Southey's Revision of His Life of Wesley." Review of English Studies 22 (1946): 134-36.

2829. Hawken, Harry. "In Wesley's Steps in Cornwall." Methodist
Recorder, 16 August 1900, 11-12.

2830. Hawkin, Edward. "Wesley and Toplady." Proceedings of the
Wesley Historical Society 8 (1911): 11-14.

2831. Hawkin, T. Driffield. "The World of Samuel Johnson and
John Wesley: Twin Pillars of the Eighteenth Century."
Methodist Recorder, 22 November 1956, 1.

2832. Hawkins, Ernest. "Methodism in Former Days. 17. The Rev.
John Wesley in Georgia." Wesleyan Methodist Magazine 69
(1846): 240-45.

2833. Hay, David. "The Hymns of the Wesleys; Illustrative of the
Spirit and Manner of Their Preaching and of Their Evangelical
Work." Methodist Recorder, 14 March 1873, 125; 21 March
1873, 137; 28 March 1873, 154; 4 April 1873, 165, 10 April
1873, 177.

230   John and Charles Wesley

2834. Haydon, Charles. "Methodism in Former Days. 4. Newcastle-
upon-Tyne--The Orphan House." Wesleyan Methodist Magazine 66 (1843): 546-52, 657-64.

2835. Hayes, Leslie W. "The 'Scare-crow House' at Birstall: A
New Wesley Letter." Proceedings of the Wesley Historical Society 31 (1957): 32-34. Commentary on a letter to John Valton, the assistant at Birstall, concerning the building of a new
chapel.

2836. _____. "Wesley and Cowper." Methodist Recorder, 8 February 1951, 9.

2837. Haywood, C. Robert. "Was John Wesley a Political Economist?"
Church History 33 (1964): 314-21. A discussion of Wesley's
Thoughts on the Present Scarcity of Provisions (1773). The
author concludes that Wesley was not a political economist,
that he did go into political theory in this pamphlet, but in
the final analysis returned to his field (religion) for his
answers.

2838. "The Headquarters of Chair Making: Methodism in High
Wycombe." Methodist Recorder, 25 November 1909, 9.

2839. Heald, George. "Obituary of Mr. William Norris." Wesleyan
Methodist Magazine 46 (1823): 63-64. Relates an anecdote
about John Wesley and William Norris, son of the itinerant
Methodist preacher John Norris.

2840. Hearnshaw, F. J. C. "The Influence of the Evangelical Revival on Eighteenth Century History." Methodist Recorder,
Wesley Bicentennial Supplement, 19 May 1938, iv-v.

2841. Heaton, Edward. "Opening of the Centenary Chapel at
Hunslet." Wesleyan Methodist Magazine 63 (1840): 324-25.

2842. Heitzenrater, Richard P. "John Wesley's Early Sermons."
Proceedings of the Wesley Historical Society 37 (1970):
110-28.

2843. _____. "Mary Wesley's Marriage." Proceedings of the
Wesley Historical Society 40 (1976): 153-63.

2844. _____. "The Oxford Diaries and the First Rise of Methodism." Methodist History 12, no. 4 (1974): 110-35.

2845. _____. "The Present State of Wesley Studies." Methodist
History 22 (1984): 221-31.

2846. _____. "A Psychological Study of John Wesley." Proceedings of the Wesley Historical Society 43 (1982): 173-75.
A review of Moore's John Wesley and Authority, no. 1181.

2846a. _____. "Wesley Studies in the Church and the Academy."
Perkins Journal 37, no. 3 (1984): 1-6.

2847. Hempton, David. "The Methodist Crusade in Ireland, 1795-
1845." Irish Historical Studies 22 (1980): 33-48. This article deals with the time after Wesley's death, but there are
numerous references to Wesley, with charges of intolerance
to Catholics.

2848. Henderson, Bernard W. "John Wesley's Last University Sermon." Cornhill Magazine, n.s. 58 (1925): 93-100. His last
university sermon was at St. Mary's Church, Oxford, 1744.
The author also quotes Charles Wesley and Benjamin Kennicott
for their impression of it.

2849. Henderson, G. D. "A Scottish Teacher of the Wesleys."
London Quarterly Review 164 (1939): 471-82. Discusses the
influence Henry Scougall had on John Wesley.

2850. Hendricks, M. Elton. "John Wesley and Natural Theology."
Wesleyan Theological Journal 18, no. 2 (1983): 7-17.

2851. Hendrix, E. R. "Jonathan Edwards and John Wesley."
Methodist Quarterly Review (Nashville) 62 (1913): 28-38.

2852. _____. "Wesley's Original American Journal." Methodist
Review 83 (1901): 513-23.

2853. Henry, Granville C. "John Wesley's Doctrine of Free Will."
London Quarterly and Holborn Review 185 (1960): 200-204.

2853a. Herbert, T. Walter. "'Sentimental.'" Times Literary Supplement, 16 May 1936, 420. Discusses Wesley's remarks
about the word sentimental. See no. 2001.

2854. Higgins, Hinchcliffe. "The Great Itinerant Preacher."
Sunday Magazine, n.s. 32 (1903): 587-89.

2855. Hildebrandt, Franz. "The Wesley Hymns." Asbury Seminarian 14, no. 1 (1960): 16-47.

2856. _____. "A Wesleyan View of Reunion." Scottish Journal
of Theology 4, no. 1 (1951): 39-54. This was a paper read
at the Cambridge University Methodist Society, October 31,
1948.

2857. _____. "Wesley's Christology." Proceedings of the Wesley Historical Society 33 (1962): 122-24.

2858. _____. "The Wesleys' Churchmanship." Drew Gateway
31 (1961): 147-62. The Wesleys respected the Church of England churchmanship, but omitted much of it from Methodism.

2859. Hill, A. Wesley. "Was John Wesley a Methodist?" Proceedings of the Wesley Historical Society 30 (1955): 82-85.

2860. Hill, Michael and Bryan Turner. "John Wesley and the Origin and Decline of Ascetic Devotion." In A Sociological Yearbook of Religion in Britain 4 (1971): 102-20. Claims that contemporary Methodists have largely abandoned the demanding ascetic religious style developed by the Wesleys and have turned their interests to social activity and Evangelism. Attempts to rediscover Wesley's religious style, however, are resurfacing.

2861. Hind, Robert. "Early Scottish Methodism." Primitive Methodist Quarterly Review, n.s. 15 (1893): 398-409.

2862. Hindley, J. Clifford. "The Philosophy of Enthusiasm: A Study in the Origins of 'Experimental Theology.'" London Quarterly and Holborn Review 182 (1957): 99-109, 199-210.

2863. Hingeley, John. "Field Preaching: Some Remarkable Services." Wesleyan Methodist Church Record 12 (1903): 179-80.

2864. _____. "The Growth of a Century: A Sketch of Redditch Methodism." Wesleyan Methodist Church Record 11 (1902): 280-81.

2865. _____. "The Heart of the 'Black Country.' Methodism in Tipton." Wesleyan Methodist Church Record 12 (1903): 100-101.

2866. Hinrichsen, Max. "Six Generations of Wesleys." Music Book 7 (1952): 30-34.

2867. Hird, Horace. "An Unpublished Wesley Picture and Pitcher." Proceedings of the Wesley Historical Society 38 (1971): 72-74.

2868. _____. "A Wesley Scent-Bottle." Proceedings of the Wesley Historical Society 37 (1969): 41-42.

2869. "His Mother Called Him 'Jackie.'" Together 3, no. 11 (1959): 16-19. Illustrations highlighting the important events in Wesley's life with some text. This article appeared again in Together 17, no. 9 (1973): 22-25.

2870. "Historical Sketches of the Reign of George II. No. 7. The Reformer [John Wesley]." Blackwood's Magazine 104 (1868): 428-56.

2871. Hobsbawm, Eric John. "Methodism and the Threat of Revolution in Britain." History Today 7 (1957): 115-24. This

author disagrees with the premise that Wesleyan Methodism
prevented a British revolution, the theory supported by
Halévy.

2872. Hodgson, E. M. "John, or Charles Wesley." Proceedings
of the Wesley Historical Society 41 (1977): 73-76. A discussion of the authorship of some Wesley hymns.

2873. _____. "Poetry in the Hymns of John and Charles Wesley." Proceedings of the Wesley Historical Society 38 (1972):
131-35, 161-65.

2874. Hogden, Margaret T. "The Negro in the Anthropology of
John Wesley." Journal of Negro History 19 (1934): 308-23.
Wesley was a positive factor in the antislavery movement,
but his bias toward other primitive cultures helped to sustain
their backwardness.

2875. Holland, Bernard C. "The Conversions of John and Charles
Wesley and Their Place in Methodist Tradition." Proceedings
of the Wesley Historical Society 38 (1971): 46-53, 65-71.

2876. _____. "'A Species of Madness': The Effect of John Wesley's Early Preaching." Proceedings of the Wesley Historical
Society 39 (1973): 77-85.

2877. Holland, Lynwood M. "John Wesley and the American Revolution." Journal of Church and State 5 (1963): 199-213.

2878. Holland, Lynwood M. and Ronald F. Howell. "John Wesley's
Concept of Religious and Political Authority." Journal of
Church and State 6 (1964): 296-313.

2879. Holliday, Andrew B. "Liverpool: The Conference City of
1912." Methodist Recorder, 18 July 1912, 10-11.

2880. Holloway, Trevor. "Preacher on Horseback." Church
Herald 35, no. 10 (1978): 4-6.

2881. Holmes, F. M. "Some Reminders of John Wesley; with a
Glance at the New Wesley Museum." Quiver 33 (1898): 921-
24.

2882. Holmes, Joshua. "Bradford: The Conference City, 1910."
Methodist Recorder, 14 July 1910, 10-12.

2883. Hoole, Elijah. "Dr. Kennicott and Mr. Wesley's Last Sermon
at St. Mary's Oxford, August 24, 1744." Wesleyan Methodist
Magazine 89 (1866): 44-50.

2884. _____. "The Origin and Local Source of Methodism, As a

Modern Revival of Ancient and Scriptural Christianity: Was
It Oxford, Epworth, London or Moravia?" Wesleyan Methodist Magazine 91: (1868): 986-98.

2885. Hooper, Henry T. "Wesley and St. Francis." Wesleyan
Methodist Magazine 143 (1920): 527-28.

2886. Hooper, J. E. "Early Methodism: Visits to Isles of Scilly
in 1743 and 1788." Scillonian 20 (1946): 130-33.

2887. Hope, Norman V. "Aldersgate: An Epoch in British History." Christianity Today 7, no. 15 (1963): 3-4.

2888. Hopkinson, Harry. "A Sunny Hampshire Village: Gosport
and Fareham." Methodist Recorder, 17 August 1911, 9.

2889. Horan, Patrick K. "Wesley and Ireland." Churchman (London) n.s. 46 (1932): 56-59.

2890. Horne, John T. "The Evangelical Revival of the Eighteenth
Century." Primitive Methodist Quarterly Review, n.s. 23
(1901): 76-92.

2891. Hornsby, J. T. "Wesley--Hervey--Sandeman." Proceedings
of the Wesley Historical Society 20 (1936): 112-13.

2892. Hoskins, J. O. "A Little Body of Experimental and Practical
Divinity." Choir 54 (1963): 188-89.

2893. Houghton, Edward. "John Wesley or Charles Wesley?" Hymn
Society of Great Britain and Ireland Bulletin 9 (1979): 93-99;
10 (1982): 70-76. Discussion of the authorship of some of the
Wesleys' hymns, contending that more are John Wesley's than
commonly believed.

2894. _____. "Poetry and Piety in Charles Wesley's Hymns."
Hymn (New York) 6 (1955): 77-86.

2895. _____. "Wrestling Jacob." Evangelical Quarterly 50
(1978): 104-8. Describes Charles Wesley's use of this scripture.

2896. Hoult, W. B. "The Rev. Samuel Wesley and the Spalding
Gentlemen's Society." Proceedings of the Wesley Historical
Society 23 (1942): 145-53.

2897. "How Best to Celebrate the Centenary of John Wesley's
Death." Wesleyan Methodist Magazine 114 (1891): 225-33.

2898. "How Wesley Preached." Methodist Recorder, 3 October
1884, 743.

2899.   Howard, Ivan. "Wesley versus Phoebe Palmer: An Extended
        Controversy." Wesleyan Theological Journal 6 (1971):   31-40.
        Phoebe Palmer was an American writer--a nineteenth-century
        proponent of entire sanctification.

2900.   Howard, Joseph. "An Ancient Suburb: Blackheath and Its
        Methodist Associations." Methodist Recorder, 30 April 1914,
        10.

2901.   Howard, R. H. "John Wesley, Evangelist and Reformer."
        Our Day 7 (1891): 184-204.

2902.   Howard, Wilbert F. "John Wesley in His Letters." Proceed-
        ings of the Wesley Historical Society 29 (1953): 3-11.

2903.   Howe, Leroy T. "Some Wesleyan Thoughts on the Grace of
        God." Perkins Journal 25, no. 1 (1971): 19-28.

2904.   Howell, L. D. "John Wesley's Complete English Dictionary."
        Notes and Queries 187 (1944): 238-39.

2905.   Hoyle, Arthur. "A Weekend Gossip: Dr. Johnson and
        Methodism." Methodist Recorder, 7 August 1913, 11.

2906.   _____. "A Weekend Gossip: Martin Luther or John Wes-
        ley." Methodist Recorder, 24 September 1914, 9.

2907.   Hoyt, W. C. "John Wesley and His Biographers." Methodist
        Quarterly Review 30 (1848): 406-35.

2908.   Hubbartt, G. F. "The Theodicy of John Wesley." Asbury
        Seminarian 12, no. 2 (1958): 15-18.

2909.   Huddleston, David. "Hinckley, Past and Present: The Story
        of Early Leicestershire Methodism." Methodist Recorder, 28
        May 1903, 13-14.

2910.   Hughes, H. Maldwyn. "The Basis, Growth and Distinctive
        Character of Doctrine in the Methodist Church." Methodist
        Recorder; Wesley Bicentennial Supplement, 19 May 1938,
        viii-ix.

2911.   _____. "The Evangelical Succession." London Quarterly
        Review 120 (1913): 230-43. Discusses the four spiritual an-
        cestors of Methodism--Paul, Augustine, Luther, and Wesley.
        Their starting point in theology was their own inner ex-
        perience.

2912.   _____. "Wesley's Standards in the Light of Today." Lon-
        don Quarterly Review 128 (1917): 214-34.

2913. Hughes, H. Trevor. "Jeremy Taylor and John Wesley."
       London Quarterly and Holborn Review 174 (1949): 296-304.
       Discusses Taylor's contribution to the spiritual life of the
       founder of Methodism through his writings Holy Living and
       Holy Dying.

2914. Hughes, Hugh Price. "John Wesley." Nineteenth Century
       29 (1891): 477-94. This article was written on the occasion
       of the 100th anniversary of Wesley's death.

2915. _____. "Methodism and Modern Culture." Wesleyan
       Methodist Magazine 105 (1882): 26-33.

2916. Hughes, John Wesley. "Welsh Methodism in Chester."
       Methodist Recorder, 23 January 1908, 10.

2917. Hughes, Robert D., III. "Wesleyan Roots of Christian
       Socialism." Ecumenist 13, no. 4 (1975): 49-53.

2918. Hulme, T. Ferrier. "John Wesley's 'Room' in Bristol, Horse-
       fair: The Oldest Memorial of the Evangelical Revival."
       Methodist Recorder, 27 June 1929, 4.

2919. Hulme, T. Ferrier, and George H. Oatley. "The Bristol
       New Room." Proceedings of the Wesley Historical Society
       17 (1930): 102-5.

2920. _____. "The Development of Personal Experience." Lon-
       don Quarterly and Holborn Review 163 (1938): 178-82.

2921. Humberstone, F. W. "John Wesley's Visits to Coventry."
       Proceedings of the Wesley Historical Society 9 (1914): 121-22.

2922. Humphreys, Arthur. "A Wide Cumberland Circuit." Method-
       ist Recorder, 12 November 1903, 9.

2923. Humphreys, Arthur Lee. "Horsemen on the Great North
       Road." Notes and Queries 180 (1941): 362-67. Describes
       Wesley's travels by horseback.

2924. Hunt, W. Stanley. "Jersey and Its Methodism." Wesleyan
       Methodist Magazine 136 (1913): 202-6.

2925. Hunter, Charles F. "In the Garden of England: Sevenoaks
       and Its Methodism." Methodist Recorder, 7 April 1904, 9-10.

2926. Hunter, Frederick. "John Wesley's Introduction to William
       Law: A Comment." Proceedings of the Wesley Historical So-
       ciety 37 (1970): 143-50.

2927. _____. "Manchester Non-Jurors and Wesley's High

Churchism." London Quarterly and Holborn Review 172
(1947): 56-61.

2928. _____. "The Origins of Wesley's Covenant Service."
Proceedings of the Wesley Historical Society 22 (1940): 126-31.
First published in London Quarterly and Holborn Review
164 (1939): 78-87.

2929. _____. "Sources of Wesley's Revision of the Prayer Book
in 1784-1788." Proceedings of the Wesley Historical Society
23 (1942): 123-33. See also 3496.

2930. _____. "Wesley: Separatist or Searcher for Unity?"
Proceedings of the Wesley Historical Society 38 (1972): 166-
69.

2931. Hunter, Frederick and Frank Baker. "The Origin of the
Methodist Quarterly Meeting." London Quarterly and Holborn
Review 174 (1949): 28-37. John Bennet was the pioneer of
the Methodist Quarterly Meeting, but it was John Wesley and
his preachers who developed it. This article is concerned
with the early period of its development, 1741-71.

2932. Hunter, Ralph W. G. "Kinder Scout: A Chronicle of Methodism in the Peak Country." Methodist Recorder, 7 November
1901, 15-16.

2933. Hunter, Richard A. "A Brief Review of the Use of Electricity
in Psychiatry with Special Reference to John Wesley."
British Journal of Physical Medicine 20, no. 5 (1957): 98-100.

2934. Hutchinson, Duane. "New Wine in Old Wineskins: A Fresh
Look at Wesley and the American Revolution." Christian Advocate 9, no. 12 (1965): 12-13.

2935. Hutchinson, F. E. "John Wesley and George Herbert."
London Quarterly and Holborn Review 161 (1936): 439-55.

2936. Hynson, Leon O. "Christian Love: The Key to Wesley's
Ethics." Methodist History 14, no. 1 (1975): 44-55.

2937. _____. "Creation and Grace in Wesley's Ethics." Drew
Gateway 46 (1975-76): 41-55.

2938. _____. "Historical Theology in the Wesleyan Mode: Response." Wesleyan Theological Journal 17, no. 1 (1982):
93-97. A response to the article by Carl O. Bangs, no.
2074.

2939. _____. "Human Liberty As Divine Right: A Study in the
Political Maturation of John Wesley." Journal of Church and
State 25 (1983): 57-85.

2940. _____. "John Wesley and Political Reality." Methodist History 12, no. 1 (1973): 37-42.

2941. _____. "John Wesley and the 'Unitas Fratrum': A Theological Analysis." Methodist History 18 (1979): 26-60.

2942. _____. "John Wesley's Concept of Liberty of Conscience." Wesleyan Theological Journal 7 (1972): 36-46.

2943. _____. "The Social Concerns of Wesley: Theological Foundations." Christian Scholar's Review 4, no. 1 (1974): 36-42.

2944. _____. "War, the State, and the Christian Citizen in Wesley's Thought." Religion in Life 45 (1976): 204-19.

2945. _____. "Wesley: The Widening Horizon." Asbury Seminarian 38, no. 5 (1984): 31-39. Discusses the pattern of Wesley's ethical development along with the political and social tracts which occupied much of his time from 1768-83.

2946. _____. "Wesley: Theology of the Moral Life." Asbury Seminarian 38, no. 5 (1984): 18-30. This is a discussion of Wesley's theological ethics--creation, salvation, and the ethics of the Spirit.

2947. _____. "Wesley, a Man for All Seasons." Asbury Seminarian 38, no. 5 (1984): 3-17. Describes the major influences on Wesley's theological development, his understanding of group psychology, his political sense, administrative talent, and commitment to social reform.

2948. _____. "A Wesleyan Theology of Evangelism." Wesleyan Theological Journal 17, no. 2 (1982): 26-42.

2949. "Impressions of Methodism in Manxland: By an Itinerant Local Preacher." Methodist Recorder, 26 September 1889, 711; 3 October 1889, 731.

2950. "In a Walled City: A Brief Methodist Retrospect." Methodist Recorder, 1 September 1910, 9.

2951. "In the Far North East: Methodism in Baffshire." Methodist Recorder, 25 August 1904, 9-10.

2952. "In the Track of John Wesley; by a Pilgrim." Methodist Recorder, 28 June 1888, 432.

2953. "In Wesley's Beloved Whittlebury: Journey into Quiet Buckingham." Methodist Recorder, 10 December 1959, 21.

2954. Ingle, Timothy C. "Methodism in West Bromwich." Wesleyan Methodist Magazine 59 (1836): 178-81.

2955. Inglis, Harry R. G. "Scotland in 1753. What John Wesley
Saw." S.M.T. Magazine 12, no. 4 (1934): 21-24.

2956. Ingram, W. G. "John Wesley's Books." Times Literary Supplement 14 August 1937, 592; 18 September 1937, 675. Letters to the Times from the librarian at Kingswood School with
an appeal to the readers for any information concerning the
works once in the Kingswood Library or the letter written by
Joseph Benton to John Wesley in reply to his appeal for a
list of books at Kingswood.

2957. Itzkin, Elissa S. "The Halévy Thesis--a Working Hypothesis?
English Revivalism: Antidote for Revolution and Radicalism,
1789-1815." Church History 44 (1975): 47-56.

2958. J. "Kingswood School." Wesleyan Methodist Magazine 76
(1853): 49-53.

2959. J., G. "Methodism in the Canterbury Circuit." Wesleyan
Methodist Magazine 60 (1837): 420-28.

2960. J., T. "A Defence of Mr. Wesley and of His Doctrines."
Wesleyan Methodist Magazine 47 (1824): 437-51, 511-27.

2961. _____. "Dr. Pye Smith and Mr. Wesley." Wesleyan Methodist Magazine 78 (1855): 124-37. A rebuttal to Pye Smith's
First Lines of Christian Theology, edited by William Farrer,
1854.

2962. Jackson, F. M. "A Bibliographical Catalogue of Books Mentioned in John Wesley's Journals." Proceedings of the Wesley
Historical Society 4 (1903-1904): 17-19, 47-51, 74-81, 107-11,
134-40, 173-76, 203-10, 232-38.

2963. Jackson, George. "John Wesley As a Bookman." London
Quarterly and Holborn Review 160 (1935): 294-305.

2964. _____. "A Parson's Log; with Wesley Two Hundred Years
Ago." Methodist Recorder, 7 January 1943, 7.

2965. Jackson, Thomas. "The Foundery and the City Road Chapel."
Wesleyan Methodist Magazine 83 (1860): 1077-82.

2966. _____. "Life of Charles Wesley." Methodist Quarterly Review 24 (1842): 112-41.

2967. _____. "The Wesleys and Peter Böhler." Wesleyan Methodist Magazine 91 (1868): 616-24.

2968. Jacobs, Horace Lincoln. "Methodism Begun in America: Bi-
centenary of Wesley's Journey to Georgia." Methodist Recorder, 10 October 1935, 20.

2969. Jacoby, L. S. "John Wesley's Separation from the Moravians."
Methodist Quarterly Review 52 (1870): 265-74.

2970. James, A. Gordon. "The Methodist Doctrine of Holy Communion." London Quarterly and Holborn Review 165 (1940):
51-60.

2971. James, Henry. "On John Wesley." Methodist Recorder, 5
March 1891, 179. Reports on a speech given at a Bury Bazaar to benefit the Bury Chapel.

2972. "James Hutton." Wesleyan Methodist Magazine 80 (1857):
156-67. Review of Daniel Benham's biography of Hutton
(1856) discussing the friendship between the Wesleys and
Hutton at Oxford.

2973. "James Hutton's Account of The Beginnings of the Lord's Work
in England to 1741." Proceedings of the Wesley Historical Society 15 (1926): 178-89, 206-14. Translated from the German
MS. in the Herrnhut Archive, describing Wesley's contacts
with the Moravians.

2974. Jefferies, Alfred. "John Wesley in Scotland." Scottish
Geographical Magazine 83 (1967): 105-12.

2975. Jefferson, Helen G. "Two Talents: The Fruitful Alliance of
Handel and Wesley." Music Ministry 6, no. 4 (1964): 4-6.

2976. Jeffery, Frederick. "John Wesley's 'Primitive Physick.'"
Proceedings of the Wesley Historical Society 21 (1937): 60-
67.

2977. _____. "Wesley at Lurgan. William Miller's Talking
Statue." Proceedings of the Wesley Historical Society 21
(1938): 192-94.

2978. *Jenkins, R. T. "John Wesley in North Wales." Bathafarn
2 (1947): 35-54.

2979. Jenkinson, Percy B. "Methodism in Grimsby." Wesleyan
Methodist Church Record 20 (1911): 93-95.

2980. Jessop, William. "A Memorial Tree: Notices of the Introduction of Methodism into Cheshire." Wesleyan Methodist Magazine 80 (1857): 217-22.

2981. "John Wesley." Bodleian Quarterly Record 5 (1926): 5-6.
Describes an exhibition of Bodleian Wesleyana.

2982. "John Wesley." Bookman 17 (1903): 568-70. Includes portraits of John Wesley and Mary Vazeille Wesley.

2983. "John Wesley." Harper's Magazine 19 (1859): 211-23. A summary of Wesley's life, ending with the statement: "It was impossible that London could become as Paris, and impossible because God had made Wesley's preaching the antidote of Voltaire's infidelity."

2984- "John Wesley." Outlook 74 (1903): 496-98.
86.
2987. "John Wesley: A Premillenarian." Christian Workers Magazine 17 (1916): 96-101.

2988. "John Wesley: an Evolutionist." Popular Science Monthly 46 (1894): 284-85. Reference is given to a paper read by William H. Mills before the Chit Chat Club of San Francisco.

2989. "John Wesley and Brother Ignatius." Methodist Recorder, 28 October 1864, 406.

2990. "John Wesley and His Critics." Littell's Living Age 40 (1854): 339-55.

2991. "John Wesley and His Predestination Critics." Wesleyan Methodist Magazine 78 (1855): 231-37, 322-35.

2992. "John Wesley and Methodism." Christian Observer and Advocate 75 (1876): 673-95. This article aims to "take a calm and dispassionate view of the life and labours of a man who viewed the world as his parish, and who, to an extent which has rarely met with a parallel, devoted his time, his energies and his substance to evangelization."

2993. "John Wesley and the Founders of Methodism." Eclectic Review, n.s. 1 (1861): 129-54. A review of Abel Steven's The History of the Religious Movement of the Eighteenth Century, Called Methodism..., no. 1582.

2994. "John Wesley and the Methodists." Church Review and Ecclesiastical Register 3 (1850): 245-67.

2995. "John Wesley and the Psychology of Revivals." Church Quarterly Review 66 (1908): 24-40.

2996. "John Wesley and the Rise of Methodism." Dublin Review, n.s. 23 (1874): 87-118.

2997. "John Wesley and the Sculptor." Apollo 37 (1943): 167. Brief mention of Wesley and Enoch Wood.

2998. "John Wesley As an Educator." Times Educational Supplement, 21 May 1938, 173.

2998a. "John Wesley: His Character and Work." Christian Examiner
76 (1864): 157-74.

2998b. "John Wesley: Hymnologist and Musician." Methodist Review
108 (1925): 389-93.

2999. "John Wesley in America." Gentleman's Magazine and Historical Chronicle 71 (1792): 23-24. An unsigned letter recounting
the writer's first-hand contacts with Wesley in Georgia, very
critical of his behavior.

3000. "John Wesley in Dublin: Memorial Tablet in St. Mary's
Church." Proceedings of the Wesley Historical Society 20
(1935): 57-62.

3001. "John Wesley in Mature and Later Life." London Quarterly
Review 38 (1872): 379-426.

3002. "John Wesley, Methodism and Dr. Johnson." United Methodist Free Churches' Magazine 34 (1891): 244-47.

3003. "John Wesley Not a Bigot." Methodist Recorder, 27 November 1863, 427. This article is from the California Christian
Advocate, in response to an article in the Oregon Weekly
Union, which accused Wesley of speaking against the Irish
Catholic Emancipation Bill of 1829, pointing out the date of
his death as 1791. It also gives examples of Wesley's toler-
ance and ecumenicism.

3004. "John Wesley on the Art of Healing." British Medical Journal 1 (1906): 987-88. Ridicules Wesley and his venture into
the medical world with Primitive Physic.

3005. "John Wesley on the 'Witness of the Spirit'." Quarterly
Christian Spectator 8 (1836): 353-68.

3006. "John Wesley Takes a Holiday; Our Founder at Hagley and
Leasorves." Methodist Recorder 10 March 1910, 12.

3007. "John Wesley's Editorial Character Vindicated: Mr. Baring
Gould's Explanation." Methodist Recorder, 5 December
1895, 867. See also nos. 2748, 2084.

3008. "John Wesley's First Visit to Gateshead." Proceedings of the
Wesley Historical Society 20 (1936): 137-39.

3009. "John Wesley's God." Ave Maria 81 (29 January 1955): 5.
Concerns Wesley's faith in God.

3010. "John Wesley's Journal." Church Quarterly Review 53
(1902): 314-30. Includes some excerpts with comments and
interpretations.

3011. "John Wesley's Love Passage." Littell's Living Age 72
(1862): 711-15. An unsympathetic account of John Wesley's
love of Grace Murray.

3012. "John Wesley's Marriage." Proceedings of the Wesley Historical Society 32 (1960): 118.

3013. "John Wesley's School." Times Educational Supplement 29
September 1934, 329. Describes Kingswood School and Wesley's love of children.

3014. Johns, Joseph. "A Saddlery Town: Methodism in the Wesley Circuit, Walsall." Methodist Recorder, 21 November 1907,
10.

3015. Johns, S. W. "John Wesley and Dr. Borlase." Old Cornwall
3 (1941): 402-6.

3016. _____. "John Wesley and Gwennap Pit." Old Cornwall 3
(1941): 381-85.

3017. Johnson, C. "The Musical Wesleys." Music Ministry 6, no.
3 (1964): 2-4.

3018. Johnson, Floyd A. "The Wesleys in Georgia: Watercolours."
Together 1, no. 12 (1957): 34-42.

3019. Johnson, J. Wesley. "The Last of the Great Reformers: The
Life and Work of John Wesley, the Founder of the Youngest of
the Great Protestant Sects." Munsey's Magazine 23 (1900):
757-68.

3020. Johnson, Moody S. "Towards a Theology of Contemporaneity:
Tillich or Wesley?" Wesleyan Theological Journal 5 (1970):
68-75.

3021. Johnson, Richard O. "The Development of the Love Feast in
Early American Methodism." Methodist History 19, no. 2
(1981): 67-83.

3022. Johnson, Ronald. "Charles Wesley and J. S. Bach." Choir
and Musical Journal 39 (1948): 34-36, 50-51.

3023. Johnson, W. Lloyd. "The Ghost of Epworth Rectory."
Methodist Magazine, December 1961, 446-48.

3024. Johnson, W. Stanley. "Christian Perfection As Love for

God." Wesleyan Theological Journal 18, no. 1 (1983): 50-
60.

3025. Joll, Watson. "Methodism in Horncastle Circuit: Its Place
in the Original East Lincolnshire Division." Methodist Recorder, 27 August 1903, 11-13.

3026. _____. "Methodism in the Spilsby Circuit; a Century of
Church Life." Methodist Recorder, 31 December 1903, 9-10.

3027. Jones, Alfred. "John Wesley." Methodist Monthly 12 (1903):
135-41, 167-72.

3028. Jones, Bernard E. "Reason and Religion Joined: The Place
of Reason in Wesley's Thought." London Quarterly and Holborn Review 189 (1964): 110-13.

3029. Jones, Dora M. "The Journals of John Wesley." Temple
Bar 122 (1901): 514-22.

3030. Jones, E. Ashton. "Llanidloes; Scene of Next Week's Welsh
Assembly." Methodist Recorder, 6 June 1901, 10-12.

3031. Jones, J. Bourne. "John Wesley As Churchman and Methodist." Wesleyan Methodist Church Record 7 (1898): 68-69.

3032. Jones, Llewelyn. "Bicentenary of Methodism in Wales."
Methodist Recorder, 6 June 1935, 7.

3033. Jones, M. H. "Howell Harris: The Trevecka Collection of
MSS." Proceedings of the Wesley Historical Society 9 (1914):
127-30.

3034. _____. "Isabella Johnson and the Wesleys." Proceedings
of the Wesley Historical Society 13 (1921): 36-39.

3035. _____. "References to the Wesleys in the First Calvinistic
Methodist Newspaper." Proceedings of the Wesley Historical
Society 12 (1920): 158-63. The first Calvinistic Methodist
newspaper was The Christian Amusement, later called The
Weekly History. It was started by Howell Harris and his
helpers.

3036. _____. "Wesley at Carmarthen." Proceedings of the Wesley
Historical Society 10 (1915): 89-90.

3037. _____. "William Jones of Wales, Trefollyn; Anglesey and
the Wesleys." Proceedings of the Wesley Historical Society 16
(1927): 53-54.

3038. Jones, W. G. "John Wesley's Chapel in Bristol. The New

Articles   245

Room in the Horse Fair." Cylchgrawn Cymdeithas Hanes
Methodistiaid Calfinaidd. 26 (1941): 43-50.

3039. Jordan, Albert F. "The Chronicle of Peter Boehler, Who Led
John and Charles Wesley to the Full Light of the Gospel."
Transactions of the Moravian Historical Society 22 (1971): 100-
178.

3040. "Journal of John Wesley." Methodist Quarterly Review 30
(1848): 455-73.

3041. Joy, James R. "Wesley: Man of a Thousand Books and a
Book." Religion in Life 8 (1939): 71-84. Describes Wesley's
commitment to learning, his lifelong attachment to reading,
and his role as author, editor, letter writer, and hymnist.

3042. Judge, G. H. Bancroft. "The Beginning of Methodism in
Ambleside." Proceedings of the Wesley Historical Society 25.
(1946): 107-10, 122-24.

3043. _____. "The Beginnings of Methodism in the Penrith District." Proceedings of the Wesley Historical Society 19
(1934): 153-60.

3044. _____. "The Early History of Methodism in Cheltenham,
1739-1812." Proceedings of the Wesley Historical Society 12
(1920): 180-91.

3045. _____. "Early Methodism in Furness." Proceedings of the
Wesley Historical Society 27 (1949): 50-55, 86-91.

3046. _____. "John Wesley's Visits to Stanley and Winchcombe
(near Cheltenham) with Notes on Early Methodism in the
Neighbourhood." Proceedings of the Wesley Historical Society 13 (1921): 63-68, 131-33.

3047. _____. "Methodism in Whitehaven." Proceedings of the
Wesley Historical Society 18 (1932): 161-66; 19 (1933): 2-9,
25-29.

3048. K, H. "Bolton Methodism - Its Early Beginnings, Its Latest
Development." Methodist Recorder, 24 February 1898, 11-12.

3049. _____. "The Chester Circuit." Methodist Recorder, 23
March 1899, 11-12.

3050. _____. "The Coming Conference: Leeds." Methodist Recorder, 15 July 1897, 499-501.

3051. _____. "Deptford Methodism." Methodist Recorder, 11
August 1898, 715-16.

246   John and Charles Wesley

3052. _____. "Grimsby and the Beginning of Its Methodism."
Methodist Recorder, 8 December 1898, 1051-52.

3053. _____. "The Little White Town: Methodism in Bideford."
Methodist Recorder, 6 April 1899, 11.

3054. _____. "Methodism in Milford Haven." Methodist Recorder,
21 September 1899, 9.

3055. _____. "Methodism in the Potteries." Methodist Recorder,
16 June 1898, 11.

3056. _____. "Methodism in the Stamford Circuit." Methodist
Recorder, 9 November 1899, 11-12.

3057. _____. "Methodism in Twickenham." Methodist Recorder,
16 February 1899, 11.

3058. _____. "The 'New Room' Bristol." Methodist Recorder,
10 November 1898, 14.

3059. _____. "Round About Methodist London: A Tour by Metropolitan Railway." Methodist Recorder, 13 July 1899, 9-12.

3060. _____. "Wesley's Chapel, City Road, London." Methodist
Recorder, 29 June 1899, 11-12.

3061. _____. "Wesley's First Month in Bristol." Methodist Recorder, 20 July 1905, 11-14.

3062. _____. "Wesley's House and the Work of God at Wesley's
Chapel." Methodist Recorder, 2 December 1897, 951-52.

3063. _____. "Why Wesley Went to Leigh." Methodist Recorder,
21 April 1898, 11-12.

3064. K., H., and H.D.W. "The Yorkshire Storm-Centre of the
Evangelical Revival." Methodist Recorder, 12 January 1899,
11-12; 19 January 1899, 11-12.

3065. Källstad, Thorvald E. "'A Brand Snatched Out of the Fire';
John Wesley's Awareness of Vocation According to the Religio-
Psychological Theory of Role." Archiv für Religionspsycholo-
gie 14 (1980): 237-45.

3066. Kay, J. Alan. "Charles Wesley." London Quarterly and Holborn Review 182 (1957): 241-46.

3067. Keeble, S. E. "John Wesley on Art and Music." Methodist
Recorder, 24 December 1895, 911-12.

3068. _____. "John Wesley's Literary Judgements." Methodist Recorder, 26 January 1899, 72.

3069. Keefer, Luke L., Jr. "John Wesley: Disciple of Early Christianity." Wesleyan Theological Journal 19, no. 1 (1984): 26-32. See also no. 3726.

3070. Keen, Stanley H. "A Pilgrimage to Herrnhut." Proceedings of the Wesley Historical Society 13 (1922): 145-49.

3071. Kellermann, Bill. "To Stir up God's Good Trouble: John Wesley and the Methodist Revival Movement." Sojourners 13, no. 3 (1984): 20-23.

3072. Kellett, E. E. "The Poetic Character of Wesley's Hymns." Methodist Recorder, 18 August 1910, 10-11.

3073. Kellock, John M. "Charles Wesley and His Hymns." Methodist Review 112 (1929): 527-39.

3074. _____. "John Wesley's Attitude to Learning." Methodist Review 111 (1928): 357-70.

3075. Kelly, Charles H. "John Wesley's Ordination of Dr. Coke As Bishop for America." Methodist Recorder, 8 December 1898, 4.

3076. Kelly, Denis. "John Wesley." Methodist Recorder, 1 July 1864, 243. This is an attempt to explain Wesley's extraordinary accomplishments in the face of so many obstacles.

3077. Kelynack, W. S. "John Wesley's Six Formative Years." London Quarterly and Holborn Review 179 (1954): 32-37. First appeared in Hymn (New York) 4 (1953): 37-43, 51. Discusses the years 1735-40 in John Wesley's life, when he learned to sing and founded the singing church of Methodism.

3078. Kendall, H. B. "John Wesley As Letter Writer." Holborn Review 59 (1917): 111-14.

3079. Kennedy, Gerald Hamilton. "Aldersgate and 1963." Christian Century 80 (1963): 677-78.

3080. Kent, John H. S. "Catchwords of 'The Conversations.' 5. John Wesley's Churchmanship." Proceedings of the Wesley Historical Society 35 (1965): 10-14.

3081. _____. "Methodism and Revolution." Methodist History 12, no. 4 (1974): 136-44.

3082. "Kentish Fire and Fidelity: A Comfortable Day at Canterbury." Methodist Recorder, 24 January 1907, 10.

3083. Ker, Ernest. "John Wesley and the Church of England."
Biblical Theology 9 (1959): 79-86.

3084. _____. "Letters [of John Wesley] to Henry Brooke of
Dublin." Proceedings of the Wesley Historical Society 20
(1935): 49-55.

3085. _____. "Loyola and the Wesley Hymns." Proceedings of
the Wesley Historical Society 30 (1955): 62-64.

3086. _____. "On Mending Charles Wesley." London Quarterly
and Holborn Review 172 (1947): 353-59.

3087. _____. "The Reynolds Portrait of Wesley." Proceedings
of the Wesley Historical Society 27 (1950): 174-76.

3088. _____. "Two Unpublished Wesley Letters." Proceedings
of the Wesley Historical Society 32 (1959): 45-47. Letters to
T. Judson and Lancelot Harrison.

3089. Kerruish, Jessie D. "John Wesley and Mann." Mannin 9
(1917): 511-16.

3090. Kershner, Frederick D. "The History of Evangelism with
Special Reference to the Contribution Made by the Restoration
Movement of the Nineteenth Century." Christian Quarterly
(Birmingham, England) 2 (1935): 83-91. The third part of
this article deals with John Wesley and evangelism.

3091. Keynes, Geoffrey. "Blake and Wesley." Notes and Queries
202 (1957): 181.

3092. Keyworth, C. W. "A Cotswold Circuit." Methodist Recorder,
20 August 1903, 11-12.

3093. _____. "The Venice of the Black Country: Tipton and
Its Methodist History." Methodist Recorder, 17 December
1903, 11-12.

3094. Kidd, T. Herbert. "Sunny Guernsey: The Island and Its
Methodism." Methodist Recorder, 1 February 1906, 9.

3095. Killian, Charles. "John Wesley: A Speech Critic." Asbury
Seminarian 24, no. 2 (1970): 7-14. Discusses Wesley's ideas
on preaching.

3096. King, W. Maurice. "Aldersgate--a Beginning." Methodist
Story 10, no. 4 (1966): 5-6.

3097. Kingdon, Frank. "Doctor Johnson and the Methodists."
Methodist Review 112 (1929): 884-89.

3098. Kingdon, Robert M. "Laissez-faire or Government Control: A Problem for John Wesley." Church History 26 (1957): 342-54. Discusses Wesley's economic ideas. His doctrines provided religious sanction to virtues which helped build capitalism.

3099. Kinlaw, Dennis E. "American Methodism at 200: The Unclaimed Heritage." Christianity Today 28, no. 16 (1984): 27-29. Discusses the four primary themes that permeate Wesley's theology and theorizes why Wesley's theology was so acceptable to Americans.

3100. Kinlaw, Dennis E. and James S. Robb. "Wesley's Other Children." Christianity Today 28, no. 18 (1984): 22-25. The "other children" are the churches outside the United Methodist Church that reflect Wesleyan heritage.

3101. Kirk, John. "Ancestry of the Wesleys." London Quarterly Review 22 (1864): 71-117.

3102. Kirkby, William. "Wesley's Primitive Physic." Proceedings of the Wesley Historical Society 18 (1932): 149-53.

3103. Kirkham, Donald H. "John Wesley's 'Calm Address': The Response of the Critics." Methodist History 14, no. 1 (1975): 13-23.

3104. Kirsop, Joseph. "John Wesley and His Contemporaries." Methodist Monthly 9 (1900): 6-8, 47-49, 77-80, 104-7, 167-70.

3105. Kishida, Yuki. "John Wesley's Ethics and Max Weber." Wesleyan Quarterly Review 4 (1967): 43-58.

3106. Kissack, Reginald. "John Wesley's Concept of the Church." Asbury Seminarian 14, no. 2 (1960): 7-20.

3107. _____. "Two Hundred Years of Methodist Field Preaching." London Quarterly and Holborn Review 164 (1939): 145-52.

3108. _____. "Wesley's Concept of His Own Ecclesiastical Position." London Quarterly and Holborn Review 186 (1961): 57-60.

3109. _____. "Wesley's Conversion: Text, Psalm, and Homily." Proceedings of the Wesley Historical Society 22 (1939): 1-6.

3110. Knapp, David. "The Ancient Town of Macclesfield and Its Methodism." Methodist Recorder, 1 September 1904, 9-10.

3111. Knapp, Sheldon. "The Place of John Wesley in Church History." Methodist Weekly (Manchester), 18 June 1903, 5.

3112. Knight, John Allan. "Aspects of Wesley's Theology after
       1770." Methodist History 6, no. 3 (1968): 33-42. Describes
       Wesley's theological shift from free grace to free will.

3113. Kroehler, Kent E. "Recall to Wesleyan Theology." Asbury
       Seminarian 24, no. 2 (1970): 15-20.

3114. Kuhn, A. J. "Nature Spiritualized: Aspects of Anti-
       Newtonianism." ELH: A Journal of Literary History 41
       (1974): 400-412. Discusses anti-Newtonianism in the writings
       of Wesley, Byrom, Law, and Hervey.

3115. L., A. "Of Mr. Wesley's Works." Methodist Magazine 35
       (1812): 288-96, 367-73.

3116. L., F. W. "The Liskeard Circuit and Some 'Lions' of the
       District." Methodist Recorder, 13 February 1908, 9.

3117. Lacour, Lawrence. "Aldersgate and Authority." Christian
       Advocate 7, no. 11 (1963): 7-8.

3118. Lacy, Herbert Edward. "Authority in John Wesley." Lon-
       don Quarterly and Holborn Review 189 (1964): 114-19.

3119. _____. "John Wesley's Ordinations." Proceedings of the
       Wesley Historical Society 33 (1962): 118-21.

3120. Lake, W. H. Oliver. "John Wesley Seen Through the Eyes
       of a Foreigner." Methodist Magazine (1952): 466-67, 501-2.
       Description of Wesley taken from the writings of Sophie v. La
       Roche.

3121. Lamont, J. D. "Methodism in the Emerald Isle, Cork." Wes-
       leyan Methodist Church Record 16 (1907): 267-68.

3122. Lang, Andrew. "The Poltergeist, Historically Considered:
       The Epworth Case." Proceedings of the Society for Psychial
       Research 17 (1901-1903): 316-21. See also no. 3467.

3123. _____. "The Wesley Ghost." Contemporary Review 68
       (1895): 288-98.

3124. Lawley, G. T. "In the Black Country: A Sketch of Bilston
       Methodism." Methodist Recorder, 21 March 1901, 13-14.

3125. _____. "In the Black Country: A Sketch of Darlaston
       Methodism." Methodist Recorder, 13 June 1901, 13-14.

3126. _____. "In the Black Country: Methodism in Wednesbury."
       Methodist Recorder, 25 April 1901, 13-15.

3127. Lawrence, Eugene. "City Road Chapel." Harper's Magazine 48 (1874): 349-65.

3128. _____. "John Wesley and His Times." Harper's Magazine 45 (1872): 105-20.

3129. Laws, C. H. "Inscriptions from Wesley's 'New Room' at Bristol." Proceedings of the Wesley Historical Society 19 (1934): 142-44.

3130. _____. "Wesley Letters in New Zealand." Proceedings of the Wesley Historical Society 17 (1930): 132-33.

3131. _____. "Wesley's Notes on the New Testament." Proceedings of the Wesley Historical Society 18 (1931): 37-39.

3132. Lawson, Albert Brown. "Catchwords of 'The Conversation.' 2. Apostolic Succession and the Threefold Ministry." Proceedings of the Wesley Historical Society 34 (1964): 141-47.

3133. Lawson, John. "John Wesley and Abstinence. But He Believed in Discipline." Christian Advocate 7, no. 15 (1963): 13.

3134. _____. "The Poetry of Charles Wesley." Emory University Quarterly 15 (1959): 31-47.

3135. _____. "Saving Faith As Wesley Saw It." Christianity Today 8, no. 15 (1964): 3-4.

3136. _____. "Wesley Rides Again." Christianity Today 4, no. 15 (1960): 12-13.

3137. Lawton, George. "The Colloquial Element in the English of Wesley's Journal." Proceedings of the Wesley Historical Society 32 (1960): 159-65, 178-85.

3138. _____. "Grace in Wesley's Fifty-three Sermons: A Concordance View." Proceedings of the Wesley Historical Society 42 (1980): 112-15. References are given to Wesley's use of the word "grace" in his 53 sermons, vols. 5 and 6 of his Works, 1872 edition.

3139. _____. "The 'Illustrious Vulgar' in John Wesley's Sermons." Proceedings of the Wesley Historical Society 33 (1961): 53-62. A study of Wesley's literary style--illustrating his use of slang and colloquialisms. His use of the "illustrious vulgar" is intermixed with biblical and scholarly language.

3140. _____. "John Wesley and Proverbs. A Concluding Essay with Special Reference to Proverb Lexicography." Proceedings

252   John and Charles Wesley

of the Wesley Historical Society 30 (1955-56): 73-81, 108-
13.

3141.   . "Matthew Bramble, Tom Paine, and John Wesley."
Proceedings of the Wesley Historical Society 33 (1961): 41-45.
Includes a poem on John Wesley, written by Matthew Bramble,
pseudonym of Richard Dearman.

3142.   . "Notes on Early Methodism in Northampton." Proceedings of the Wesley Historical Society 25 (1946): 88-94,
104-7.

3143.   . "Proverbial Element in Wesley's Journal." Proceedings of the Wesley Historical Society 29 (1953): 58-65.

3144.   . "Proverbs and Proverbial Echoes in John Wesley's
Letters." Proceedings of the Wesley Historical Society 26
(1948): 111-14, 129-34. Discusses Wesley's use of biblical,
classical, and Shakespearean proverbs.

3145.   . "The Slang and Colloquial Expressions in Wesley's
Letters." Proceedings of the Wesley Historical Society 32
(1959): 5-11, 25-33.

3146.   . "Slang and Colloquialism in John Wesley's Tracts
and Treatises." Proceedings of the Wesley Historical Society
35 (1966): 154-58, 165-67, 185-88.

3147.   . "A Wesley Autograph on Sinless Perfection?"
Proceedings of the Wesley Historical Society 34 (1963): 29-33.
This is a discussion of an alleged manuscript of John Wesley's
on perfection.

3148.   . "Wesley's Homiletic Use of Proverbial Lore."
Proceedings of the Wesley Historical Society 28 (1951): 2-7,
25-27.

3149.   . "The Wesleys in the 'Orange Street Hymnal'."
Proceedings of the Wesley Historical Society 37 (1970): 93-98,
140-42, 182-93. The "Orange Street Hymnal" was edited and
produced by Augustus Montague Toplady under the title
Psalms and Hymns for Public and Private Worship. Most of
the 419 hymns contained in it are greatly altered. This
article discusses four of John Wesley's translated hymns contained in Toplady's hymnal.

3150.   . "Wesley's Use of Proverbs in His Treatises and
Kindred Works." Proceedings of the Wesley Historical Society 29 (1954): 169-77.

3151. Leach, Elsie A. "John Wesley's Use of George Herbert."
Huntington Library Quarterly 16 (1953): 183-202.

Articles   253

3152. Leary, William. "John Cennick, 1718-55: A Bicentenary Appreciation." Proceedings of the Wesley Historical Society 30 (1955): 30-37.

3153. Lee, Atkinson. "Methodism and Its Psychological Problems." London Quarterly and Holborn Review 163 (1938): 189-93.

3154. Lee, G. Elliott. "Beginnings of Methodism in Herefordshire." Methodist Magazine 161 (1938): 225-29.

3155. Lee, L. G. H. "Wesley's Travels in His Own Country." Lincolnshire Magazine 1 (1934): 379-82.

3156. Lee, Philip H. "Thomas Maxfield." Proceedings of the Wesley Historical Society 21 (1938): 161-62.

3157. Lee, Umphrey. "John Wesley in Arcadia." Southwest Review (Dallas) 13 (1928): 413-32. Describes John Wesley's time in Georgia.

3158. _____. "John Wesley's Love Affairs." Methodist Quarterly Review 74 (1925): 476-93. Betty Stanton, Mary Granville, Sophia Hopkey, Grace Murray, and Mrs. Vazeille.

3159. Leedal, John J. "Wesley and Keith." Proceedings of the Wesley Historical Society 9 (1914): 155-58.

3160. Leedal, T. G. "An Ancient Yorkshire Borough: Wakefield and Its Methodism." Methodist Recorder, 28 March 1907, 10.

3161. Lees, Samuel. "Wednesbury and West Bromwich As Wesley Knew Them." Proceedings of the Wesley Historical Society 4 (1904): 153-59.

3162. _____. "The Wesleyan Centenary in Sheffield: Memories of Norfolk Street Chapel." Methodist Recorder, 16 July 1880, 502.

3163. Léger, J. Augustin. "Wesley's Place in Catholic Thought." Constructive Quarterly 2 (1914): 329-60.

3164. Lelièvre, Matthieu. "Wesley's Attachment to the Church of England." Methodist Recorder, 3 July 1862, 215.

3165. "The Lesson of John Wesley's Life." United Methodist Free Churches' Magazine 34 (1891): 121-23. Compares Wesley and Voltaire, indicating similarities and attributing Wesley's vast accomplishments to his industry, zeal, and sense of mission.

3166. Lester, George. "Methodism in Grimsby." Methodist Recorder, 27 February 1890, 136; 6 March 1890, 153.

3167. _____. "Samuel Wesley's Second Benefice, Epworth."
Methodist Recorder, 9 January 1890, 20.

3168. Lewis, Thomas H. "John Wesley As a Scholar." Methodist
Quarterly Review 73 (1924): 648-58. Discusses Wesley's in-
tellect, diligence, and dedication to preaching the Gospel.

3169. Lidgett, J. S. "The Genius of Methodism: Lecture."
Methodist Recorder, 26 October 1905, 5.

3170. _____. "John Wesley and John Henry Newman." London
Quarterly Review 146 (1926): 1-10.

3171. _____. "The Theological Issues." London Quarterly and
Holborn Review 163 (1938): 171-74. This is a discussion of
John Wesley's conversion.

3172. "The Life of Wesley." London Quarterly Review 1 (1853):
38-68. This article reviews Wesley's life and recent biographies of him--those by Southey, Watson, Moore, Taylor.

3173. Lightwood, James. "An Interesting Wesley Relic." Methodist
Recorder, 30 October 1902, 15. The relic is a portion of the
first list of members of the Bristol Society in 1741, in John
Wesley's handwriting.

3174. Lightwood, James T. "Handel's Original Tunes to Charles
Wesley's Hymns." Choir and Musical Journal 31 (1930): 53-
55, 101-3.

3175. _____. "John Wesley at St. Paul's." The Choir and Musical Journal 29 (1938): 98-99. Speculates as to the hymns
John Wesley heard while at St. Paul's Cathedral in the Spring
of 1738.

3176. _____. "Notes on the Foundery Tune-Book." Proceedings
of the Wesley Historical Society 1 (1898): 116-17; 2 (1900):
147-60.

3177. _____. "The Story of Methodist Music." Wesleyan Methodist Magazine 149 (1926): 61, 125, 187, 315, 758-59. Also
published as a book by Epworth Press, 1928.

3178. _____. "Tune Books of the Eighteenth Century." Proceedings of the Wesley Historical Society 3 (1902): 237-40;
5 (1905): 101-8.

3179. Lindstrom, Harald G. A. "The Message of John Wesley and
the Modern Man." Drew Gateway 25 (1955): 186-95.

3180. Little, C. Deane. "The Origin of Methodism in Manchester."

Proceedings of the Wesley Historical Society 25 (1946): 116-
22; 26 (1947): 1-6, 17-22, 33-35.

3181. Little, C. Deane and Victor E. Vine. "John Wesley's Marriage." Proceedings of the Wesley Historical Society 32
(1960): 118.

3182. "'Lively, Loving' Margate: Methodism in East Kent."
Methodist Recorder, 28 June 1906, 10.

3183. Lloyd, A. Kingsley. "Charles Wesley's Debt to Matthew
Henry." London Quarterly and Holborn Review 171 (1946):
330-37. Discusses Wesley's use of Henry's Commentary in
his Short Hymns on Select Passages of the Holy Scripture.

3184. _____. "Philip Doddridge (1702-51) and John Wesley: A
Bi-centenary Appreciation." Proceedings of the Wesley
Historical Society 28 (1951): 50-52.

3185. Lock, W. "1780 Wesley Hymnal." Journal of Church Music
22, no. 8 (1980): 2-4.

3186. Lockwood, John P. "Memorials of Peter Böhler." Wesleyan
Methodist Magazine 77 (1854): 685-94.

3187. Lockyer, Thomas F. "The Churchmanship of John Wesley."
London Quarterly Review 141 (1924): 57-69. Describes Wes-
ley's role in the divergence of Methodism from the Church of
England.

3188. _____. "The Genealogy of the Wesley Family." Proceedings of the Wesley Historical Society 1 (1898): 67-69.

3189. _____. "John Wesley at Aldersgate Street. The Words
That Warmed the Heart." London Quarterly Review 116
(1911): 81-94. Concerns Luther's writings that influenced
Wesley.

3190. _____. "John Wesley's Revised Version of the New Testament." London Quarterly Review 143 (1925): 55-62. An
evaluation of Wesley's version which came about 100 years
before the Revised Standard Version.

3191. _____. "Luther and Wesley." Proceedings of the Wesley
Historical Society 8 (1911): 61-66.

3192. _____. "What Are 'Our Doctrines'?" London Quarterly
Review 134 (1920): 46-53.

3193. Lofthouse, William F. "Dante, Shakespeare, and Wesley."
Wesleyan Methodist Magazine 125 (1902): 654-57.

3194. _____. "John Wesley's Letters to His Brother." London
Quarterly and Holborn Review 185 (1960): 60-65, 133-39. A
discussion of their relationship as reflected in John's letters
to Charles.

3195. _____. "Wesley and His Women Correspondents." Wesley's
Chapel Magazine January and April, 1959. There were many.
Among those listed are Dorothy Furly, Sarah Ryan, Miss
March, Mrs. Woodhouse, Lady Maxwell, Mary Bosanquet, Ann
Bolton, Mary Bishop, Elizabeth Ritchie, and others.

3196. _____. "Wesley's Doctrine of Christian Perfection." London Quarterly and Holborn Review 159 (1934): 178-88.

3197. London Ministers Meeting. "The Churchmanship of John Wesley." Methodist Recorder, 24 March 1892, 192-93. States
that John Wesley's position was unique--there was a touch of
the high, low, broad, and narrow church in him.

3198. Lord, William. "Opening of a Methodist Chapel at Baptist-
Mills [Bristol North Circuit]." Wesleyan Methodist Magazine
61 (1838): 136-37.

3199. Ludwig, Charles. "Positive Memories." Mennonite 94, no. 1
(1979): 2-3. The author attributes Wesley's success to his
positive thinking.

3200. Luik, John C. "Marxist and Wesleyan Anthropology and the
Prospects for a Marxist-Wesleyan Dialogue." Wesleyan Theological Journal 18, no. 2 (1983): 54-66.

3201. Lunn, Arnold H. M. "The Mind of John Wesley." Review
of the Churches, n.s., 5 (1928): 497-507.

3202. _____. "The Theology of John Wesley." Review of the
Churches, n.s., 6 (1929): 72-85.

3203. Lunn, Henry S. "The Wesleys and Bishop Winnington Ingram." London Quarterly Review 133 (1920): 13-25.

3204. "Luther, Wesley and the Child." Methodist Recorder, 18
October 1906, 12.

3205. Lyles, Albert M. "The Hostile Reaction to the American Views
of Johnson and Wesley." Journal of the Rutgers University
Library 24 (1960): 1-13. Describes the attacks on Johnson's
Taxation No Tyranny and Wesley's Calm Address to Our
American Colonies.

3206. Lyles, Jean Caffey. "The Bicentennial of American Methodism:
1784-1984." Ecumenical Trends 13 (1984): 49-55.

3207. M, H. "Bicentenary of Wesley's First Sermon: Memorable
Scene at Southleigh and Open Letter from Whitney." Methodist Recorder, 22 October 1925, 4-5.

3208. _____. "Methodism in a Fascinating Cornish Town;
Evangelism at Launceston." Methodist Recorder, 31 January
1935, 5-6.

3209. _____. "Peeps at Living Methodism: A Bit of Yorkshire;
a Memorable Rally at Oakworth; a Glimpse of Keighley."
Methodist Recorder, 9 April 1931, 4.

3210. _____. "Peeps at Living Methodism: Old and New in Cardiff." Methodist Recorder, 27 March 1930, 5-6.

3211. McAllum, Daniel. "Methodism in York." Wesleyan Methodist
Magazine 50 (1827): 456-58, 526-28.

3212. McCarthy, Daryl. "Early Wesleyan Views of Scripture."
Wesleyan Theological Journal 16, no. 2 (1981): 95-105.

3213. "Macclesfield Methodism: Centenary of Sunderland Street
Chapel." Methodist Recorder, 21 December 1899, 12.

3214. McCommon, Paul C. "Come, Thou Long-Expected Jesus."
Church Musician 35, no. 3 (1983): 8-11, 48-49. About
Charles Wesley's hymn of that title.

3215. McConnell, Francis J. "New Interest in John Wesley."
Journal of Religion 20 (1940): 340-58. Bibliographical essay
reviewing some of the then recent works on Wesley and
Methodism.

3216. McCrea, Alexander. "Bicentenary of Methodism in Ireland."
Methodist Recorder, 12 June 1952, 4.

3217. _____. "Wesleyana in Ireland." Proceedings of the Wesley Historical Society 19 (1934): 121-23. Concerns materials
in Edgehill College, Belfast.

3218. McCullagh, Thomas. "The Biographers of Wesley." London
Quarterly Review 97 (1902): 129-52.

3219. _____. "The First Methodist Society: The Date and Place
of Its Origin." Proceedings of the Wesley Historical Society
3 (1902): 166-74. Reprinted in 12 (1939): 77-83. See also
no. 3462.

3220. _____. "The Wesleys and the Nobility. Pt. 5 - Selina,
Countess of Huntingdon." Wesleyan Methodist Magazine 122
(1899): 420-27.

258   John and Charles Wesley

3221. _____. "The Wesleys in Relation to Nonconformity." Wesleyan Methodist Magazine 110 (1887): 61-65, 177-85.

3222. McDermott, William F. "Circuit Rider of the Centuries." Together 1, no. 8 (1957): 12-16.

3223. _____. "He Carried a World of Hope in His Saddlebags."
Reader's Digest 62 (June 1953): 103-6. Condensed from the
Christian Advocate, 6 October 1949.

3224. McDonald, Frederic W. "Bishop Butler and John Wesley: A
Comparison and Contrast." Methodist Recorder, 27 February
1896, 142; 5 March 1896, 156; 12 March 1896, 172.

3225. _____. "Butler and Wesley: A Comparison and Contrast."
Methodist Recorder, 5 July 1900, 3-4.

3226. _____. "John Wesley, the Theologian." Methodist Recorder,
2 April 1891, 257. A sermon delivered at City Road Chapel,
March 8, 1891.

3227. McEllhenney, John G. "John Wesley and Samuel Johnson: A
Tale of Three Coincidences." Methodist History 21, no. 3
(1983): 143-55.

3228. McElrath, Hugh T. "Praise the Lord Who Reigns Above."
Church Musician 34, no. 1 (1982): 19-23. Concerns Charles
Wesley and his hymn by that title.

3229. _____. "Rejoice the Lord is King." Church Musician 34,
no. 7 (1983): 8-11. About the Charles Wesley hymn of that
title.

3230. McGonigle, Herbert. "Pneumatological Nomenclature in Early
Methodism." Wesleyan Theological Journal 8 (1973): 61-72.

3231. _____. "Wesley's Revision of the Shorter Catechism."
Preacher's Magazine 56, no. 1 (1980): 59, 62-63.

3232. McGrath, Alister E. "Justification in Earlier Evangelicalism."
Churchman 98 (1984): 217-28.

3233. McIntosh, Lawrence D. "John Wesley: Conversion as a
Continuum." Midstream 8, no. 3 (1969): 50-65.

3234. McKean, G. R. "Primitive Physic." Canadian Magazine 64
(1925): 238, 256.

3235. McKellar, Hugh D. "The First Denominational Hymnbook."
Hymn 31 (1980): 33-37. Claims that the Countess of Huntingdon was responsible for the first denominational hymnbook,
not John Wesley.

3236. McKenna, David L. "John Wesley and Megatrends: A Guest Editorial." Christianity Today 28, no. 17 (1984): 18-19. Discusses parallels between eighteenth-century England and twentieth-century America, and attempts to show how Wesley would counsel Americans today.

3237. McNabb, Vincent. "John Wesley and Christian Peace." Blackfriars 18 (1937): 820-27. Discusses Piette's book on Wesley (no. 1301), Wesley's successful movement, and his closeness to Catholicism.

3238. McNeill, John T. "Luther at Aldersgate." London Quarterly and Holborn Review 164 (1939): 200-217.

3239. Maddox, Randy L. "Responsible Grace: The Systematic Perspective of Wesleyan Theology." Wesleyan Theological Journal 19, no. 2 (1984): 7-22.

3240. Madison, Thomas W. "John Wesley on Race: A Christian View of Equality." Methodist History 2, no. 4 (1964): 24-34.

3241. _____. "Some Economic Aspects of John Wesley's Thought Revisited." Methodist History 4, no. 1 (1965): 33-45. The primary purpose of this article is to describe "the manner in which Wesley related his theology and his ethics to a concern for the economic life and the economic well-being of his followers."

3242. Malekin, Peter. "William Law and John Wesley." Studia Neophilologica 37 (1965): 190-98.

3243. Manaton, G. Aubrey. "Methodism in North Devon: The Centenary of the Barnstaple Circuit." Methodist Recorder, 19 October 1911, 10.

3244. "Manchester Methodism a Century Ago: Some of Its Fathers and Features." Methodist Recorder, 11 April 1901, 13-14.

3245. Mann, Henry. "A John Wesley Relic." Methodist Monthly 3 (1894): 9-11. The relic is the original clock purchased by John Wesley, placed by him in the Orphan House, Newcastle-on-Tyne, and, at the time this article was written, in the possession of the trustees of Wallsend Church.

3246. Manning, Bernard L. "The Evangelical Doctrines of Charles Wesley's Hymns." London Quarterly and Holborn Review 166 (1941): 459-63. Reviews Rattenbury's Hymns for the Use of the People Called Methodists.

3247. _____. "Hymns for the Use of the People Called Methodists." London Quarterly Review 158 (1933): 309-32.

3248. _____. "The Recall to Religion in the Hymns of Charles Wesley." London Quarterly and Holborn Review 163 (1938): 475-91.

3249. _____. "Wesley's Hymns Reconsidered." London Quarterly and Holborn Review 165 (1940): 19-30, 154-65. Discusses the variety of meter, breadth of vocabulary, and ability to express emotions.

3250. Manning, H. S. "The Preacher on Horseback." Bedfordshire Magazine 3 (1953): 323-28.

3251. Manor, James. "The Coming of Britain's Age of Empire and Protestant Mission Theology." Zeitschrift für Missionswissenschaft und Religionswissenschaft 61 (1977): 38-54. John Wesley is one of the four theologians discussed in this article.

3252. Mansfield, Herbert W. "The Wesleys and Aldersgate." Methodist Magazine July 1953, 296-98.

3253. Marriott, C. W. "John Wesley and His Significance As an Educator." Religion in Education 10 (1942): 13-16.

3254. Marriott, Thomas. "Methodism in Former Days. 10. Georgia." Wesleyan Methodist Magazine 67 (1844): 919-23.

3255. _____. "Methodism in Former Days. 16. The Rev. John Wesley and Christian Union." Wesleyan Methodist Magazine 69 (1846): 43-45.

3256. _____. "Methodism in Former Days. 18. Medicine and Medical Advice." Wesleyan Methodist Magazine 69 (1846): 359-64.

3257. _____. "Methodism in Former Days. 19. The Education of Children." Wesleyan Methodist Magazine 69 (1846): 450-54.

3258. _____. "Methodism in Former Days. 26. Hayes, Hillingdon and Uxbridge." Wesleyan Methodist Magazine 70 (1847): 865-69.

3259. _____. "Methodism in Former Days. 36. General Redemption." Wesleyan Methodist Magazine 72 (1849): 164-66.

3260. _____. "Methodism in Former Days. 38. Wesley at Everton." Wesleyan Methodist Magazine 72 (1849): 489-92.

3261. _____. "The Rev. John Wesley and Robert Southey, LLD." Wesleyan Methodist Magazine 68 (1845): 239-40.

3262. _____. "The Rev. John Welsey, M.A., and William

Articles   261

Wilberforce, Esq., on Christian Perfection and Practical
Christianity." Wesleyan Methodist Magazine 68 (1845): 364-
65.

3263. Marsh, Daniel L. "Methodism and Early Methodist Theological
Education." Methodist History 1, no. 1 (1962): 3-13.

3264. Marshall, I. Howard. "Sanctification in the Teaching of John
Wesley and John Calvin." Evangelical Quarterly 34, no. 2
(1962): 75-82.

3265. Marshall, Romey Pitt. "Backtracking John Wesley." Together 2, no. 7 (1958): 33-37.

3266. _____. "Wesley and the Reformation." Religion in Life
39 (1970): 426-33. Compares Wesley, Luther, and Calvin.

3266a. Maser, Frederick E. "Discovery--John Wesley's Authorship
of the Poem Georgia.'" Methodist History 21 (1983): 169-
71.

3267. _____. "The Early Biographers of John Wesley."
Methodist History 1, no. 2 (1963): 29-42.

3268. _____. "The Human Side of John Wesley." Religion in
Life 27 (1958): 544-56. Describes examples of Wesley's humor and wit, his love of children, his affairs of heart, and
periods of depression.

3269. _____. "John Wesley's Only Marriage, an Examination of
Dr. Frank Baker's Article 'John Wesley's First Marriage.'"
Methodist History 16, no. 1 (1977): 33-41. See nos. 2036,
2197.

3270. _____. "Preface to Victory: An Analysis of John Wesley's
Mission to Georgia." Religion in Life 25 (1956): 280-93.

3271. _____. "Problem in Preaching: An Analysis of the
Preaching Power of John Wesley." London Quarterly and
Holborn Review 182 (1957): 110-17.

3272. Massa, Mark S. "The Catholic Wesley: A Revisionist Pro-
legomenon." Methodist History 22 (1983): 38-53. Explores
John Wesley's relationship with the Roman Catholic Church.

3273. Mather, P. Boyd. "John Wesley and Aldersgate." Christian
Century 80 (1963): 1581-83.

3274. Matsumoto, Hiroaki. "John Wesley's Understanding of Man."
Wesleyan Quarterly Review 4 (1967): 83-102.

3275. Mawer, Walter. "The 'Queen of the South' and Her Method-
       ism." Methodist Recorder, 7 July 1898, 11.

3276. May, G. Lacey. "Some Letters of John Wesley." Treasury
       35 (1920): 368-76. Discusses Wesley's character and work as
       discerned in his letters.

3277. Me. "Mr. Wesley's Character. Preaching and Authorship."
       Wesleyan Methodist Magazine 70 (1847): 1203-11.

3278. Meadley, T. D. "Society for the Reformation of Manners:
       With a Glance at the Rev. Samuel Wesley and the Restoration
       Drama." London Quarterly and Holborn Review 176 (1951):
       144-48.

3279. Mecklenburg, Willard. "Wesley and Luther." Together 12,
       no. 11 (1968): 50.

3280. Mercer, Jerry L. "The Destiny of Man in John Wesley's Es-
       chatology." Wesleyan Theological Journal 2 (1967): 56-65.

3281. Meredith, W. H. "John Wesley As a Preacher for the
       Present Time." Homiletic Review 43 (1902): 494-501.

3282. _____. "John Wesley, Christian Socialist." Methodist Re-
       view 83 (1901): 426-39. Describes Wesley's efforts at social
       reform.

3283. _____. "John Wesley, Educator." Methodist Review 85
       (1903): 399-409.

3284. _____. "Wesley's First Missionary, and His Visit to New
       England." Methodist Review 87 (1905): 413-18. Richard
       Boardman was the first Methodist missionary to enter New
       England.

3285. Metherell, E. Howard. "Robert Carr Brackenbury's Chapel
       at Raithby." Proceedings of the Wesley Historical Society
       20 (1936): 170-73.

3286. "Methodism at Tantobie." Methodist Recorder, 26 June 1890,
       432.

3287. "Methodism in a 'Town of Gardens': Cheltenham in Wesley's
       Time and Today." Methodist Recorder, 31 August 1905, 9.

3288. "Methodism in Chester." Methodist Recorder, 2 February
       1888, 79.

3289. "Methodism in Cornwall." Wesleyan Methodist Church Record
       1 (1892): 68-70.

3290. "Methodism in Sticklepath: Some Account of an Old Method-
        ist Centre." Methodist Recorder, 20 September 1900, 11.

3291. "Methodism in Teesdale." Methodist Recorder, 4 October
        1923, 6.

3292. "Methodism in the Eighteenth Century." London Quarterly
        Review 20 (1863): 405-34. Reviews George Smith's History
        of Wesleyan Methodism, no. 1533, and Abel Steven's The
        History of the Religious Movement Called Methodism, no.
        1582.

3293. "Methodism in the Malverns: The Beauty Spot of Worcester-
        shire." Methodist Recorder, 27 June 1907, 9.

3294. "Methodism in Wales: An Important Literary Find."
        Methodist Recorder, 8 August 1895, 569.

3295. Methodist Times; Special Supplement; Centenary of Wesley's
        Death, February 26th 1891. 24p.

3296. "The Methodists." Priest 22 (1966): 11-14. This is an ar-
        ticle about John and Charles Wesley.

3297. Metz, Donald. "John Wesley and Romance." Preacher's
        Magazine 54, no. 1 (1978): 50. Brief description of Wesley's
        failure to achieve happiness in romantic love.

3298. _____. "Wesley and His Opposition." Preacher's Maga-
        zine 55, no. 1 (1979): 35. Brief discussion of the opposition
        to Wesley by the Church, the press, and the mob.

3299. Meyler, L. J. "Wesley in Pembrokeshire." Proceedings of
        the Wesley Historical Society 21 (1938): 207-9.

3300. Miller, M. "The Life and Times of John Wesley." Wesleyan
        Methodist Association Magazine 17 (1854): 276-86.

3301. Mills, Frederick H. "Wesley's Wife in Wesley's Letters."
        Proceedings of the Wesley Historical Society 21 (1938): 120-
        27.

3302. Mills, Stella. "A Petty Attack on Wesley's Hymns." Pro-
        ceedings of the Wesley Historical Society 41 (1977): 22-25.
        The attack discussed here was by Thomas Pennington Kirk-
        man, an Anglican clergyman.

3303. Mims, Edwin. "Dr. Johnson and John Wesley." Methodist
        Review 85 (1903): 543-54.

3304. "Mr. Birrell on John Wesley." Times, 30 May 1896, 7. An

account of a lecture given by Augustine Birrell at the Royal
Institution on "John Wesley: Some Aspects of the 18th Century." See no. 170.

3305.   "Mr. Wesley's Authorship, Journals, etc. Observations on a
Remark in an Article Extracted from the North British Review." Wesleyan Methodist Magazine 70 (1847): 1109-22.

3306.   "Mr. Wesley's Bishops." Methodist Magazine and Quarterly
Review 14 (1832): 238-40.

3307.   "Mr. Wesley's Christian Library." Wesleyan Methodist Magazine 50 (1827): 310-16.

3308.   "Mr. Wesley's Conversion." Wesleyan Methodist Magazine
61 (1838): 342-54.

3309.   Mitchell, T. Crichton. "Response to Dr. Timothy Smith on
the Wesleys' Hymns." Wesleyan Theological Journal 16, no.
2 (1981): 48-57. See no. 3712.

3310.   Moore, Robert L. "Justification without Joy: Psychohis-
torical Reflections on John Wesley's Childhood and Conversion." History of Childhood Quarterly: The Journal of
Psychohistory 2 (1974): 31-52.

3311.   Moore, Sydney H. "Wesley and Fénelon." London Quarterly
and Holborn Review 169 (1944): 155-57. Describes these two
men as educators.

3312.   _____. "Wesley and Jena: Our Founder's Footprints in
Germany." Methodist Recorder, 30 December 1909, 9.

3313.   _____. "Wesley's Favorite Village: Shoreham and Its
Early Methodist History." Methodist Recorder, 5 September
1912, 9.

3314.   Morgan, David T. "'The Dupes of Designing Men': John
Wesley and the American Revolution." Historical Magazine
of the Protestant Episcopal Church 44 (1975): 121-31.

3315.   _____. "John Wesley's Sojourn in Georgia Revisited."
Georgia Historical Quarterly 64 (1908): 253-62.

3316.   Morgan, E. Athan. "The Wesleys and Fonmon Castle,
Glamorgan." Bathafarn 9 (1954): 38-41.

3317.   Morgan, Robert. "Oliver Goldsmith and Methodism." Proceedings of the Wesley Historical Society 18 (1932): 106-8.

3318.   Morsley, Clifford. "In the Footsteps of the Wesleys: A

Methodist Pilgrimage." Coming Events in Britain, July 1963, 16-20.

3319. Moseley, William H. "The Coming of the Newcastle Conference; the Conference Towns: Gateshead and Newcastle." Methodist Recorder, 18 July 1901, 11-16.

3320. Moss, Arthur Bruce. "The Ordination of Francis Asbury." Methodist History 1, no. 3 (1963): 25-28.

3321. "The Mother of the Wesleys." Monthly Religious Magazine 21 (1859): 306-15.

3322. "The Mother of the Wesleys." Spectator 59 (1886): 1360-62. A review of Eliza Clarke's biography of Susanna Wesley, no. 352.

3323. "The Mother of the Wesleys." Sunday Magazine 2 (1866): 123-28.

3324. Moulton, W. Fiddian. "A Notable Midland Chapel: The Jubilee of Trinity, Wolverhampton." Methodist Recorder, 10 July 1913, 10.

3325. Moulton, Wilfrid J. "John Wesley's Doctrine of Christian Perfection: Lecture." Methodist Recorder 13 November 1924, 19.

3326. _____. "John Wesley's Doctrine of Perfect Love." London Quarterly Review 144 (1925): 14-27.

3327. Mounfield, Arthur. "John Wesley's Visits to Warrington." Proceedings of the Wesley Historical Society 8 (1911): 57-61, 81-85; 9 (1913): 90-92.

3328. Mullen, Wilbur H. "John Wesley and Liberal Religion." Religion in Life 35 (1966): 561-74. Describes Wesley's desire for "latitude of religious belief and practice within the general framework of the church."

3329. _____. "John Wesley's Method of Biblical Interpretation." Religion in Life 47 (1978): 99-108.

3330. Mullineau, James. "Wesley's Bicentenary: Letter from New York Christian Advocate." Wesleyan Methodist Church Record 12 (1903): 134.

3331. Mumford, Norman W. "Organization of the Methodist Church in the Time of John Wesley." London Quarterly and Holborn Review 171 (1946): 35-40, 128-35. Discusses development of the societies, the class meeting, the itinerancy of the preachers, and the early conferences.

3332. Murdick, Olin J. "Was Wesley a 'Romish' Ruse?" Homiletic
       and Pastoral Review 49 (1949): 368-74.

3333. Murgatroyd, T. "John Wesley's Complete English Dictionary."
       Notes and Queries 187 (1944): 172.

3334. Myall, William. "John Wesley." International Review 11
       (1881): 320-38.

3335. Myers, Arthur. "The Conference City and Its Methodism."
       Methodist Recorder, 19 July 1906, 11-14. Discusses Wesley
       in Nottingham.

3336. Myers, Lucia. "A New Birthday Hymn." Hymn 24 (1973):
       57-58. The author composed a new Aldersgate hymn to
       celebrate the birth of Methodism.

3337. N., G. "John Wesley's Complete English Dictionary." Notes
       and Queries 187 (1944): 103.

3338. N., M. "Methodism in South Shields: Centenary of Chapter
       Row Chapel." Methodist Recorder 8 October 1908, 10.

3339. _____. "Saas Street Mission, Sunderland: Coming of Age,
       Growth and Development." Methodist Recorder, 23 September
       1909, 9.

3340. N., M. R. "Methodism in Cleobury Mortimer: One of Dr.
       Pope's Advanced Posts." Methodist Recorder, 6 November
       1902, 13-14.

3341. _____. "Methodism in Walsall: The Middle Age." Method-
       ist Recorder, 3 November 1904, 9-10.

3342. _____. "The Roots of a Great Tree: The Beginnings of
       Methodism in Birmingham." Methodist Recorder, 21 February
       1901, 11-12.

3343. _____. "Walsall and the Wesleys: The Story of the 1743
       Riots." Methodist Recorder 29 September 1904, 9-10.

3344. Nash, Vaughan. "Illustrious Quack." New Statesman and
       Nation, n.s. 2 (1931): 252-53. Discusses Primitive Physic
       and the reasons Wesley felt compelled to take upon himself
       medical concerns.

3345. Nattrass, J. Conder. "A Few Notes on Early Methodism in
       Haworth." Proceedings of the Wesley Historical Society 10
       (1916): 141-46, 165-68, 200-205.

3346. "Newcastle Churches in John Wesley's Day." Proceedings of
       the Wesley Historical Society 12 (1919): 65-67.

3347. _____ . "Portrait of Charles Wesley." Proceedings of the
Wesley Historical Society 9 (1913): 4.

3348. Nayler, John. "Twenty-three Wesleyan Methodist Conferences Held at Leeds." Wesleyan Methodist Magazine 105
(1882): 352-63, 445-55, 520-28.

3349. Nelson, James. "John Wesley and the Georgia Moravians."
Transactions of the Moravian Historical Society 23 (1984):
17-46.

3350. Neufer, P. Dale. "Creedal Freedom in American Methodism."
Religion in Life 43 (1974): 42-51. Discusses Wesley's concept
of freedom from rigid creed and its impact on the growth of
American Methodism.

3351. "New Wesleyan Chapel at Brentford." Methodist Recorder,
19 September 1889, 684.

3352. Newland, F. W. "The Cradle of Methodism." Sunday at Home,
December 1901, 112-15.

3353. Newton, John Anthony. "The Ecumenical Wesley." Ecumenical
Review 24 (1972): 160-75.

3354. _____ . "Perfection and Spirituality in the Methodist Tradition." Church Quarterly 3 (1970): 95-103.

3355. _____ . "Samuel Annesley (1620-1696)." Proceedings of the
Wesley Historical Society 45 (1985): 29-45.

3356. Nicholas, Geraldine. "Ten Criminals ... Used of God!"
Herald of Holiness 69, no. 14 (1980): 6-7. Tells the story of
Charles Wesley's visit to Newgate Prison, July 19, 1738, and
how the event made him aware of the power of God within himself.

3357. Nicholson, Norman. "Wesley and Watts." Times Literary Supplement, 6 August 1954, 44-45.

3358. Nicholson, Roy S. "The Holiness Emphasis in the Wesleys'
Hymns." Wesleyan Theological Journal 5 (1970): 49-61.

3359. _____ . "John Wesley: Spiritual Revolutionary." Christian
Life 26, no. 12 (1965): 32-36.

3360. _____ . "John Wesley and Ecumenicity." Wesleyan Theological Journal 2 (1967): 66-81.

3361. _____ . "John Wesley on Prevenient Grace." Wesleyan Advocate, September 13, 1976, 5-6.

3362. _____. "John Wesley's Personal Experience of Christian Perfection." Asbury Seminarian 6, no. 1 (1952): 65-89.

3363. _____. "Wesley on Witnessing to Holiness." Preacher's Magazine 53, no. 1 (1978): 19-20.

3364. Nilson, E. Anker. "Prevenient Grace." London Quarterly and Holborn Review 184 (1959): 188-94.

3365. Nininger, Ruth. "Wesley Hymn Festivals." Hymn 9 (1958): 58-60. Discusses hymn festivals held in 1957, on the 250th anniversary of the birth of Charles Wesley.

3366. Nix, James. "Methodism in Oxford." Methodist Recorder, 22 September 1904, 9-10.

3367. Noble, Mark. "Centenary of a Cathedral Circuit: Durham and Its Methodism." Methodist Recorder, 3 October 1912, 9.

3368. _____. "A Methodist Homestead: The Western Borders of a Newcastle Circuit." Methodist Recorder, 19 April 1906, 14.

3369. _____. "Newcastle-upon-Tyne." Wesleyan Methodist Magazine 108 (1885): 414-22, 501-6.

3370. _____. "Newcastle-upon-Tyne; Past and Present." Wesleyan Methodist Church Record 3 (1894): 114-15.

3371. _____. "A Northern Methodist Cathedral: The Story of Brunswick, Newcastle-on-Tyne." Methodist Recorder, 15 January 1914, 10.

3372. _____. "Sunderland and Its Methodism: Past and Present." Methodist Recorder, 13 March 1902, 13-14.

3373. _____. "Tyneside Methodism: The Ryton Circuit." Methodist Recorder, 17 August 1905, 10.

3374. Noll, Mark A. "John Wesley and the Doctrine of Assurance." Bibliotheca Sacra 132 (1975): 161-77.

3375. _____. "Romanticism and the Hymns of Charles Wesley." Evangelical Quarterly 46 (1974): 195-223.

3376. Noro, Yoshio. "The Character of John Wesley's Faith." Wesleyan Quarterly Review 4 (1967): 10-26.

3377. _____. "Wesley's Understanding of Christian Perfection." Wesleyan Quarterly Review 4 (1967): 27-42.

3378. Norton, J. Baker. "Bridge Street Chapel, Bolton." Methodist Recorder, 29 September 1904, 14.

3379. "Nottingham Methodist Notes. Early Preaching Places."
        Proceedings of the Wesley Historical Society 5 (1906): 164-
        69.

3380. _____. "John Wesley and the Nottingham General Hospital."
        Proceedings of the Wesley Historical Society 5 (1906): 163-
        64.

3381. Nuttall, Geoffrey F. "Charles Wesley in 1739." Proceedings
        of the Wesley Historical Society 42 (1980): 181-85. Contains
        an extract from the journal of Joseph Williams of Kidderminster
        (1692-1755), in which he records hearing Charles Wesley
        preaching in Bristol and subsequently attended a society
        meeting with him.

3382. Nutter, Charles S. "Charles Wesley As a Hymnist." Method-
        ist Review 108 (1925): 341-57.

3383. _____. "Letter to the Rev. Mr. Heath [18 May 1787]."
        Proceedings of the Wesley Historical Society 16 (1928): 155-
        56. This is a letter with commentary from John Wesley to
        Heath, the head of Cokesbury College.

3384. Nygren, E. Herbert. "John Wesley's Changing Concept of
        the Ministry." Religion in Life 31 (1962): 264-74.

3385. _____. "Wesley's Answer to Existentialism." Christian
        Advocate 9, no. 3 (1965): 7-8.

3386. O. "Society-Meetings." Wesleyan Methodist Magazine 84
        (1861): 339-48.

3387. "Obituary of John Wesley." Gentleman's Magazine 69 (1791):
        282-84.

3388. "'An Oldham Resident.' The Story of Glodwich from an Old
        Garret to a Model Sunday School." Methodist Recorder, 31
        August 1905, 10.

3389. Ollard, S. L. "John Wesley: The Preacher of 'Plain
        Truths.'" Times, 21 May 1938, 15-16. This article about
        Wesley was written on the 200th anniversary of Wesley's Al-
        dersgate experience.

3390. "On Methodism." Methodist Recorder, 20 September 1888,
        707. Attributes Wesley's success to his gift of leadership
        and organizational abilities.

3391. Ong, Walter J. "Peter Ramus and the Naming of Methodism;
        Medieval Science through Ramist Homiletic." Journal of the
        History of Ideas 14 (1953): 235-48.

3392. Onstott, Anna M. "A 'Script' Portrait of Wesley." Proceed-
       ings of the Wesley Historical Society 19 (1934): 129-32. This
       script portrait was done by Glück Rosenthal.

3393. "The Original Settlement of the Wesleys." Proceedings of the
       Wesley Historical Society 9 (1914): 113-16. This article was
       provided by a member of the Wesley family who was not iden-
       tified.

3394. Osborn, George. "The Example of Elisha: The Substance of
       a Sermon Preached on October 25, 1839." Wesleyan Methodist
       Magazine 63 (1840): 199-219.

3395. _____. "Lessons from the Life and Work of John Wesley."
       Methodist Recorder, 26 February 1891, 165-66.

3396. Osborn, George R. "Methodism and Education; John Wesley's
       Contribution." London Quarterly and Holborn Review 181
       (1956): 259-64.

3397. Osborn, T. G. "The Work of Methodism--Methodism and
       Education." Methodist Recorder, 5 March 1891, 171-72.

3398. Osborne, N. J. "A Circuit Centenary Celebration: The
       Story of Southend and Leigh." Methodist Recorder, 4 Sep-
       tember 1913, 10.

3399. Osgood, Samuel. "John Wesley." Christian Examiner 43
       (1847): 1-19. This article is a review of Southey's, White-
       head's, and Watson's biographies, but it does not review
       these books critically as much as it recounts Wesley's life
       and contributions.

3400. Oswalt, John N. "John Wesley and the Old Testament Con-
       cept of the Holy Spirit." Religion in Life 48 (1979): 283-92.

3401. _____. "Wesley's Use of the Old Testament in His Doc-
       trinal Teachings." Wesleyan Theological Journal 12 (1977):
       39-53.

3402. "The Other Wesley." Time, 7 October 1957, 74, 75.

3402a. Ott, Philip W. "A Corner of History--John Wesley and the
       Non-Naturals." Preventive Medicine 9 (1980): 578-84.

3403. _____. "John Wesley on Health: A Word for Sensible
       Regimen." Methodist History 18, no. 3 (1980): 193-204.

3404. Outler, Albert C. "Beyond Pietism: Aldersgate in Context."
       Motive 23, no. 8 (1963): 12-16.

3405. _____. "Evangelism in the Wesleyan Spirit." Andover
Newton Quarterly 14 (1974): 212-24.

3406. _____. "John Wesley: Folk-Theologian." Theology Today
34 (1977): 150-60.

3407. _____. "John Wesley As Theologian--Then and Now."
Methodist History 12, no. 4 (1974): 63-82.

3408. _____. "Pastoral Care in the Wesleyan Spirit." Perkins
Journal 25, no. 1 (1971): 4-11.

3409. _____. "Towards a Re-appraisal of John Wesley As Theologian." Perkins School of Theology Journal 14, no. 2 (1961):
5-14.

3410. _____. "Wesley, the Evangelist." Together 16, no. 4
(1972): 39-41. This is drawn from his lecture of 1971 to the
United Methodist Conference on Evangelism.

3411. Overton, Frederick Arnold. "John Wesley in His Own Day."
Cornhill Magazine, n.s. 14 (1903): 743-51.

3412. Overton, John Henry. "The Wesleys at Epworth." Longman's Magazine 7 (1885): 41-52.

3413. Owen, Goff, Jr. "The Evolution of Methodist Hymnody in
the U.S." Hymn 13 (1962): 49-55.

3414. Owens, Richard E. "Primitive Methodist Hymnody." American Organist 14, no. 10 (1980): 17.

3415. "Oxford and the Wesleys." Methodist Recorder, 25 August
1910, 9.

3416. "Oxford Celebrates Wesley's Student Days." Christian Century 43 (1926): 529. An account of the bicentenary celebration of Wesley's admission to Lincoln College, Oxford.

3417. Oyston, H. G. "John Wesley and Handel." Methodist Weekly (Manchester), 26 June 1902, 3. Claims a close connection
between the work and labors of John Wesley and the success
of Handel in England.

3418. P., S. J. "In Wesley's Footsteps: Jubilee of Fletcher Street
Church, Bolton." Methodist Recorder, 1 June 1911, 10.

3419. Packard, George T. "John Wesley." Harper's Weekly 35
(1891): 163-64. Contains a large reproduction of a painting
of John Wesley at the age of 40.

3420. Page, Arthur. "Where Wesley Preached His Last Sermon: A Visit to Leatherhead and a Chat with the Rev. L. A. Parsons." Methodist Recorder, 8 August 1929, 5.

3421. Page, W. Scott. "Wesley and the Sense of Humour." Methodist Recorder, 15 March 1906, 13.

3422. Palmer, Edgar C. "Methodism in Huddersfield." Wesleyan Methodist Magazine 135 (1912): 620-24.

3423. Panosian, Edward M. "In Pursuit of Souls." Faith for the Family 2, no. 6 (1975): 13-15.

3424. _____. "John Wesley's Doctrine of Christian Perfection." Biblical Viewpoint 6 (1972): 120-29.

3425. Parker, Judson F. "The Hymns of the Wesleys in Two Generations: Theological Inferences Drawn from the Editions of 1932 and 1964 of the Methodist Hymnal." Methodist History 9, no. 2 (1971): 3-15.

3426. Parkes, James F. "The Newest Conference City: Lincoln." Methodist Recorder, 15 July 1909, 4-5.

3427. Parkinson, George. "A Veteran Local Preacher in an Historic Spot." Methodist Recorder, 2 May 1901, 12.

3428. Parlby, William. "Early Visits of the Founders of Methodism to Herefordshire, 1743-1750." Proceedings of the Wesley Historical Society 17 (1929): 87-96.

3429. _____. "The Wesleys--an Attempt to Account for Their High Church Principles, 1808." Proceedings of the Wesley Historical Society 11 (1918): 155-59. A letter by J. T. Rutt, dated 1808, is printed in full and discussed by William Parlby.

3430. Partridge, Eric. "John Wesley's Dictionary." London Quarterly and Holborn Review 156 (1932): 544-47. Reprinted in the Wesley Chapel Magazine, October 1955, and the Proceedings of the Wesley Historical Society 27 (1950): 170-73.

3431. Pask, A. H. "The Influence of Arminius on John Wesley." London Quarterly and Holborn Review 185 (1960): 258-63.

3432. Passmore, Joseph. "Methodism in Whalley: An Historic Lancashire Village." Methodist Recorder, 22 June 1905, 12.

3433. Pates, Herbert W. "Methodism in Upper Nidderdale." Methodist Recorder, 15 December 1904, 9-10.

Articles   273

3434. _____. "Rothwell and Its Methodism." Methodist Recorder,
        12 December 1907, 12.

3435. Paull, J. David. "At the Mouth of the Yare: The Stormy
        Youth of Yarmouth Methodism." Methodist Recorder, 18 June
        1903, 13-15.

3436. Peabody, A. P. "Wesley and Methodism." North American
        Review 75 (1852): 226-47. A review of Isaac Taylor's Wes-
        ley and Methodism, 1852, no. 1635.

3437. Pearse, Mark Guy. "The First Cornish Methodist." Wes-
        leyan Methodist Magazine 104 (1881): 44-50, 113-17.

3438. _____. "The First Cornish Methodists." Cornish Maga-
        zine 2 (1899): 67-75.

3439. Pearson, Edith McCall. "The Wesley Family and Dorset."
        Dorset Year Book 1973-74, 8-12.

3440. Peel, Albert. "John Wesley As Letter Writer." Congrega-
        tional Quarterly 10 (1932): 86-90. Reviews Vulliamy's John
        Wesley, no. 1738, and Telford's Letters, no. 1645.

3441. _____. "Wesley and the Free Churches." London Quar-
        terly and Holborn Review 163 (1938): 218-21.

3442. Pellowe, William C. S. "John Wesley's Use of Doctrine."
        Methodist Review 107 (1924): 101-7.

3443. _____. "John Wesley's Use of the Bible." Methodist Re-
        view 106 (1923): 353-74.

3444. _____. "Wesley's Use of Science." Methodist Review 110
        (1927): 394-403.

3445. Penn, Mayson. "Canterbury and Its Methodism." Wesleyan
        Methodist Magazine 130 (1907): 805-12.

3446. Pennington, Edgar Legare. "John Wesley's Georgia Ministry."
        Church History 8 (1939): 231-54.

3447. Perkins, E. Benson. "The Restored Epworth Rectory."
        Proceedings of the Wesley Historical Society 31 (1957): 50-
        52.

3448. Perkins, J. P. "The Humour of John Wesley." Wesleyan
        Methodist Magazine 143 (1920): 697-98.

3449. Perks, Robert W. "Wesley an Empire Builder." Wesleyan
        Methodist Magazine 149 (1926): 459-60. Concerns Wesley's
        efforts in the arena of politics and social reform.

3450. Perry, J. H. "John Wesley and Methodism." Methodist Quar-
       terly Review 53 (1871): 289, 351.

3451. "Peter Martin and John Wesley." Old Cornwall 4 (1947):
       205-8. Quotes Peter Martin's recollections about John Wesley
       from Richard Treffy's Memoirs of Richard Trewavas.

3452. Phelps, Sydney K. "Two of Our Invisible Hosts." Nine-
       teenth Century 98 (1925): 128-36. A discussion of Wesley's
       City Road House and Samuel Johnson's house in Gough
       Square.

3453. Phipps, William E. "John Wesley on Slavery." Quarterly
       Review (Nashville) 1, no. 3 (1981): 23-31.

3454. Phoebus, G. A. "Was He Ordained a Bishop by Erasmus?"
       Methodist Quarterly Review 60 (1878): 88-111.

3455. Pierson, Arthur T. "Wesley and His Mission." Missionary
       Review of the World 26 (1903): 641-45.

3456. Piggott, H. J. "Opinions of Italian Public Men on the Life
       and Work of John Wesley." Wesleyan Methodist Magazine 103
       (1880): 734-39. Includes comments by Raffaele Mariano,
       Emile Laveleye, Giuseppe De Leva, and Marco Minghetti on
       Sciarelli's translation of Lelièvre's Life of Wesley.

3457. Pike, David. "The Religious Societies, 1678-1738." Pro-
       ceedings of the Wesley Historical Society 35 (1965): 15-20,
       32-38.

3458. "Pilgrimage to Epworth." Methodist Recorder, 27 September
       1888, 726-27.

3459. Pilkington, Frederick. "An Annotation to Wesley's Journal."
       London Quarterly and Holborn Review 178 (1953): 263-70.
       Relates the story of Thomas Rutherford and the impact Wesley
       had on his life.

3460. _____. "Methodism and Episcopacy." Contemporary Re-
       view 193 (1958): 303-7.

3461. Platt, Frederic. "Charles Wesley's Bristol House." Pro-
       ceedings of the Wesley Historical Society 18 (1932): 137-42.

3462. _____. "The First Methodist Society; the Date and Place
       of Its Origin." Proceedings of the Wesley Historical Society
       22 (1940): 155-64. A reply to no. 3219.

3463. _____. "Wesley's 'Ordinations'--a Retrospect." London
       Quarterly and Holborn Review 160 (1935): 63-73.

Articles   275

3464. _____. "The Work of the Holy Spirit." London Quarterly and Holborn Review 163 (1938): 175-78.

3465. Playter, G. F. "John Wesley As a Man of Literature." Methodist Quarterly Review 40 (1858): 272-90; 41 (1859): 548-67; 42 (1860): 260-77, 624-39.

3466. Pocock, W. W. "Early Methodist Finance." Wesleyan Methodist Magazine 108 (1885): 760-67, 886-94.

3467. Podmore, Frank. "Remarks on Mr. Lang's Paper." Proceedings of the Society for Psychial Research 17 (1901-1903): 328-32. Comments on Lang's discussion of Old Jeffrey. See no. 3122. Podmore's article is followed by Lang's rebuttal on pp. 333-36.

3468. "Points of Resemblance between the Sender of the Gospel to the English in the Sixth Century and the Restorer of the Gospel to the English in the Eighteenth Century." Wesleyan Methodist Magazine 114 (1891): 445-48. Compares Wesley and Gregory the Great.

3469. Polkinghorne, G. Waddy. "Blackburn and Its Methodism." Wesleyan Methodist Magazine 134 (1911): 96-102.

3470. Pollard, Charles. "John Wesley and Robert Carr Brackenbury: Some Unpublished Letters." Proceedings of the Wesley Historical Society 28 (1951): 53-58, 67-73.

3471. _____. "A Wesley Legacy." London Quarterly and Holborn Review 171 (1946): 317-25. Describes a collection of Wesleyana that was bequeathed to Wesley House in 1946, and reproduces some of the letters.

3471a. Pollock, John C. "From Wesley to Graham." Christianity Today 1, no. 17 (1957): 6-7, 24.

3472. Polsom, Edward R. "Early Methodism in Paulton: The Story of a West Country Circuit." Methodist Recorder, 17 March 1910, 11.

3473. _____. "An Old West Country Circuit: Methodism in Midsomer Norton." Methodist Recorder, 2 June 1910, 10.

3474. _____. "A Somerset Village Centenary: Methodism in Clutton." Methodist Recorder, 15 September 1910, 9.

3475. Porter, Frank G. "John Wesley, the Anticipator." Christian Century 40 (1923): 1162-64. Describes Wesley's involvement with social issues of his day.

3476. _____. "Wesley, a Forerunner of Social Reform." <u>Method-
ist Review</u> 103 (1920): 908-18.

3477. Porter, Laurence E. "James Hervey, 1714-1758; a Bicentenary
Appreciation." <u>Evangelical Quarterly</u> 31, no. 1 (1959): 4-20.

3478. Porter, Stephen. "Wesley at Dudley." <u>Blackcountryman</u> 10,
no. 2 (1977): 40-42.

3479. Potter, Charles Francis. "The Story of Religion: Wesley."
<u>Woman's Home Companion</u>, June 1928, 26, 66-68.

3480. Prescott, C. J. "Wesley and Newman: A Problem." <u>Method-
ist Quarterly Review</u> 74 (1925): 29-42.

3481. Preston, Novella D. "Charles Wesley, Preacher As Well As
Poet." <u>Church Musician</u> 13 (April 1962): 14-15.

3482. Prestwood, Charles M., Jr. "The Greater Legacy of Wesley
and Luther." <u>Christian Advocate</u> 6, no. 21 (1962): 7-8.

3483. Priestley, A. Weston. "John Wesley and Health." <u>Methodist
Recorder</u>, 10 January 1895, 20. The author attributes Wesley's longevity to heredity, simple eating and sleeping habits,
and continual exercise in the fresh air caused by his constant
travel.

3484. Prothero, R. E. "John Wesley." <u>Good Words</u> 32 (1891): 101-
6, 190-95.

3485. "Pusey and Puseyism: Wesley and Methodism." <u>Methodist
Recorder</u>, 29 September 1882, 728-29.

3486. Pyke, Richard. "The Western World." <u>London Quarterly
and Holborn Review</u> 163 (1938): 199-203.

3487. R., M. D. "'Semper Fidelis': Methodist History and Progress in Exeter." <u>Methodist Recorder</u>, 30 August 1900, 11-12.

3488. Rack, Henry D. "Wesley and Romanticism." <u>Proceedings of
the Wesley Historical Society</u> 45 (1985): 63-65.

3489. Radford, J. Grange. "John Wesley and the Empire." <u>Spec-
tator</u> 160 (1938): 907-8. Describes the results of Wesley's
life on the British Empire.

3490. _____. "John Wesley's Witness to Christ: Yesterday and
Today." <u>Methodist Magazine</u> 161 (1938): 261-64.

3491. Rainer, P. A. "Early Methodist Preaching in Altrincham,
Cheshire." <u>Proceedings of the Wesley Historical Society</u> 23
(1941): 37-38.

Articles 277

3492. Rakestraw, Robert V. "John Wesley as a Theologian of Grace." Journal of the Evangelical Theological Society 27 (1984): 193-203.

3493. Randolph, J. Ralph. "John Wesley and the American Indian: A Study in Disillusionment." Methodist History 10, no. 3 (1972): 3-11.

3494. Rattenbury, Harold B. "The World Parish." London Quarterly and Holborn Review 163 (1938): 207-11.

3495. Rattenbury, John Ernest. "John Wesley's Whitsuntide Experience: Modern Methodism's Need: What is 'Evangelical Conversion'." Methodist Recorder, 12 May 1937, 17.

3496. _____. "Note on Article on 'Sources of Wesley's Revision of the Prayer Book of 1784-88'." Proceedings of the Wesley Historical Society 23 (1942): 173-75. See no. 2929.

3497. Raymond, Allan. "'I Fear God and Honour the King': John Wesley and the American Revolution." Church History 45 (1976): 316-28.

3498. Raymond, P. B. "Wesley's Religious Experience." Methodist Review 86 (1904): 28-35. Discusses the Moravian influence on Wesley and his Aldersgate experience.

3499. "Rebirth in Virginia." Time: Special 1776 Issue 105 (19 May 1975): 61. A description of Methodist activities in the Colonies, as it would have been written in 1776.

3500. "Records Preserved ... the Admission of John Wesley to His Fellowship at Lincoln College, Oxford, 1725-26." Proceedings of the Wesley Historical Society 15 (1926): 146-61.

3501. Redfearn, James. "Wesley As a Correspondent." Wesleyan Methodist Church Record 9 (1900): 147. Describes the friendship between John Wesley and Jane (Hilton) Barton, and their correspondence, quoting a letter from Wesley to her of 9 November 1779.

3502. Reeve, Florence A. "West Street Chapel, St. Giles, Seven Dials." Proceedings of the Wesley Historical Society 16 (1928): 137-41.

3503. Reeve, Ronald. "John Wesley, Charles Simeon, and the Evangelical Revival." Canadian Journal of Theology 2 (1956): 203-14.

3504. "The Reformer." Blackwood's Magazine 104 (1868): 428-56.

3505. Reid, H. M. B. "Watts and Wesley: A Contrast." Good
Words 41 (1900): 658-62.

3506. Reist, Irwin W. "Confession of Sin in the Life of Christian
Excellence and the Order of Salvation in the Theology of
John Wesley." Asbury Seminarian 29, no. 2 (1974): 24-36.

3507. _____. "John Wesley and George Whitefield: A Study in
the Integrity of Two Theories of Grace." Evangelical Quarterly 47, no. 1 (1975): 26-40.

3508. _____. "John Wesley's View of Man: A Study in Free
Grace Versus Free Will." Wesleyan Theological Journal 7
(1972): 25-35.

3509. _____. "John Wesley's View of the Sacraments: A Study
in the Historical Development of a Doctrine." Wesleyan
Theological Journal 6 (1971): 41-54.

3510. Reubelt, J. A. "Ignatius Loyola and John Wesley." Christian
Quarterly 3 (1871): 176-92.

3511. "Rev. John Wesley and His Likeness." Hogg's Instructor,
n.s. 3 (1849): 264-65. Relates Culy's approach to John Wesley and his success in taking his likeness for a bust, by
paying him ten quineas, which Wesley used to aid debtors.

3512. "Review of the Lives of Wesley and Whitefield." Christian
Spectator 3 (1821): 471-89, 530-48. This contains a lengthy
review of Southey's Life of Wesley (1820): no. 1553.

3513. "Review on the Economy of Methodism." Quarterly Christian
Spectator 1 (1829): 509-26. Discusses Wesley's "ecclesiastical
economy" of Methodism, his authority, and structure of his
movement.

3514. Reynolds, Herbert G. "The History of Plymouth and Its
Methodism." Methodist Magazine 152 (1929): 411-20.

3515. Reynolds, William J. "Love Divine, All Loves Excelling."
Hymn 33 (1982): 187.

3516. Rhodes, Frank. "Epworth and Its Associations." United
Methodist Magazine 13 (1920): 45-48.

3517. Rice, William North. "Bicentennial of John Wesley." North
American Review 176 (1903): 817-31.

3518. Richards, E. "A Sketch of Dudley Methodism." Methodist
Recorder, 26 September 1901, 12-13.

3519. Richards, Ernest. "The Influence of Methodism on Life and
      Thought." Holborn Review 74 (1932): 42-53.

3520. Richards, Frank. "Kingswood School." Wesleyan Methodist
      Magazine 130 (1907): 404-12.

3521. Richards, H. C. "John Wesley in Cornwall." Methodist Re-
      corder, 24 October 1901, 18.

3522. _____. "John Wesley in London Churches." Transactions
      of the St. Paul's Ecclesiological Society 5 (1905): 85-92. The
      purposes of this article are to illustrate John Wesley's connec-
      tion with London churches, as a preacher, using his diary to
      show how he worked with the Church of England, and second-
      ly, to prove that the bishops did not drive him from the
      church.

3523. Richards, Peter S. "John Wesley in the East Midlands."
      Proceedings of the Wesley Historical Society 41 (1978): 185-
      87.

3524. Richardson, Cyril C. "Poverello and Methodist. A Study in
      Francis of Assisi and John Wesley." Religion in Life 7
      (1938): 218-30. A comparison of the two men, their theology
      as well as their personalities and appearance, their attitudes
      toward mysticism, learning, and the church. The differences
      outweigh the similarities.

3525. Richardson, N. S. "John Wesley on Separation from the
      Church." Church Review 14 (1861): 63-74.

3526. Riddell, William Renwick. "Wesley's System of Medicine."
      New York Medical Journal 99 (1914): 64-68.

3527. Rigg, James H. "The Churchmanship of John Wesley."
      Contemporary Review 28 (1876): 648-81.

3528. _____. "John Wesley." Methodist Recorder, 20 June
      1884, 439; 27 June 1884, 455; 4 July 1884, 470-71.

3529. _____. "John Wesley As an Evangelist." Sunday at Home
      32 (1885): 279-80, 294-96, 309-14, 332-35, 347-49.

3530. _____. "The Sacrament of the Lord's Supper." Methodist
      Recorder, 5 March 1891, 190-91.

3531. Rigg, John. "Methodism in Sheffield." Wesleyan Methodist
      Magazine 58 (1835): 606-12.

3532. Riggall, Marmaduke. "Langham Row." Proceedings of the
      Wesley Historical Society 7 (1910): 130-32.

3533. _____. "A 'Poem' on Wesley." Proceedings of the Wesley Historical Society 16 (1927): 38-53. Reprints and discusses a poem on John Wesley by T.R.I., which originally appeared in the Hereford Journal, 1840. The author of this article credits it to Thomas R. Jones, Wesleyan minister, 1835-83.

3534. Rights, Douglas L. "A Moravian's Report on John Wesley-- 1737." South Atlantic Quarterly 43 (1944): 406-9. Contains translation of Spangenberg's report on Wesley, written in 1737 in Georgia to authorities of the Moravian Church in Herrnhut, Saxony.

3535. Rishell, Charles W. "Wesley and Other Methodist Fathers on Childhood Religion." Methodist Review 84 (1902): 778-84.

3536. Rivers, Isabel. "John Wesley and the Language of Scripture, Reason and Experience." Prose Studies 4 (1981): 252-86.

3537. Robbins, Alfred F. "John Wesley's Marriage." Notes and Queries 11th ser., 2 (1910): 226. Reprints newspaper accounts of his marriage.

3538. Robbins, Peggy. "God, Man, Woman, and the Wesleys." American Heritage 35, no. 3 (1984): 96-103. The Wesley's Georgia adventure is termed "unrelieved bungling" in this article.

3539. Roberts, Gomer M., and Frank Baker. "John Wesley's 'Sacred Harmony'." Proceedings of the Wesley Historical Society 27 (1950): 167-68.

3540. Roberts, Griffith T. "Charles Wesley's 'Right to Preach Throughout England and Ireland'." Proceedings of the Wesley Historical Society 21 (1937): 31-32. Charles Wesley made a claim before a justice at Churchill, September 9, 1744, for the right to preach.

3541. _____. "The Wesleys and Anglesey Methodism." Proceedings of the Wesley Historical Society 24 (1944): 121-25; 25 (1945): 4-8, 23-29.

3542. * _____. The Wesleys and Sir John Philipps of Picton Castle." Bathafarn 1 (1946).

3543. _____. "Wesley's First Society in Wales." Proceedings of the Wesley Historical Society 27 (1950): 111-16, 125-28. Cardiff, 1739-1829.

3544. Robinson, Joshua. "New Chapels in the Dewsbury Circuit." Wesleyan Methodist Magazine 61 (1838): 537-39.

3545. "Rochester Methodism: The Centenary of Bethel." Methodist Recorder, 26 May 1910, 9.

3546. Rogal, Samuel J. "Bread to the Hungry: John Wesley and the Poor." Christian Advocate 17, no. 5 (1973): 11-13.

3547. _____. "The Contributions of John and Charles Wesley to the Spread of Popular Religion." Grace Theological Journal 4 (1983): 233-44. Discusses the many ways the Wesleys spread Methodism throughout England, but the primary force was John Wesley's organizational abilities.

3548. _____. "'The Elder unto the Well-Beloved': The Letters of John Wesley." Journal of Religious Studies 7, no. 2 (1979): 73-87.

3549. _____. "Enlightened Enthusiasm: Anti-Methodism in the Literature of the Mid and Late Eighteenth Century." Enlightenment Essays 5, no. 1 (1974): 3-13.

3550. _____. "The Epworth Women: Susanna Wesley and Her Daughters." Wesleyan Theological Journal 18, no. 2 (1983): 80-89.

3551. _____. "George Romney's Portrait of John Wesley." Eighteenth-Century Life 5 (1978): 38-47.

3552. _____. "Horace Walpole and the Methodists." University of Dayton Review 12, no. 3 (1976): 107-19. Discusses Horace Walpole's anti-Methodist sentiments, and especially his opinions of John Wesley, Whitefield, and the Countess of Huntingdon.

3553. _____. "John Wesley and the Attack on Luxury in England." Eighteenth-Century Life 3 (1977): 91-94.

3554. _____. "John Wesley and the Organ: the Superfluous Pipes." Church Music (St. Louis) no. 2 (1974): 27-31. States that the evidence indicates Wesley could never give his official approval for the use of the organ in the liturgy of the Methodist societies.

3555. _____. "John Wesley and the Press-Gangs." Asbury Seminarian 36, no. 3 (1981): 24-33. Quasi-legal gangs impressed men for service in the navy. Some of these gangs were used to harrass early Methodist meetings.

3556. _____. "John Wesley at Edinburgh: 1751-1790." Trinity Journal (Deerfield, Ill.) 4, no. 1 (1983): 18-34.

3557. _____. "John Wesley on War and Peace." Studies in Eighteenth Century Culture 7 (1978): 329-44.

3558. _____. "John Wesley's Daily Routine." Methodist History
13, no. 1 (1974): 41-50.

3559. _____. "John Wesley's London." Asbury Seminarian 34,
no. 1 (1979): 23-32.

3560. _____. "John Wesley's Women." Eighteenth-Century Life
1 (1974): 7-10. A discussion of those women in John Wesley's life for whom he had romantic feelings, as well as those
who were of special interest to him because of their commitment to his movement.

3561. _____. "A Journal and Diary Checklist of John Wesley's
Reading: 14 October 1735--23 February 1791." Serif 11,
no. 1 (1974): 11-33.

3562. _____. "Kingswood School--John Wesley's Educational Ex-
periment." Illinois Quarterly 40 (Summer 1978): 5-14.

3563. _____. "The Occasional Hymns of Charles Wesley: Their
Historic Viewpoint." Cresset (January 1979): 8-12.

3564. _____. "Old Testament Prophecy in Charles Wesley's
Paraphrase of Scripture." Christian Scholar's Review 13
(1984): 205-16.

3565. _____. "Pills for the Poor: John Wesley's Primitive
Physick." Yale Journal of Biology and Medicine 51 (1978):
81-90.

3566. _____. "Pope and the Wesleys." University of Dayton
Review 9, no. 1 (1972): 47-57.

3567. _____. "Pope's 'Contribution' to English Hymnody."
University of Dayton Review 10, no. 1 (1973): 85-97. Discusses Pope's involuntary contribution to the hymns of
Charles and John Wesley, noting similarities in pronunciation,
language, and thought.

3568. _____. "The Role of Paradise Lost in Works by John and
Charles Wesley." Milton Quarterly 13 (1979): 114-19.

3569. _____. "Scriptural Quotation in Wesley's Earnest Appeal."
Research Studies (Pullman, Washington) 47 (1979): 181-88.

3570. _____. "Thoughts on Prior: John Wesley's Distortion of
Johnson." Essays in Literature 11 (1984): 137-43.

3571. Rogers, Charles A. "John Wesley and William Tilly." Proceedings of the Wesley Historical Society 35 (1966): 137-41.

Articles   283

3572. Rogers, James. "A Cradle of Yorkshire Methodism: The His-
       tory of a Century and a Half." Methodist Recorder, 27 De-
       cember 1900, 9-10.

3573. Rogers, James A. "John Wesley Can Help Improve the Hymn
       Singing in Your Church." Music Ministry, 8, no. 7 (1976):
       28, 31.

3574. Rogers, T. Guy. "John Wesley and the Church of England."
       London Quarterly and Holborn Review 163 (1938): 221-24.

3575. Rose, Delbert R. "What were the Results of Aldersgate in
       Wesley's Life and Ministry?" Asbury Seminarian 18, no. 1
       (1964): 18-35.

3576. Rousseau, G. S. "John Wesley's Primitive Physic (1747)."
       Harvard Library Bulletin 16 (1968): 242-56. There were at
       least 38 English editions and over 24 American editions of
       Primitive Physic, and this account of the book ends with a
       checklist of editions.

3577. Routley, Erik. "The Case against Charles Wesley." Hymn
       Society of Great Britain and Ireland Bulletin 4 (1960): 252-59.

3578. _____. "Charles Wesley and Matthew Henry." Congrega-
       tional Quarterly 33 (1955): 345-51. Comments on the book
       The Hymns of Methodism, by Henry Bett, no. 162.

3579. Rowe, G. Stringer. "A Note on Wesley's Deed Poll." Pro-
       ceedings of the Wesley Historical Society 1 (1897): 37-38.
       Discusses Wesley's "Deed of Declaration," and raises the
       question of whether the deed was put fully into force between
       the time it was executed in 1784 and Wesley's death.

3580. "Royal Cowes: The Methodist History of 170 Years." Method-
       ist Recorder, 12 September 1907, 9.

3581. Rudman, Arthur. "Methodism in Sheffield: First Period--the
       Sheffield Circuit." Methodist Recorder, 15 May 1902, 13-14.

3582. Runyon, Theodore. "Theology and Praxis at the Oxford In-
       stitute." Christian Century 99 (1982): 916.

3583. Rupp, E. Gordon. "Some Reflections on the Origin and De-
       velopment of the English Methodist Tradition, 1738-1898."
       London Quarterly and Holborn Review 178 (1953): 166-75.

3584. Russell, Thomas. "Where the Wesleys Once Lived: Epworth
       Pilgrimage." Methodist Recorder, 9 May, 1968, 5.

3584a. Rutt, J. T. "The Wesleys--An Attempt to Account for Their

High Church Principles, 1808." Proceedings of the Wesley Historical Society 11 (1918): 155-57. Reprints a letter which appeared in the Monthly Repository, 1808.

3585. Ryder, Mary R. "Avoiding the 'Many-Headed Monster': Wesley and Johnson on Enthusiasm." Methodist History 23 (1984): 214-22.

3586. S. "Glimpses of Old Burslem." Methodist Recorder, 22 July 1884, 522; 25 July 1884, 535; 29 July 1884, 554.

3587. _____. "Historical Reminiscences of the Wesleyan-Methodist Book-Room." Wesleyan Methodist Magazine 65 (1842): 1010-16.

3588. _____. "How Methodism Came to Newcastle-upon-Tyne." Methodist Recorder, 21 July 1885, 523.

3589. _____. "Methodism in a Great Cotton Town: The Story of the Blackburn Circuit." Methodist Recorder, 12 September 1907, 10.

3590. _____. "Methodism in Former Days. 2. The Phenomenon near Black-Hamilton, Yorkshire." Wesleyan Methodist Magazine 66 (1843): 206-8.

3591. S., B. "Methodism in Bromley." Methodist Recorder, 31 October 1935, 10.

3592. S., G. B. "Busy and Beautiful: Northampton's Methodist Associations." Methodist Recorder, 30 May 1907, 10.

3593. S., G. M. "Charles Wesley." Monthly Religious Magazine 22 (1859): 217-33.

3594. S., S. "The Potter's Clay: The Moulding of Methodism in North Staffordshire." Methodist Recorder, 3 January 1901, 11-12.

3595. S., W. E. "Constable's Country: Methodism in Manningtree." Methodist Recorder, 8 September 1904, 9-10.

3596. S., W. W. "An Ancient City: Winchester and the South Hants Mission." Methodist Recorder, 6 February 1908, 10.

3597. Sackett, A. Barrett. "John Wesley and the Greek Orthodox Bishop." Proceedings of the Wesley Historical Society 38 (1971-72): 81-87, 97-102.

3598. _____. "John Wesley's Preferment to St. Daniels Church, Near Pembroke." Proceedings of the Wesley Historical Society 39 (1974): 158-65.

3599. Sakakibara, Gan. "A Study of John Wesley's Economic Ethics." Wesleyan Quarterly Review 4 (1967): 59-72.

3600. Salmon, Albert E. "A City of Many Memories: York and Its Methodism." Methodist Recorder, 1 June 1905, 11.

3601. Sampson, George. "The Century of Divine Songs." Warton Lecture on English Poetry. Proceedings of the British Academy 29 (1943): 37-64. John and Charles Wesley are among the hymn writers discussed in this lecture.

3602. "Samuel Wesley, M.A., Brother to the Founders of Methodism." Notes and Gleanings 4 (1891): 33-34.

3603. Sanders, Evelyn. "The Hymn Composed in a Dungeon." Church Herald 36, no. 7 (1979): 6-7.

3604. Sanders, J. Kingsley. "John Wesley's Bristol Conferences." Methodist Recorder, 2 July 1959, 5.

3605. Sanders, Paul. "The Puritans and John Wesley." Work/Worship 17, no. 2 (1967): 13-19. A review article on Monk's John Wesley, His Puritan Heritage, no. 1175.

3606. Sanders, Paul S. "John Wesley and Baptismal Regeneration." Religion in Life 23 (1954): 591-603.

3607. _____. "Sacraments in Early Methodism." Church History 26 (1957): 355-71. Discusses Baptism and the Lord's Supper under Wesley's evangelical ministry, and contends that American practice of the sacraments has not followed the Wesleyan heritage.

3608. _____. "Wesley's Eucharistic Faith and Practice." Anglican Theological Review 48 (1966): 157-74.

3609. _____. "What God Hath Joined Together." Religion in Life 29 (1960): 491-500.

3610. Sandwith, Humphrey. "Methodism and Its Relations to the Church and the Nation." Wesleyan Methodist Magazine 52 (1829): 310-15, 378-82, 452-58, 518-24, 600-606, 666-73, 736-43, 806-18.

3611. Sangster, W. E. "Wesley and Sanctification." London Quarterly and Holborn Review 171 (1946): 214-21.

3612. Sargisson, C. S. "Bath and John Wesley." Wesleyan Methodist Magazine 136 (1913): 51-58.

3613. _____. "John Wesley and Dr. Johnson." Methodist Recorder, 9 September 1909, 10-11.

3614. _____. "John Wesley As 'Field Preacher'." Wesleyan Methodist Magazine 134 (1911): 689-94.

3615. _____. "John Wesley Busts in Staffordshire Pottery." Connoisseur 19 (1907): 11-17.

3616. _____. "John Wesley, Curate." Wesleyan Methodist Magazine 136 (1913): 779-85.

3617. Saul, G. Beamish. "A Missionary Circuit: The Story of Pickering Methodism." Methodist Recorder, 20 June 1912, 9.

3618. Saunders, Arthur W. "The Wesley Family and Its Coat of Arms." Proceedings of the Wesley Historical Society 35 (1966): 110-14.

3619. "Scarborough: From a Methodist Visitor's Point of View." Methodist Recorder, 2 June 1910, 9.

3620. "Scarborough Methodism: Its Origin and Early Struggles-- Wesley's Frequent Visits." Methodist Recorder, 16 February 1905, 9.

3621. Schelp, Hanspeter. "Wordsworth's 'Daffodils' Influenced by a Wesleyan Hymn." English Studies 42 (1961): 307-9. This author points out striking similarities between William Wordsworth's poem "Daffodils" and Charles Wesley's hymn "When Quiet in My House I Sit."

3622. Schiller, Francis. "Reverend Wesley, Doctor Marat and Their Electric Fire." Clio Medica 15 (1981): 159-76.

3623. Schofield, Robert E. "John Wesley and Science in Eighteenth Century England." Isis 44 (1953): 331-40.

3624. Scott, J. T. "Primitive Physick." American Journal of Physical Therapy 6 (1929): 137-40.

3625. Scroggs, Robin. "John Wesley As Biblical Scholar." Journal of Bible and Religion 28 (1960): 415-22.

3626. Sears, Donald A. "The Rise of the English Hymn 1707-1779." Journal of Church Music 13, no. 2 (1971): 10-15.

3627. "The Secret of Wesley." Christian Evangelist 63 (1926): 1383. Wesley's secret was the Bible and his faith in God.

3628. Selbie, W. B. "What We May Learn from John Wesley." London Quarterly Review 151 (1929): 145-53.

3629. Selby, E. T. "The New Room, Bristol." Proceedings of the Wesley Historical Society 26 (1948): 96-97.

3630. Seller, John W. "An Ancient Society: The Centenary of
       Whitby, Brunswick." Methodist Recorder, 2 July 1914, 10.

3631. _____. "Methodism in Robin Hood's Bay: The Earliest
       Society of the Yorkshire Coast." Methodist Recorder, 22 April
       1909, 10.

3632. _____. "The Old Order Changeth: The Planting of Meth-
       odism in Prescot and How It Grew." Methodist Recorder, 7
       March 1901, 13-14.

3633. _____. "Rural Methodism: The Story of the Sherburn
       Circuit." Methodist Recorder, 30 April 1908, 10.

3634. _____. "A Story of Early Methodism." Wesleyan Methodist
       Church Record 21 (1912): 119-20. Describes Wesley's work
       in Prescot.

3635. Sellers, Ian. "Anglicans, Methodists, and Swedenborgians:
       Their Early Interrelationships in Liverpool." New-Church
       Magazine 93 (1974): 134-37.

3636. Sellers, William E. "The Wesleys and Garth." Wesleyan
       Methodist Magazine 140 (1917): 372-76. Charles Wesley's
       wife was from Garth.

3637. _____. "The Wesleys and Trevecca." Wesleyan Methodist
       Magazine 135 (1912): 538-42.

3638. Sellors, R. "A New Wesley Portrait." Wesleyan Methodist
       Magazine 131 (1908): 517-19.

3639. "Semper Fidelis: Semper Paratus: Notes on Exeter Method-
       ism." Methodist Recorder, 6 September 1906, 10.

3640. Severs, George. "Anticipation and the Proleptic Adjective in
       Charles Wesley's Hymns." Proceedings of the Wesley His-
       torical Society 8 (1912): 184-88.

3641. _____. "Wesley's Visits to Keighley and Bingley 1780-2."
       Proceedings of the Wesley Historical Society 13 (1922): 134.

3642. "Shaftesbury: 'The City of a Dream': Birthplace of John
       Haime and Charles Garrett." Methodist Recorder, 21 March
       1907, 10.

3643. "Shaftesbury and Gillingham: A Circuit Centenary." Meth-
       odist Recorder, 12 August 1909, 9.

3644. Shafto, G. R. Holt. "Methodism in Dickens-Land." Method-
       ist Recorder, 28 August 1902, 11-12.

288   John and Charles Wesley

3645. Sharp, Percy. "The Birthplace of John Wesley: Axholme:
       a Centre of World-Wide Influence." Methodist Recorder, 16
       April 1903, 15-16.

3646. Sheffield, Wesley. "John Wesley and Abstinence: He Was
       No Abstainer." Christian Advocate 7, no. 15 (1963): 12.

3647. Sheldon, J. Bernard. "Rev. Dr. Clegg, of Chapel-en-le-
       Frith." Proceedings of the Wesley Historical Society 20
       (1936): 159-65.

3648. Sheldon, W. C. "Travelling in Wesley's Time." Proceedings
       of the Wesley Historical Society 7 (1909): 2-8, 50-53.

3649. Shelton, R. Larry. "John Wesley's Approach to Scripture in
       Historical Perspective." Wesleyan Theological Journal 16
       (1981): 23-50.

3650. _____. "John Wesley's 'Bible Christianity'." Preacher's
       Magazine 56, no. 4 (1981): 48.

3651. _____. "Wesley on Maintaining a Catholic Spirit." Preach-
       er's Magazine 53, no. 4 (1978): 12-13.

3652. _____. "Wesley on the Use of Money." Preacher's Maga-
       zine 57, no. 4 (1982): 37, 59.

3653. _____. "Wesley's Covenant Theology." Preacher's Maga-
       zine 54, no. 4 (1979): 42-43. Wesley's covenant theology had
       two aspects: the dependence of the believer on God's grace,
       and the obligation and duties which must be performed as a
       result of one's faith.

3654. _____. "Wesley's Doctrine of Man." Preacher's Magazine
       55, no. 4 (1980): 36-37.

3655. Shepherd, Thomas Boswell. "And Can It Be? An Analysis
       of a Hymn by Charles Wesley." London Quarterly and Holborn
       Review 170 (1945): 445-48.

3656. _____. "The Children's Verse of Dr. Watts and Charles
       Wesley." London Quarterly and Holborn Review 164 (1939):
       173-84.

3657. _____. "George Crabbe and Methodism." London Quar-
       terly and Holborn Review 166 (1941): 166-74. Crabbe des-
       cribed Methodism as "This spiritual influenza." Later he came
       to appreciate Wesley and Methodism.

3658. _____. "John Wesley and Matthew Prior." London Quar-
       terly and Holborn Review 162 (1937): 368-73.

3659. _____. "John Wesley and the Charterhouse." Proceedings of the Wesley Historical Society 21 (1937): 25-30.

3660. _____. "Methodists and the Theatre in the Eighteenth Century." Proceedings of the Wesley Historical Society 20 (1936): 166-68, 181-85; 21 (1937): 3-7, 36-38.

3661. Sherwin, Oscar. "Milton for the Masses: John Wesley's Edition of Paradise Lost." Modern Language Quarterly 12 (1951): 267-85.

3662. Shipley, David C. "The Holy Communion and the Wesleyan Heritage." Perkins School of Theology Journal 11, no. 1 (1957): 4-7.

3663. _____. "The Methodist Ministry in the Eighteenth Century." Perkins School of Theology Journal 13, no. 1 (1959): 5-14.

3664. _____. "Wesley and Some Calvinistic Controversies." Drew Gateway 25 (1955): 195-210.

3665. Showell, Rudland. "Wesley Day Service at Charterhouse School, Godalming." Proceedings of the Wesley Historical Society 21 (1938): 152-54.

3666. Shrubsall, A. "The Garden of England: The Land of Apples, Cherries and Bricks." Methodist Recorder, 3 October 1907, 9.

3667. Sibthorp, R. E. "The Wesley Saga." English Church Music, 1969, 40-43. A review of Erik Routley's The Musical Wesleys, no. 1425.

3668. Simon, John Smith. "At Mr. Grevil's, Wine Street, Bristol." Methodist Recorder, 10 February 1898, 11-12. Grevil was a grocer in Bristol, in whose shop Wesley and Whitefield met on March 31, 1739.

3669. _____. "The Death of John Wesley." Proceedings of the Wesley Historical Society 13 (1922): 158-62.

3670. _____. "Early Ordinations." Proceedings of the Wesley Historical Society 10 (1916): 157-58; 12 (1919): 67.

3671. _____. "The Establishment of Methodism in the Channel Islands. Pt. 4. From Mr. Wesley's Visit to the Conclusion of Mr. Brackenbury's Mission." Wesleyan Methodist Magazine 93 (1870): 332-41.

3672. _____. "John Wesley and Doncaster Methodism." Christian Miscellany and Family Visitor, November 1887, 518-23.

3673. _____. "John Wesley and Field Preaching." Proceedings
of the Wesley Historical Society 11 (1917): 54-63.

3674. _____. "John Wesley Submits to Be More Vile." Methodist Recorder, 7 April 1898, 11. Wesley consents to preaching in the open at Whitefield's instigation.

3675. _____. "John Wesley's 'Deed of Declaration'." Proceedings of the Wesley Historical Society 12 (1919): 81-93.

3676. _____. "Methodism in Birmingham." Wesleyan Methodist
Magazine 107 (1884): 919-28.

3677. _____. "Methodism in Dorset; by a Dorset Preacher."
Wesleyan Methodist Magazine 92 (1869): 335-44, 431-43.

3678. _____. "Mr. Wesley's Notes upon the New Testament."
Proceedings of the Wesley Historical Society 9 (1914): 97-105.

3679. _____. "The New Room in the Horsefair, Bristol." Methodist Recorder, 27 October 1898, 11; 3 November 1898, 11.

3680. _____. "Two Old Kingswood Chapels." Methodist Recorder,
28 April 1898, 11-12.

3681. _____. "Wesley's House." Methodist Recorder, 16 December 1897, 992.

3682. _____. "Wesley's Ordinations." Proceedings of the Wesley Historical Society 9 (1914): 145-54; 10 (1915): 65-66.

3683. Simons, Edward J. "The Great Sayings of John Wesley."
Wesleyan Methodist Church Record 12 (1903): 18, 39, 71, 98,
127, 135, 164, 203, 226, 251, 278, 305.

3684. Simpson, W. O. "A Few of Mr. Wesley's Christmas Days."
Methodist Recorder, 20 December 1878, 759.

3685. "Sir A. Quiller-Couch on the Wesley Hymns." Choir and
Musical Journal 12 (1921): 86-88. Reports on a lecture by
Arthur Quiller-Couch.

3686. Skinner, C. A. "John Wesley." Universalist Quarterly and
General Review 21 (1864): 486-500. A brief overview of John
Wesley's life and work.

3687. "A Slander upon Mr. Wesley Refuted." Wesleyan Methodist
Magazine 74 (1851): 354-61. This is a rebuttal to George
Payne's Lectures on Christian theology, 1845, dealing with the
doctrine of original sin.

3688. Slater, C. W. "The Pembroke Circuit." Methodist Recorder, 30 May 1901, 11-13.

3689. Sleigh, John. "Pedigree of the Wesley Family." Reliquary 8 (1868): 188.

3690. Smart, Henry T. "Methodism and Social Work--Methodism and the Working Man." Methodist Recorder, 12 March 1891, 209.

3691. Smith, Benjamin. "Early Methodism in Whitchurch (Salop)." Proceedings of the Wesley Historical Society 20 (1936): 114-17, 139-43.

3692. Smith, C. Ryder. "The Richmond Letters of Charles Wesley." Proceedings of the Wesley Historical Society 22 (1940): 150-54, 183-88; 23 (1941): 7-14. Fifteen letters held at Richmond College reprinted with annotations.

3693. _____. "The Richmond 'Wesleyana'." Proceedings of the Wesley Historical Society 21 (1937): 57-60. A list of Wesleyana at Richmond College.

3694. Smith, H. Arthur. "Footprints of the Wesleys in Cornwall." Cornish Magazine 1 (1898): 241-51.

3695. _____. "German Hymns and Wesley's Translations." Methodist Recorder, 23 January 1896, 55-56.

3696. Smith, H. H. "B.C. and A.D. of John Wesley." Methodist Quarterly Review (Nashville) 79 (1930): 713-15. Refers to before and after Aldersgate, phrase used by Frank W. Boreham, Australian essayist.

3697. _____. "How Wesley Dealt with Erring Preachers." Methodist Quarterly Review (Nashville) 76 (1927): 401-11.

3698. Smith, Harmon L. "Wesley's Doctrine of Justification: Beginning and Process." London Quarterly and Holborn Review 189 (1964): 120-28. First appeared in Duke Divinity School Bulletin 28 (1963): 88-98.

3699. Smith, Henry. "The Country of Cromwell and Cowper: Methodism in Huntingdon." Methodist Recorder, 25 January 1912, 9.

3700. _____. "Early Methodism in Hertfordshire and Its Immediate Vicinity." Wesleyan Methodist Magazine 107 (1884): 604-13.

3701. _____. "Early Methodism in Huntingdonshire and Its Immediate Vicinity." Wesleyan Methodist Magazine 104 (1881): 585-92.

3702. _____. "Early Southern Methodism: Hampshire Highways and Byways." Methodist Recorder, 8 April 1909, 10.

3703. _____. "Wesley Pottery in Brighton." Proceedings of the Wesley Historical Society 21 (1938): 140-41.

3704. Smith, J. Weldon, III. "Some Notes on Wesley's Doctrine of Prevenient Grace." Religion in Life 34 (1964): 68-80.

3705. Smith, John T. "John Wesley's First Service in Blackburn, and After." Methodist Magazine 152 (1929): 751-56.

3706. Smith, Neil G. "The Literary Taste of John Wesley." Queen's Quarterly 45 (1938): 353-58.

3707. Smith, Thornley. "Mr. Wesley in Bolton." Methodist Recorder, 12 December 1861, 313.

3708. _____. "Wesley's Labours in Bolton." Methodist Recorder, 13 March 1862, 82.

3709. Smith, Timothy L. "Chronological List of John Wesley's Sermons and Doctrinal Essays." Wesleyan Theological Journal 17, no. 2 (1982): 88-110.

3710. _____. "The Doctrine of the Sanctifying Spirit in John Wesley and John Fletcher." Preacher's Magazine 55, no. 1 (1979): 16-17, 54-58.

3711. _____. "George Whitefield and Wesleyan Perfectionism." Wesleyan Theological Journal 19, no. 1 (1984): 63-86.

3712. _____. "Holy Spirit in the Hymns of the Wesleys." Wesleyan Theological Journal 16, no. 2 (1981): 20-47. See also no. 3309.

3713. _____. "How John Fletcher Became the Theologian of Wesleyan Perfectionism 1770-1776." Wesleyan Theological Journal 15, no. 1 (1980); 68-87.

3714. _____. "John Wesley and the Wholeness of Scripture." Interpretation--A Journal of Bible and Theology 39 (1985): 246-62.

3715. _____. "Notes on the Exegesis of John Wesley's Explanatory Notes upon the New Testament." Wesleyan Theological Journal 16, no. 1 (1981): 107-13.

3716. Smith, Warren Thomas. "Attempts at Methodist and Moravian Union." Methodist History 8, no. 2 (1970): 36-48.

Articles 293

3717. _____. "The Christmas Conference. Wesley's Emissaries Sail for America." Methodist History 6, no. 4 (1968): 3-27.

3718. _____. "The Wesleys in Georgia: An Evaluation." Journal of the Interdenominational Theological Center 6 (1979): 157-67.

3719. Smyth, Richard Renwick. "A Sermon in Song." Hymn 15 (1964): 47-52. The author shows how Charles Wesley carried through in his hymns some of the points of faith and doctrine expounded in John Wesley's sermon "The Marks of the New Birth."

3720. Snow, M. Lawrence. "Aldersgate Mythology." Christian Advocate 7, no. 21 (1963): 7-8.

3721. _____. "Methodist Enthusiasm: Warburton Letters, 1738-1740." Methodist History 10, no. 3 (1972): 30-47.

3722. Snyder, Howard A. "John Wesley: A Man for Our Times." Christianity Today 16, no. 19 (1972): 8-11.

3723. _____. "John Wesley: Hope in Action." Other Side 13, no. 7 (1977): 52-55. A discussion of Wesley's concern for the salvation of the masses--touching upon both the ethical and social dimensions of his work.

3724. _____. "John Wesley and the Radical Protestant Tradition." Asbury Seminarian 33, no. 3 (1978): 13-38.

3725. _____. "The Making of a Radical Protestant Tradition." Asbury Seminarian 33, no. 1 (1978): 5-33. Deals with John Wesley as a theologian.

3726. _____. "Spirit and Form in Wesley's Theology: A Response to Keefer's 'John Wesley: Discipline of Early Christianity'." Wesleyan Theological Journal 19, no. 1 (1984): 33-35. See no. 3069.

3727. _____. "A Wesleyan Perspective on Church Growth." Asbury Seminarian 33, no. 5 (1978): 6-10.

3728. _____. "Wesley's Concept of the Church." Asbury Seminarian 33, no. 1 (1978): 34-59.

3729. Snyder, Melvin H. "The Joyful Mother: Susanna Wesley." Wesleyan Advocate, 26 April 1976, 4.

3730. Sobey, T. R. "Winchelsea's Link with John Wesley." Sussex County Magazine 25 (1951): 252.

3731. "Some Account of Mrs. Sarah Wesley (Relict of the Rev.
Charles Wesley, M.A.)." Methodist Magazine 6 (1823): 447-
52.

3732. Southey, Robert. "Field Preaching." Primitive Wesleyan
Methodist Magazine 37 (1859): 355-57. Taken from Southey's
Life of John Wesley.

3733. _____. "Letters on the Life of John Wesley, Founder of
English Methodism, to the Viscount C...; Signed R.S."
Correspondent 1 (1817): 26-48, 157-76.

3734. Sowton, Stanley. "In Wesley's Footsteps through Inner London; His Associations in the City." Methodist Recorder, 6
July 1933, 5.

3735. _____. "John Wesley and Charterhouse." Methodist Recorder, 3 June 1937, 4.

3736. _____. "John Wesley's Will: Somerset House Reveals One
of Its Treasures." Methodist Recorder, 6 December 1934, 17.

3737. _____. "The Schooldays of Two Famous Boys: John and
Charles Wesley at Charterhouse and Westminster." Methodist
Recorder, 7 December 1933, 10.

3738. _____. "Some Interesting Pages from the Past." Methodist Recorder; Wesley Bicentennial Supplement, 19 May 1938,
xiv. Discusses manuscripts showing Wesley's admission to
Charterhouse, the marriage of Samuel and Susannah in the
Parish Register, John Wesley and the Society for the Propagation of the Gospel, the burial of John's wife, and Charles's
burial in Marylebone.

3739. _____. "Wesley Links with Inner London: A City Pilgrimage." Methodist Recorder, 1 September 1932, 5.

3740. _____. "Where Wesley's Heart was 'Strangely Warmed';
Has the Very Room Been Discovered?" Methodist Recorder,
27 April 1933, 4.

3741. Sparrow, John. "George Herbert and John Donne among the
Moravians." Bulletin of the New York Public Library 68
(1964): 625-53. Discusses John Wesley's use of Donne and
Herbert.

3742. "A Spartan Mother." Temple Bar 115 (1898): 506-15.

3743. Spencer, Harry C. "Story behind John Wesley's Famous Portrait." Together 10, no. 8 (1966): 34-35. Story of the
Frank O. Salisbury portrait of Wesley.

3744.   Spooner, George.   "Some Account of the Gracious Dealings
        of a Merciful God with a Vile Sinner."   Proceedings of the
        Wesley Historical Society 20 (1935): 75-79.   Recounts Wesley's
        visits to Ditcheat, Somerset.

3745.   Stafford, Darby.   "By Pendle Water: In the Land of the
        'Lancashire Witches'."   Methodist Recorder, 14 November 1907,
        11.

3746.   _____.   "A Dead Controversy and a Living Hymn: John
        Wesley and Augustus Toplady."   Methodist Recorder, 12 July
        1906, 9.

3747.   _____.   "In 'David Copperfield's Village'; Blundeston and
        Its Methodism."   Methodist Recorder, 25 January 1906, 9.

3748.   _____.   "John Wesley and Bath: The Great Evangelist and
        'Society' Sinners."   Methodist Recorder, 15 September 1904,
        9-10.

3749.   _____.   "John Wesley and Field Preaching: With Some of
        His Outdoor Pulpits."   Methodist Recorder, 15 August 1907,
        9.

3750.   _____.   "Methodism in Orchard-land: The Past and Present
        of the Evesham Circuit."   Methodist Recorder, 1 October 1903,
        15-19.

3751.   _____.   "Methodism in Shakespeare Land: Round about
        Stratford-on-Avon."   Methodist Recorder, 12 March 1903,
        15-19.

3752.   _____.   "A Notable Last Appearance: John Wesley and the
        Tree at Winchelsea."   Methodist Recorder, 3 December 1908,
        21-22.

3753.   _____.   "Reminiscences of the Newbury Circuit: How the
        Young Preacher Fared in the Old Days."   Methodist Recorder,
        12 October 1905, 11.

3754.   Stamp, John S.   "Note on John Wesley's Primitive Physic."
        Wesleyan Methodist Magazine 68 (1845): 10.

3755.   Stamp, Lord.   "Westley Hall and the Wesley Family."   Pro-
        ceedings of the Wesley Historical Society 22 (1939): 28-31.

3756.   Stamp, William W.   "Methodism in Leicester."   Wesleyan Meth-
        odist Magazine 57 (1834): 102-8.

3757.   Stampe, George.   "The 'Preaching' Portrait of John Wesley."
        Proceedings of the Wesley Historical Society 8 (1911): 1.   The
        painter was John Russel (sic).

3758. _____. "The Rev. Samuel Wesley, M.A., Rector of Epworth." Proceedings of the Wesley Historical Society 11
(1917): 1-7.

3759. "The Standard and the Wesleys." Methodist Recorder, 6
September 1867, 316. Discusses the article in the Standard
which reviews Robert Wright's Memoir of General James
Ogelthorpe, with details about Wesley in Georgia.

3760. Stanger, Frank Bateman. "The Reopening of John Wesley's
City Road Chapel: A Call for Methodist Renewal." Method-
ist History 17, no. 3 (1979): 178-99. Also appeared in
Asbury Seminarian 34, no. 1 (1979): 3-22.

3761. Staples, Rob L. "Sanctification and Selfhood: A Phenome-
nological Analysis of the Wesleyan Message." Wesleyan
Theological Journal 7 (1972): 3-16.

3762. Starkey, Lycurgus M., Jr. "The Holy Spirit and the Wesleyan Witness." Religion in Life 49 (1980): 72-80.

3763. Stead, W. T. "St. John of England: On the Centenary of
the Death of John Wesley, March 2nd, 1891." Review of Reviews 3 (1891): 282-93.

3764. _____. "The Wesley Centenary." Review of Reviews 3
(1891): 246. A review of articles written on behalf of the
centenary of Wesley's death.

3765. Stephenson, John. "The Doctrine of Christian Holiness As
Taught by John Wesley." Primitive Methodist Quarterly Review, n.s. 4 (1882): 697-705; 5 (1883): 90-97, 450-65.

3766. Stephenson, T. Bowman. "John Wesley." Sunday Magazine,
n.s. 20 (1891): 159-64, 252-58.

3767. _____. "Wesley Centenary Papers--Wesley Chapel."
Methodist Recorder, 22 January 1891, 65.

3768. Stevens, Abel. "John Wesley and the Church." Methodist
Quarterly Review 44 (1862): 41-61. Discusses Wesley's re-
lationships to the Church of England and the Protestant
Episcopal Church.

3769. Stevens, William Bacon. "The Church in Georgia Before the
Revolution--The Wesleys and Whitefield in Georgia." Church
Review 46 (1885): 1-15.

3770. Stevenson, George John. "City Road Chapel--a Few Historical Notes." Methodist Recorder, 8 November 1878, 661.

3771. _____. "John Wesley and Luther." Methodist Recorder, 9 November 1883, 826.

3772. _____. "John Wesley and Oxford Methodism." Methodist Recorder, 29 December 1876, 741.

3773. _____. "Wesley and Wellington." Methodist Recorder, 9 March 1877, 131.

3774. Stevenson, R. T. "An Eighteenth Century Club." Bibliotheca Sacra 54 (1897): 66-85. Discusses impact of Wesley's Holy Club.

3775. Stevenson, Robert M. "John Wesley's First Hymnbook." Review of Religion 14 (1950): 140-60. A discussion of his Collection of Psalms and Hymns, 1737, Charleston, South Carolina, and later editions. The author of the article claims that "John Wesley was the instigator and, throughout, the controlling influence in the outburst of Evangelical song."

3776. Stewart, David. "John Wesley, the Physician." Wesleyan Theological Journal 4 (1969): 27-38.

3777. Stewart, William. "A Methodist Shrine." Methodist Magazine 151 (1928): 401-4. Discusses Wesley's house on City Road, London.

3778. Stillings, Dennis. "John Wesley: Philosopher of Electricity." Medical Instrumentation 7 (1973): 307.

3779. Stoeffler, F. Ernest. "The Wesleyan Concept of Religious Certainty--Its Prehistory and Significance." London Quarterly and Holborn Review 33 (1964): 128-39.

3780. Stokes, Durward T. "The Baptist and Methodist Clergy in South Carolina and the American Revolution." South Carolina Historical Magazine 73 (1972): 87-96.

3781. "The Story of Wesley's Book-Room: Origin and Growth of the Methodist Publishing House." Methodist Recorder, 10 December 1908, 9-10.

3782. Stoughton, John. "John Wesley's Sermons Preached on His Father's Tombstone." United Methodist Free Churches' Magazine 30 (1887): 385-87.

3783. Strawson, William. "Wesley's Doctrine of the Last Things." London Quarterly and Holborn Review 184 (1959): 240-49. Considers Wesley's views on eschatology.

3784. _____. "Wesley's Two-fold Belief about the Church. 1 -
       The Gospel. 2 - Unity of the Church." Methodist Recorder,
       16 March 1961, 9; 23 March 1961, 11.

3785. Strickling, George F. "Charles Wesley--The Indomitable!"
       Choral and Organ Guide 6, no. 3 (1953): 30-31.

3786. _____. "Wesley's Greatest Hymn." Choral and Organ
       Guide 7, no. 8 (1954): 21-22. The story of "Wrestling Ja-
       cob." Reprinted in the same journal, 20 (1967): 12-13.

3787. Stringer, J. Harrison. "Promise of Sanctification; a Study
       in a Famous Wesley Passage." London Quarterly and Holborn
       Review 180 (1955): 26-30.

3788. Strobe, Donald B. "When John Wesley Preached on Sin He
       Called It Original." Christian Advocate 5, no. 10 (1961):
       5-6.'

3789. Studwell, William E. "Glory to the New-Born King!" Journal
       of Church Music 21, no. 10 (1979): 2-6. Concerns the origin
       of "Hark the Herald Angels Sing."

3790. "Suburban Surrey: The Past and Present of the Sutton Cir-
       cuit." Methodist Recorder, 26 September 1907, 9.

3791. Sugden, Edward H. "John Wesley at Oxford." Proceedings
       of the Wesley Historical Society 18 (1932): 169-72. Repro-
       duces a letter from his mother with commentary.

3792. _____. "Samuel Wesley's Notes on Shakespeare." London
       Quarterly Review 139 (1923): 157-72. This is Samuel Wesley
       III, son of Charles Wesley. There are references in the ar-
       ticle to John and the other Wesleys.

3793. Sullivan, Ponsonby. "Church and Religion in England, 1660-
       1880." Church Quarterly Review 120 (1935): 38-53.

3794. Supplee, G. William. "Charles Wesley: Persecuted Hymn
       Writer." Eternity 21, no. 10 (1970): 36.

3795. Surtees, H. W. "Wesley's Will and the Conference." Pro-
       ceedings of the Wesley Historical Society 17 (1930): 134-35.

3796. "Susanna Wesley." Boston Review 5 (1865): 586-604. Dis-
       cusses Kirk's The Mother of the Wesleys, no. 969.

3797. "Susanna Wesley." Saturday Review 62 (1886): 555-57. A
       review of the book by Eliza Clarke, 1886, no. 352.

3798. Sutherland, Allan. "Famous Hymns of the World: 'Jesus,
       Lover of My Soul.'" Delineator 65 (1905): 76-78.

3799. Sweet, Leonard I. "The Four Fundamentalisms of Oldline
       Protestants." Christian Century 102 (1985): 266-70.

3800. Sweet, William W. "John Wesley and Scientific Discovery."
       Christian Century 40 (1923): 591-92. Discusses Wesley's
       attitude toward Franklin's discovery regarding electricity.

3801. _____. "John Wesley in Ireland." Methodist Review 106
       (1923): 380-91.

3802. _____. "John Wesley--Stained Glass Saint or Living
       Prophet?" Christian Century 53 (1936): 1197. This is a re-
       view of Umphrey Lee's John Wesley and Modern Religion,
       no. 1018.

3803. _____. "John Wesley, Tory." Methodist Quarterly Re-
       view 71 (1922): 255-68.

3804. Sweringen, H. V. "Rev. John Wesley As a Physician."
       Cincinnati Lancet-Clinic, n.s. 46 (1901): 238.

3805. Swift, Wesley F. "Brothers Charles and John." London
       Quarterly and Holborn Review 182 (1957): 275-80.

3806. _____. "Early Aberdeen Methodism." Proceedings of the
       Wesley Historical Society 16 (1928): 118-22.

3807. _____. "Early Methodism in Dumfries." Proceedings of
       the Wesley Historical Society 21 (1937): 68-74.

3808. _____. "Early Methodism in Edinburgh." Proceedings of
       the Wesley Historical Society 17 (1929): 78-86.

3809. _____. "Early Methodism in Northwich." Proceedings of
       the Wesley Historical Society 22 (1939): 38-45.

3810. _____. "'Feed the Lambs' at Haverfordwest: A New Wes-
       ley Letter." Proceedings of the Wesley Historical Society 30
       (1956): 132-33.

3811. _____. "Five Wesley Letters." Proceedings of the Wesley
       Historical Society 33 (1961): 11-16. Letters to Asbury, Peard
       Dickenson, Brian Bury Collins, John Watson, and John Elli-
       son, with comments.

3812. _____. "John Wesley at Perth." Proceedings of the Wesley
       Historical Society 28 (1951): 28-29.

3813. _____. "John Wesley's Lectionary with Notes on Some La-
       ter Methodist Lectionaries." London Quarterly and Holborn
       Review 183 (1958): 298-304. Presents a discussion of the

Book of Common Prayer and John Wesley's Sunday Service of the Methodists.

3814. _____. "Methodism in Allendale." Wesleyan Methodist Magazine 95 (1872): 710-19.

3815. _____. "Portraits and Biographies of Charles Wesley." Proceedings of the Wesley Historical Society 31 (1957): 86-92.

3816. _____. "The Sunday Service of the Methodists." Proceedings of the Wesley Historical Society 29 (1953): 12-20.

3817. _____. "Three Unpublished Letters from John Wesley to His Wife." Proceedings of the Wesley Historical Society 27 (1949): 58-62.

3818. _____. "Three Wesley Letters." Proceedings of the Wesley Historical Society 32 (1960): 186-89. Letters to John Stretton, Elizabeth Padbury, and Jane Hilton, with commentary.

3819. _____. "Wesley and Scottish Methodism." Proceedings of the Wesley Historical Society 18 (1931): 1-6.

3820. _____. "Wesley Chapel, Whitby." Proceedings of the Wesley Historical Society 21 (1938): 168-73.

3821. _____. "Wesley in Keith, and Dr. Ha." Proceedings of the Wesley Historical Society 16 (1927): 63-65.

3822. _____. "Wesley Went to Scotland Two Hundred Years Ago." Methodist Recorder, 19 April 1951, 4.

3823. T. "Observations on Long Sermons." Wesleyan Methodist Magazine 56 (1833): 852-54.

3824. T., E. "On the Perfection of the Spiritual Life." Wesleyan Methodist Magazine 67 (1844): 36-45, 106-13, 208-17.

3825. T., J. "Wesley's First 'Plan' for London." Methodist Recorder, 11 June 1903, 11.

3826. T., J. E. "John Wesley's Cosmogony." Westminster Review 94 (1870): 306-21. Discusses Methodism's antagonism to science, asserting that it is always opposed to scientific progress, that it exhibits a "horror of science and free inquiry."

3827. T., R. A. "Notes on Some Bristol Conferences: A Study in Methodist Evolution." Methodist Recorder, 20 July 1905, 17-19.

Articles   301

3828. Taberer, Alfred A. "Uncle and Nephew: Samuel Wesley,
       Junior's Comments on John." Proceedings of the Wesley His-
       torical Society 32 (1960): 140-41.

3829. Tasker, John G. "John Wesley As Physician: An Apprecia-
       tion by G. Gisler." Proceeding of the Wesley Historical So-
       ciety 16 (1928): 141-44.

3830. Taylor, A. E. "St. John of the Cross and John Wesley."
       Journal of Theological Studies 46 (1945): 30-38.

3831. Taylor, Alva W. "John Wesley's Social Work." Christian
       Evangelist 40 (1903): 330.

3832. Taylor, George. "Mr. Wesley in Early Life: A Letter."
       Wesleyan Methodist Magazine 55 (1832): 793.

3833. Taylor, H. J. "Wesley's Last Open Air Sermon." Methodist
       Magazine 160 (1937): 674-75.

3834. Taylor, James P. "The Capital of West Cornwall: Penzance
       and Its Methodism." Methodist Recorder, 19 October 1905,
       13.

3835. Taylor, Philip H. "Padiham Circuit: A Scene of Very Early
       Methodist Activity." Methodist Recorder, 14 February 1907,
       9.

3836. Taylor, Robert A. "Barley Hall: A Yorkshire Haunt of John
       Wesley." Methodist Recorder, 28 May 1903, 11.

3837. Teeter, Herman B. "Mr. Wesley and the Tax Collector."
       Together 7, no. 5 (1963): 33. Tells how Wesley responded to
       a tax collector when asked about his silverplate.

3838. _____. "That Man Wesley." Together 7, no. 10 (1963):
       45. This brief article deals with the forcefulness of Wesley's
       preaching.

3839. Telford, John. "An Ancient Spa: Tunbridge Wells and Its
       Methodism." Methodist Recorder, 16 June 1904, 11-12.

3840. _____. "Beautiful Surrey: Wesley and His Successors in
       the Dorking and Horsham Circuit." Methodist Recorder, 9
       July 1903, 15-19.

3841. _____. "Cardinal Newman and John Wesley: A Comparison
       and a Contrast." Sunday Magazine n.s. 20 (1891): 331-36.

3842. _____. "Dean Hutton on John Wesley." London Quarterly
       Review 148 (1927): 96-102. A review of Hutton's book on
       Wesley, no. 890.

3843. _____. "John Wesley in Marylebone." Quiver 22 (1887):
159-62, 207-9.

3844. _____. "John Wesley in Training." Methodist Review 112
(1929): 9-19. Tells of John Wesley's days at Charterhouse,
Christ Church, and Lincoln College.

3845. _____. "John Wesley's School at Kingswood." Methodist
Review 81 (1899): 410-20.

3846. _____. "Methodism, a Providential Mosaic." Wesleyan
Methodist Church Record 1 (1892): 280-81, 292-94.

3847. _____. "Methodism in West Central London: West Street
Chapel and Its Associations." Wesleyan Methodist Magazine
108 (1885): 111-20, 202-10, 280-87.

3848. _____. "New Light on Wesley's Character." London Quarterly Review 113 (1910): 1-21.

3849. _____. "Nottingham and the Wesleys." Methodist Recorder,
25 June 1891, 477; 2 July 1891, 497.

3850. _____. "An Old Bristol Weekly." Methodist Recorder, 17
July 1890, 493. An account of John Wesley's marriage.

3851. _____. "On Editing Wesley's Letters." London Quarterly
Review 156 (1931): 145-58.

3852. _____. "Plymouth and the Wesleys." Church Record 22
(1913): 167.

3853. _____. "Some Facts about Bradford." Methodist Recorder,
23 June 1902, 433; 30 June 1892, 450; 7 July 1892, 466; 14
July 1892, 494.

3854. _____. "Some Notes on Derby." Methodist Recorder, 30
July 1891, 573.

3855. _____. "Wesley and His Preachers in Newark. Methodist
Recorder, 16 July 1891, 528-29.

3856. _____. "Wesley Day: Its Threefold Claim." Methodist
Recorder, 21 May 1931, 12. Discusses the Wesleys' conversion
and Pentecost.

3857. _____. "Wesley's Interest in Life." Wesleyan Methodist
Magazine 126 (1903): 414-21.

3858. _____. "Wesley's Room in Lincoln College." London Quarterly Review 152 (1929): 250-53.

3859.   Thickens, John, and C. Ryder Smith. "The Wesleys and
        Others." Times Literary Supplement 25 December 1943, 619.
        Letters to the editor concerning Dilks's article, no. 2506.

3860.   Thiessen, Carol R. "John Wesley Alive!" Christianity Today
        25, no. 17 (1981): 84. Reviews the play The Man from Al-
        dersgate, no. 4559.

3861.   Thomas, Burton G. "John Wesley on the Art of Healing."
        American Physician (Rahway, N.J.) 32 (1906): 295-98.
        Criticizes Wesley's Primitive Physick.

3862.   Thomas, Gilbert. "George Fox and John Wesley." Methodist
        Recorder, 10 April 1924, 11.

3863.   _____. "John Wesley." Quarterly Review 261 (1933):
        320-35. Review article of recent books on Wesley.

3864.   Thomas, John Wesley. "Original Anecdote of John Wesley."
        Wesleyan Methodist Magazine 88 (1865): 915-16. Relates the
        story of Wesley's last visit to Exeter and his attempt to
        quiet a crying infant.

3865.   _____. "Reminiscences of Methodism in Exeter." Wesleyan
        Methodist Magazine 94 (1871): 229-37.

3866.   Thompson, Claude H. "Aldersgate and the New Reformers."
        Christian Advocate 6, no. 10 (1962): 7-8.

3867.   _____. "Wesley's Doctrines of Christian Perfection." To-
        gether 6, no. 5 (1962): 45-47.

3868.   Thompson, Edgar W. "Episcopacy: John Wesley's View."
        London Quarterly and Holborn Review 181 (1956): 113-17.

3869.   _____. "John Wesley, Superintendent." London Quarterly
        and Holborn Review 184 (1959): 325-30. Discusses Wesley's
        choice of the word "superintendent" over "bishop."

3870.   _____. "Wesley's Famous Saying--'Church or No Church.'"
        Proceedings of the Wesley Historical Society 22 (1940): 105-7.

3871.   Thompson, Peter. "The Works of Methodism: Methodism and
        the Masses." Methodist Recorder, 5 March 1891, 171.

3872.   Thornley, J. "John Wesley's Views on Temperance." United
        Methodist Free Churches' Magazine 29 (1886): 423-25.

3873.   Tibbetts, Kenneth. "Methodism in Berwick-upon-Tweed."
        Proceedings of the Wesley Historical Society 33 (1962): 161-
        69.

3874. Tildesley, J. C. "John Wesley in Ireland." Methodist Recorder, 9 April 1896, 237; 16 April 1896, 252.

3875. _____. "The Recreation of John Wesley." Quiver 28 (1893): 57-61. Describes some of the simple activities that provided pleasure to John Wesley.

3876. Tindall, Edwin H. "Methodism in Manchester." Methodist Recorder, 2 February 1883, 69.

3877. Tippett, Alan R. "The Church Which Is His Body." Missiology 2 (1974): 147-59. The author indicates that for this article he needed a theologian to compare with the physical anthropologist, so he selected John Wesley.

3878. Todd, John M. "John Wesley." Jubilee 6, no. 9 (1959): 40-43.

3879. _____. "John Wesley's Legacy." Commonweal 64 (1956): 369-70.

3880. Towlson, Clifford W. "Early Days of the Methodist Church and Its Impact on Nineteenth Century England." Methodist Recorder; Wesley Bicentennial Supplement, 19 May 1938, vi-vii.

3881. "'Town and Gown' Salutes Wesley Memorial." Methodist Recorder, 30 May 1968, 7. Celebration of 150th year of Wesley Memorial Church, Oxford.

3882. Towns, Elmer L. "John Wesley and Religious Education." Religious Education 65 (1970): 318-28.

3883. Tracy, Wesley. "Christian Education in the Wesleyan Mode." Wesleyan Theological Journal 17, no. 1 (1982): 30-53. See response by J. Duane Beals, no. 2106.

3884. _____. "J. W. and the Kids." Preacher's Magazine 58, no. 1 (1982): 2-4, 37. Discusses Wesley's interest and work with Christian education.

3885. "A Tradition concerning John Wesley." Old Cornwall 4 (1946): 140-41. Discusses a traditional rhyme about a dangerous crossing by Wesley between Hayle and Lelant.

3886. Tralascia, F. "Saint Francis of Protestantism." Methodist Review 109 (1926): 925-28. A discussion of St. Francis of Assisi and John Wesley.

3887. Trethewey, W. "St. Austell: A Typical Cornish Circuit." Methodist Recorder, 9 May 1912, 10.

3888. Trickett, Rachel. "To Instruct and Inflame." Times Literary
       Supplement, 21 December 1984, 1467-68. Review of Richard
       E. Brantley's Locke, Wesley, and the Method of English Ro-
       manticism, no. 215, and vol. 7 of Wesley's Works, Oxford
       edition, no. 819.

3889. Troughton, Marion. "Lesser Brother." Contemporary Review
       211 (1967): 314-18. An article discussing Charles Wesley and
       his hymns.

3890. True, C. K. "Wesleyan Methodism." North American Review
       90 (1860): 181-205.

3891. Truscott, John. "Wesley's Chapel, City Road, London."
       Methodist Monthly 16 (1907): 269-73.

3892. Tsoumas, George J. "Methodism and Bishop Erasmus."
       Greek Orthodox Theological Review 2, no. 2 (1956): 62-73.
       This article contends that Erasmus was not a canonical bishop
       of the Greek Orthodox Church.

3893. Turner, Ewart Edmund. "John Wesley and Mysticism."
       Methodist Review 113 (1930): 16-31.

3894. Turner, J. Arthur. "The Expansion of Bolton Methodism."
       Methodist Recorder, 15 October 1908, 12.

3895. _____. "In a Methodist County: Some Leaves of Early
       Louth Methodism." Methodist Recorder, 1 December 1904,
       9-10.

3896. Turner, J. Munsey. "John Wesley, People's Theologian."
       One in Christ 14 (1978): 328-39.

3897. Turney, Thomas A. "Methodism in Stockton." Wesleyan
       Methodist Church Record 16 (1907): 123-24.

3898. Turrell, W. J. "Three Electrotherapists of the Eighteenth
       Century: John Wesley, Jean Paul Marat and James Graham."
       Annals of Medical History 3 (1921): 361-67.

3899. "Two Christmas Days: John Wesley aboard the 'Simmonds'
       and the 'Samuel.'" Methodist Recorder, 5 December 1935, 7.

3900. "250th Birthday." Time 62 (6 July 1953): 52-53. John Wes-
       ley's 250th birthday celebration in Philadelphia.

3901. Tyerman, Luke. "Early Methodism and the Established
       Church." Methodist Recorder, 10 March 1871, 111. Extracts
       from Tyerman's biography of Wesley, no. 1722.

3902. _____. "The Life and Character of Wesley." Methodist Recorder, 23 June 1871, 329. Extracts from his biography, no. 1722.

3903. Tyson, John R. "Charles Wesley and the German Hymns." Hymn 35 (1984): 153-57.

3904. _____. "John Wesley and William Law: A Reappraisal." Wesleyan Theological Journal 17, no. 2 (1982): 58-78.

3905. Tyson, John R., and Douglas Lister. "Charles Wesley, Pastor: A Glimpse Inside His Shorthand Journal." Quarterly Review (Nashville) 4, no. 2 (1984): 9-21. Describes the pastoral side of Charles Wesley as revealed through a recent discovery of a manuscript fragment of his Journal, found in the Methodist Archives at the John Rylands Library, Manchester.

3906. "Unveiling of the Statue." Methodist Recorder, 5 March 1891, 186-87. Reports on the ceremony of the unveiling of Wesley's statue in London, done by Adams Acton.

3907. Urlin, R. Denny. "The Centenary of John Wesley's Death." Newbery House Magazine 4 (1891): 257-65.

3908. Urwin, E. C. "The 'Warmed Heart' and Its Social Consequences." London Quarterly and Holborn Review 163 (1938): 211-14.

3909. V. "A John Wesley Find." Notes and Queries 179 (1940): 67-68. Comments on T.C.C.'s note, see no. 2351.

3910. V., A. T. "Epworth a Century Ago." Methodist Magazine 143 (1920): 289.

3911. Van Pelt, John Robert. "The Eucharistic Hymns of the Wesleys." Religion in Life 22 (1953): 449-54.

3912. Van Valin, Howard F. "Mysticism in Wesley." Asbury Seminarian 12, no. 2 (1958): 3-14.

3913. Verax. "Mr. Wesley's Attachment to the Church." Primitive Wesleyan Methodist Magazine 13 (1835): 255-58.

3914. Vickers, John A. "Gibbes Family of Hilton Park, an Unpublished Correspondence of John Wesley." Methodist History 6, no. 3 (1968): 43-61.

3915. _____. "The John Wesley Conversion Place Memorial." Proceedings of the Wesley Historical Society 43 (1981): 27-28. This memorial was placed outside the Museum of London.

3916. _____. "John Wesley's Third London Chapel." Proceedings of the Wesley Historical Society 43 (1981): 59-61. This chapel was known as Snowsfields Chapel.

3917. _____. "Lambeth Palace Library: Some Items of Methodist Interest from the Fulham Papers." Methodist History 9, no. 4 (1971): 22-29. Describes correspondence in the Fulham Papers dealing with John Wesley and his Georgia experience.

3918. _____. "Notes and Quotes. John Wesley and Robert Hall, Junior." Methodist History 8, no. 1 (1969): 87-88.

3919. _____. "Notes on Wesley's Visits to Taunton, Sept. 1743 and Sept. 1775." Proceedings of the Wesley Historical Society 30 (1956): 186-87.

3920. _____. "On Indexing John Wesley." Indexer 11 (1979): 189-97.

3921. Vine, Victor E. "Catchwords of 'The Conversations.' 3. Episcopacy." Proceedings of the Wesley Historical Society 34 (1964): 167-69.

3922. _____. "'Episcopé' in Methodism." Proceedings of the Wesley Historical Society 30 (1956): 162-70.

3923. _____. "John Wesley, Ordinary." Proceedings of the Wesley Historical Society 32 (1960): 190-91. Discusses Wesley's appointment to serve in Georgia.

3924. _____. "Wesley, King and Coke." Proceedings of the Wesley Historical Society 31 (1957-58): 65-70, 102-3, 147-48.

3925. "A Visit to the Grave of John Wesley." Sunday at Home 1 (1854): 334-35.

3926. Voight, A. G. "John Wesley and the Salzburgers." Lutheran Quarterly 27 (1897): 370-76. Makes a case that it was the Moravians not the Salzburgers who influenced Wesley.

3926a. Vulgamore, Melvin L. "Wesley and Tillich in the Legalistic Influence of Justification." Rocky Mountain Review 2, no. 1 (1964-65): 35-47.

3927. W., H. D. "Good-natured Gravesend: Methodism in a Famous River-side Town." Methodist Recorder, 12 May 1910, 12.

3928. W., J. "The Naval and Garrison Church of the West: Sunday School Centenary at Devonport." Methodist Recorder, 18 May 1911, 10.

3929. W., J. G. "Methodism in Wolverhampton." Methodist Recorder 13 February 1902, 13-15.

3930. W., J. P. "A Plant of Slow Growth: Methodism in Southampton." Methodist Recorder, 26 April 1906, 9.

3931. W., N. "A Wesley Memorial Church at Kingswood." Methodist Monthly 16 (1907): 188-90.

3932. W., T. A. "Methodism in the Highland Capital: The Story of the Inverness Church." Methodist Recorder, 20 January 1910, 9.

3933. Waddy, J. Leonard. "The First Meeting-House in Wednesbury." Proceedings of the Wesley Historical Society 42 (1979): 24-27.

3934. Wakefield, Gordon S. "John Wesley: Post-Reformation Spirituality." Month, 2d n.s. 8 (1975): 293-96.

3935. _____. "Methodist Spirituality." One in Christ 2 (1966): 251-65. This is an overview of the influences on Wesley's spirituality--Anglicanism, Puritanism, mysticism.

3936. Wakinshaw, William. "A Fruitful Bough: Methodism Up and Down Teesdale." Methodist Recorder, 14 January 1909, 12.

3937. _____. "A Gem of English Scenery: Swaledale and Its Methodism." Methodist Recorder, 3 January 1907, 9.

3938. _____. "A Haunt of Methodism: Danby and Its Dales." Methodist Recorder, 28 February 1907, 9.

3939. _____. "The Hull Mission: A Methodist Story in Four Chapters." Methodist Recorder, 29 December 1904, 9-10.

3940. _____. "London's Links with Wesley." United Methodist Magazine 3 (1910): 122-24.

3941. _____. "Methodism in Lancaster." Methodist Recorder, 13 November 1902, 13-15.

3942. _____. "The Newcastle District." Wesleyan Methodist Magazine 150 (1927): 362-67.

3943. _____. "Picturesque Wensleydale: A Methodist Stronghold." Methodist Recorder, 19 March 1908, 9.

3944. _____. "Two Old Fortresses: Yarm and Osmotherley." Methodist Recorder, 15 August 1907, 10.

Articles   309

3945. _____. "Under the Clevelands: Methodism in the Stokes-
ley Circuit." Methodist Recorder, 21 May 1908, 11.

3946. _____. "Wesley and Newcastle." Wesleyan Methodist Magazine 161 (1938): 276-79.

3947. _____. "Wesley's Links with Bristol." Wesleyan Methodist
Magazine 138 (1915): 923-28.

3948. _____. "Wesley's Orphan House." Wesleyan Methodist
Magazine 155 (1932): 536-39.

3949. Walker, Clayton. "Sunshineland: Wesleyan Methodism in
Torquay." Methodist Recorder, 17 September 1903, 17-24.

3950. Wallace, Charles. "Simple and Recollected: John Wesley's
Life-Style." Religion in Life 46 (1977): 198-212. Discusses
Wesley's attitude toward diet, work, sleep, leisure, medicine,
and wealth.

3951. Wallace, Charles, Jr. "Susanna Wesley's Spirituality: The
Freedom of a Christian Woman." Methodist History 22, no.
3 (1984): 158-73.

3952. Waller, Dr. "Wesley's Footsteps in Savannah." Methodist
Recorder, 14 March 1901, 6.

3953. Waller, John. "Wesley and His Friend the High Sheriff."
Wesleyan Methodist Magazine 109 (1886): 591-94. The high
sheriff was a Mr. Cole, and the towns of Sundon and Luton
are mentioned.

3954. Wallington, Arthur. "Romney's Portrait of Wesley." Proceedings of the Wesley Historical Society 13 (1922): 182-84.

3955. _____. "Wesley and Anne Dutton." Proceedings of the
Wesley Historical Society 11 (1917): 43-48.

3956. _____. "Wesley, Benson and Grotius." Proceedings of
the Wesley Historical Society 10 (1915): 113-15.

3957. _____. "Wesley's London 'Retreats'." Proceedings of the
Wesley Historical Society 10 (1915): 84-85. Concerns Newington House and Highbury House.

3958. Walls, Jerry L. "The Free Will Defense: Calvinism, Wesley
and the Goodness of God." Christian Scholar's Review 13
(1983): 19-33.

3959. _____. "John Wesley's Critique of Martin Luther."
Methodist History 20, no. 1 (1981): 29-41.

3960. Wallwork, Norman. "Hymns on the Lord's Supper." Proceedings of the Wesley Historical Society 43 (1982): 92-94. This is a review of Burton's The Richest Legacy, no. 267.

3961. Walmsley, Robert. "John Wesley's Parents: Quarrel and Reconciliation." Proceedings of the Wesley Historical Society 29 (1953): 50-57. First appeared in the Manchester Guardian, 2 and 3 July 1953.

3962. Walsh, John D. "Elie Halévy and the Birth of Methodism." Transactions of the Royal Historical Society 5th ser., 25 (1975): 1-20.

3963. Walters, Orville S. "The Concept of Attainment in John Wesley's Christian Perfection." Methodist History 10, no. 3 (1972): 12-29.

3964. _____. "John Wesley's Footnotes to Christian Perfection." Methodist History 12, no. 1 (1973): 19-36.

3965. Walters, Stanley D. "Strange Fires: A Biblical Allusion in John Wesley's Hymns." Methodist History 17, no. 1 (1978): 44-58.

3966. Walton, Albert N. "Early Methodism in Bridport." Proceedings of the Wesley Historical Society 24 (1943): 64-69.

3967. _____. "Wesley and Winchelsea." Proceedings of the Wesley Historical Society 13 (1922): 135-38.

3968. Walton, Sydney. "Darlington Methodism: The Centenary of Bondgate." Methodist Recorder, 19 June 1913, 9.

3969. Wansbrough, Charles E. "Notes on Wesley's Deed Poll." Proceedings of the Wesley Historical Society 1 (1897): 39-41.

3970. Ward, J. D. U. "The Furniture of John Wesley's House." Antiques 33 (1938): 192-94.

3971. Wardle, W. Lansdell. "The Lay Preacher." London Quarterly and Holborn Review 163 (1938): 196-98.

3972. Ware, Thomas. "The Christmas Conference of 1784." Methodist Magazine and Quarterly Review 14 (1832): 96-104.

3973. Warnick, Mrs. John. "Four Unpublished Letters of John Wesley." Perkins School of Theology Journal 13, no. 2 (1960): 28-32. Letters to Peard Dickinson, Francis Asbury, John Collins, and John Watson.

3974. "Was John Wesley the Founder of American Methodism?" Methodist Review 73 (1891): 618-23.

3975.   Watchurst, Percy L. "Francis of Assisi and John Wesley."
        Wesleyan Methodist Magazine 128 (1905): 484-86.

3976.   Watkin-Jones, Howard. "Two Oxford Movements: Wesley
        and Newman." Hibbert Journal 31 (1932): 83-96.

3977.   Watkins, Howell A. "Did Wesley Really Mean Four A.M.?"
        Together 8, no. 8 (1964): 39-41. Advocates Wesley's habit
        of rising early.

3978.   Watkinson, W. L. "The Work of Methodism - Methodism and
        Literature." Methodist Recorder, 5 March 1891, 172.

3978a. Watson, David Lowes. "Christ Our Righteousness: The
        Center of Wesley's Evangelistic Message." Perkins Journal
        37, no. 3 (1984): 34-47.

3979.   _____. "Spiritual Formation in Ministerial Training; the
        Wesley Paradigm: Mutual Accountability." Christian Century
        102 (1985): 122-24. Describes the adaptation of Wesley's
        class meeting to the curriculum at Perkins School of Theology.

3980.   Watson, Philip S. "Pentecost at Aldersgate." Central Chris-
        tian Advocate 137, no. 9 (1962): 5-7.

3981.   _____. "Wesley and Luther on Christian Perfection."
        Ecumenical Review 15 (1963): 291-302.

3982.   "The Way of the Warmed Heart: Aldersgate Year, 1963, Com-
        memorates an Event of Supreme Importance in the Life of
        Methodism's Founder." Together 7, no. 5 (1963): 35-45.

3983.   Wearmouth, Robert F. "The First Methodist Conference,
        June 25-30, 1744." London Quarterly and Holborn Review
        169 (1944): 205-10.

3984.   Weaver, Edward. "Wesley and Charterhouse School."
        Wesleyan Methodist Magazine 135 (1912): 936-41.

3985.   Weaver, Sampson. "Wesley and Wordsworth." Wesleyan
        Methodist Magazine 127 (1904): 835-37.

3986.   Webb, James R., Jr. "The Young John Wesley--A New Monu-
        ment." Methodist History 8, no. 2 (1970): 33-35. Describes
        the new John Wesley monument dedicated Sunday, August 3,
        1969, in Savannah, Georgia.

3987.   Wedley, John F. "An Ancient Royal Burgh: The History of
        Bewdley and Its Methodism." Methodist Recorder, 22 Novem-
        ber 1906, 10.

3988. _____. "Methodism in Stourport: A Beauty Spot Near the
      Black Country." Methodist Recorder, 26 April 1906, 10.

3989. Weinstein, Alfred A. "John Wesley, Physician and Apothe-
      cary." Georgia Review 10 (1956): 48-54. The author claims
      that Wesley influenced enormously the practice of medicine in
      England.

3990. Welch, Edwin. "The Early Methodists and Their Records."
      Journal of the Society of Archivists 4 (1971): 200-211.

3991. _____. "A Forgotten Thread in Congregational History:
      The Calvinistic Methodists." Congregational Historical Society
      Transactions 21 (1972): 84-93.

3992. Wesley, L. H. Wellesley. "The Wesley Coat of Arms." Pro-
      ceedings of the Wesley Historical Society 1 (1898): 97-100.

3993. Wesley, Sarah. "Some Account of Mrs. Sarah Wesley,
      Relict ... of Charles Wesley...." Wesleyan Methodist Maga-
      zine 46 (1823): 506-11. The Sarah Wesley who wrote this
      article was the daughter of Sarah Wesley, widow of Charles.

3994. "Wesley and Leatherhead." Methodist Recorder, 6 October
      1904, 15.

3995. "Wesley and Methodism." Eclectic Review, n.s. 4 (1852):
      15-36. A review of Isaac Taylor's book Wesley and Methodism,
      no. 1635.

3996. "Wesley and Methodism." North British Review 16 (1852):
      506-36. A review of Isaac Taylor's book Wesley and Method-
      ism, no. 1635.

3997. "Wesley and Modern Philosophy." Methodist Quarterly Review
      61 (1879): 5-21, 205-23.

3998. "Wesley and Music." British Musician 12 (1935): 276-81.

3999. "Wesley and the American Revolution." Primitive Methodist
      Quarterly Review, n.s. 3 (1881): 325-36.

4000. "Wesley and the Press." Christian Advocate (Belfast), 22
      February 1918, 31; 8 March 1918, 39; 15 March 1918, 43;
      22 March 1918, 47; 5 April 1918, iii; 12 April 1918, iii; 26
      April 1918, 67.

4001. "Wesley and Wesleyanism." British Quarterly Review 54
      (1871): 417-60.

4002. "Wesley and Whitefield Contrasted." Wesleyan Methodist
      Magazine 70 (1847): 985-90.

4003. "Wesley and William Cudworth." Proceedings of the Wesley Historical Society 12 (1919): 34-36.

4004. "Wesley at His Birthplace." Methodist Weekly (Manchester) 3, no. 33 (1903): 4-5.

4005. "Wesley Chapel, Reading; Local Methodist History." Methodist Recorder, 21 July 1888, 510.

4006. "Wesley Day at Wesley's Chapel." Methodist Recorder, 30 May 1963, 3.

4007. "The Wesley Family." Museum of Foreign Literature and Science 23 (1933): 379-88.

4008. "The Wesley Family Ghost." All the Year Round, n.s. 8 (1872): 199-204.

4009. "The Wesley Handstamp (1973)." Black Country Man 7 (Spring 1974): 47-48. Contains a letter to the editor by J. T. Aungiers.

4010. "Wesley--His Messages and His Methods." Methodist Monthly 12 (1903): 163-64.

4011. "Wesley Letters Discovered among Treasures in City Road." Methodist Recorder, 17 October 1963, 14.

4012. "Wesley, Methodism, the Church." Church Review 24 (1872): 564-95.

4013. "Wesley on Wealth." Methodist Weekly (Manchester) 3, no. 33 (1903): 1.

4014. "Wesley Preaching-Places Near Manchester." Methodist Recorder, 18 January 1906, 16.

4015. "Wesleyan Methodism." English Review 8 (1847): 314-53.

4016. "Wesleyan Methodism on the 'Witness of the Spirit.'" Quarterly Christian Spectator 9 (1837): 169-93.

4017. "Wesleys and Westminster." Methodist Recorder, 11 June 1903, 10.

4018. "Wesley's Chapel, City Road: By Our Own Commissioner." Methodist Monthly 1 (1892): 202-7.

4019. "Wesley's Character and Opinions in Early Life." London Quarterly Review 37 (1871-72): 298-345. A critique of Southey and others on their appraisals of Wesley's character.

4020. "Wesley's Demeanour in a Riot at Wednesbury." United
       Methodist Free Churches' Magazine 34 (1891): 140-42.

4021. "Wesley's Electricity." Scientific American 64 (1891): 210.
       Ridicules Wesley's Desideratum; or, Electricity Made
       Plain.

4022. "Wesley's First Conference." Methodist Recorder, 23 July
       1867, 245.

4023. "Wesley's House: By Our Own Commissioner." Methodist
       Monthly 1 (1892): 265-68.

4024. "Wesley's 'New Room.'" Methodist Recorder, 20 February
       1930, 12.

4025. "Wesley's Ordination of Dr. Coke." Methodist Quarterly Re-
       view 57 (1875): 579-95.

4026. "Wesley's Services to England." Spectator 83 (1899): 81-82.
       This author states that Wesley's supreme title to fame is that
       he "arrested the moral and spiritual decline of England, and
       that he was the chief agent in the renewal of her inward and
       spiritual life."

4027. "Wesley's Visits to Knutsford." Proceedings of the Wesley
       Historical Society 21 (1937): 8-9.

4028. "Wesley's Visits to the Isle of Man." Proceedings of the Wes-
       ley Historical Society 5 (1905): 80-84.

4029. "Wesley's Wig." Once a Week, n.s. 5 (1870): 282-84.

4030. "Wesley's World Parish." Newsweek 41 (29 June 1953): 82-83.
       An article on the 250th anniversary of the birth of John Wes-
       ley.

4031. West, J. I. "John Wesley in the Isle of Man." Proceedings
       of the Isle of Man Natural History and Antiquarian Society,
       n.s. 6 (1959): 15-27.

4032. West, W. M. S. "Methodists and Baptists in Eighteenth Cen-
       tury Bristol." Proceedings of the Wesley Historical Society
       44 (1984): 157-67.

4033. "West Riding Methodism: The Stainland Circuit." Methodist
       Recorder, 14 May 1908, 10.

4034. Westbrook, Francis B. "The Bicentenary of Wesley's Select
       Hymns with Tunes Annext." Mosaic; a Quarterly Review of
       Church Music, Liturgy and the Arts, October 1965, 113-15.

4035. _____. "Handel and the Wesleys: Some Bicentenary Reflections." Methodist Recorder, 9 April 1959, 11.

4036. _____. "The Music at Wesley's Conversion." Choir 54 (1963): 39-40.

4037. Wheatley, Henry B. "John Wesley's English Dictionary." Bookworm 1 (1888): 15-19.

4038. Whedon, D. A. "John Wesley's Views of Entire Sanctification." Wesleyan Methodist Magazine 85 (1862): 1015-20, 1090-93.

4039. "When Did the Rev. J. Wesley Become Savingly Converted?" Wesleyan Methodist Association Magazine 17 (1854): 256-70.

4040. "When Wesley Failed." Christian Century 41 (1924): 944-45. Brief discussion of Wesley's experience at Wroote.

4041. White, Arnold. "John Wesley in Ireland." Spectator 129 (8 July 1922): 43. A brief letter to the editor.

4042. White, David. "John Wesley and the Catholic Spirit." Workers with Youth 19, no. 11 (1966): 12-14.

4043. White, Herbert W. "Wesley's Death through the Eyes of the Press." London Quarterly and Holborn Review 184 (1959): 45-46.

4044. White, J. Penberthy. "The Kineton Circuit: Methodism Around and About Edgehill." Methodist Recorder, 12 October 1911, 10.

4045. _____. "Methodism in Ashbourne: A Derbyshire Circuit and Its Villages." Methodist Recorder, 29 January 1903, 13-14.

4046. _____. "Retford and Its Methodism." Methodist Recorder, 6 June 1901, 12-13.

4047. "The White Cliffs of Dover: Methodism in a Great Fortress." Methodist Recorder, 16 August 1906, 9.

4048. Whitebrook, J. C. "An Account of Tracts and Pamphlets on the Doctrine of Grace. Published by Hervey, Sandeman, Wesley, and others." Journal of the Calvinistic Methodist Historical Society 10 (1925): 9-20.

4049. Whiteley, J. H. "The Background of the Revival." London Quarterly and Holborn Review 163 (1938): 185-89.

4050. Whitney, G. W. "Opinions of John Wesley." Universalist
       Quarterly and General Review 30 (1873): 317-30, 434-54; 31
       (1874): 185-98; 32 (1875): 90-98, 323-43. Discusses Wes-
       ley's theological doctrines.

4051. Whittaker, Colin C. "Not Afraid to Die." Pentecostal Evangel
       no. 3386 (1 April 1979): 6-7.

4052. "Whit-week and the Wesleys." Methodist Recorder, 28 May
       1925, 12. Discusses the conversion of the Wesley brothers.

4053. Whyte, Alexander. "Brilliant Characterisation of John Wes-
       ley." Methodist Recorder, 24 October 1901, 15-16.

4054. _____. "'Gentle Jesus, Meek and Mild;' Some Notes of a
       Lecture on Charles Wesley's Children's Hymn in Free St.
       George's, Edinburgh." Sunday Magazine n.s. 28 (1899):
       324-26.

4055. Wigley, Henry T. "Hugh Bourne and John Wesley: A Com-
       parison." Proceedings of the Wesley Historical Society 31
       (1958): 182-85.

4056. Wilcoxon, Clair D. "The Whole Man: A Study of John Wes-
       ley's Healing Ministry." Religion in Life 28 (1959): 580-86.
       Stresses Wesley's concern for both mind and body in his at-
       tempts at healing, and describes his theological position re-
       garding sickness and health.

4057. Wilkes, Samuel. "Dr. Bowden's Last Circuit: The Wiltshire
       Mission." Methodist Recorder, 26 May 1904, 9-10.

4058. "William Cowper and John Wesley." Primitive Wesleyan Meth-
       odist Magazine 39 (1861): 106-7, 128. Includes Cowper's poem
       "Whitefield and Wesley."

4059. Williams, Albert Hughes. "John Wesley, Incumbent?" Pro-
       ceedings of the Wesley Historical Society 41 (1978): 133-38.
       Discusses the possibility of John Wesley's being an incumbent
       in Pembrokeshire.

4060. _____. "John Wesley's Visits to Builth, 1743-1750."
       Bathafarn 20 (1965): 45-53.

4061. Williams, M. O., Jr. "The Warmed Heart: Aldersgate--Then
       and Now." Chinese Recorder 69 (1938): 296-300.

4062. Williams, Melvin G. "He Taught Methodists to Read." To-
       gether 11, no. 6 (1967): 28-30.

4063. Williams, Willard A. "Influences that Led to Wesley's

Aldersgate Experience." Central Christian Advocate 138, no.
8 (1963): 8-10.

4064. Williamson, Karina. "Herbert's Reputation in the Eighteenth
Century." Philological Quarterly 41 (1962): 769-75. Cites
examples of John Wesley's "pruning" of Herbert's poems.

4065. Wilson, Arthur. "Those Were Rough Days on Tyneside:
When John Wesley Came to Newcastle." Methodist Recorder,
2 August 1962, 5.

4066. Wilson, Charles. "Biddick--in the Newcastle-upon-Tyne
'Round.'" Proceedings of the Wesley Historical Society 14
(1924): 117-21.

4067. Wilson, Charles R. "The Relevance of John Wesley's Distinctive Correlation of Love and Law." Wesleyan Theological
Journal 12 (1977): 54-59.

4068. Wilson, David Dunn. "The Importance of Hell for John Wesley." Proceedings of the Wesley Historical Society 34
(1963): 12-16.

4069. _____. "John Wesley and Mystical Prayer." London Quarterly and Holborn Review 193 (1968): 61-69.

4070. _____. "John Wesley, Gregory Lopez and the Marquis de
Renty." Proceedings of the Wesley Historical Society 35
(1966): 181-84.

4071. _____. "John Wesley's Break with Mysticism Reconsidered."
Proceedings of the Wesley Historical Society 35 (1965): 65-67.

4072. Wilson, W. D. "John Wesley and Methodists." Church Review 3 (1850): 245-67.

4073. Winchester, Caleb Thomas. "John Wesley." Century Magazine 66 (1903): 389-408, 492-510.

4074. Winter, Lovick Pierce. "Charles Wesley in America." Methodist Quarterly Review 65 (1916): 71-84.

4075. Winter, W. Jessop. "The Metropolis of Dartmoor: Methodism
in the Okehampton Circuit." Methodist Recorder, 18 February 1904, 9-10.

4076. Wintersgill, M. "A Short History of Liverpool Methodism."
Methodist Recorder, 23 July 1896, 510.

4077. Wiseman, Frederick Luke. "The Conference Town: Birmingham." Wesleyan Methodist Magazine 117 (1894): 524-30.

4078. _____. "George Herbert and John Wesley: The Herbert
Tercentenary." Methodist Recorder, 8 June 1933, 14.

4079. _____. "John Wesley on the Cause and Cure of Decline.
1--Field Preaching." Methodist Recorder, 5 January 1911,
12.

4080. _____. "John Wesley on the Cause and Cure of Decline.
2--Christian Perfection." Methodist Recorder, 2 February
1911, 12.

4081. _____. "John Wesley on the Cause and Cure of Decline.
3--Church Unity." Methodist Recorder, 23 March 1911, 12.

4082. _____. "Methodist Doctrine Illustrated; from John Wesley's Hymn Book." Methodist Recorder; Wesley Bicentennial
Supplement, 19 May 1938, ix.

4083. _____. "Theology in Hymns." Spectator 169 (1942):
332-33. A discussion of Charles Wesley and his hymns.

4084. Withrow, W. H. "The Wesleys and the New Portraits."
Outlook 69 (1901): 314-19.

4085. Wood, A. Skevington. "John Wesley's Reversion to Type:
The Influence of His Nonconformist Ancestry." Proceedings
of the Wesley Historical Society 35 (1965): 88-93. (A re-
joinder by Albert B. Lawson on p. 125.)

4086. _____. "Lessons from Wesley's Experience." Christianity
Today 7, no. 15 (1963): 4-6.

4087. Wood, Donald. "Ascending to the Source." Preacher's
Magazine 59, no. 1 (1983): 38-39. Concerns John Wesley's
attitude toward learning and his desire of knowledge.

4088. _____. "In the Worst of Times." Preacher's Magazine 58,
no. 1 (1982): 42-43. Briefly describes some of the corrup-
tions rampant in Wesley's day.

4089. _____. "A Matter of Obedience: John Wesley on the
Lord's Supper." Preacher's Magazine 56, no. 1 (1980): 33-
34.

4090. _____. "Put Yourself in the Place of Every Poor Man."
Preacher's Magazine 55, no. 1 (1979): 44-45. Describes
Wesley's acts of charity.

4091. _____. "Wesley's Instructions on Singing." Preacher's
Magazine 53, no. 2 (1978): 12-13.

4092. _____. "Wesley's View of War." Preacher's Magazine 57, no. 1 (1981): 35, 62.

4093. Wood, Laurence W. "Thoughts upon the Wesleyan Doctrine of Entire Sanctification with Special Reference to Some Similarities with the Roman Catholic Church Doctrine of Confirmation." Wesleyan Theological Journal 15, no. 1 (1980): 88-99. A discussion of "a remarkable similarity that exists between the Roman Catholic doctrine of confirmation and the Wesleyan doctrine of entire sanctification."

4094. _____. "Wesley's Epistemology." Wesleyan Theological Journal 10 (1975): 51-53.

4095. Wood, R. W. "God in History. Wesley a Child of Providence." Methodist Quarterly Review 78 (1929): 94-104.

4096. Woodward, Max W. "Wesley's Electrical Machine." Nursing Mirror 114, no. 2978, Supplement (1962): 10, 16.

4097. Woomer, D. Darrell. "United Methodist Hymnody." American Organist 14, no. 7 (1980): 18.

4098. Worden, Barbara S. "The Emotional Evangelical: Blake and Wesley." Wesleyan Theological Journal 18, no. 2 (1983): 67-79.

4099. Workman, H. B. "Wyclif, Hus, Luther and Wesley." Proceedings of the Wesley Historical Society 15 (1926): 141-45.

4100. Workman, W. P. "The 'Russell' Portrait of John Wesley at Kingswood School." Proceedings of the Wesley Historical Society 10 (1915): 67-68.

4101. "The Works of Arminius." Wesleyan Methodist Magazine 48 (1825): 748-57.

4102. Wright, C. J. "Comenius and Methodism: A Significant Tercentenary." London Quarterly and Holborn Review 166 (1941): 436-50. Discusses Comenius' influence on John Wesley's thinking.

4103. _____. "The Great Itinerant: An Oxford Bicentenary." Modern Churchman 16 (1926): 69-77. Claims that John Wesley was a born leader, a believer in institutions, an organizer, and of a practical mind.

4104. _____. "Methodism and the Church of England." Modern Churchman 45 (1955): 345-52; 46 (1956): 52-54.

4105. Wright, J. "Wesley in Sussex." Sussex County Magazine 18 (1944): 43-44.

320

320 John and Charles Wesley

4106. Wright, J. Anderson. "Grimsby and Its Methodism: The
George Street Church and Victoria Chapel Jubilee." Methodist Recorder, 13 October 1910, 9.

4107. _____. "A Study in Methodist Growth: Park Street Circuit, Bolton." Methodist Recorder, 12 June 1913, 9.

4108. Wright, J. C. "Wesley the Lover." Holborn Review 62
(1920): 73-78. Mentions Betty Kirkham, Grace Murray,
Mrs. Pendarves, Sophia Hopkey, and his wife.

4109. Wright, Joseph G. "A Miniature Portrait of John Wesley."
Proceedings of the Wesley Historical Society 6 (1908): 142.

4110. _____. "Two Scarce Wesley Medals." Proceedings of the
Wesley Historical Society 6 (1908): 85-86.

4111. _____. "Wesley Portraits." Proceedings of the Wesley
Historical Society 2 (1899): 49-51; 3 (1902): 185-92; 4
(1903): 1-5.

4112. Wright, Joseph G., and R. Green. "Busts of John Wesley."
Proceedings of the Wesley Historical Society 3 (1902): 173-
74.

4113. Wright, Louis B. "John Wesley: Scholar and Critic."
South Atlantic Quarterly 29 (1930): 262-81.

4114. Wylie, William P. "The Strange Case of the Two Johns: An
Anglican Comment on the Anglican Methodist Reunion Scheme."
Month, n.s. 40 (1968): 259-63. The two Johns are John Wes-
ley and John Henry Newman.

4115. Wynkoop, Mildred Bangs. "Hermeneutical Approach to John
Wesley." Wesleyan Theological Journal 6 (1971): 13-22.

4116. _____. "John Wesley--Mentor or Guru?" Wesleyan Theological Journal 10 (1975): 5-14. Summarizes what it means
to be truly Wesleyan.

4117. _____. "Theological Roots of Wesleyanism's Understanding
of the Holy Spirit." Wesleyan Theological Journal 14, no. 1
(1979): 77-98.

4118. Yates, Arthur S. "Wesley and His Bible." Methodist Recorder, 11 August 1960, 8.

4119. _____. "Wesley and Whitsuntide." Methodist Recorder, 22
May 1947, 1.

4120. _____. "A Wesley Relic in London's Theatreland." Methodist Recorder, 27 August 1953, 4. The article is about the West Street Chapel, near Leicester Square.

4121. Young, Betty I. "Sources for the Annesley Family." Proceedings of the Wesley Historical Society 45 (1985): 47-57.

4122. Young, David. "Wesley's Journeys in Mid-Wales." Proceedings of the Wesley Historical Society 9 (1913): 45-47.

4123. Young, Dinsdale T. "Wesley Phrase--'Daubed with Gold and Silver.'" Methodist Recorder, 7 March 1907, 17.

4124. Young, Jesse Bowman. "John Wesley's Invalid Year." Methodist Review (N.Y.) 84 (1902): 592-96.

4125. Young, Robert, and John H. James. "Revival of Religion in the Penzance Circuit." Wesleyan Methodist Magazine 73 (1850): 33-39.

4126. Zabilka, Ivan L. "John Wesley and the Plurality of Worlds." Asbury Seminarian 36, no. 3 (1981): 34-38. Deals with Wesley's beliefs regarding many worlds and possible life on them.

4127. Zaring, E. R. "John Wesley Discourses upon Old Age." Methodist Review 106 (1923): 375-79.

4128. Zehrer, Karl. "The Relationship between Pietism in Halle and Early Methodism." Methodist History 17, no. 4 (1979): 211-224. Shows the areas of disagreement between John Wesley and the Pietists in Halle.

DISSERTATIONS AND THESES

4129. Abelove, Henry D. "John Wesley's Influence during His Lifetime on the Methodists." Ph.D. diss., Yale University, 1978. 253p.

4130. Adams, Nelson Falls. "The Musical Sources for John Wesley's Tunebooks; the Genealogy of 148 Tunes." S.M.D. diss., Union Theological Seminary, 1973.

4131. Albright, William Edward. "The Relation of John Wesley and the Methodist Societies to the Anglican Church (1738-1791)." B.D. thesis, Duke University, 1944. 102p.

4132. Allen, L. S. "Wesley and the Eucharist." Master's thesis, Northwestern University, 1961. 103p.

4133. Allison, Earl A. "John Wesley's Doctrine of Christian Perfection." B.D. thesis, Butler University, 1954. 93p.

4134. Anderson, Lillian. "The Doctrine of Christian Holiness As Found in the Writings of John Wesley and Reflected in His Hymns." Master's thesis, St. John's University, Collegeville, Minn., 1969. 72p.

4135. Armstrong, Clinton Cornelius. "The Religious Leadership of John Wesley." Ph.D. diss., University of Illinois, 1959. 176p.

4136. Arnett, William M. "John Wesley--Man of One Book." Ph.D. diss., Drew University, 1954. 261p.

4137. Ashman, R. G. "An Examination of the Views of John Wesley in Relation to the Protestant Reformation." Ph.D. diss., University of Wales, 1949. 195p.

4138. Baker, D. S. "Hymns on Patriotism: Unpublished Poems of Charles Wesley." Master's thesis, University of Birmingham, 1960.

4139. Baker, Dale Winston. "The Doctrine of the Holy Spirit in the Theology of John Wesley." Master's thesis, Northwestern University, 1953. 145p.

4140. Baker, Eric W. "The Relation of William Law to John Wesley and the Beginnings of Methodism." Ph.D. diss., University of Edinburgh, 1941.

4141. Barton, J. Hamby. "The Definition of the Episcopal Office in American Methodism." Ph.D. diss., Drew University, 1960. 231p. Chap. 1, pp. 2-33, is entitled "The Authority of the Fathers--Wesley."

4142. Bates, Gerald E. "A Comparative Study of Calvin's and Wesley's Conceptions of the Perfectability of Man." Master's thesis, Western Theological Seminary, 1964. 125p.

4143. Bebb, Evelyn Douglas. "John Wesley's Religious Teaching and His Social and Economic Views." B.Litt. thesis, University of Oxford, 1944.

4144. Bence, Clarence L. "John Wesley's Telelogical Hermeneutic." Ph.D. diss., Emory University, 1981. 291p.

4145. Benner, Forest T. "The Immediate Antecedents of the Wesleyan Doctrine of the Witness of the Spirit." Ph.D. diss., Temple University, 1966. 253p.

4146. Bennett, E. Fay. "The Call of God in the Ministry of John Wesley: A Study of Spiritual Authority in Methodist History." Ph.D. diss., Southwestern Baptist Theological Seminary, 1963. 184p.

4147. Bennett, Edward L. "The Personal Religion of John Wesley." B.D. thesis, Butler University, 1956. 126p.

4148. Bennett, James V. "Social Influences of the Wesley Movement." B.D. thesis, Butler University, 1954. 79p.

4148a. Black, Robert Edwin. "The Social Dimensions of John Wesley's Ministry As Related to His Personal Piety." Ph.D. diss., Union Theological Seminary in Virginia, 1984. 204p.

4149. Blaising, Craig Alan. "John Wesley's Doctrine of Original Sin." Th.D. diss., Dallas Theological Seminary, 1979. 388p.

4150. Boleyn, Charles Wheatly. "John Wesley's View of Man." S.T.M. thesis, Union Theological Seminary, 1941.

4151. Bonner, Warren Arthur. "John Wesley's Conversion Experience." B.D. thesis, Southern Methodist University, 1926.

4152. Boraine, Alexander Lionel. "The Nature of Evangelism in the Theology and Practice of John Wesley." Ph.D. diss., Drew University, 1969. 286p.

4153. Boshears, Onva K., Jr. "John Wesley, the Bookman; a Study
       of His Reading Interests in the Eighteenth Century." Ph.D.
       diss., University of Michigan, 1972. 425p.

4154. Bowmer, John C. "Church and Ministery in Wesleyan Meth-
       odism from the Death of John Wesley (1791) to the Death of
       Jabez Bunting (1858)." Ph.D. diss., University of Leeds,
       1967.

4155. Boyce, John B. "John Wesley As a Literary Man." S.T.M.
       thesis, Western Theological Seminary, 1932. 93p.

4156. Braxton, J. W. "John Wesley's Conception of the Ideal
       Christian." B.D. thesis, Duke University, 1932. 109p.

4157. Brendall, Earl Hall. "The Persecution of Methodists in the
       Time of John Wesley." B.D. thesis, Duke University, 1936.
       132p.

4158. Brendlinger, I. A. "A Study of the Views of Major Eighteenth
       Century Evangelicals on Slavery and Race, with Special
       Reference to John Wesley." Ph.D. diss., University of Edin-
       burgh, 1982.

4159. Brigg, G. T. "The Contribution of John Wesley to the Social
       and Educational Life of Bristol and Its Neighbourhood."
       Master's thesis, University of Bristol, 1960.

4160. Brightman, Robert Sheffield. "Gregory of Nyssa and John
       Wesley in Theological Dialogue of the Christian Life." Ph.D.
       diss., Boston University, 1969. 393p.

4161. Bullock, Frederick William Bagshawe. "Religious Conversion
       in Great Britain (1700-1850): A Psychological and Historical
       Enquiry." M.Litt. thesis, Cambridge University, 1934.
       618p. Contains section on John Wesley's conversion ex-
       perience, pp. 97-114.

4162. _____. "Religious Societies (Ecclesiolae in Ecclesia) from
       1500 to 1800, excluding Those of the Church of Rome." Ph.D.
       diss., Cambridge University, 1938. 644p. Methodist religious
       societies, 1740-1800 discussed on pp. 471-93.

4163. Burns, Lacy Harvey. "The Social Elements in the Thought
       and Practice of John Wesley." B.D. thesis, Duke University,
       1937. 122p.

4164. Burtner, Robert W. "Justification and Sanctification; a Study
       of the Theologies of Martin Luther and John Wesley." Mas-
       ter's thesis, Union Theological Seminary, 1948.

4165. Byrum, Roy D. "Theological Implications in the Hymns of
       Charles Wesley." B.D. thesis, Duke University, 1945.
       122p.

4166. Calaqui, Jeremias Datu. "The Doctrine of Man in John Wes-
       ley's Theology." Master's thesis, Northwestern University,
       1961. 166p.

4166a. Campbell, Ted Allen. "John Wesley's Conceptions and Uses
       of Christian Antiquity." Ph.D. diss., Southern Methodist
       University, 1984. 368p.

4167. Capp, Philip L. "An Inquiry into John Wesley's Understand-
       ing of the Nature of Methodism with Reference to the Chris-
       tian World Mission." Master's thesis, Seattle Pacific College,
       1958.

4168. Carlin, James Albert. "John Wesley's Understanding of Hu-
       man Nature." Master's thesis, Southern Methodist University,
       1950.

4169. Carruth, Samuel Enoch. "John Wesley's Concept of the
       Church." Th.D. diss., Iliff School of Theology, 1952. 218p.

4170. Carwithen, Edward Franklin. "The Attitudes of the Methodist
       Episcopal Church toward Peace and War." S.T.D. diss.,
       Temple University, 1944. 148p. Chap. 1 deals with John
       Wesley's attitudes toward peace and war, pp. 1-17.

4171. Cascio, Robert Jude. "Mystic and Augustan: A Study of
       the Impact of William Law on John Wesley, Edward Gibbon and
       John Byrom." Ph.D. diss., Fordham University, 1974.
       209p.

4172. Casto, Robert Michael. "Exegetical Method in John Wesley's
       Explanatory Notes upon the Old Testament: A Description
       of His Approach, Uses of Sources, and Practice." Ph.D.
       diss., Duke University, 1977. 562p.

4173. Chilcote, Paul Wesley. "John Wesley and the Women Preachers
       of Early Methodism." Ph.D. diss., Duke University, 1984.
       454p.

4174. Cho, Chong Nahm. "A Study in John Wesley's Doctrine of
       Baptism in the Light of Current Interpretations." Ph.D.
       diss., Emory University, 1966. 219p.

4174a. Clapper, Gregory S. "John Wesley on Religious Affection:
       His Views on Experience and Emotion and Their Role in the
       Christian Life and Theology." Ph.D. diss., Emory Univer-
       sity, 1985. 237p.

4175. Clark, Robert Burton. "The History of the Doctrine of
       Christian Perfection in the Methodist Episcopal Church in
       America up to 1845." Ph.D. diss., Temple University, 1946.
       306p. The first two chapters of this dissertation are con-
       cerned with Christian perfection as taught by John Wesley and
       the dependence of the American Methodist Episcopal Church
       on Wesley's doctrine.

4176. Claypool, James V. "Berkeley and Wesley." S.T.D. diss.,
       Temple University, 1932. 238p.

4177. Cloke, H. "Wesleyan Methodism's Contribution to National
       Education." Master's thesis, University of London, King's
       College, 1936.

4178. Coggin, James E. "John Wesley's Doctrine of Perfection and
       Its Influence on Subsequent Theology." Ph.D. diss., South-
       western Baptist Theological Seminary, 1950.

4179. Coleman, Burton Henry. "Wesley's Contribution to Theology."
       Master's thesis, Southern Methodist University, 1936. 50p.

4180. Collins, Edward M. "A Critical Edition of the Thirteen Ser-
       mons by John Wesley on the Sermon on the Mount." Ph.D.
       diss., Ohio University, 1965. 214p.

4180a. Collins, Kenneth Joseph. "John Wesley's Theology of Law."
       Ph.D. diss., Drew University, 1984. 292p.

4181. Cooper, Allen Lamar. "John Wesley: A Study in Theology
       and Social Ethics." Ph.D. diss., Columbia University, 1965.
       251p.

4182. Coppedge, W. Allan. "John Wesley and the Doctrine of Pre-
       destination." Ph.D. diss., University of Cambridge, Em-
       manuel College, 1976. 357p.

4183. Cory, Carol. "The Christology of John Wesley Compared
       with That of Methodist Church School Literature." Master's
       thesis, Northwestern University, 1964. 221p.

4184. Cousins, David N. "Going on to Perfection: Investigating
       a Wesleyan Model for Christian Spirituality." D.Min. diss.,
       Princeton Theological Seminary, 1982. 146p.

4185. Cox, Leo George. "John Wesley's Concept of Sin." Mas-
       ter's thesis, State University of Iowa, 1957. 193p.

4186. Cranmer, Florence E. "A History of the Methodist Publishing
       House." Master's thesis, Drexel Institute of Technology,
       1955. 55p. Chap. 1, pp. 1-7, "Origin and Foundation,"
       deals with John Wesley and his publishing efforts.

4187. Crow, Earl P. "John Wesley's Conflict with Antinomianism in Relation to the Moravians and Calvinists." Ph.D. diss., University of Manchester, 1964. 360p.

4188. Cubie, David Livingstone. "John Wesley's Concept of Perfect Love: A Motif Analysis." Ph.D. diss., Boston University, 1965.

4189. Custer, Watson Stanley. "The Doctrine of the Atonement in the Writings of John Wesley." Master's thesis, Northwestern University, 1955. 128p.

4190. Dale, James. "The Theological and Literary Qualities of the Poetry of Charles Wesley in Relation to the Standards of His Age." Ph.D. diss., University of Cambridge, 1960. 271p.

4191. Darby, James Carter. "A Study of the Historical Development of John Wesley's Doctrine of Christian Perfection As Proclaimed in His Preaching and Tested in the Life of the Christian Community." Master's thesis, Northwestern University, 1956. 132p.

4192. Davies, W. R. "The Relation of Methodism and the Church of England between 1738 and 1850." Master's thesis, University of Manchester, 1960.

4192a. Dean, William Walter. "Disciplined Fellowship: The Rise and Decline of Cell Groups in British Methodism." Ph.D. diss., University of Iowa, 1985. 577p.

4193. Denyer, A. S. "The Catholic Element in the Hymns of Charles Wesley." B.D. thesis, University of Leeds, 1943.

4194. Dicker, Gordon Stanley. "The Concept 'Simul Iustus et Peccator' in Relation to the Thought of Luther, Wesley and Bonhoeffer, and Its Significance for a Doctrine of the Christian Life." Th.D. diss., Union Theological Seminary, 1971. 229p.

4195. Downes, J. C. T. "Eschatological Doctrines in the Writings of John and Charles Wesley." Ph.D. diss., University of Edinburgh, 1960. 271p.

4196. DuBose, Robert Newsome. "The Doctrine of Conversion in the Teachings of John Wesley." B.D. thesis, Duke University, 1946. 116p.

4197. Dunker, Carl Frederick. "John Wesley's Doctrine of Man and Sin." Master's thesis, Butler University, 1957. 73p.

4198. Dunlap, E. Dale. "Methodist Theology in Great Britain in the

Nineteenth Century." Ph.D. diss., Yale University, 1956. The first chapter deals with Wesley's ancestral nonconformity, Anglican conformity, and his doctrines of divine grace, redemption, sanctification, Christian Perfection, and his Christo-centric religion of grace.

4199. Dunn, Lawrence L. "A Contemporary Analysis of John Wesley's Doctrine of the Church." Master's thesis, Asbury Theological Seminary, 1969. 119p.

4200. Dunning, H. Ray. "Nazarene Ethics As Seen in a Theological, Historical, and Sociological Context." Ph.D. diss., Vanderbilt University, 1969. 229p. The first chapter examines the doctrinal source of Nazarene ethics, demonstrating the extent to which it is similar or at variance with Wesley's position.

4201. Durham, Donald William. "The function of the Conception of the Judgment to Come, in the Thought of: Thomas Aquinas, John Calvin, and John Wesley." B.D. thesis, Duke University, 1947. 65p.

4202. Dygoski, Louise Annie. "The Journals and Letters of John Wesley on Preaching." Ph.D. diss., University of Wisconsin, 1961.

4203. Earle, Ralph. "The Doctrine of Sanctification in the New Testament." Th.D. diss., Gordon College of Theology and Missions, Boston, 1941.

4204. Eberly, Paul F. "John Wesley's Philosophy of Religion." Ph.D. diss., Syracuse University, 1934.

4205. Edgar, Fred Russell. "The Home Life of Susannah Wesley." B.D. thesis, Southern Methodist University, 1936. 64p.

4205a. _____. "A Study of John Wesley from the Point of View of the Educational Methodology Used by Him in Fostering the Wesleyan Revival in England." Ph.D. diss., Columbia University, 1952.

4206. Edwards, Maldwyn L. "The Political Ideas and Influence of John Wesley." Master's thesis, University of Wales, 1927.

4207. Ekrut, James Charles. "Universal Redemption, Assurance of Salvation, and Christian Perfection in the Hymns of Charles Wesley, with Poetic Analyses and Tune Examples." M.M. thesis, Southwestern Baptist Theological Seminary, 1978. 174p.

4208. Ellsworth, Donald Paul. "Music in the Church for Purposes of Evangelism: Historical Antecedents and Contemporary

Practices." D.M.A. diss., University of Southern California, 1977. 291p. Includes a discussion of the Wesleys and their evangelical hymns, which the author describes as popular and secular in origin.

4209. English, John Cammel. "The Historical Antecedents and Development of John Wesley's Doctrine of Christian Initiation." Ph.D. diss., Vanderbilt University, 1965.

4210. Fakahua, Sione Aio. "John Wesley and Worship in the Free Wesleyan Church of Tonga." B.D. thesis, Pacific Theological College, 1968. 129p.

4211. Fernández, Angel Agustín. "The Wesley Girls and the Eighteenth Century." Master's thesis, Southern Methodist University, 1950.

4212. Fleming, Richard Lee. "The Concept of Sacrifice in the Eucharistic Hymns of John and Charles Wesley." D.Min. diss., Southern Methodist University, 1980.

4213. Franz, Rolaine Marie. "All the Ship's Company: A Wesleyan Paradigm for the Poetry of Christopher Smart, William Cowper, and William Blake." Ph.D. diss., Brown University, 1978. 268p.

4214. Fuhrman, Eldon R. "The Concept of Grace in the Theology of John Wesley." Ph.D. diss., University of Iowa, 1963. 505p.

4215. Gaddis, Merrill E. "Christian Perfectionism in America." Ph.D. diss., University of Chicago, 1929. Chap. 5 is concerned with Wesleyan perfectionism, pp. 120-65.

4216. Galliers, Brian J. N. "The Theology of Baptism in the Writings of John Wesley." Master's thesis, Leeds University, 1957.

4217. Garlow, James Lester. "John Wesley's Understanding of the Laity as Demonstrated by His Use of the Lay Preachers." Ph.D. diss., Drew University, 1979. 360p.

4218. Garrison, Richard Benjamin. "Love as the Radical Element in John Wesley's Doctrine of Perfection." Master's thesis, Drew University, 1955. 130p.

4219. Gerdes, Egon Walter. "John Wesley's Attitude toward War: A Study of the Historical Formation, the Theological Determination, and the Practical Manifestation of John Wesley's Attitude toward War and Its Place in Methodism." Ph.D. diss., Emory University, 1960. 205p.

4220. Glenn, Lucinda Alice. "John Wesley's Development of a Doc-
       trine of the Church." Master's thesis, Pacific School of Re-
       ligion, 1980. 181p.

4221. Goodloe, Robert Wesley. "The Office of Bishop in the
       Methodist Church." Ph.D. diss., University of Chicago,
       1929. 215p.

4222. Goss, W. A. "Early Methodism in Bristol, with Special
       Reference to J. Wesley's Visits to the City, 1739-90, and
       Their Impression on the People." Master's thesis, University
       of Bristol, 1932.

4223. Graham, E. Dorothy. "The Contribution of Lady Glenorchy
       and Her Circle to the Evangelical Revival." B.D. thesis,
       University of Leeds, 1964. 217p. This thesis describes
       Lady Glenorchy's conversion, contacts with John Wesley,
       and devotion to her religion.

4223a. Gray, Wallace Gale. "The Place of Reason in the Theology
       of John Wesley." Ph.D. diss., Vanderbilt University, 1953.

4224. Greathouse, William M. "A Study of Wesley's Doctrines of
       Sin and Perfection As Treated by Cell, Lee and Cannon."
       M.A. thesis, Vanderbilt University, 1948. 94p.

4225. Greve, Lionel. "Freedom and Discipline in the Theology of
       John Calvin, William Perkins and John Wesley: An Examina-
       tion of the Origin and Nature of Pietism." Ph.D. diss.,
       Hartford Seminary, 1976. 299p.

4226. Grimes, Walter Bruce. "Some Contributions of Early Meth-
       odism to American Christianity, 1729-1816." M.A. thesis,
       University of Chicago, 1915. 68p.

4227. Haas, Alfred Burton. "John Wesley and the Sacrament of
       Holy Communion." Master's thesis, Drew University, 1946.

4228. Hahn, Peninsula Sukwon. "Mr. Wesley's Conception of
       Episcopacy." Master's thesis, Southern Methodist University,
       1935. 80p.

4229. Haley, Carl Wrenn. "John Wesley's Conception of the Natural
       State of Man." B.D. thesis, Duke University, 1936. 136p.

4230. Hansen, William Albert. "John Wesley and the Rhetoric of Re-
       form." Ph.D. diss., University of Oregon, 1972. 346p.

4231. Hardin, Harvey M. "John Wesley's Experience and Interpreta-
       tion of the Witness of the Spirit." B.D. thesis, Duke Univer-
       sity, 1932. 105p.

4232. Harkness, Paul H. "John Wesley, from Theology to Ethics."
       Master's thesis, Pacific School of Religion, 1979. 84p.

4233. Harper, Steve. "The Devotional Life of John Wesley, 1703-
       38." Ph.D. diss., Duke University, 1981. 729p.

4234. Hartman, Lewis Oliver. "The Mystical Elements in John Wes-
       ley's Doctrines." Ph.D. diss., Boston University, 1909.

4234a. Hartzog, Nancy Helen. "John Wesley's Understanding of Sal-
       vation As a Guideline to Treating Adult Female Incest Survi-
       vors." D.Min. diss., School of Theology at Claremont, 1985.
       116p.

4235. Harvey, Marvin Ellis. "The Wesleyan Movement and the
       American Revolution." Ph.D. diss., University of Washington,
       1962. 401p.

4236. Hazlitt, Joseph Allen. "John Wesley's Doctrine of the Atone-
       ment." Master's thesis, Southern Methodist University,
       1955. 70p.

4237. Hegarty, Charles Kiely, Jr. "John Wesley's Doctrine of Pre-
       venient Grace." B.D. thesis, Southern Methodist University,
       1938. 74p.

4238. Heitzenrater, Richard P. "John Wesley and the Oxford
       Methodists, 1725-1735." Ph.D. diss., Duke University, 1972.
       548p.

4239. Henderson, D. Michael. "The Class Meeting in Methodism and
       Chartism." Master's thesis, Indiana University, 1976. 47p.

4240. _____. "John Wesley's Instructional Groups." Ph.D.
       diss., Indiana University, 1980. 260p.

4241. Henrikson, Patricia B. "The Influence of Thomas Halyburton
       upon John Wesley's Understanding of His Own Experience and
       the Formulation of His Theology." Master's thesis, North-
       western University, 1968. 155p.

4242. Henson, Chet C. "Wesley the Evangelist." B.D. thesis,
       Southern Methodist University, 1929. 58p.

4243. Hill, Donald Merle. "A Study of John Wesley's Concept of
       Pastoral Care." Master's thesis, Asbury Theological Seminary,
       1952. 159p.

4244. Hillman, Robert John. "Grace in the Preaching of Calvin and
       Wesley, a Comparative Study." Ph.D. diss., Fuller Theological
       Seminary, 1978.

4245.   Hodgson, E. M. "The Poetry of John and Charles Wesley,
        with Special Reference to Their Hymns." Ph.D. diss., Uni-
        versity of London, 1970.

4246.   Hoffman, Thomas G. "The Moral Philosophy of John Wesley:
        The Development and Nature of His Moral Dynamic." Ph.D.
        diss., Temple University, 1968. 278p.

4247.   Hoggard, Earl Reid. "Mr. Wesley's Conception of Salvation."
        B.D. thesis, Southern Methodist University, 1936.

4248.   Holsclaw, David Francis. "The Demise of Disciplined Christian
        Fellowship: The Methodist Class Meeting in Nineteenth-
        Century America." Ph.D. diss., University of California,
        Davis, 1979. The first chapter deals with the English origins
        of the Methodist class meetings, pp. 1-48.

4249.   Hoon, Paul W. "The Soteriology of John Wesley." Ph.D.
        diss., University of Edinburgh, 1936.

4249a. Horst, Mark Lewis. "Christian Understanding and the Life
        and Faith in John Wesley's Thought." Ph.D. diss., Yale
        University, 1985. 338p.

4250.   Hosman, Glenn Burton, Jr. "The Problem of Church and
        State in the Thought of John Wesley As Reflecting His Under-
        standing of Providence and His View of History." Ph.D.
        diss., Drew University, 1970. 423p.

4251.   Hull, J. E. "The Controversy between John Wesley and the
        Countess of Huntingdon: Its Origin, Development, and Con-
        sequences." Ph.D. diss., University of Edinburgh, 1959.

4252.   Hunt, Raymond Fletcher. "John Wesley As Spiritual Director."
        Master's thesis, Northwestern University, 1967. 100p.

4253.   Hylson-Smith, Kenneth. "Studies in Revivalism As a Social
        and Religious Phenomenon, with Special Reference to the Lon-
        don Revival." Part 1 covers the Revival in London, 1736-
        1750, pp. 22-89.

4254.   Hynson, Leon O. "Church and State in the Thought and Life
        of John Wesley." Ph.D. diss., University of Iowa, 1971.
        340p.

4255.   Ireson, R. W. "The Doctrine of Faith in John Wesley and the
        Protestant Tradition: A Comparative Study." Ph.D. diss.,
        University of Manchester, 1974.

4256.   Irvin, Richard Lee. "John Wesley's Doctrine of Man." Mas-
        ter's thesis, Southern Methodist University, 1940. 113p.

4256a. Isaacs, Everett Cahall. "John Wesley's Theology and Practice
       of Ministry for Spiritual Maturity: Contributions for Today."
       D.Min., Drew University, 1985. 205p.

4257. James, Henry C. "Wesley's Conception of Religious Education
       and Conversion." Master's thesis, Asbury Theological Semi-
       nary, 1960. 66p.

4258. Jaycox, Edwin. "Wesley's Experience and Teaching of Holi-
       ness." B.D. thesis, Asbury Theological Seminary, 1933.
       56p.

4258a. Jebanathan, Gabriel. "John Wesley: An Adaptive Strategy
       for Church Growth." Master's thesis, Fuller Theological
       Seminary School of World Mission, 1985. 230p.

4259. Jenson, Evelyn Gene Van Til. "John Wesley's Use of Three
       Types of Classical Oratory--Forensic, 'Epideictic,' and
       Deliberative--in his Journal." Ed.D. diss., Ball State Uni-
       versity, 1980. 195p.

4260. Jorden, Eric Evans. "The Ideal of Sanctity in Methodism and
       Tractarianism with Special Reference to John Wesley and John
       Henry Newman: A Comparative Study." Ph.D. diss., Uni-
       versity of London, 1958. 426p.

4261. Källstad, Thorvald E. "John Wesley and the Bible. A Psy-
       chological Study." Thesis, University of Uppsala, 1974.
       356p.

4262. Kang, Stephen Sungbo. "John Wesley As an Evangelist."
       Master's thesis, Northern Baptist Theological Seminary, 1958.
       134p.

4263. Kapp, John R. "John Wesley's Idea of Authority in the
       State." Ph.D. diss., Boston University, 1938.

4264. Keefer, Luke L., Jr. "John Wesley: Disciple of Early
       Christianity." 2 vols. Ph.D. diss., Temple University,
       1982.

4265. Kellett, Norman Lawrence. "John Wesley and the Restoration
       of the Doctrine of the Holy Spirit to the Church of England
       in the Eighteenth Century." Ph.D. diss., Brandeis Univer-
       sity, 1975. 212p.

4266. Kendall, Rex Stone. "John Wesley and John Henry Newman,
       Resemblances and Contrasts." B.D. thesis, Southern Meth-
       odist University, 1935. 51p.

4267. Kennedy, James William. "John Wesley's Doctrine of

334 John and Charles Wesley

Sanctification versus the United Methodist Clergy Family in Today's World." D.Min. diss., Eden Theological Seminary, 1980.

4268. Kidwell, Dorothea Isabel. "The Idea of Grace in the Theology of Saint Augustine and John Wesley." Master's thesis, Northwestern University, 1950. 163p.

4269. Kim, Seung Lak. "John Wesley's Doctrine of the Witness of the Spirit, or, the Assurance of Salvation." Ph.D. diss., Southern Baptist Theological Seminary, 1932.

4270. Kingdon, Robert Wells. "The Development of John Wesley's Social Gospel." B.D. thesis, Chicago Theological Seminary, 1928. 48p.

4271. Kirkham, Donald H. "Pamphlet Opposition to the Rise of Methodism. The Eighteenth Century English Evangelical Revival under Attack." Ph.D. diss., Duke University, 1973. 455p.

4272. Lawrence, William B. "An Inquiry into the Theological Relationship between John Wesley and Jonathan Edwards." B.D. thesis, Union Theological Seminary, 1971. 64p.

4273. Lawson, Albert Brown. "John Wesley and Some Anglican Evangelicals of the Eighteenth Century." Ph.D. diss., University of Sheffield, 1974.

4274. Lawson, Arvest Neal. "A Program for Renewal and Outreach in Amboy United Methodist Church in Light of John Wesley's Thought." D.Min. diss., Drew University, 1983. 178p.

4275. _____. "The Relation of Justification and Sanctification in Wesley's Theology." Master's thesis, Princeton Theological Seminary, 1956. 101p.

4276. Lawton, George. "Aspects of Wesley's English Style with Special Reference to Vocabulary." Master's thesis, University of Liverpool, 1958.

4277. Leach, Keith Alan. "Early Methodism: A Response to an Emerging Industrial Society." S.T.M. thesis, Seabury-Western Theological Seminary, 1967. 145p.

4278. Lee, John D., Jr. "The Conversion-Experience of May 24, 1738, in the Life of John Wesley." Ph.D. diss., Boston University, 1937.

4279. Lee, Peter A. "The Political Ethics of John Wesley." Ph.D. diss., Yale University, 1940. 211p.

4280. Leupp, Roderick Thomas. "'The Art of God': Light and
       Darkness in the Thought of John Wesley." Ph.D. diss.,
       Drew University, 1985. 245p.

4280a. _____. "The Vitality of a Tradition: Wesleyan-Arminianism
       and Christian Perfection. Master's thesis, Pacific School of
       Religion, 1978. 138p.

4281. Lewis, Mary Frances. "Charles Wesley's Contribution to
       Hymnology." S.M.M. thesis, Union Theological Seminary,
       1957. 83p.

4282. Liddick, Joseph G. "John Wesley and Charismatic Experience."
       Master's thesis, Wheaton College, 1980. 117p.

4283. Longfield, Marguerite Landon. "Significance of Wesley's Work
       in America." Master's thesis, Northwestern University, 1925.
       71p.

4284. Loring, Herbert R. "A Comparison of the Biographies of
       John Wesley Since 1850 in the Light of Biographical and
       Critical Materials." Th.D. diss., Boston University, 1951.
       357p.

4285. Lyddon, Richard Eugene. "The Relevance for the Contem-
       porary Church of the Eighteenth Century British Methodist
       Class Meeting." D.Min. diss., School of Theology at Clare-
       mont, 1978.

4286. McCallie, James David. "John Wesley's Doctrine of Christian
       Perfection and Its Implications in the Life of the Church."
       B.D. thesis, Butler University, 1958. 139p.

4287. McClendon, James William. "The Doctrine of Sin and the
       First Epistle of John; a Comparison of Calvinist, Wesleyan,
       and Biblical Thought." Th.D. diss., Southwestern Baptist
       Theological Seminary, 1953. 278p.

4288. McCleskey, Wayne H. "John Wesley's Theology of Expe-
       rience." Master's thesis, Southern Methodist University,
       1936. 66p.

4289. McCommon, Paul C. "The Influence of Charles Wesley's
       Hymns on Baptist Theology." Ph.D. diss., Southern Baptist
       Theological Seminary, 1948. 156p.

4289a. McCormick, Kelley Steve. "John Wesley's Use of John
       Chrysostom on the Christian Life: Faith Filled with the Energy
       of Love." Ph.D. diss., Drew University, 1983. 45p.

4290. McDonald, Thaddeus LeVerne. "The Beginnings of Methodist

Polity under John Wesley." B.D. thesis, Duke University, 1944.

4291. McEldowney, James E. "John Wesley's Theology in Its Historical Setting." Ph.D. diss., University of Chicago, 1944. 355p.

4292. McGovern, Terrence Xavier. "The Methodist Revival and the British Stage." Ph.D. diss., University of Georgia, 1978. 408p. Discusses Samuel Wesley pp. 121-28, John Wesley pp. 144-61.

4293. McIntosh, Lawrence Dennis. "The Nature and Design of Christianity in John Wesley's Early Theology: A Study in the Relationship of Love and Faith." Ph.D. diss., Drew University, 1966. 266p.

4294. MacKenzie, P. D. "The Methodist Class Meeting: A Historical Study." Master's thesis, University of St. Andrews, 1970.

4295. McNulty, Frank John. "The Moral Teaching of John Wesley." S.T.D. diss., Catholic University of America, 1963. 157p.

4296. Madron, Thomas W. "The Political Thought of John Wesley." Ph.D. diss., Tulane University, 1965. 265p.

4297. Magnuson, Arthur C. "John Wesley and William Law." Master's thesis, Boston University, 1983. 121p.

4298. Manahan, Isaias G. "A Survey of the Wesleyan Religious Revival in England in the Eighteenth Century." Master's thesis, Asbury Theological Seminary, 1954. 198p.

4299. Manifold, Orrin A. "The Development of John Wesley's Doctrine of Christian Perfection." Ph.D. diss., Boston University, 1946. 203p.

4300. Martin, John T. "The Wesleyan Doctrine of the Eucharist: Its Salvific and Ethical Implications." D.Min. diss., Wesley Theological Seminary, 1976. 189p.

4301. Mathai, Karimpinamannil P. "An Inductive Study in the Doctrinal Teachings of John Wesley's Explanatory Notes upon the Old Testament." Master's thesis, Asbury Theological Seminary, 1966. 138p.

4302. Maycock, J. "Augustus Montague Toplady, Hymn-Writer and Theologian, with Special Reference to His Controversy with John Wesley." Ph.D. diss., University of Edinburgh, 1946.

4303. Mayo, Harold Jonathan. "John Wesley and the Christian
       East: On the Subject of Christian Perfection." Master's
       thesis, St. Vladimir's Orthodox Theological Seminary, n.d.
       69p.

4304. Mears, R. A. F. "The History of Methodism in the Eighteenth
       Century." B.Litt. thesis, University of Oxford, 1925.

4305. Mercer, Jerry L. "The Destiny of the Church in Wesley's
       Eschatology." Master's thesis, Southern Methodist University,
       1965. 103p.

4306. _____. "A Study of the Concept of Man in the Sermons of
       John Wesley." Th.D. diss., School of Theology at Claremont,
       1970. 231p.

4307. Meredith, Clyde W. "The Wesleyan Theology of Personal Ex-
       perience." Master's thesis, Butler University, 1943. 101p.

4308. Meredith, Lawrence. "Essential Doctrine in the Theology of
       John Wesley: With Special Attention to the Methodist Stand-
       ards of Doctrine." Ph.D. diss., Harvard University, 1962.
       199p.

4308a. Meyers, Arthur Christian. "John Wesley and the Church
       Fathers." Ph.D. diss., Saint Louis University, 1985. 296p.

4309. Miller, Harry Frank. "Fox and Wesley Examined in the Quest
       for Religious Certainty." B.D. thesis, Southern Methodist
       University, 1937. 61p.

4310. Miller, James MacBeath. "The Roots and Development of
       Wesley's Organization." Ph.D. diss., University of Edin-
       burgh, 1951. 349p.

4311. Mizuki, Joao. "The Wesleyan Movement and Its Influence on
       Social Problems of Eighteenth Century England." Master's
       thesis, Asbury Theological Seminary, 1954. 117p.

4312. Molin, Sven Eric. "John Wesley's Techniques in Revising
       Literary Masterpieces for His Methodist Audience, with Special
       Reference to Paradise Lost." Ph.D. diss., University of Penn-
       sylvania, 1956. 334p.

4313. Moore, Jack Warren. "The Relationship of John Wesley's Con-
       cept of Holiness to His Concept of the Church." B.D. the-
       sis, Duke University, 1946. 107p.

4314. Moore, Robert L. "From Resignation to Exaltation: A Psy-
       chological Study of Authority and Initiative in the Life and
       Thought of John Wesley." Ph.D. diss., University of Chi-
       cago, 1975.

John and Charles Wesley

4315. Morris, Gilbert Leslie. "Imagery in the Hymns of Charles Wesley." Ph.D. diss., University of Arkansas, 1969. 437p.

4316. Moss, Reginald. "The Origins and Influence of Methodism in the North Staffordshire Potteries before 1820." Master's thesis, University of London, 1952. 160p.

4316a. Mullins, James Herbert. "The Influences of Three Groups on John Wesley." Master's thesis, Northeast Missouri State University, 1983. 58p.

4317. Mussman, Robert Byron. "A Study and Evaluation of the Primary Nonscriptural Influences on John Wesley's Doctrine of Christian Perfection." Ph.D. diss., Southern Baptist Theological Seminary, 1959. 154p.

4318. Nagamachi, Wataru Isaac. "Christian Perfection As Taught by John Wesley." Master's thesis, Southern Methodist University, 1931. 75p.

4319. Naglee, David Ingersoll. "The Significance of the Relationship of Infant Baptism and Christian Nurture in the Thought of John Wesley." Ph.D. diss., Temple University, 1966. 355p.

4320. Neff, Blake J. "John Wesley and John Fletcher on Entire Sanctification: A Metaphoric Cluster Analysis." Ph.D. diss., Bowling Green State University, 1982. 104p.

4321. Nomura, Makoto. "Sanctification and Sacraments in John Wesley." S.T.M. thesis, Drew University, 1982. 101p.

4322. Norman, D. D. R. "The Development of the Evangelical Doctrine of the Atonement in England from the Conversion of John Wesley to the Present Day." Master's thesis, University of Nottingham, 1957.

4323. Nygren, Ellis Herbert. "John Wesley's Interpretation of Christian Ordination." Ph.D. diss., New York University, 1960.

4324. Odhner, Ormond deCharms. "The Relations between John Wesley and Emanuel Swedenborg." Master's thesis, Northwestern University, 1957. 114p.

4325. Oliveira, Clory Trindade de. "A Theological Comparison of the Doctrines of Christian Perfection in John Wesley and Vocation in Karl Barth." Master's thesis, Southern Methodist University, 1965. 149p.

4326. Palmer, David J. "A Study of John Wesley's Doctrine of

Christian Perfection and Its Social Implication." B.D. thesis,
Butler University, 1956. 90p.

4327. Pask, A. H. "The Influence of Arminius upon the Theology
of John Wesley." Ph.D. diss., University of Edinburgh,
1940.

4328. Paul, Morris Otis. "Some Changing Views of John Wesley."
B.D. thesis, Southern Methodist University, 1935. 47p.

4329. Pennington, Chester Arthur. "The Essentially Wesleyan Form
of the Doctrine of Redemption in the Writings of Emil Brün-
ner." Ph.D. diss., Drew University, 1948.

4330. Perkinson, Edward Myron. "The Place of Reason and/or
Revelation in the Theologies of Karl Barth and John Wesley."
Master's thesis, Northwestern University, 1962. 88p.

4331. Phibbs, Andrew Frank. "John Wesley's Conception of Scriptural Holiness." B.D. thesis, Duke University, 1937. 152p.

4332. Phillips, Charles Gordon. "The Relation of John Wesley to
American Methodism." Master's thesis, Northwestern University, 1923. 97p.

4333. Pierce, Martha Dorothy. "The Eschatology of John Wesley
as Found in Sermons and Notes on the New Testament."
B.A. thesis, Drew University, 1960. 65p.

4334. Pike, D. "The Religious Societies in the Church of England,
1678-1743, and Their Influence on John Wesley and the
Methodist Movement." Master's thesis, University of Leeds,
1960.

4335. Polhemus, Oscar Maurice. "Some Social Aspects of the Wesleyan Movement in the Eighteenth Century." Master's thesis,
Indiana University, 1922.

4336. Pucelik, Thomas M. "Christian Perfection according to John
Wesley...." Thesis, Pontificia Studiorum Universitas A. S.
Thoma Aq. in Urbe, 1963. 72p.

4337. Pullen, Paul T. "The Place of Baptism in the Thought and
Work of John Wesley." S.T.M. thesis, Pittsburgh-Xenia
Theological Seminary, 1957. 85p.

4337a. Rakestraw, Robert Vincent. "The Concept of Grace in the
Ethics of John Wesley." Ph.D. diss., Drew University, 1985.
435p.

4338. Reed, Ralph Lee. "The Doctrine of Christian Perfection in

340

Early Methodist Theology." B.D. thesis, Duke University, 1943. 116p.

4339. Renshaw, John Rutherford. "The Atonement in the Theology of John and Charles Wesley." Th.D. diss., Boston University, School of Theology, 1965. 305p.

4340. Reynolds, James William. "The Legacy of John Wesley As the Organizer and Leader of the Methodist Movement." B.D. thesis, Duke University, 1948. 66p.

4341. Robertson, John Dallas. "The Concept of the Calling in the Theology of John Wesley." Master's thesis, Vanderbilt University, 1953. 93p.

4342. Rogers, Charles A. "The Concept of Prevenient Grace in the Theology of John Wesley." Ph.D. diss., Duke University, 1967. 339p.

4343. Rorapaugh, Albert Chapman. "Grace and Works; a Comparison of St. Thomas Aquinas and John Wesley." S.T.M. thesis, Oberlin College, 1952. 133p.

4344. Roth, Herbert John. "A Literary Study of the Calvinistic and Deistic Implications in the Hymns of Isaac Watts, Charles Wesley, and William Cowper." Ph.D. diss., Texas Christian University, 1978. 186p.

4345. Rowlett, Kenneth Gordon. "John Wesley's Doctrine of Sin; an Analysis and a Comparison." S.T.M. thesis, Oberlin College, 1962. 209p.

4346. Russell, Bernard C. "The Theory and Practice of Christian Discipline, According to John Wesley: Its Theological Bases and Its Modern Relevance." Ph.D. diss., Drew University, 1951.

4347. Rutter, Robert Sherman. "The New Birth: Evangelicalism in the Transatlantic Community during the Great Awakening, 1739-1745." Ph.D. diss., Rutgers University, 1982. 449p.

4348. Sanders, Paul S. "An Appraisal of John Wesley's Sacramentalism in the Evolution of Early American Methodism." Ph.D. diss., Union Theological Seminary, 1954. 617p.

4349. Santos, Julian B. "The Relationship of Salvation and Social Responsibility in the Wesleyan Tradition." D.Min. diss., School of Theology at Claremont, 1981. 88p.

4350. Scales, William Albert. "Selected Unpublished Anthems of Charles Wesley, Jr." Ph.D. diss., University of Southern California, 1969. 510p.

4351. Scanlon, Michael Joseph. "The Christian Anthropology of John Wesley." S.T.D. diss., Catholic University of America, 1969. 164p.

4352. Score, John Nelson Russell. "A Study of the Concept of the Ministry in the Thought of John Wesley." Ph.D. diss., Duke University, 1963. 388p.

4352a. Seaborn, Joseph William, Jr. "John Wesley's Use of History As a Ministerial and Educational Tool." Th.D. diss., Boston University School of Theology, 1985. 265p.

4353. Selleck, J. Brian. "The Book of Common Prayer in the Theology of John Wesley." Ph.D. diss., Drew University, 1983. 2 vols.

4354. Shackford, Joseph Temple. "The Relation of Morality and Religion in the Thought of John Wesley." B.D. thesis, Duke University, 1943. 105p.

4355. Sheffler, Samuel Lee. "Communicating the Gospel to a Rural Church through the Sermons of the Wesleys." D.Min. diss., Drew University, 1982. 137p.

4356. Shermer, Robert Charles. "John Wesley's Speaking and Writing on Predestination and Free Will." Ph.D. diss., Southern Illinois University, Carbondale, 1969. 375p.

4357. Shimizu, Mitsuo. "Epistemology in the Thought of John Wesley." Ph.D. diss., Drew University, 1980. 245p.

4358. Shipley, David C. "Methodist Arminianism in the Theology of John Fletcher." Ph.D. diss., Yale University, 1942. 450p. The first chapter concerns Wesley and Arminianism, pp. 1-36.

4359. Shudo, Daniel K. "John Wesley: Man of Discipline; an Investigation of the Concept of Discipline in the Life and Works of Mr. John Wesley, M.A." Master's thesis, Asbury Theological Seminary, 1959. 87p.

4360. Shult, John. "John Wesley's Doctrine of Baptism and Its Relation to Sanctification." Master's thesis, Lutheran School of Theology at Chicago, 1979. 181p.

4361. Smith, Chester Burl. "Influences of Moravian Mysticism Appearing in the Hymnody of the Wesleys." Master's thesis, Butler University, 1958. 148p.

4362. Smith, Paxton. "John Wesley: Man of Letters." B.D. thesis, Southern Methodist University, 1931. 61p.

4363. Spellmann, Norman Woods. "The General Superintendency in
       American Methodism, 1784-1870." Ph.D. diss., Yale Univer-
       sity, 1961. 371p.

4364. Sproull, Jerry. "The Class Meeting." Master's thesis, As-
       bury Theological Seminary, 1967.

4365. Staples, Rob L. "John Wesley's Doctrine of Christian Per-
       fection: A Reinterpretation." Th.D. diss., Pacific School
       of Religion, 1963. 368p.

4366. Starkey, Lycurgus M. "The Work of the Holy Spirit in the
       Theology of John Wesley." Ph.D. diss., Columbia University,
       1953. 237p.

4367. Stockton, C. R. "The Origin and Development of Extra-
       liturgical Worship in Eighteenth Century Methodism." D.Phil.
       diss., Oxford University, 1969. 382p.

4368. Sweetland, William Ernest. "A Critical Study of John Wesley
       As Practical Thinker and Reformer." Ph.D. diss., Michigan
       State University, 1955. 202p.

4369. Taylor, David Lyman. "Lay Leadership in Methodist Wor-
       ship." S.T.M. thesis, Seabury-Western Theological Seminary,
       1960. 150p. Chap. 3 discusses Wesley and the Reformation.

4370. Taylor, George Brenton. "The Functions of the State in
       Social Reform As Found in Some Official Publications of Meth-
       odism." Th.D. diss., Boston University School of Theology,
       1955. 272p.

4371. Taylor, Warren F. "The Resurrection: A Study in the His-
       tory of Preaching." Ph.D. diss., School of Theology at
       Claremont, 1980.

4372. Tenney, Mary Alice. "Early Methodist Biography, 1739-1791:
       A Study in the Literature of the Inner Life." Ph.D. diss.,
       University of Wisconsin, 1939. Chap. 5 discusses John Wes-
       ley's journal.

4373. Tews, Jane Alison. "The Origin and Outcome of the Liturgies
       of John Wesley." D.Min. diss., School of Theology at Clare-
       mont, 1978. 94p.

4374. Totten, Samuel Nathaniel. "A Study of the Standard Sermons
       of John Wesley with Special Attention to Their Structure, De-
       velopment, Content, Use of Scripture and Elements of Evan-
       gelism." B.D. thesis, Butler University, 1958. 90p.

4375. Townsend, James A. "Feelings Related to Assurance in

Charles Wesley's Hymns." Ph.D. diss., Fuller Theological Seminary, 1979.

4376. Tseng, Y. D. "Charles Wesley and His Poetry." B.D. thesis, University of Oxford, 1936.

4377. Tsoumas, George J. "A Critical Evaluation of John Wesley's Ordination from a Greek Orthodox Viewpoint." Ph.D. diss., Boston University, 1953.

4378. Tucker, Robert Leonard. "The Separation of the Methodists from the Church of England." Ph.D. diss., Columbia University, 1918. 184p.

4379. Tuttle, Robert G. "The Influence of the Roman Catholic Mystics on John Wesley." Ph.D. diss., University of Bristol, 1969. 476p.

4380. Tyson, John R. "Charles Wesley's Theology of the Cross: An Examination of the Theology and Method of Charles Wesley As Seen in His Doctrine of the Atonement." Ph.D. diss., Drew University, 1983.

4381. Uphaus, Dwight Leslie. "A Set of Wesley Hymns Suited to Worship in the Church of the Nazarene Arranged for Choir and Congregation." D.M.A. diss., University of Missouri, Kansas City, 1981. 120p.

4382. Van House, Robert W. "The Wesleyan Doctrine of Man and Leadership Practice in a United Methodist Church." D.Min. diss., Phillips University, 1974. Chap. 3 entitled "John Wesley's Doctrine of Man," pp. 19-31.

4383. Van Valin, Howard F. "A Historical Study of the Influence of Monastic Piety on John Wesley." B.D. thesis, Asbury Theological Seminary, 1955. 86p.

4384. Velázquez, José R. "The Theological Basis of John Wesley's Social Concern." Master's thesis, Asbury Theological Seminary, 1967. 103p.

4385. Vogel, John Richard. "Faith and the Image of God: An Investigation of John Wesley's Doctrine of Salvation." Master's thesis, Depauw University, 1967. 86p.

4386. Wade, William Nash. "A History of Public Worship in the Methodist Episcopal Church and Methodist Episcopal Church, South, from 1784 to 1905." Ph.D. diss., University of Notre Dame, 1981. Chap. 1 deals with John Wesley's Sunday Service.

4387. Walsh, John Dixon. "Yorkshire Evangelicals in the Eighteenth
       Century, with Special Reference to Methodism." Ph.D. diss.,
       University of Cambridge, 1956. 407p.

4388. Warner, T. E. "The Impact of Wesley on Ireland." Ph.D.
       diss., University of London, 1954. 337p.

4389. Watson, David Lowes. "The Origins and Significance of the
       Early Methodist Class Meeting." Ph.D. diss., Duke Univer-
       sity, 1978. 470p.

4390. Wearmouth, Robert F. "Methodism from the Death of Wesley,
       1791, to the Wesleyan Centenary, 1839." Master's thesis,
       University of Birmingham, 1928.

4391. Weigand, Thomas, Jr. "The Preaching of John Wesley."
       B.D. thesis, Butler University, 1955. 108p.

4392. Welch, Barbara Ann. "Charles Wesley and the Celebration of
       Evangelical Experience." Ph.D. diss., University of Michigan,
       1971. 147p.

4393. Wellons, Albert Wilson. "The Development of John Wesley's
       Idea of the Nature and Means of Salvation." B.D. thesis,
       Duke University, 1945. 123p.

4394. West, Cleo Aubrey. "John Wesley's Doctrine of Conversion."
       B.D. thesis, Southern Methodist University, 1937.

4395. Whited, Harold V. "A Rhetorical Analysis of the Published
       Sermons Preached by John Wesley at Oxford University."
       Ph.D. diss., University of Michigan, 1959. 373p.

4396. Whitney, Arthur P. "The Basis of Opposition to Methodism
       in England in the Eighteenth Century." Ph.D. diss., New
       York University, 1951. 77p. Chap. 3, "Traits of a
       Methodist," is concerned mainly with the situation as it de-
       veloped under the leadership of John Wesley.

4397. Wilberforce, D. L. "A Study of the Formative Influences
       Governing the Development of John Wesley's Social, Political
       and Ecclesiastical Methods and Practices." M.Litt. thesis,
       University of Newcastle-upon-Tyne, 1976.

4398. Wilder, James Sampson. "Early Methodist Lay Preachers and
       Their Contribution to the Eighteenth Century Revival in
       England." Thesis, University of Edinburgh, 1948. 409p.

4399. Williams, Atticus Morris. "John Wesley: the Critical Years
       of 1738-1744." Honors thesis, Duke University, 1962. 70p.

4400. Williams, Colin Wilbur. "Methodism and the Ecumenical Move-
       ment." Ph.D. diss., Drew University, 1958. 138p.

4401. Williams, Ronald Gordon. "John Wesley's Doctrine of the
       Church." Th.D. diss., Boston University, School of Theolo-
       gy, 1964.

4401a. Wilson, Charles Randall. "The Correlation of Love and Law
       in the Theology of John Wesley." Ph.D. diss., Vanderbilt
       University, 1959. 212p.

4402. Wilson, David Dunn. "The Influence of Mysticism on John
       Wesley." Ph.D. diss., University of Leeds, 1968. 422p.

4403. Wilson, Robert Henry. "John Wesley's Doctrine of Sanctifica-
       tion." D.Min. diss., Fuller Theological Seminary, 1972. 170p.

4404. Windemiller, Duane Arlo. "The Psychodynamics of Change in
       Religious Conversion and Communist Brainwashing: With Par-
       ticular Reference to the Eighteenth Century Evangelical Revi-
       val and the Chinese Thought Control Movement." Ph.D.
       diss., Boston University, 1960. 178p. Chap. 3 concerns
       religious conversion during the Evangelical revival, pp. 48-
       90.

4404a. Winstead, Michael Ernest. "A Methodist Approach to Steward-
       ship: An Evaluation of John Wesley's Sermon 'The Use of
       Money' and Its Application to Contemporary Fund Raising."
       D.Min. diss., School of Theology at Claremont, 1984. 81p.

4405. Woodward, Barry John. "Using the 83 Wesley Hymns in the
       Book of Hymns/The Methodist Hymnal in Present Day Min-
       istry." D.Min. diss., Drew University, 1981. 352p.

4406. Wyatt, Lloyd D. "John Wesley's Doctrine of Salvation."
       B.D. thesis, Butler University, 1955. 84p.

POETRY

(See also nos. 3141, 3533)

4407. A., R. "In Memory of John Wesley M.A." Methodist Magazine 36 (1813): 799-800.

4408. An Acrostic, Humbly Inscribed to the Rev'd. Mr. John Wesley. [London? S. Coate? 1791?]. Poem in the form of an acrostic on the death of John Wesley. NjMUM

4409. Bainbridge, H. S. "John Wesley." Methodist Recorder, 26 February 1891, 168.

4410. Barrow, James. An Elegy Occasioned by the Death of the Rev. Charles Wesley, M.A., Who Departed This Life March the 29th, 1788, in the 80th Year of His Life. London: Scollick, 1788. 8p. NjMUM

4411. Beard, George. The History of Methodism; or, The Wesleyan Centenary. A Poem in twelve books, Including Notices of the West Indies, etc.... London: J. C. Beard; Simpkin, Marshall and Co., [1840]. 180p.

4412. Bishop, Helen. "Pictures from John Wesley's Journal." Proceedings of the Wesley Historical Society 31 (1958): 161-63. Two poems: "South Carolina--April 1737," and "London--February 1791."

4413. Churchey, Walter. Lines on the Rev. John Wesley. [1791?] Printed on satin, eight lines.

4414. Court, Lewis H. "John Wesley." Wesleyan Methodist Magazine 149 (1926): 399.

4415. _____. "Wesley's Statue at Bristol." Methodist Magazine 160 (1937): 279.

4416. Cozens, Z. "An Elegy on the Rev. John Wesley, M.A." Arminian Magazine 14 (1791): 445-47.

4417. Creighton, James. A Dialogue in Verse Occasioned by the Death of the Rev. John Wesley. 1794. 20p.

4418.   _____. Elegiac Stanzas Occasioned by the Death of the
          Rev. Charles Wesley. London, 1788. 24p.

4419.   An Elegiac Pastoral Occasioned by the Death of the Reverend
          John Wesley, Who Died March 2d, 1791. London: W. Brid-
          ges, 1791. 16p.

4420.   An Elegy on the Death of the Rev. John Wesley, M.A.
          Philadelphia: Barrett and Jones, Printers, 1844. 16p.

4421.   Farrington, Harry Webb. "John Wesley." Methodist Review
          110 (1927): 404.

4422.   Fish, M. E. "Wesley." Methodist Magazine 155 (1932): 709.

4423.   "The Following Verses Were Written by a Poor Man, upon Mr.
          Wesley's First Preaching the Gospel in Kingswood." Method-
          ist Magazine 26 (1803): 48.

4424.   Gilder, Richard Watson. "John Wesley." In Wesley Bicen-
          tennial..., 124-25. See no. 52.

4425.   Gough, Benjamin. "In Memoriam. Charles Wesley, Hymnol-
          ogist." In Wesley Memorial Volume, 529-31. See no. 257.
          Also contained in The Methodist Hymn Book and Its Associa-
          tions, vii-ix. See no. 1594.

4426.   Hare, John Middleton. "Memories of Haworth Church."
          Methodist Recorder, 3 October 1879, 748.

4427.   Harris, W. Gregory. "John Wesley: The Practical Mystic."
          Wesleyan Methodist Magazine 135 (1912): 468.

4428.   Hunter, Ralph W. G. "In Memoriam John Wesley--Charles
          Wesley, Westminster Abbey, March 30th 1876." Methodist
          Recorder, 21 April 1876, 205.

4429.   K., C. Wesley's Escape from the Fire, Chronicled in Verse.
          Methodist Rhymes, no. 1. London: C. A. Bartlett, 1865.
          8p.

4430.   Kenton, James. Thoughts (in Verse) Sacred to the Memory
          of Charles Wesley, Who Died March 29th, 1788. London: J.
          Moore, 1788. 16p.

4431.   _____. A Token of Affectionate Regard, Sacred to the
          Memory of the Rev. John Wesley. London: J. Moore, 1791.
          15p.

4432.   Kresensky, Raymond. "Poem for Charles Wesley." Christian
          Century 59 (1942): 629.

348   John and Charles Wesley

4433. Lawton, David. "Wesley's Prayer Room: Written After a
       Visit to Wesley's House, in City Road." Wesleyan Methodist
       Church Record 15 (1906): 61.

4434. Lindsay, T. A. "John Wesley." Wesleyan Methodist Maga-
       zine 146 (1923): 432.

4435. Lines in Memory of the Reverend John Wesley, A.M. Shef-
       field: J. Gales, 1791. 16p.

4436. Lines on the Erection of a Statue to the Memory of John Wes-
       ley. N.p., n.d. 22p. IEG

4437. "Lines Written on Visiting the Tomb of the Rev. John Wesley,
       in December, 1827; by a Class Leader in the Primitive Wes-
       leyan Methodist Society." Primitive Wesleyan Methodist Maga-
       zine 6 (1828): 93.

4438. Mackay, James. Flesh into Flame. London: Epworth Press,
       1950. 15p.

4439. Marsden, Joshua. An Elegiac Poem on the Death of the Late
       Eminent and Reverend John Wesley, A.M., Inscribed to the
       Rev. J. Taylor. Nottingham: S. Tupman, 1791. 32p. IEG

4440. Martin, Thomas. The Centenary: A Commemorative Poem:
       Including Occasional Sketches of Men and Events in the His-
       tory of Methodism. London: John Mason, 1839. 160p.

4441. Martindale, Miles. An Elegy on the Death of the Revd. John
       Wesley. Nottingham, Eng.: S. Tupman, 1791. 15p. NjMUM

4442. Mole, John. "John Wesley Preaching at Gwennap Pit." En-
       counter 64, no. 3 (1985): 7.

4443. "A Monody to the Memory of the Rev. John Wesley (During
       the Funeral Solemnities)." Arminian Magazine 14 (1791):
       557-60, 593-96.

4444. Moore, William Kennedy. "Wesley and Whitefield." Methodist
       Recorder, 23 February 1872, 93.

4445. Mowbray, Henry. "Description of Rev. John Wesley and of
       the Conversion of Mary Desmond, under His Ministry; from
       Whitchurch's David Dreadnought." Methodist Magazine 39
       (1816): 277-78.

4446. Olivers, Thomas. A Descriptive and Plaintive Elegy on the
       Death of the Late Rev. John Wesley. London: G. Paramore,
       1791. 12p.

4447. _____. "Elegy on the Death of John Wesley." Methodist
Recorder, 26 February 1891, p. 167.

4448. Pearson, Charles William. Methodism: A Retrospect and an
Outlook. New York: Hunt and Eaton; Cincinnati: Cranston
and Stowe, 1891. 86p. Several pages of this long poem are
about John Wesley.

4449. Pellowe, William C. S. "John Wesley Draws the Decades After
Him." In Three Sermons That Gave Birth to Methodism, 5.
See no. 1284.

4450. Pescod, Joseph. An Elegy on the Death of the Rev. John
Wesley.... Lincoln, Eng.: Smith, 1791. 8p.

4451. R., T. "An Elegy on the Death of the Rev. John Wesley,
A.M." Arminian Magazine 14 (1791): 647-52.

4452. Reid, W. Hamilton. "Monody on the Late Rev. John Wesley."
Gentleman's Magazine 69 (1791): 367.

4453. S., H. "Sonnet on Jackson's Portrait of Wesley." Wesleyan
Methodist Magazine 56 (1833): 688.

4454. Santley, Mary McDermott. An Elect Lady. Cleveland, 1892.
2p.

4455. Sutcliffe, Joseph. Lines on the Erection of a Statue to the
Memory of John Wesley, in the Wesleyan College of Richmond,
June 14, 1849. London: M. Snell, 1850. 24p.

4456. Trim, [Edward Baldwyn]. "Curious Eloge on John Wesley."
In A Congratulatory Address to the Rev. John Crosse....
To Which is Added ... an Eloge to the Memory of John Wes-
ley..., 143-50. London, 1791. 197p.

4457. Vine, Alfred H. "Wesley's Home." In Wesley Studies, 16-17.
See no. 190.

4458. Williams, Dwight. "Epworth." In Wesley Memorial Volume,
343. See no. 257.

4459. Williams, William Thomas. John Wesley, Unwearied Ambassador.
Cincinnati: God's Bible School and Missionary Training Home,
1938. 50p.

4460. Wills, S. "A Sonnet [to John Wesley]." Methodist Recorder,
26 February 1891, 168.

4461. Winchester, Elhanan. An Elegy on the Death of John Wesley.... London, 1791. 14p.

4462. Wiseman, George W. "John Wesley." <u>Together</u> 7, no. 1
       (1963): 59.

DRAMA

(See also no. 1845)

4463. Allan, Marion. Wesley, a Play. Dramatized from Telford's Life of Wesley. London: Epworth Press, 1938. 43p.

4464. Baker, Thomas Henry. Grace Murray, a Play in Three Acts. London: Epworth Press, 1950. 51p. "The Play is concerned with the love of John Wesley and Grace Murray, and with happenings that culminated in what Telford has described as 'the greatest trial of Wesley's life'."

4465. Berry, Douglas. Man of One Book. A Play in Two Acts. Nashville: Discipleship Resources, 1983. 66p.

4466. Bibbins, Ruthella Bernard. The Romance of Methodism Building a Lovely Lane around the World.... Richmond, Va.: Methodist Publishing House, 1934. 48p.

4467. Blatherwick, Douglas Pursey. The Twenty-fourth of May; a Short Play about John Wesley. London: H. V. Capsey, 1937. 14p.

4468. Bowmer, John C. When First Sent Forth; a Presentation for Wesley Day. London: Epworth Press, 1965. 18p. A play depicting the beginnings of Methodism.

4469. Brenton, Howard. "Wesley." In Plays for Public Places, 31-70. London: Eyre Methuen and Co., 1972. 103p. Episodes from the life of John Wesley in England and Colonial America.

4470. Cumbers, Frank Henry. My Wondering Soul; Scenes from the Life of Charles Wesley. London: Epworth Press, 1957. 39p. Three-act play written to mark the 250th anniversary of Charles Wesley's birth.

4471. Ehrensperger, Harold Adam. The Spreading Flame: The Pageant of the Methodist Beginnings.... New York and Cincinnati: Methodist Book Concern, 1934. 46p.

4472. _____. The Spreading Word: A Pageant of the People
Called Methodists--They of a Thousand Books and Two,
Celebrating the Sesquicentennial of the Publishing House
of the Church. Kansas City, Mo.?, 1939? Program.

4473. Eliason, M. W. "Make the Welkin Ring; a Dramatic Service
Reliving Christmas with the Wesleys." Music Ministry, n.s.
10, no. 12 (1978): 6-7.

4474. Emurian, Ernest K. Awakening at Aldersgate, a Play in
Three Scenes. Nashville: Methodist Evangelistic Materials,
1963. 23p. NjMUM

4475. _____. "Charles Wesley." In Ten New Plays for Church
and School, 91-107. Natick, Mass.: W. A. Wilde Co., 1959.
194p. A one-act play.

4476. Everson, F. Howell. The Late Mr. Wesley. A Phantasy.
London: Epworth Press, 1950. 32p.

4477. Ivens, H. John. John Wesley; Glimpses of the Life and Work
of a Great World Citizen. London: Epworth Press, 1932.
64p.

4478. Macdonald, Alec. Wesley, the Preacher; a Broadcast Play.
London: Epworth Press, 1938. 19p.

4479. McTavish, John, and Judith Ann Brocklehurst. The Passions
of John Wesley. Nashville: Abingdon Press, 1985. 48p.

4480. Raynor, Frank Charles. John Wesley, Fellow of Lincoln; a
Play in Five Scenes. Leeds: J. Broadbent, 1938. 80p.

4481. Ride! Ride!: A Musical Based on a Story about John Wesley.
Lyrics by Alan Thornhill; Music by Penelope Thwaites; Ar-
rangements by Will Reed. London: Croydon, 1976. 64p.
NjMUM. See no. 4564.

4482. Robinson, Emma A. "Beginnings of Methodism in England."
Episode 1 in The Pageant of Methodism. Rev. ed. Nashville:
Epworth League, 1915. 48p.

4483. Shields, James Kurtz. Scenario of the Life of John Wesley.
Bridgeport, Conn.: John Wesley Pictures Corp., 19--? 26p.

4484. Whitworth, Phyllis. John Wesley: A Play in Three Acts.
London: Epworth Press, 1947. 101p.

4485. Willcox, Helen Lida. Along the Years: A Pageant of Methodism. New York and Cincinnati: The Methodist Book Concern,
1930. 60p. John Wesley is a character in Episode 1.

FICTION

4486. Allan, Dot. Passionate Sisters. London: Robert Hale, 1955. 192p.

4487. Andrew, Prudence. A New Creature. London: Hutchinson; New York: Putnam, 1968. 331p.

4488. Bett, Henry. The Watch Night: Being Some Account of the Earlier Life and Adventures of Mr. Richard Vivian, a Preacher of the Gospel among the People Called Methodists, and Particularly of What Befell Him in the Years 1744, 1745, and 1746. London: S. Paul and Co., 1912. 311p. John Wesley plays a prominent role in this story.

4489. Bone, Florence. The Morning of Today. New York: Eaton and Mains; Cincinnati: Jennings and Graham, 1907. 204p.

4490. Charles, Elizabeth Rundle. Diary of Mrs. Kitty Trevylyan: A Story of the Times of Whitefield and the Wesleys. New York: M. W. Dodd, 1864. 436p.

4491. Cleveland, John. The Master Preacher. Illustrated by Grenville Manton. London: Isbister and Co., 1904. 96p. The Christmas issue of the Sunday Magazine. NjMUM

4492. Drakeford, John W. Take Her, Mr. Wesley. Waco, Tex.: Word Books, 1973. 142p.

4493. Eayrs, George. A Son of Issachar: A Story of the Times of Wesley and Kilham. London: George Burroughs, n.d. 236p.

4494. Hocking, Joseph. The Birthright: Being the Adventurous History of Jaspar Pennington of Pennington in the County of Cornwall. London: Ward, Lock, 1919. 256p.

4495. Jacob, Uncle [pseud.]. Tales of the Wesleyan Methodists. London: Jonathan Neal, 1861. 85p.

4496. Leslie, Emma. Walter: A Tale of the Times of Wesley. New

York: Phillips and Hunt; Cincinnati: Walden and Stowe,
1880.   364p.

4497.   Moore, Frank Frankfort.   The Messenger: The Love That
Prevailed.   Illustrated by H. B. Matthews.   New York: Empire, 1907.   320p.

4498.   Newman, Leslie Arthur.   Gypsy Tells Her Story.   London:
Epworth Press, 1947.   83p.

4499.   Oemler, Marie Conway.   The Holy Lover.   New York: Boni
and Liveright, 1927.   315p.

4500.   Quiller-Couch, Arthur Thomas.   Hetty Wesley.   New York
and London: Macmillan, 1903.   337p.

4501.   Sizer, Kate Thompson.   Denis Patterson, Field Preacher; a
Story of Early Methodism and John Wesley.   London: R.
Culley, n.d.   197p.

JUVENILE WORKS

4502. Baker, Frank. "Was John Wesley Real?" Cross/Talk 2, no. 3 (1973).

4503. Barstad, Glenna. They Dared for God. Mountain View, Calif.: Pacific Press, 1958. 128p.

4504. Bennett, William W. A History of Methodism for Our Young People. Cincinnati: Jennings and Pye, 1878. 273p.

4505. Bonsall, Elizabeth Hubbard. Famous Hymns, with Stories and Pictures. 2d ed. Philadelphia: Union Press, 1927. 136p.

4506. Brett, Sidney Reed. John Wesley. Lives to Remember Series. London: Adam and Charles Black, 1958. 96p.

4507. Bull, Norman J. "John Wesley." In One Hundred Great Lives, 190-92. Bath: Hulton Educational Publications, 1972. 355p.

4508. Church, Leslie Frederic. John Wesley, Vivid Life Story in Modern Caption Form. London: Epworth Press, 1953. 23p. Cartoon-type black and white drawings by Greta Jones.

4509. Clifford, Joan. The Young John Wesley. Illustrated by Arthur Roberts. London: Parrish; New York: Roy Publishers, 1966. 126p.

4510. Crawshaw, John. Fireside Conversations about Wesley. London: Whittaker and Co., [185-?]. 126p. IEG

4511. Curnock, Nehemiah. The Father of Methodism; or, The Life of the Rev. John Wesley, M.A., Written for Children. London: C. H. Kelly, 1891. 64p.

4512. Davey, Cyril J. Horseman of the King. The Story of John Wesley. Stories of Faith and Fame. London: Lutterworth Press, 1957. 94p.

4513. Fitzgerald, William Blackburn. Through England on Horseback in the Eighteenth Century. London: C. H. Kelly, 1913. 156p.

356   John and Charles Wesley

4514. Garlick, Phyllis L. Six Great Missionaries: St. Francis
       Xavier, John Wesley, Alexander MacKay, Sir Wilfred Grenfell,
       Ida Scudder, Albert Schweitzer. London: Hamish Hamilton,
       1955. 216p.

4515. Hill, David C. "John Wesley Minister to Millions." In Mes-
       sengers of the King, 89-97. Minneapolis, Minn.: Augsburg
       Publishing House, 1968.

4516. Hodges, George. "John Wesley." In Saints and Heroes Since
       the Middle Ages, 296-318. New York: Henry Holt and Co.,
       1912. 318p.

4517. Kerr, Ronn. Winning the Frontier: John Wesley. Book 1.
       Illustrated by Bill McPheeters. N.p.: Ronn Kerr Associates,
       1976. 11p. Comic book format.

4518. Kirlew, Marianne. The Story of John Wesley, Told to Boys
       and Girls. New York: Methodist Book Concern, 1920. 168p.

4519. MacDonald, William. The Young Peoples' Wesley. Introduc-
       tion by Bishop W. F. Mallalieu. New York: Eaton and
       Mains, 1901. 204p.

4520. McDougall, David. The Story of John Wesley Told to Young
       People. Stirling: Stirling Tract Enterprise, 1938. 16p.

4521. McNeer, May Younge, and Lynd Ward. John Wesley. New
       York: Abingdon-Cokesbury Press, 1951. 95p.

4522. McPherson, Anna Talbott. "John Wesley: The Apostle of the
       Open Road." Chap. 16 in Spiritual Secrets of Famous
       Christians, 124-32. Grand Rapids, Mich.: Zondervan Pub-
       lishing House, 1964. 152p.

4523. Miller, Basil William. "John Wesley." In Ten Famous Evan-
       gelists, 14-22. Grand Rapids, Mich.: Zondervan Publishing
       House, 1949. 88p.

4523a. _____. "Susanna Wesley." In Ten Girls Who Became Fa-
       mous, 7-13. Grand Rapids, MI: Zondervan Publishing House,
       1946.

4524. Myers, Elisabeth P. Singer of Six Thousand Songs; a Life
       of Charles Wesley. Illustrated by Leonard Vosburgh. Lon-
       don and New York: T. Nelson, 1965. 160p.

4525. Polkinghorne, Ruby Kathleen, and M. I. R. Polkinghorne.
       "John Wesley." In In the Steps of the Apostles, 128-37.
       London: University of London Press, 1957. 174p.

Juvenile Works   357

4526. Powell, Jessie. The Horseman with the Torch; a Book about
       John Wesley. London: Lutterworth Press, 1946. 83p.

4527. St. Clair, Clara. "Little John's Shield." Our Own Magazine
       9 (1888): 136-38. The Story of the Epworth fire, with an
       engraving of John Wesley preaching in Cornwall.

4528. Sims, Lydel. The Burning Thirst; a Story of John Wesley.
       New York: Abingdon Press, 1958. 136p.

4529. Sowton, Stanley. It Happened to John Wesley. London:
       Epworth Press, 1938. 95p.

4530. Stephen, James. "John Wesley, the Traveling Evangelist."
       Chap. 1 in Twelve Famous Evangelists, with Incidents in
       Their Remarkable Lives, 7-10. London: Pickering and
       Inglis, n.d. 96p.

4531. Tucker, Robert Leonard. "John Wesley and the Evangelical
       Revival." Chap. 14 in Builders of the Church, 135-44. New
       York and Cincinnati: Abingdon Press, 1924. 336p.

4532. Vasey, Thomas. The Story of Our Founder: Being a Life
       of John Wesley, Written for Children. 3d ed. London:
       Elliot Stock, 1871. 108p.

4533. Vernon, Louise A. A Heart Strangely Warmed. Illustrated
       by Allan Eitzen. Scottdale, Pa.: Herald Press, 1975. 125p.

4534. Vickers, John A. John Wesley: Founder of Methodism.
       Illustrated by Ronald Jackson. Loughborough: Ladybird
       Books, 1977. 50p.

4535. Walters, Helen B. When John Wesley Was a Boy. Grand
       Rapids, Mich.: Baker Book House, 1961. 97p.

4536. Wilson, Richard. "Wesley, Whitefield, and Wilberforce." In
       Servants of the People: A Book of Biographies for Young
       Citizens, 143-50. London: J. M. Dent and Sons, 1920.
       224p.

4537. Wise, Daniel. Heroic Methodists of the Olden Time ... In-
       tended to Please and Profit Boys and Girls. New York:
       Phillips and Hunt, 1882. 307p. Includes chapters on John,
       Charles, and Susanna Wesley.

4538. _____. The Story of a Wonderful Life; or, Pen Pictures
       of the Most Interesting Incidents in the Life of the Celebrated
       John Wesley, Adapted to the Tastes and Wants of Young
       People. Cincinnati: Curts and Jennings, 1873. 318p.

MISCELLANEA

(See also no. 1845)

4539. Baker, Frank. John Wesley and the Birth of the Methodist Episcopal Church. Wilmore, Ky.: Asbury Theological Seminary, 1984. Sound cassette.

4540. Cannon, William R. Glorious Realization. Nashville: Tidings, 1974. Sound cassette.

4541. Celebrating Wesley's Chapel: November 1st 1778 - November 1st 1978. London: Miramar Records, 1978. Sound recording.

4542. Charles Wesley Remembers. Macon, Ga.: Good News TV, 1983. 4 videocassettes. Rev. James Reese as Charles Wesley.

4543. Cleland, James T. The Event of Aldersgate. Richmond, Va.: Union Theological Seminary, [1976?]. Sound cassette.

4544. Driver, Tom F. Libretto to The Invisible Fire; an Oratorio Expressing John Wesley's Experience of Conversion and Recalling the Beginnings of Methodism, by Cecil Effinger. Edited by O. L. Simpson. N.p.: Methodist Publishing House, 1960. 64p.

4545. Haines, Lee. Reformers and Revivalists: the Wesleyan Methodist Connection. Wilmore, Ky.: Asbury Theological Seminary, 1984. Sound cassette.

4546. Heitzenrater, Richard P. At Full Liberty: Wesley and Doctrinal Standards in American Methodism. Wilmore, Ky.: Asbury Theological Seminary, 1984. Sound cassette.

4547. Houston, James Macintosh. John Wesley and Christian Perfection. Arlington, Va.: C. S. Lewis Institute, 1979. Sound cassette.

4548. Hunter, George G. Our Roots in Wesleyan Evangelism. Wilmore, Ky.: Asbury Theological Seminary, 1982. Sound cassette.

4549. Hynson, Leon O. Wesley: Man for All Seasons. Wilmore,
Ky.: Asbury Theological Seminary, 1983. Sound cassette.

4550. _____. Wesley: The Widening Horizon. Wilmore, Ky.:
Asbury Theological Seminary, 1983. Sound cassette.

4551. _____. Wesley: Theology of the Moral Life. Wilmore,
Ky.: Asbury Theological Seminary, 1983. Sound cassette.

4552. John Wesley. London: BBC-TV Production Co.; Lansdale,
Pa.: Gateway Films, Inc., [197-?]. Motion picture, 16mm.

4553. John Wesley. London: Common Ground, 1948. Released in
the U.S. by United World Films, 1950. Filmstrip.

4554. John Wesley: Practical Evangelist. Film by Paul Klein.
N.p.: Media Division of the United Methodist Communications
Councils in Association with the United Methodist Heritage
Fellowship, [197?]. Motion picture.

4555. John Wesley, That Excellent Minister of the Gospel, Carried
by Angels in Abraham's Bosom.... London: Robert Sayer,
1791. Engraving.

4556. Joy, Donald. Toward Christian Pilgrimage: John Wesley's
Pilgrimage. Wilmore, Ky.: Asbury Theological Seminary,
1982. Sound cassette.

4557. Kaye, John. Life and Death of the Rev. John Wesley, A.M.
London: Wesleyan Times Office, 1859. 12 engravings.

4558. Maire, Douglas Allen, and David A. Neil. The Life of John
Wesley: A Slide Presentation and Lecture. Denver: Iliff
School of Theology, 1977. Sound cassette, script, and 148
slides.

4559. Nelson, Roger. The Man from Aldersgate. N.p.: Brad L.
Smith, 1978. Sound recording.

4560. Outler, Albert C. Evangelism in the Wesleyan Tradition.
Ayden, N.C.: Institutional Electronics, Inc., n.d. 3 sound
cassettes.

4561. _____. John Wesley. Waco, Texas: Creative Resources,
[1972?]. 4 sound cassettes with study guide.

4562. _____. On Working Out Our Own Salvation. Wilmore, Ky.:
Asbury Theological Seminary, 1982. Sound cassette.

4563. Pudney, John. John Wesley and His World. Slide set, made
by Linda Woods Glen. 19 slides from the book, no. 1342.
Student project, Iliff School of Theology, Denver, 1979.

4564. Ride! Ride!: A Musical Based on a Story about John Wesley.
Book and Lyrics by Alan Thornhill; Music by Penelope
Thwaites; Directed by Peter Coe. London: Pilgrim Records,
1976. Sound cassette. See also no. 4481.

4565. Snyder, Howard A. Ryan Lectures. Wilmore, Ky.: Asbury
Theological Seminary, 1977. 3 sound cassettes: 1. The
Making of a Radical. 2. Wesley's Concept of the Church.
3. Wesley and the Radical Protestant Tradition.

4566. Twenty Four Scenes in the Life and Death of the Wesley
Family.... London: R. Owen, [1850?]. GtBMM

4567. Wesley and His Times. N.p.: Trafco Productions, [1983?].
Videocassette. Adapted from the Film John Wesley produced
by Religious Films, Ltd.

PART II:

NON-ENGLISH-LANGUAGE
PUBLICATIONS

NON-ENGLISH-LANGUAGE PUBLICATIONS

4568. Acquaah, Gaddiel Robert. John Wesley. Methodifo asore ne
farebaa, 1703-1791. Cape Coast: Methodist Book Depots,
1942. 43p. GtBMM

4569. Alcuni Giudizi di Giovanni Wesley, Fondatore Delle Chiese
Evangeliche Metodiste. Rome: Chiera, 1880. 23p. It

4570. Allan, Charles Wilfrid. Yüeh-han Wei-ssu-li. 1953. 153p.
NcD

4571. Barbieri, Sante Uberto. Una extraña estirpe de audaces.
Buenos Aires: Ediciones "El Camino," 1958. 198p.

4572. Benedyktowicz, Witold. Bracia z Epworth. Warszawa:
Odrodzenie, 1971. 231p.

4573. Berg, Johannes van den. Het christelijk leven naar de op-
vatting van John Wesley. Kampen: J. H. Kok, 1959. 28p.

4574. _____. "John Wesley's contacten met Nederland."
Nederlands Archief voor Kerkgeschedenis 52, no. 1 (1971):
36-96.

4575. Borgen, Ole Edvard. Taufe, Konfirmation und Mitgliedschaft
in methodistischen Verständnis.... Frankfurt, [Main?] 1969.
75p. NjMUM

4575a. Bryant, Eunice R. "La teología en acción: la teología de
Juan Wesley." D.Min. diss., Nazarene Theological Seminary,
1982.

4576. Burkhard, Johann Gottlieb. Vollständige Geschichte der
Methodisten in England, aus Glaubwürdigen quellen; nebst
den Lebensbeschreibungen ihrer beyden stifter, des herrn
und George Whitefield. 2 vols. in 1. Nürnberg: Raw'sche
Buchhandlung, 1795.

4577. Cahn, Ernst. "John Wesley, als Vorkämpfer einer christlichen
Sozialethik." Christliche Welt 46 (1932): 208-12.

363

364   John and Charles Wesley

4578. Carile, S. "Wesley e i valdesi in Georgia. Integrazione
ante litteram?" Bolletino della Società di Studi Valdesi 95,
no. 135 (1974): 35-36.

4579. Cowley, Thomas. "Les débuts du Méthodisme et les courants
évangéliques dans la société britannique." Istina 14 (1969):
387-412.

4580. Cruvellier, Jean Marc Etienne. L'Exégèse de Romains 7 et
le mouvement de Keswick. Academisch proefschrift.
'S-gravenhage: Drukkerij Pasmans, 1961. 215p. Thesis,
University of Amsterdam.

4581. Curzon, Alfred de. "John Wesley, précurseur de la Croix-
Rouge." Nouvelle Revue, 4th ser., 82 (1926): 16-28.

4582. Davies, Owen. Ymddiddanion Rhwyng dau Gymmydog,
Hyffordd a Bereand, yn Dangos Cyfeiliornadau Calfinistiaeth;
y'nghyd a dau Lythyr at Mr. Thomas Jones, yn Gwrthbrofi
ei Brawf ef O Anghysonedd Mr. Wesley. Caerlleon: Heming-
way, 1807. 376p.

4583. Durrlemann, Valdo. John Wesley; ou, L'Histoire d'un homme
qui avait eu peur de mourir. Poste-parisien. Carrières-
sous-Poissy, S.-et-O., La Cause, 1938. 46p.

4584. Eicken, Erich von. Rechtfertigung und Heiligung bei Wesley
dargestellt unter Vergleichung mit den Anschauungen Luthers
und des Luthertums. Th.D. diss., Heidelberg, 1934. 69p.

4585. Eissele, Karl G. Karl Wesley, der Sänger des Methodismus.
Bremen: Anker-Verlag, 1932. 119p. GV

4586. Eltzholz, Carl Frederik. Livsbilleder af John Wesley. Chicago: Boghandel's Forlag, 1903. 178p. IEG

4587. Erb, Jörg. "Johannes Wesley." In vol. 2 of his Die Wolke
der Zeugen; Lesebuch zu einem evangelischen Namenkalender,
385-92. Kassel: J. Stauda, 1957-63.

4588. Evans, Christmas. Mene Tecel; neu adolygead ar Lyfran
bychan o waith Mr. Wesley. Caernarfon: T. Roberts, 1806.
48p.

4589. Evans, John. John Wesley: ei fywyd a'i lafur. Treffynnon:
P. M. Evans, 1880. 552p.

4590. Flachsmeier, Horst Reinhold. Ein brennend Herz; das Leben
John Wesleys. Zürich: Gotthelf-Verlag, 1955.

4591. _____. "Charles Wesley als Prediger und Evangelist."

Der Evangelist: Sonntagsblatt der Methodistenkirche in
Deutschland 108 (1957): 397-98. GDZS

4592. _____. John Wesley als Sozialhygieniker und Arzt. Diss.,
Hamburg, 1957. 91p.

4593. _____. "Methodistische Geschichte. John Wesley als
Sozialhygieniker und Arzt." Wort und Tat: Zeitschrift für
den Dienst am Evangelium 13 (1959): 266-69.

4594. _____. "Was ist England durch Wesley geworden?" Der
Evangelist. Sonntagsblatt der Methodistenkirche in Deutschland 104 (1953): 189. GDZS

4595. Fotsch, Wilhelm. "Aus Johann Wesleys Leben." In Glaubens-
helden, geschildert vom Standpunkt des vollen Heils in
Christo, 3-203. Cincinnati: Cranston, 1893. 678p.

4596. Frost, Stanley Brice. Die Autoritätslehre in den Werken John
Wesleys. Aus der Welt Christlicher Frömmigkeit, 13. Mu-
nich: Ernst Reinhardt, 1938. 112p. His dissertation,
Marburg.

4597. Funk, Theophil. "John Wesley nach 'Aldersgate'." Der
Evangelist. Sonntagsblatt der Methodistenkirche in Deutschland 114 (1963): 267. GDZS

4598. _____. "Stimme der Geschichte. Wesleys Herrnhutreise
1738." Die Furche; evangelische Monatsschrift für das
geistige Leben der Gegenwart 22 (1937): 274-78. GDZS

4599. _____. "Wilhelm Gross schuf eine Wesley-Büste." Der
Evangelist. Sonntagsblatt der Methodistenkirche in Deutschland 104 (1953): 245.

4600. Gerdes, Egon W. "John Wesleys Lehre von der Gotteseben-
bildlichkeit des Menschen." Diss., Christian-Albrechts-
Universität Kiel, 1958. 306p.

4601. Gounelle, Edmond. John Wesley et le réveil d'un peuple.
Les Vainqueurs, 19. Geneve: Editions Labor et fides, 1948.
212p.

4602. _____. Wesley et ses rapports avec les Français: thèse
historique. Nyons, 1898. 112p.

4603. Grant, R. V. John Wesley teterina. East Cape, Papua:
Methodist Mission, 1950. 34p. Translated into Bwaidogan
language, 1952.

4604. Guiton, François. Histoire du Méthodisme Wesleyan dans les
Iles de la Manche. London: John Mason, 1846. 312p.

366 John and Charles Wesley

4605. Guiton, William Henri. John Wesley; esquisse de sa vie et de son oeuvre. Neuilly: Dépôt de Publications Méthodistes, n.d. 86p.

4606. Haddal, Ingvar. "Nattverden i Charles Wesleys Salmer." Kirke og Kultur 63 (1958): 147-55.

4607. Haemmerlin, Michael. Essai dogmatique sur John Wesley, d'après ses sermons. Colmar: C. Decker, 1857. His thesis, Strasbourg.

4608. Hughes, D. R. "John Wesley a hen gapel Crosby Row, Llundain." Bathafarn 4 (1949): 7-13. Concerns John Wesley and the Old Chapel at Crosby Row, London.

4609. Hughes, Rowland. Cofnodau O Amrywiol Ymddyddanion, Rhwng Y Parch. John Wesley, A.M. a'r Pregethwyr Mewn cyfundeb ag ef: Yn cynwys y ffurf o ddysgyblaeth a sefydlwyd yn mhlith y pregethwyr a'r bobl yn y cymdeithasau Methodistaidd. Llanidloes: Albion-Wasg, 1843. 84p.

4610. Iglesia Metodista de México. La Iglesia Metodista de México y su herencia Wesleyana. Comité Organizador de la Celebración del CCL Aniversario (1703--28 de junio--1953) del nacimiento del Rev. Juan Wesley. Mexico City: Nueva Educación, [1953?]. 194p. TxDaM-P

4611. Impeta, Christoffel Nicolaas. De leer der heiliging en volmaking bij Wesley en Fletcher. Leiden: P. J. Mulder, [1913?]. 440p. Proefschrift-Vrije Universiteit te Amsterdam.

4612. Jones, J. Ellis. "John Wesley a William Law." Traethodydd 102 (1947): 97-105.

4613. Jones, John. Y Bywgraffydd Wesleyaidd: yn cynwys brashanes am un-a-thringain o Weinidogion Wesleyaidd Cymreig, yn nghyda 35 o weinidogion a gwyr lleyg Saesonig. Machynlleth: J. Williams, 1866. 196p.

4614. Jones, Thomas. Y Canmlwyddiant O Drefnyddiaeth Wesleyaidd, Sef, Golwg Fer ar Ddechread, cynydd, A Selfyllfa Bresenol y Cymdeithasau Trefnyddol Wesleyaidd Trwy y Byd. Llanidloes: a Gyhoeddwyd ac ar Werth gan J. Lloyd, 1840. 111p. AbN

4615. _____. Ymddyddanion crefyddol rhwng dau gymmydog ystyriol a hyffordd,... y'nghyd ag ychydig sylwadau ar lythyr Mr. Owen Davies at yr awdur: a phrawf o anghysonedd.... J. Wesley mewn amryw bynciau o athrawiaeth. Bala: R. Saunderson, 1807. 446p.

4616. Kamm, Otto. John Wesley und die englische Romantik.
Marburg-Lahn: Druckerei H. Bauer, 1939. 56p. His dissertation, Marburg.

4617. Ang Kasaysayan nang buhay at nang manga gawa ni Juan
Wesley at nang kaniyang kapatid na Carlos.... Manila:
Methodist Publishing House, 1906. 75p.

4618. Kneule, Irmgard. "John Wesley: Hat Wesley den Eltern und
Erziehern des 20 Jahrhunderts noch etwas zu sagen?"
Dienst am Kinde 25, no. 7 (1954): 20-21. GDZS

4619. Kreutzer, Karl. "John Wesley: Das Erbe Johannes Wesleys
an die Welt." Oekumenische Rundschau 2 (1953): 81-84.

4620. Kromrei, Gerhart. John Wesley--ein Erweis göttlicher Gnade.
Munich: Ankers-Verlag, 1948. 31p.

4621. La Gorce, Agnes de. "L'Enfance d'un grand Anglais."
Les Nouvelles Littéraires, no. 915 (27 April 1940): 1-2.

4622. _____. "John Wesley, réformateur de l'Angleterre." Revue
des Deux Mondes, 8th ser., 44 (1938): 639-57.

4623. _____. "Le réformateur Wesley et la monarchie Anglaise."
Revue Universelle 78 (1939): 449-60.

4624. _____. Wesley, maître d'un peuple (1703-91). Paris: A.
Michel, 1940. 366p.

4625. Léger, Augustin. "La Doctrine de Wesley; la controverse
Morave." Annales de Philosophie Chrétienne, 4th ser., 12
(1911): 449-92.

4626. _____. La Jeunesse de Wesley. L'Angleterre réligieuse et
les origines du Méthodisme au XVIIIe siècle. Paris: Librairie
Hachette, 1910. 137p.

4627. Lelièvre, Matthieu. La Théologie de Wesley. Etude sur les
doctrines et l'enseignement du réveil du XVIII siècle connu
sous le nom de Méthodisme. Paris: Publications Méthodistes,
1924. 436p.

4628. _____. "Visite de John Wesley." Chap. 6 in Histoire du
Méthodisme dans les Iles de la Manche, précédé de l'histoire
de la Réformation Hugenote dans cet Archipel..., 248-67.
Paris: Librairie Evangélique; London: Theophilus Woolmer,
1885. 580p.

4629. Lerch, David. Heil und Heiligung bei John Wesley, dargestellt unter Berücksichtigung seiner Anmerkungen zum Neuen

Testament. Zurich: Gedruckt bei der Christlichen Vereins-
buchhandlung, 1941. 180p. His dissertation, Zurich.

4630. Lezius, F. E. "Wesley's Perfektionismus und die Otley-
Bewegung." In Zur Praxis des Christenthums, 213-30. Vol.
2 of Reinhold-Seeberg-Festschrift. Leipzig: D. W. Scholl,
1929.

4631. Lindström, Harold Gustaf Ake. John Wesleys budskap och
nutiddsmänniskan. Stockholm: Bokförlags Aktiebolaget,
1953. 22p. NjMUM

4632. _____. "Metodismen och Kyrkans ämbete." Tro Och Liv,
no. 2 (1959): 54-63.

4633. Listov, Andreas Lauritz Carl. Om Brödrene Wesley og
Methodismen: en Kort historisk Fremstilling. Copenhagen,
1861.

4634. Lovsky, Fadiey. Wesley, apôtre des foules, pasteur des
pauvres. 2d ed. Le Havre: Editions Foi et Victoire, 1977.
175p.

4635. McCallum, John. Cunntas aithghearr air Iain Wesley agus
sgriobhaidhean eile, leis an urr. Glaschu: G. Mac-na-
Ceardadh, 1911. 115p.

4636. Mann, Heinrich. "Zum Gedenken an Charles Wesley. Du
bist ja des Lebens Quelle." Wort und Tat: Zeitschrift für
den Dienst am Evangelium 12 (1958): 44-47.

4637. Marquardt, Manfred. "John Wesleys 'Synergismus'." In
Die Einheit der Kirche: Dimensionen ihrer Heiligkeit
Katholizität u. Apostolizität: Festgabe Peter Meinhold zum
70. Geburtstag, edited by Lorenz Hein, 96-102. Wiesbaden:
Steiner, 1977. 313p.

4638. _____. Praxis und Prinzipien der Sozialethik John Wesleys. Göttingen: Vandenhoeck und Ruprecht, 1977. 176p.
Originally presented as the author's thesis, Kiel, 1975, under
the title Praxis und Prinzipien sozialer Verantwortung.

4639. Matsumoto, Hiroaki. [The Doctrine of Man in the Thought of
John Wesley.] Tokyo: Japan Wesley Study Society, 1961.
79p. In Japanese. NjMUM

4640. Mayer, Erika. Charles Wesleys Hymnen. Eine Untersuchung
und literarische Wurdigung. Diss., Tübingen, 1957.

4641. Metodismen. Utgitt i anledning av 200 arsjubileet for John
Wesleys oplev-else den 24. Mai 1738. Oslow: Norsk For-
lagsselskap, 1938. 79p.

4642. Metodizmút. Shcho e? Ot' gde e? Russe: Pechatitsa
       "Nadezhda," 1896. 55p. NjMUM

4643. Möller, R. H. John Wesleys Selbersterziehung; ein Muster
       für unsere Jugend. Vortrag. Winnenden: Lämmle und
       Müllerschön, 1913. 16p. GV

4644. Nast, William. Das Leben und Wirken des Johannes Wesley
       und seiner haupt-Mitarbeiter.... Cincinnati: L. Swormstedt
       and J. H. Power, 1852. 300p.

4644a. Nausner, Helmut. "John Wesley--ein Reformator? Christ-
       liche Vollkommenheit als Lebensthema." In Was Bedeutet uns
       heute die Reformation? edited by Rudolf Zinnhobler, 99-127.
       Linz: Oberösterreichischer Landesverlag, 1973. 132p.

4645. Neely, Thomas Benjamin. Juan Wesley: el gran reformador
       religioso. New York: Eaton and Mains, 1905. 191p.

4646. Nes, Hendrik Marius van. John Wesley. Nijkerk: G. F.
       Callenbach, 1907. 215p.

4647. Nielsen, Emil. John Wesleys Liv og Virke. Copenhagen,
       1933. 140p.

4648. Nielsen, Fredrik. John Wesley og den Engelske Statskirke.
       Smaaskrifter til Oplysning for Kristne, no. 3. Copenhagen:
       Karl Schonberg Forlag, 1891. 56p.

4649. Nilsen, E. Anker. "En Psykodynamisk Analyse av John
       Wesleys Religiose opplevelser." Norsk Teologisk Tidsskrift
       76 (1975): 35-42. Discusses Källstad's John Wesley and the
       Bible, no. 4261.

4650. Nippert, Ludwig. Das Walten der göttlichen Vorsehung in
       John Wesleys Leben und Wirken. Bremen: Verlag des Trak-
       tathauses, 1876. 85p. NjMUM

4651. Norel, Okke. John Wesley. Getuigen van Christus, 2d ser.,
       15. Amsterdam: W. ten Have, 193-? 32p.

4652. _____. John Wesley, de vader van het methodisme. Den
       Haag: J. N. Voorhoeve, 1936. 159p.

4653. Norel-Straatsma, A. Susanna Wesley. Lichstralen op den
       akker wereld, no. 3. Zeist: Drukkerij van de Stichting
       Hoenderloo, 1936. 39p.

4654. Noro, Yoshio. Wesley no Shōgai to shingaku. Tokyo:
       Kirisuto Kyōdan Shuppan Kyōku, 1975. 668p. NjMUM

4655.   Nuelsen, John L. "Geschichte des britischen Methodismus
        von seiner entstehung bis zum Tode Wesleys." Pt. 1 in
        Kurzgefasste Geschichte des Methodismus von seinen Anfangen
        bis Zur Gegenwart, 1-205. 2d ed. Bremen: Verlagshaus der
        Methodistenkirche, 1929. 875p.

4656.   _____. Das Heilserlebnis im Methodismus. Zürich:
        Christliche Vereinsbuchhandlung, 1938. 45p.

4657.   Orcibal, Jean. "Les Spirituels français et espagnols chez
        John Wesley et ses contemporains." Revue de l'Histoire des
        Religions 139 (1951): 50-109.

4658.   Orlamünder, P. "Johannes Wesleys Zeugnis von der christ-
        lichen Vollkommenheit." Der Evangelist. Sonntagsblatt der
        Methodistenkirche in Deutschland 111 (1960): 76. GDZS

4659.   Pak, Ch'ang-bŏn. Kidok kyohoe ŭi ilch'iron. 1972. 89p.

4660.   Petri, Laura. John Wesley.... Uppsala: J. A. Lindblad,
        1928. 280p.

4661.   Plat, Hugo. "John Wesley als Evangelist." Der Evangelist.
        Sonntagsblatt der Methodistenkirche in Deutschland 104
        (1953): 187. GDZS

4662.   Pollmer, K. H. "Johannes Wesley und sein sozialer Dienst."
        Glaube und Gewissen. Eine Protestantische Monatsschrift 2
        (1956): 225-26.

4663.   _____. "Kirchengründer wider Willen. Zum 175. Todestag
        John Wesleys am 2 Marz." Glaube und Gewissen. Eine Pro-
        testantische Monatsschrift 12 (1966): 50-51.

4664.   Remusat, Charles de. "John Wesley et le méthodisme."
        Revue des Deux Mondes, 2d ser., 85 (1870): 350-86.

4665.   Roberts, Gomer Morgan. "Llythyrau Trefeca a Wesley."
        Bathafarn 15 (1960): 45-54.

4666.   Roberts, Griffith Thomas. "Llanfihangel, Anglesey." Batha-
        farn 3 (1948): 57-59. Concerns Wesley's visits to Anglesey.

4667.   _____. "Seiadau cynnar John Wesley yng Nghymru."
        Bathafarn 1 (1946): 25-39. Concerns early societies held by
        John Wesley in Wales.

4668.   _____. "Wesley a Harris." Cylchgrawn Cymdeithas Hanes
        Methodistiaid Calfinaidd 30 (1945): 65-72, 93-99.

4669.   Roessle, Julius. Johannes Wesley, de Vater der methodistischen Erweckungsbewegung. 2d ed. Giessen: Brunnen, 1954. 88p.

4670. _____. John Wesley. Der Kirchengründer wider Willen. Gissen and Basel, 1939. 78p.

4671. Rosinski, O. F. "Zum 250. Geburtstag John Wesley--17 Juni 1703." Deutsches Pfarrerblat (1953): 267-68.

4672. Rott, Ludwig. "John Wesleys Heilserfahrung am 24 Mai 1738." Der Evangelist. Sonntagsblatt der Methodistenkirche in Deutschland 114 (1963): 247-48. GDZS

4673. Roux, Théophile. La Conversion évangélique de Wesley. Paris: Dépôt des Publications Méthodistes [1938?]. 37p.

4674. Rupp, E. Gordon. "John Wesley--Ein christlicher Prophet." Concilium. Internationale Zeitschrift für Theologie 4 (1968): 510-16.

4675. _____. John Wesley und Martin Luther. Stuttgart: Studiengemeinschaft für Geschichte der evangelisch-methodistischen Kirche, 1983. 24p.

4676. Ryder-Smith, Janet. The Story of John Wesley. Madras: Christian Literature Society for India, 1938. 27p. Text in Tamil.

4677. Salomon, Alfred. Der Rauhreiter Gottes; die Geschichte John Wesleys. Helden des Glaubens, vol. 3. Constance: Christliche Verlagsanstalt, 1959. 95p. Juvenile literature.

4678. Samouélian, S. John Wesley: petit album du Méthodisme. Nimes: Dépôt des Publications Méthodistes, 1960. 32p. NjMUM

4679. _____. Le Réveil méthodiste. Nimes: Publications Evangéliques Méthodistes, 1974. 105p. NjMUM

4680. Schempp, Johannes. Seelsorge und Seelanführung bei John Wesley. Stuttgart: Christliches Verlagshaus, 1949. 248p. His dissertation, Tübingen. NjMUM

4681. Schmidt, Carl Christian Gottlieb. Des Johannes Wesley Leben und Wirken. Halle, 1849. 99p.

4682. Schmidt, Martin. "Die Bedeutung Luthers für Wesleys Bekehrung." Luther Jahrbuch 20 (1938): 125-59.

4683. _____. "John Wesley als Organisator der methodischen Bewegung." In Für Kirche und Recht: Festschrift für

Johannes Heckel zum 70. Geburtstag, edited by Siegfried
Grundmann, 313-50. Cologne: Böhlau Verlag, 1959. 360p.

4684.   . "John Wesley und die Biographie des französischen
Grafen Gaston Jean-Baptiste de Renty (1611-49)." Theologia
Viatorum. Jahrbuch der Kirchlichen Hochschule Berlin 5
(1954): 194-252.

4685.   . John Wesleys Bekehrung. Bremen: Verlaghaus
der Methodistenkirche, 1938. 107p. His dissertation, Zurich.

4686.   . "Der Missionsgedanke des jungen Wesley auf dem
Hintergrunde seines Zeitalters." Theologia Viatorum. Jahrbuch der Kirchlichen Hochschule Berlin 1948-49, 80-97.

4687.   . "Die ökumenische Bedeutung John Wesleys."
Theologische Literaturzeitung 78 (1953): 449-59.

4688.   . "Zum Gedächtnis von Wesleys Bekehrung."
Sächsisches Kirchenblatt, n.s. 2 (1938): 165-67.

4689. Schneeberger, Vilêm. "Der Begriff der christlichen Freiheit
bei John Wesley." Communio Viatorum 20 (1977): 47-61.
Discusses Wesley's concept of religious and civil liberty.

4690.   . "Haushalter Gottes (Beitrag zum Thema Verzicht
im Blick auf christliche Lebenshaltung.)" Communio Viatorum
23 (1980): 23, 65-70.

4691.   . Theologische Wurzeln des sozialen Akzents bei John
Wesley. Zurich: Gotthelf Verlag, 1974. 191p. Slightly
abridged translation of the author's thesis, Husova ceskoslo-
venska evangelicka fakulta bohoslovecka, Prague, 1972.

4692. Scholz, Ernst. "John Wesley. Der Vater des Methodismus."
In vol. 1 of Okumenische Profile: Brückenbauer der einen
Kirche, edited by Günter Gloede, 129-37. Stuttgart: Evang.
Missionverlag, 1961.

4693.   . "John Wesley und die Heilsgewissheit." Der
Evangelist. Sonntagsblatt der Methodistenkirche in Deutschland 104 (1953): 164. GDZS

4694. Schweikher, Marie. Johann Wesley: Sein Leben und sein
Werke. Baiblingen: Verlag der Wesleyanischen Methodisten-
Gemeinschaft, 1874. 208p. NjMUM

4695. Scott, Jefferson Ellsworth. Sarguzasht, pâdri John Wesley
sâhib ki, Methodist Kalisiyá ká mukhtasar ahwál. Lucknow
(India): Methodist Publishing House, 1893. 464p. NjMUM

4696. Scott, Percy. John Wesleys Lehre von der Heilgung: Ver-
glichen mit einem lutherisch-pietistischen Beispiel. Studien
zur Geschichte des neueren Protestantismus, vol. 17. Berlin: A. Töpelmann, 1939. 97p.

4697. Sites, Sarah Moore. A Story of the Wonderful Life, of the
Celebrated John Wesley. Foochow, China: M. E. Mission
Press, 1894. Text in Chinese.

4698. Sommer, Carl Ernst. Der designierte Nachfolger John Wesleys. Beiträge zur Geschichte der Evangelisch-Methodistischen
Kirche, no. 6. Stuttgart: Christliche Verlagshaus, 1977.
27p.

4699. _____. "John Wesleys Weg nach Aldersgate." Der Evangelist: Sonntagsblatt der Methodistenkirche in Deutschland
114 (1963): 234-35. GDZS

4700. _____. "Wesley und Luther." Der Evangelist. Sonntagsblatt der Methodistenkirche in Deutschland 111 (1960): 536.
GDZS

4701. Sommer, Johann Wilhelm Ernst. "Die Bedeutung der Heilserfahrung John Wesleys." Wort und Tat. Zeitschfirt für den
Dienst am Evangelium 7 (1953): 51.

4702. _____. John Wesley und die soziale Frage. Munich:
Anker-Verlag, n.d. 52p.

4703. _____. "John Wesleys Heilserlebnis in seiner Bedeutung
für die Mission." Evangelisches Missionsmagazin n.s. 82
(1938): 342-51.

4704. Song, Hŭng-guk. Wesŭlle sinhak kwa kuwŏnnon. 1975.

4705. Spencer, Miss. Life of Suzanne Wesley. Translated by
Yone Motora. Tokyo: Methodist Publishing House, 1892.
Written in Japanese. NjMUM

4706. Spörri, Theophil. "John Wesley, 1703-91." Kirchenblatt
für die reformierte Schweiz 109 (1953): 198-99.

4707. Stockwell, Bowman Foster. La teología de Juan Wesley y la
nuestra. Buenos Aires: Editorial La Aurora, 1962. 110p.
TxDaM-P

4708. Tanaka, Kamenosuke. Jon Uesure den. 1929. 274p. NcD

4709. Thiele, Eugen. Gottes Kavallerie; Geschichten und Skizzen
aus der Pionierzeit des Methodismus. Zürich: Gotthelf
Verlag, [1969]. 127p.

4710. Thiersch, Heinrich Wilhelm Josias. John Wesley. Augsburg,
       1879. 37p.

4711. Thomas, Wilhelm. Heiligung im Neuen Testament und bei
       John Wesley. Zürich: Christliche Vereinsbuchhandlung,
       1965. 54p.

4712. Thorkildsen, John. John Wesley og litteraturen. Oslo:
       Forlagsselskap, 1933. 30p. NjMUM

4713. Wakefield, Gordon S. "La Littérature du désert chez John
       Wesley." Irénikon 51, no. 2 (1978): 155-70.

4714. Wärenstam, Eric. John Wesley; landsvägsriddaren som
       väckte England. Stockholm: Förlaget Filadelfia, 1949. 9p.

4715. Watson, Philip S. Die Autorität der Bibel bei Luther und
       Wesley. Beiträge zur Geschichte der Evangelisch-Methodis-
       tischen Kirche, vol. 14. Stuttgart: Christliches Verlags-
       haus, 1983. 27p.

4716. Wauer, Gerhard Adolph. Die Anfänge der Brüderkirche in
       England. Leipzig: F. Jansa, 1900. 152p. His dissertation,
       Leipzig.

4717. Weissbach, Jürgen. Der neue Mensch im theologischen
       Denken John Wesleys. Beiträge zur Geschichte des
       Methodismus, no. 2. Stuttgart: Christliches Verlagshaus
       in Komm., 1970. 218p.

4718. Werner, August. "Die Methodisten: John Wesley und George
       Whitefield." In Helden der christlichen Kirche..., 283-92.
       4th ed. Leipzig: Otto Spamer, 1904. 334p.

4719. Wesley et Wesleyanisme justifiés, ou réponse aux attaques
       du journal La Réformation aux XIXe Siècle. Nimes: Typog-
       raphie C. Durand-Belle, 1849. 84p. NjMUM

4720. Westin, Gunnar. "Johan Henrik Lidén och John Wesley."
       Kyrkohistorisk Arsskrift 37 (1937): 266-71.

4721. Williams, Albert Hughes. "Wesley a Harris." In Er clod,
       saith bennod ar hanes Methodistiaeth yng Nghymru, edited
       by Thomas Richards. Wrecasam: Hughes a'i fab, 1934. 176p.

4722. Zimmermann, A. "John Wesley und (General) William Booth."
       Historisch-politische blätter für das Katholische Deutschland
       140 (1907): 481-89.

4723. _____. "Neues Licht über John Wesley im Anschluss an die
       neuesten Forschungen." Literarischer Handweiser zunächst
       für alle Katholiken deutscher Zunge 48 (1910): 585-92.

TOPICAL INDEX

(JW is used for John Wesley; CW for Charles Wesley)

375

Catholicity   627, 1568, 1930, 2751, 3163, 3651, 4042
Caton, Eng. 95
Cell, George Croft   2549
Cennick, John   2418, 3152
Channel Islands   1180, 2763, 3671
Chapel-en-le-Frith, Eng. 3647
Charity schools   937, 1225
Charleston, S.C. 2038
Charlestown Collection see A Collection of Psalms and Hymns
Chelsea, Eng. 724, 2135
Cheltenham, Eng. 941, 3044, 3287
Cheshire, Eng. 2665
Chester Circuit   64, 3049
Chester, Eng. 223, 912, 2269, 2687, 2916, 2950, 3288
Children   1204, 2519, 2702, 3535, 3884
China   2298
"Christ the Lord Is Risen Today"   1245
"Christ Whose Glory Fills the Sky"   1422
Christian antiquities   4166a
Christian Community   2233
Christian education   314, 609, 1094, 1337, 2106, 4205a, 4257, 4319
Christian ethics   127, 295, 433, 892, 1053, 1729, 4200
Christian Library   509, 2591, 3307
Christian life   300, 610, 931, 932, 1744, 4346
Christian perfection see Perfection
Christian union   43, 464, 766, 879, 1067, 1436, 2856, 3255, 3716,
     4081, 4401
Christmas   2172, 2199, 2529, 2816, 3684, 3899
Christmas Conference   1163, 1692, 3713, 3972
Christology see Jesus Christ
Christus Victor   2742
Chrysostom, St. John   4289a
Church   1532, 1900, 2107, 3106, 3728, 4169
Church and State   1632, 2944, 4250, 4254
Church Fathers see Fathers of the Church
Church history   161, 343, 351, 441, 570, 738, 1182, 1448, 1457,
     1728, 1891, 3111, 3221. See also Great Britain, church
     history
Church music   436, 518, 4130, 4208
Church of England   35, 36, 58, 83, 99, 289, 293, 294, 354, 380,
     407, 441, 485, 493, 569, 767, 841, 843, 877, 889, 895, 925,
     927, 974, 1062, 1067, 1084, 1118, 1258, 1261, 1311, 1317, 1383,
     1385, 1388, 1389, 1427, 1442, 1518, 1547, 1619, 1638, 1865,
     1966, 2384, 2473, 2595, 2620, 3031, 3083, 3108, 3164, 3203,
     3429, 3522, 3525, 3574, 3610, 3635, 3768, 3793, 3901, 3913,
     4104, 4131, 4192, 4265, 4273, 4334, 4378
Church of Scotland, catechisms and creeds   1097
Church of the Nazarene   628, 4200, 4381
Church polity   1392, 1579, 1800
Church renewal   1551, 1631
Churches, Methodist   511, 1289

Epworth, Eng. 86, 265, 565, 581-583, 655, 760, 830, 988, 1010,
    1032, 1153, 1589, 1726, 1903, 2093, 2236, 2429, 3023, 3122,
    3123, 3167, 3352, 3412, 3447, 3458, 3516, 3550, 3584, 3782,
    3910, 4004
Erasmus, Bishop 3454, 3597, 3892
Erskine, Ebenezer 2015
Erskine, James, Lord Grange 2420
Erskine, Ralph 2015
Eschatology 3280, 3783, 4195, 4305, 4333
Ethics 3105, 4246
Evangelical revival 36, 58, 112, 178, 197, 220, 263, 398, 445, 460,
    518, 733, 747, 765, 766, 853, 864, 1015, 1105, 1219, 1259,
    1275, 1291, 1364, 1421, 1449, 1460, 1471, 1514, 1546, 1557,
    1672, 1747, 1758, 1794, 2474, 2735, 2840, 2890, 3503, 4205a,
    4253
Evangelicalism 484, 508, 570, 1161, 1380, 1546, 4347
    in literature 216
Evangelism 1249, 1454, 2423, 2601, 2948, 3090, 3405, 3410, 3471a,
    3978a, 3529, 4242, 4262
Everton, Eng. 1546, 3260
Evesham Circuit 3750
Evolution 2988
Ewhurst, Eng. 1977
Exeter, Eng. 237, 323, 1029, 3487, 3639, 3864, 3865
Existentialism 3385
Experience (religion) 630, 1053, 2686, 3536, 4174a, 4307
Explanatory Notes upon the New Testament 1135, 3715, 4136
Explanatory Notes upon the Old Testament 1963, 4172, 4301

Faith 102, 221, 633, 1222, 1273, 3135, 3376, 4249a, 4255, 4293,
    4385, 4401
Faith and reason 4223a
Falmouth, Eng. 2617
"Father of Boundless Grace" 2635
Fathers of the Church 4308a
Fénelon, François de Salignac de la Mothe 3311
Fenwick, Eng. 1670
Field, John 2243
Field Bible 2016, 2243, 2293
Field preaching 2503, 2668, 2863, 3107, 3614, 3673, 3674, 3732,
    3749, 3833, 4079
Figures of speech 4315
Fletcher, John 1262, 1724, 2466, 2642, 2652, 3710, 3713, 4320, 4358
Folkstone, Eng. 689
Food conservation 37, 2837
Forster, J. W. L. 4084
Foundery Collection See A Collection of Psalms and Hymns
Fox, George 2200, 3862, 4309
Francis of Assisi, Saint 2359, 2885, 3524, 3886, 3975
Fraser, James, Bp. of Manchester 2170

Free churches 1448
Free Grace 3508
Free will 2853, 3958, 4182, 4356
Freeman, Richard 2020
Freeman family 2413
Freemasonry 2461
Frome, Eng. 1709
Fulham papers 3917
Fuller, Thomas 2530
Fulneck, Eng. 2030
Furness, Eng. 2297, 3045

Gainsborough, Eng. 578
Galloway, Joseph 2284
Garrett, Charles 3642
Garrettson, Freeborn 2097
Garth, Eng. 3636
Gateshead, Eng. 599, 2252, 2613, 2787, 3008, 3319, 3427
Gell, Robert 2144
Gellar, W. O. 355
"Gentle Jesus, Meek and Mild" 4054
Georgia 198, 268, 334, 640, 791, 858, 976, 1534, 1910, 2090, 2337,
     2346, 2365, 2441, 2443, 2550, 2779, 2813, 2184, 2832, 2968,
     2999, 3018, 3157, 3254, 3270, 3315, 3446, 3538, 3718, 3759,
     3769, 3917, 3923
Germany 1233, 3312. See also Herrnhut, Germany
Ghosts 760, 844, 1201, 1313, 1589, 1726, 1903, 3023, 3122, 3123,
     3467, 4008
Gibbes family 3914
Gibbon, Edward 4171
Gibson, Edmund 397
Gilbert family 2242
Gillingham, Eng. 3643
Glamorgan, Wales 3316
Glas, John 2614
Glasgow, Scot 2326
Glossop Circuit 1637
Glouster Circuit 829
God 550, 1043, 1369, 1706, 3009, 4095, 4385
Goethe, Johann Wolfgang von 122
Goldsmith, Oliver 2332, 3317
Gomersal, Eng. 1980
Gordon, Alexander 2220
Gordon, Lord George 2026
Gornalwood, Eng. 470
Gosport, Eng. 2888
Grace (theology) 658, 679, 825, 1086, 1890, 2517, 2903, 2937,
     3138, 3361, 3364, 3492, 3704, 4048, 4214, 4237, 4244, 4268,
     4337a, 4342, 4351
Grantham, Eng. 360

Granville, Mary 3158
Graves, James Robinson 248
Gravesend, Eng. 3927
Great Britain
    Church history 1258, 1514, 1605, 1606, 1842, 3251. See also
        Church history
    Social conditions 220, 562, 981, 1797, 4088
Great Horton, Eng. 2710
Greek Language, JW's translations from 2802
Green, William 2196
Greenock, Scot. 1929, 2113
Gregorius, Saint., Bp. of Nyssa 4160
Gregory I, Saint 3468
Grimsby Circuit 836, 2979, 3052, 3166
Grimsby, Eng. 1031, 1481, 4106
Grimshaw, William 769, 3064
Groot, Gerard 2314
Guernsey, Isle of 3094
Guidance, divine 2752
Gwennap Pit, Cornwall 3016

Haddock family 1974
Hagley, Eng. 3006
Haime, John 3642
Halévy, Elie 2957, 3962
Halifax, Eng. 315, 778, 1749, 2788
Hall, Robert, Jr. 3918
Halyburton, Thomas 4241
Hampshire, Eng. 3702
Hampson, John 2246
Handel, George Frideric 2975, 3174, 3417, 4035
Hanley, Eng. 1535
Hanson, Thomas 2031
Hardon, John A. 2232
"Hark! the Herald Angels Sing" 348, 1188
Harris, Howell 977, 1864, 3033, 3035
Harrison, Lancelot 2109
Hartlepool, Eng. 1263
Harwich, Eng. 775
Haslingden, Eng. 783, 1604, 2277
Haverfordwest, Wales 2255, 3810
Haworth, Eng. 1715, 3064, 3345
Hayes, Eng. 3258
Headingley College Library, Leeds 2064
Heath, Levi 2024, 3383. See also Cokesbury College
Hell, 4068
Henry, Matthew 3183, 3578
Heptonstall, Eng. 654, 1480
Herbert, George 2369, 2935, 3151, 3741, 4064, 4078
Hereford, Eng. 1267

388   John and Charles Wesley

3777, 3970, 4023
conversion memorial   3915
Foundery, the   2965
guidebooks   86, 302, 1734
Hinde Street Chapel   427, 1659
St. Paul's Cathedral   3175
Snowsfields Chapel   3916
West Street Chapel   1659, 3502, 3847, 4120
Westminster School   424, 2208, 3737, 4017
London Circuit   395
Lopez, Gregory   4070
Lord's Supper   119, 146, 203, 356, 657, 1358, 1360, 1362, 1433,
    2096, 2190, 2204, 2690, 2761, 2970, 3530, 3607, 3608, 3662,
    3911, 4089, 4132, 4212, 4227, 4300
Loughborough, Eng.   1982
Louth Circuit   369, 3895
Love   386, 649, 2164, 2571, 3297, 4108
"Love Divine, All Loves Excelling"   100, 1422, 1423, 3515
Love feasts   85, 366, 643, 2678, 3021, 4367
Love (theology)   3326, 4188, 4218, 4293, 4401, 4401a
Loxdale, Ann   2022
Loyola, Saint Ignatius   3085, 3510
Luckock, Herbert Mortimer   2373
Lurgan, Ire.   2977
Luther, Martin   56, 816, 1053, 1970, 2124, 2154, 2424a, 2447, 2475,
    2622, 2778, 2785, 2906, 2911, 3109, 3189, 3191, 3204, 3238,
    3266, 3279, 3482, 3771, 3959, 3980, 3981, 4099, 4164, 4194
Luton, Eng.   1641, 2072, 2174, 3953
Lycoming College, Williamsport, Pa.   1068
Lyttleton, George Lyttleton   2533

Macarius, Saint   2288, 4308a
M'Caine, Alexander   575
Macclesfield, Eng.   1530, 2712, 3110, 3213
McKendree, William   2720
McNab, Alexander   2544
Madan family   2137
Maesmynis, Eng.   2335
Man, Isle of   1418, 2538, 2540, 2949, 3089, 4028, 4031
Man (theology)   114, 1143, 3274, 3508, 3654, 4150, 4166, 4197, 4229,
    4256, 4306, 4351, 4382
Manchester, Eng.   592, 594, 1555, 2313, 3180, 3244, 3876, 4014
Mankinholes, Eng.   2795
Manningtree, Eng.   3595
Manuscripts   2138, 2299, 2470
Margate, Eng.   224, 2239, 2263, 3182
The Marks of the New Birth   3719
Martin, Peter   3451
Marx, Karl   1505, 3200
Marylebone, Eng.   73, 2809, 3738, 3843

Robin Hood's Bay, Eng. 1914, 3631
Rochdale, Eng. 71, 1185
Rochester, Eng. 3545, 3644
Rodda, Richard 2419, 2531
Rogers, Hester Ann 2389
Rogers, James 1705
Rolvenden, Eng. 1972
Roman catechism 1140
Romanticism 215, 670, 2810, 2823, 3375, 3488
Romney, George 3551, 3954
Rosenthal, Gluck 3392
Rossendale, Eng. 917
Rotherham Circuit 1441, 2076
Rothwell, Eng. 3434
Roubillac, Louis François 2749
Rous, Francis 2594
Russell, John 3757, 4100
Rutherford, Thomas 2052, 3459
Ryan, Sarah 2104
Rye, Eng. 1974, 2675, 4105
Ryton-on-Tyne, Eng. 3373

Sacraments 194, 1268, 3509, 4321, 4348, 4401
Sacred Harmony 3539
Sacrifice 750, 818
St. Albans Circuit 697
St. Austell Circuit 3887
St. Ives, Eng. 1187
St. Just, Eng. 1702
St. Simons Island, GA. 306
Salisbury Circuit 1938
Salisbury, Eng. 2213
Salvation 438, 579, 679, 881, 1042, 1310, 1455, 1475, 2368, 3259,
    3506, 4234a, 4385, 4393, 4207, 4209, 4247, 4249, 4329,
    4349, 4385, 4393, 4406
Salzburgers 3926
Sanctification 63, 116, 191, 304, 482, 574, 610, 862, 1042, 1162,
    1264, 1450, 1462, 1536, 1640, 1831, 1849, 1893, 1962, 2364,
    2742, 2899, 3264, 3611, 3710, 3761, 3787, 4038, 4093, 4164,
    4184, 4203, 4267, 4275, 4308, 4321, 4360, 4401a, 4403
Sandeman, Robert 2891
Sargant, William Walters 1355
Satire 1069
Saugh House 2261
Savannah, Ga. 42, 175, 198, 1022, 1944, 1950, 3952, 3986
Scarborough, Eng. 2125, 3619, 3620
Science 2355, 2661, 2784, 2807, 3444, 3623, 3826
Scilly Islands 2886
Scotland 270, 748, 827, 1265, 1599, 1624, 1868, 2015, 2492, 2739,
    2861, 2955, 2974, 3819
Scott, Abraham 1710, 1712

Scougall, Henry 2849
Scripture see Bible
Sculpture 2457, 2599, 2746, 2749, 3615, 4112
Scunthorpe, Eng. 2732
Selby, Eng. 1186
Select Hymns with Tunes Annext 4034
Sermon on the Mount 1795, 2506a, 4180
Sevenoaks, Eng. 940, 2925
Seward, William 2201
Shaftesbury, Eng. 3642, 3643
Shakespeare, William 2336, 3193, 3792
Sheerness-on-Sea, Eng. 1951
Sheffield, Eng. 591, 1468, 1847, 2268, 2318, 2351, 2353, 3162,
      3531, 3581, 3909
Sherburn Circuit 3633
Shoreham, Eng. 3313
Shorthand 2371, 2380
Shotley Bridge, Eng. 177
Shropshire, Eng. 1523
Silverton, Eng. 1827
Simeon, Charles 1546, 3503
Simpson, David 2483
Sin 297, 325a, 1414, 1838, 2446, 3506, 3687, 3788, 4149, 4185,
      4197, 4224, 4287, 4345
Singing 320, 1089, 1410, 2509, 2519, 3573, 4091
Sittingbourne, Eng. 3666
Slack, John 662
Slavery 1464, 1544, 2044, 2289, 3240, 3453, 4158
Smart, Christopher 1598, 4213
Smith, John 411
Smith, Pye 2961
Smith House, Lightcliffe 2283
Smuggling 2118
Social ethics 4181
Social problems 46, 277, 280, 2171, 4148, 4148a, 4277, 4311, 4335,
      4370
Social reform 1679, 3449
Socialism 603, 604
Society for the Propagation of the Gospel in Foreign Parts 2340,
      3738
Society for the Reformation of Manners 3278
Society of Friends see Quakers
Sociology, Christian 161, 738, 752, 947, 1050, 1363, 1608, 1687,
      1729, 2536, 2623, 2638, 2917, 2943, 3282, 3723, 4143, 4270,
      4349
Solar system 2185
"Soldiers of Christ Arise" 998, 1226, 1666
Soldiers, religion among 1780, 2577, 2579
The Song of the Three Children 2065
Soteriology see Salvation
South Africa 1783

Vanderbilt University 2377
Van Mildert, William, Bp. of Llandaff and Durham 2498
Varanese 2009, 2820
Vazeille, Mary 675, 1085, 2077, 2091, 2571, 2982, 3158, 3301, 3738,
    3817. See also Wesley, John, marriage
Vegetarianism 2157
Vocabulary 2112, 4276
Voltaire 126, 1515, 2456, 3165

Wakefield, Eng. 2404, 3160
Wales 1857, 1858, 1921, 2342, 2344, 2484, 2978, 3032, 3037, 3294,
    3542, 3543, 4122
Walpole, Horace 2797, 3552
Walsall, Eng. 3014, 3341, 3343
Wandsworth Circuit 994, 995
War 560, 2944, 3557, 4092, 4170, 4219
Warburton, William 397, 3721
Wardle, Eng. 2347
Warrington, Eng. 2681, 2711, 3327
Waterford, Ire. 2452, 2460
Watson, John 3811, 3973
Watson, Richard 1463
Watts, Isaac 1122, 1426, 2325, 2705, 3357, 3505, 3656, 4344
Weather 2451
Webb, Thomas 2381
Weber, Max 3105
Wedgwood, Josiah 3586
Wednesbury, Eng. 499, 1334, 1740, 3126, 3161, 3933, 4009, 4020
Wellington, 1st duke of 3773
Wensleydale, Eng. 3943
Wentworth House 2338
Wesley, Charles
    anecdotes 1957, 3381
    anniversaries, etc. 1719, 1793, 3365
    as author 2047
    biographers 3815
    children 319
    churchmanship 2191, 3584a
    conversion hymn 2511, 2736
    death 996
    hymns 44, 72, 144, 197, 247, 267, 311, 329, 330, 377, 404, 406,
        486, 613, 614, 623, 641, 672, 720, 839, 842, 930, 944, 946,
        952, 1000, 1041, 1056, 1122, 1129, 1168, 1235, 1245, 1269,
        1270, 1329, 1331, 1360, 1361, 1373, 1420, 1542, 1543, 1571,
        1652-1654, 1778, 1879, 1887, 1888, 1970, 2010, 2112, 2114,
        2142, 2143, 2150, 2151, 2158, 2162, 2163, 2275, 2315, 2334,
        2427, 2510, 2583, 2584, 2637, 2660, 2663, 2670, 2725, 2757,
        2773, 2786, 2833, 2855, 2872, 2893, 2894, 3072, 3073, 3086,
        3246, 3248, 3249, 3302, 3309, 3413, 3414, 3563, 3601, 3640,
        3655, 3685, 3712, 3719, 3786, 3789, 3798, 3889, 3903, 3911,
        4083, 4165, 4193, 4207, 4212, 4245, 4281, 4289, 4315, 4344,

2160, 2322, 2772, 2819, 3321, 3323, 3352, 3550, 3729, 3738,
3742, 3791, 3951, 3961, 4084, 4205
Wesley College, Headingley 2693
Wesley family 60, 128, 129, 199, 341, 350, 408, 512, 522, 556, 564,
565, 584, 942, 1010, 1425, 1593, 1595, 1603, 1815, 1876, 1877,
1902, 1904, 1931, 2056, 2068, 2114, 2165, 2273, 2304, 2342, 2380,
2602, 2647, 2650, 2782, 2866, 2892, 3017, 3101, 3188, 3393,
3412, 3439, 3550, 3618, 3689, 3755, 3992, 4007, 4085, 4211
    exhibitions 400
Wesley studies 1253, 2324, 2845, 2846a, 3215
Wesleyan Methodism 531, 719, 841, 911, 1173, 1765, 1906, 2487,
2960, 4015
Wesleyan Methodist Church 259, 1383, 1385, 1522, 1533, 1577,
1638, 1661, 1735, 1774, 1886
    history 770, 776
    hymns 330
Wesleyana 94, 430, 584, 986, 1137, 1566, 1907, 2063, 2064, 2234,
2237, 2693, 2694, 2867, 2868, 2981, 3217, 3245, 3471, 3693,
4009, 4110
West Bromwich, Eng. 1334, 2954
Westley, Bartholomew 128
Westley, John 128
Westmorland, Eng. 1993
Weston, James 2371
Whaley Bridge 2603
Whalley, Eng. 3432
Whateley, Mary 2265
Whitby, Eng. 495, 2409, 3630, 3820
Whitchurch, Eng. 2699, 3691
Whitefield, George 237, 270, 407, 500, 871, 1230, 1665, 1801, 1884,
2071, 2201, 2411, 2796, 2797, 3507, 3674, 3711, 3769, 4002
Whitehaven Circuit 3047
Whitehead, John 1705
Whittlebury, Eng. 2953
Wigan, Eng. 1048
Wight, Isle of 540, 2012
Wigs 2286, 4029
Wilberforce, William 659, 3262
Wilson, Woodrow 2435
Wiltshire, Eng. 4057
Winchcombe, Eng. 3046
Winchelsea, Eng. 1974, 1979, 2679, 3730, 3752, 3967
Winchester, Eng. 3596
Wit and humor 2127
Witheridge, Eng. 1058
Witness, inward 2489
Witness of the Spirit see Holy Spirit
Witton, Eng. 443
Wolverhampton, Eng. 1325, 3324, 3929
Women 241, 242, 563, 746, 788, 2188, 2497, 3195, 3560, 4173
Wood, Enoch 421, 2375, 2746, 2997

Jarboe, Betty.
    John and Charles Wesley : a
bibliography / by Betty M.
Jarboe. -- [Philadelphia] : American
Theological Library Association ;
Metuchen, N.J. : Scarecrow Press,
1987.
    xv, 404 p. ; 23 cm. -- (ATLA
bibliography series ; no. 22)

$39.50 09/03/88

    Includes index.
    ISBN 0-8108-2039-0

(Cont. on next card)
87-13005

02205   60317   759493   B   © THE BAKER & TAYLOR CO.   8247